BY THE SAME AUTHOR

Blake's Apocalypse: A Study in Poetic Argument
"COMMENTARY," IN *The Poetry and Prose of William Blake,*
EDITED BY D. V. ERDMAN
The Ringers in the Tower: Studies in Romantic Tradition
Shelley's Mythmaking
Yeats

THE VISIONARY COMPANY

A READING OF ENGLISH ROMANTIC POETRY

And so it was I entered the broken world
To trace the visionary company of love, its voice
An instant in the wind (I know not whither hurled)
But not for long to hold each desperate choice.

HART CRANE

CORNELL PAPERBACKS

CORNELL UNIVERSITY PRESS

ITHACA & LONDON

THE
VISIONARY
COMPANY

A READING OF
ENGLISH ROMANTIC
POETRY

HAROLD BLOOM

REVISED & ENLARGED EDITION

Revised and enlarged edition, 1971
First printing, Cornell Paperbacks, 1971
Fourth printing, 1990

International Standard Book Number 0-8014-9117-7
Library of Congress Catalog Card Number 73-144032
Printed in the United States of America

♾ The paper in this book meets the minimum requirements of the American National Standard for Information Sciences— Permanence of Paper for Printed Library Materials, ANSI Z39.48-1984.

FOR

M. H. ABRAMS

PREFACE TO THE REVISED EDITION

THE VISIONARY COMPANY was written in 1959–1960, and published in 1961. For this new edition I have added an introductory essay on the historical backgrounds of English Romantic poetry and an epilogue relating my study to some current phenomena. Where I am persuaded I was mistaken, I have made revisions, and I have tried to eliminate redundancies. I have also taken advantage of David V. Erdman's textual scholarship to correct my quotations from Blake's writings.

My debts are manifold, and some I have recognized only upon rereading. I owe most to the general criticism of Romantic poetry by G. Wilson Knight, Northrop Frye, and my teachers William K. Wimsatt and M. H. Abrams; to the last this book is rededicated with a student's continued homage. On particular poets, I have been influenced most by Frye on Blake, Geoffrey Hartman on Wordsworth, Humphrey House on Coleridge, my teacher Frederick A. Pottle on Shelley, Walter Jackson Bate on Keats, George Ridenour on Byron, Geoffrey Grigson on Clare, and John Heath-Stubbs on Darley. I have tried to benefit, in revising, by the suggestions of Paul de Man, John Hollander, Alvin Feinman, and Jerome Schneewind.

The subject of this book, as I have come to see on rereading, is the dialectic of nature and the imagination in Romantic poetry. That the Romantics were not poets of nature is its central contention, which I have developed in some later books, on Blake and on Yeats and in the volume of essays *The Ringers in the Tower.* As practical criticism, my studies of individual Romantic poets here do not translate them into Blakean categories (as a number of negative critics charged, most notably C. S. Lewis and René Wellek) but do seek out the crucial analogues and rivalries that connect these poets, and that make them not only sharers in a Spirit of the Age but contemporaries in the spirit, tracers of the visionary company of love.

H. B.

New Haven, Connecticut, August 24, 1970

CONTENTS

Prometheus Rising: The Backgrounds of Romantic Poetry   xiii

Prologue   1

I   WILLIAM BLAKE

1   The Heritage of Sensibility   7

    COLLINS' ODE ON THE POETICAL CHARACTER   7

    POETICAL SKETCHES   15

2   The Individual Vision   20

    THE CONCEPT OF BEULAH   20

    THE GIANT FORMS   31

3   The Contraries   33

    SONGS OF INNOCENCE AND OF EXPERIENCE   33

4   Negations   49

    THE BOOK OF THEL   49

    VISIONS OF THE DAUGHTERS OF ALBION   53

    THE CRYSTAL CABINET   56

    THE MENTAL TRAVELLER   58

5   Bible of Energy   64

    THE MARRIAGE OF HEAVEN AND HELL   64

6   Bible of Hell   71

    THE BOOK OF URIZEN   71

7   States of Being   80

    THE FOUR ZOAS   80

8   The Recovery of Innocence   97

    MILTON   97

9   Blake's Apocalypse   108

    JERUSALEM   108

II   WILLIAM WORDSWORTH

1   The Great Marriage   124

THE RECLUSE   124
NUTTING   128

2 Myth of Memory   131
TINTERN ABBEY   131
THE PRELUDE   140

3 Spots of Time   164
RESOLUTION AND INDEPENDENCE   164
ODE: INTIMATIONS OF IMMORTALITY   170

4 Natural Man   178
THE OLD CUMBERLAND BEGGAR   178
MICHAEL   182

5 The Myth Denied   184
PEELE CASTLE   184
ODE TO DUTY   187
LAODAMIA   188

6 The Frozen Spirit   193
THE EXCURSION   193
EXTEMPORE EFFUSION   196

III SAMUEL TAYLOR COLERIDGE

1 The Conversation Poems   200
THE EOLIAN HARP   200
FROST AT MIDNIGHT   202
THE NIGHTINGALE   205

2 Natural Magic   206
THE ANCIENT MARINER   206
CHRISTABEL   212
KUBLA KHAN   217

3 Wisdom and Dejection   220
FRANCE: AN ODE   220
DEJECTION: AN ODE   222
TO WILLIAM WORDSWORTH   228

4 Positive Negation   232
LIMBO   232
NE PLUS ULTRA   235

IV GEORGE GORDON, LORD BYRON

1 Promethean Man   238

CHILDE HAROLD'S PILGRIMAGE 238

PROMETHEUS 245

MANFRED 248

CAIN 253

2 The Digressive Balance 255

BEPPO 255

DON JUAN 257

3 The Byronic Ethos 272

THE VISION OF JUDGMENT 272

STANZAS TO THE PO 276

LAST POEMS 279

V PERCY BYSSHE SHELLEY

1 Urbanity and Apocalypse 282

2 The Quest 285

ALASTOR 285

3 The Hidden Power 290

HYMN TO INTELLECTUAL BEAUTY 290

MONT BLANC 293

ODE TO THE WEST WIND 296

TO A SKYLARK 302

4 Titan on the Rock 306

PROMETHEUS UNBOUND 306

5 Dialectics of Vision 323

THE TWO SPIRITS: AN ALLEGORY 323

THE WITCH OF ATLAS 326

6 Darkening of the Quest 335

EPIPSYCHIDION 335

ADONAIS 342

7 Transmemberment of Song 350

FINAL LYRICS 350

THE TRIUMPH OF LIFE 352

VI JOHN KEATS

1 Gardens of the Moon 363

SLEEP AND POETRY 363

ENDYMION 368

2 Hymns of Eros 378

THE EVE OF ST. AGNES   378

LA BELLE DAME SANS MERCI   384

LAMIA   387

3 Temples of the Sun   390

HYPERION   390

ODE TO PSYCHE   399

4 Naturalistic Humanism   407

ODE TO A NIGHTINGALE   407

ODE ON MELANCHOLY   413

ODE ON A GRECIAN URN   416

ODE ON INDOLENCE   420

5 Tragic Humanism   421

THE FALL OF HYPERION   421

TO AUTUMN   432

BRIGHT STAR   435

VII BEDDOES, CLARE, DARLEY, AND OTHERS

1 Thomas Lovell Beddoes   439

DANCE OF DEATH   439

2 John Clare   444

THE WORDSWORTHIAN SHADOW   444

3 George Darley and Others   456

THE STRANGLING TIDE   456

Epilogue: The Persistence of Romanticism   461

Chronological Table   467

Notes   471

Index   473

PROMETHEUS RISING: THE BACKGROUNDS OF ROMANTIC POETRY

THE political background of English Romantic poetry is darkened by European revolution and English reaction against that revolution. The England in which Blake and Wordsworth grew up was a country one hundred years removed from its one great revolution, the Puritan movement. The most important political event in early-nineteenth-century England was one that failed to take place: the repetition among Londoners of the revolution carried through by Parisians. Out of the ferment that failed to produce a national renewal there came instead the major English contribution to world literature since the Renaissance, the startling phenomenon of six major poets appearing in just two generations.

No intelligent thoroughgoing Marxist critic has yet studied all of English Romantic literature in any detail, and I shudder to contemplate a reading of Blake's epics or Byron's *Don Juan* in the light of economic determinism alone. Still, such a study would reveal much that now is only matter for speculation, for the Romantic age saw the end of an older, pastoral England and the beginning of the England that may be dying now. When Blake was born, in 1757, and even as late as 1770, when Wordsworth was born, England was still fundamentally an agricultural society. When Blake died, in 1827, England was largely an industrial nation, and by 1850, when Wordsworth died, England was in every sense the proper subject for Marxist economic analysis that it became in *Das Kapital*. The power of England had passed from an established aristocracy holding huge estates, and an upper middle class of London merchants, to a much more amorphous grouping that combined both of these with a new class of industrial employers. And the common people of England were no longer just a peasantry and city artisans, but now a huge and tormented industrial working class as well. In the last quarter of the eighteenth century that emerging class was troubled by two foreign revolutions, neither like any known previously in modern Europe. The American Revolution looks tame enough to us today, but to Blake it was the first voice of the morning, and in his symbolism it assumed an importance greater even than that taken on by the French Revolution. The French Revolution, much more genuinely a modern social upheaval, is the single most important external factor that conditions Romantic poetry, as in Blake's *The Marriage of Heaven and Hell,* Wordsworth's *The Prelude,* and Shelley's *Prometheus Unbound.*

The English government under which Blake and Wordsworth lived was engaged either in continental warfare or in suppressing internal dissent, or both together, for most of their lives. The London of the last decade of the eighteenth century and the first of the nineteenth is the London shown in Blake's poem of that title in *Songs of Experience:* a city in which the traditional English liberties of free press, free speech, and the rights of petition and assembly were frequently denied. A country already shaken by war and anarchic economic cycles was beginning to experience the social unrest that had overthrown the French social order, and the British ruling class responded to this challenge by a vicious and largely effective repression.

Voices raised against this repression included Tom Paine, who had to flee for his life to France, where he then nearly lost it again, and a much more significant figure, the philosophical anarchist William Godwin, who was the major English theorist of social revolution. Godwin subsided into a timid silence during the English counterterror, but his philosophic materialism was crucial for the early Wordsworth and the young Shelley alike, though both poets were to break from Godwin in their mature works.

Behind the materialist vision of Godwin was a consciousness that older modes of thought were dying with the society that had informed them. When Blake was eight years old, the steam engine was perfected, and what were to be the images of prophetic labor in Blake's poetry, the hammer and the forge, had their antagonist images prepared for them in the furnaces and mills of another

England. In the year of Wordworth's birth, we have the ironical juxtaposition of Goldsmith's poem *The Deserted Village,* a sad celebration of an open, pastoral England vanishing into the isolated farm holdings, and wandering laborers resulting from enclosure. "Nature," insofar as it had an outward, phenomenal, meaning for Pope, was a relaxed word, betokening the gift of God that lay all about him. Wordsworthian nature, the hard, phenomenal otherness that opposes itself to all we have made and marred, takes part of its complex origin from this vast social dislocation.

The real misery in England brought about through these economic and social developments was on a scale unparalleled since the Black Death in the fourteenth century. The French wars, against which all of Blake's prophetic poetry protests with Biblical passion, were typical of all modern wars fought by capitalistic countries. Enormous profits for the manufacturing classes were accompanied by inflation and food shortages for the mass of people, and victory over Napoleon brought on all the woes endemic to a capitalist society when peace breaks out—an enormous economic depression, unemployment, hunger, and more class unrest.

This unrest, which there was no means of channeling into organization or a protest vote, led to giant public meetings, riots, and what was called frame-breaking, a direct attempt to end technological unemployment by the destruction of machines. The government reacted by decreeing that frame-breaking was punishable by death. The climax of popular agitation and government brutality came in August 1819, in the Peterloo Massacre at Manchester, where mounted troops charged a large, orderly group that was meeting to demand parliamentary reform, killing and maiming many of the unarmed protesters. For a moment, England stood at the verge of revolution, but no popular leaders of sufficient force and initiative came forward to organize the indignation of the mass of people, and the moment passed. A similar moment was to come in 1832, at the start of another age, but then revolution was to be averted by the backing-down of parliament, and its passage of the first Reform Act that helped to establish the Victorian compromise. So the political energies of the age were not without issue, even in England, but to idealists of any sort living in England during the first three decades of the nineteenth century it seemed that a new energy had been born into the world and then had died in its infancy. The great English writers of the period reacted to a stagnant situation by withdrawal, either internal or external. In Blake and Wordsworth this internal movement helped create a new kind of poetry; it created modern poetry as we know it.

The useful term "Romantic," describing the literary period that was contemporary with the French Revolution, the Napoleonic wars, and the age of Castlereagh and Metternich afterward, was not employed until the later Victorian literary historians looked back at the early years of the nineteenth century. Since that time, the word has meant not only that cultural period, in England and on the Continent, but a kind of art that is timeless and recurrent as well, usually viewed as being in some kind of opposition to an art called classical or neoclassical. The word goes back to a literary form, the romance, the marvelous story suspended part way between myth and naturalistic representation. By the middle of the eighteenth century in England, "romantic" had become an adjective meaning wild or strange or picturesque, and was applied more to painting and to scenery than to poetry. The critical terms by which mid-eighteenth-century literature named itself, in direct opposition to the classicism of Pope, Swift, and Dr. Johnson, were "the Sublime" and "sensibility." No poet of the Romantic period ever characterized his own poetry or that of any of his contemporaries as "Romantic." All that the six major poets thought they shared was what William Hazlitt called "The Spirit of the Age." In the semiapocalyptic dawn of the French Revolution, it really did seem that a renovated universe was possibe—that life could never again be what it had been. It is not very easy now for any of us to summon up the fervor of that moment, through whatever leap of historical imagination. We have no real analogue to it as a universal psychic shock that at first promised liberation from everything bad in the past. The Russian Revolution, even if it were not now almost as historically remote from us as the French, would not be an adequate analogue, for it took place in a world already suffering through a war. The French Revolution was, in its day, a new kind of ideological revolution—hence the terror it aroused in its opponents, and the hope in its sympathizers.

To understand fully the link between the Revolution and English Romantic literature, it is perhaps most immediately illuminating to consider the case, not of one of the great poets, but of the critic

William Hazlitt, who kept his faith in the Revolution and even in Napoleon long after every other literary figure of the time had turned reactionary or indifferent, or had died young. Hazlitt not only lived and died a Jacobin, but his entire background and career are archetypal of English Romanticism, and his personality and psychology are representative of English Romanticism, as those of Rousseau perfectly incarnate the French variety.

Like that of all the English Romantic poets, Hazlitt's religious background was in the tradition of Protestant dissent, the kind of nonconformist vision that descended from the Left Wing of England's Puritan movement. There is no more important point to be made about English Romantic poetry than this one, or indeed about English poetry in general, particularly since it has been deliberately obscured by most modern criticism. Though it is a displaced Protestantism, or a Protestantism astonishingly transformed by different kinds of humanism or naturalism, the poetry of the English Romantics is a kind of religious poetry, and the religion is in the Protestant line, though Calvin or Luther would have been horrified to contemplate it. Indeed, the entire continuity of English poetry that T. S. Eliot and his followers attacked is a radical Protestant or displaced Protestant tradition. It is no accident that the poets deprecated by the New Criticism were Puritans, or Protestant individualists, or men of that sort breaking away from Christianity and attempting to formulate personal religions in their poetry. This Protestant grouping begins with aspects of Spenser and Milton, passes through the major Romantics and Victorians, and is clearly represented by Hardy and Lawrence in our century. It is also no accident that the poets brought into favor by the New Criticism were Catholics or High Church Anglicans—Donne, Herbert, Dryden, Pope, Dr. Johnson, Hopkins in the Victorian period, Eliot and Auden in our own time. Not that literary critics have been engaged in a cultural-religious conspiracy, but there are at least two main traditions of English poetry, and what distinguishes them are not only aesthetic considerations but conscious differences in religion and politics. One line, and it is the central one, is Protestant, radical, and Miltonic-Romantic; the other is Catholic, conservative, and by its claims, classical. French culture has been divided between those who have accepted the French Revolution and its consquences and those who have sought to deny and resist them. Similarly, but more subtly, English culture has been divided between those who have accepted the Puritan religious revolution of the late sixteenth and seventeenth century and those who have fought against it. Though I oversimplify, the conflict I seek to expose is most certainly there; it runs all through the criticism of T. S. Eliot, in many concealments, and it accounts finally for *all* of Eliot's judgments on English poetry. Hazlitt's criticism, which by any standards remains at least as vital as Eliot's, illustrates the same dialectical point in reverse—the sensibility involved is that of a Protestant dissenter, and the judgments are shaped accordingly.

The main characteristic of English religious dissent was its insistence on intellectual and spiritual independence, on the right of private judgment in questions of morality, on the inner light within each soul, by which alone Scripture was to be read—and most of all, on allowing no barrier or intermediary to come between a man and his God. Academic criticism of literature in our time became almost an affair of church wardens; too many students for instance learned to read Milton by the dubious light of C. S. Lewis' *Preface to Paradise Lost,* in which the major Protestant poem in the language becomes an Anglo-Catholic document. The best preparation for reading Romantic poetry always will be a close rereading of Book I of Spenser's *Faerie Queene* and of Milton's *Paradise Lost* which judges the spiritual content of those poems wholly and maturely. Milton begins his poem with an invocation to the Muse, an epic device that he transforms into the summoning of the Holy Spirit of God, which "before all temples dost prefer / the upright heart and pure." He means just that; he is repudiating the temples, all of them, and offering instead his own arrogantly pure and upright heart as the true dwelling place of the creative Word of God. The Spirit that moved over the face of the waters and brought forth our world is identical with the shaping spirit dwelling within the soul of the inspired Protestant poet. Spenser is not so forthright, but Book I of his poem offers a Calvinist-oriented allegory that is scarcely less iconoclastic in juxtaposing a Puritan knight-errant to a corrupt machinery of salvation. The spirit of Hazlitt, of Blake, of the younger Wordsworth, of Shelley and Keats, is a direct descendant of this Spenserian and Miltonic spirit—the autonomous soul seeking its own salvation outside of and beyond the hierarchy of grace. The spiritual nakedness of Hazlitt, Blake, and the others is a more extreme version of that English nonconformist temper which had so triumphed in Milton that it made him a church with one believer, a political party of one, even at last a nation unto himself.

It was not until 1828 that Dissenters gained legal equality in matters of religion and education in England. Hazlitt, in 1818, wrote the following eloquent praise of his coreligionists, the sectaries —the men and women who embodied what Edmund Burke had called "the dissidence of dissent and the Protestantism of the Protestant religion." The nonconformists, Hazlitt wrote, "are the steadiest supporters of [England's] liberties and laws, they are checks and barriers against the insidious or avowed encroachments of arbitrary power: and they are depositaries of the love of truth." Dissent or religious individualism was always more a state of mind than a doctrine, and it was opposed to the Establishment steadily from the Restoration, in 1660, down to the repeal of the Test Acts, in 1828. From then on dissent, in the form of the evangelical revival, attempted to take over the Church of England itself, and secured enough of a hold to engender the counterreaction of the Oxford movement of Newman and his friends and followers.

Dissent had begun as a protest against ecclesiastical authority, but it grew into an affirmation of both civil and religious freedom. Milton's prose works utilize as their central concept the Protestant doctrine of "Christian Liberty," which holds that it is the prerogative of every regenerated man under the New Law of the Gospel to be free of every ecclesiastical constraint. After the Stuart Restoration, Milton turned his energies to exploring the Paradise within each man, for Christian Liberty could still offer this. The outward energies of Protestant individualism, balked by the Restoration, tended to go into the fight for the natural liberties of Englishmen. The inward energies largely died out of poetry after Milton, and did not appear again until the Miltonic revival of the 1740's, of which Collins' *Ode on the Poetical Character* is one of the great monuments. In the meantime they were partly secularized by the more radical wing of the Whig party, led by Charles James Fox in the later eighteenth century. In religion proper they became incarnated in George Fox and the Quakers, and more significantly for Romanticism, in the two great nonconformist theologians of the late eighteenth century—Richard Price and Joseph Priestley. Price and Priestley led the radical Unitarian agitation for reform of church and state that enlisted the young Coleridge and Wordsworth as supporters and helped stir them to an early discontent with eighteenth-century culture and its institutions.

When the Bastille fell, the Dissenters hailed the events in France with elation. Richard Price preached a sermon on November 4, 1789, that greeted the Revolution in the name of English nonconformist tradition from Cromwell and Milton on, a sermon that provoked Edmund Burke into the eloquent counterattack of his *Reflections on the Revolution in France.* In their later lives, when both had turned into Tories, Coleridge and Wordsworth became disciples of Burke. But when they were young men, they followed Priestley and Godwin in attacking Burke and in defending the French Revolution. When the Anglican Bishop Watson published his sermon against the revolution, charmingly entitled *The Wisdom and Goodness of God in Having Made Both Rich and Poor,* Wordsworth replied with his angry pamphlet, *A Letter to the Bishop of Llandaff,* in which the Bishop and Burke are invited to contemplate the daily terrors afflicting the English working class—"the scourge of labour, of cold, of hunger," as Wordsworth phrased it. Even more ironic was Coleridge's role in those times, for the older Coleridge was to make the ideological foundations for English conservatism and established Anglicanism in the Victorian period. But the young Coleridge followed Priestley to the extent of imitating his famous sermon of 1794, in which the French Revolution is interpreted as being the time of troubles preceding the millennium that is the first stage of the apocalypse, the last judgment prophesied in the Revelation of St. John the Divine. In his long poem *Religious Musings,* written in 1794–1796, Coleridge also wrote of the Revolution as a necessarily violent threshold to a thousand years of peace, after which Christ would come again to judge the nations of the earth. The same apocalyptic language appears also in Wordsworth's *Recluse* and *Prelude* and in Blake's *Marriage of Heaven and Hell* and in his poems on the French and American Revolutions. A generation later, the apocalyptic impulse abandons the contemporary world, which belongs to Metternich and his colleagues, and enters the purely ideal world explored so magnificently by Shelley in his lyrical drama *Prometheus Unbound.*

It is these apocalyptic longings, themselves expressions of a radically Protestant temperament, that most clearly distinguish Romantic poetry from most of the English poetry that had been written since the Renaissance. It is not a deprecation of Restoration and Augustan poets to generalize that they treated man as a distinctly limited being, set in a context of reason, nature, and society that ordered his horizons and denied any possibility of a radical alteration in his mundane hopes. Indeed, it is the strength and even the glory of such poets that they so powerfully attacked man's vain pride and his dangerous longings to escape the harsh realities of a reasonable existence. One can call this a glory, even if one has not a conservative or classical or Catholic temperament, if one takes a little history into account. Restoration literature and its Augustan successors—the whole line of neoclassicists from Dryden through Addison, Pope, and Swift down to its rear-guard fighter, Samuel Johnson—were in reaction against the most disordered age of England's history, a time of civil warfare, religious struggle, and a complete change in the philosophical and scientific world view. The age of Cromwell and Milton is from one standpoint the glorious culmination of the Elizabethan age of Renaissance and Reformation, but from a more traditional standpoint it was a brutal and anarchic collapse of a settled society into a chaos of rebellion and sectarianism, brought about through overweening spiritual pride and the original sin of civil and ecclesiastical arrogance and disobedience. Pope and Swift, and Johnson afterward, set themselves against every innovation, every mark of dissent, every extreme position in ethics, politics, metaphysics, or art. The Augustan fear of madness, so strong in Swift and Johnson, plays a considerable part in this opposition, which goes so far at to attack what Johnson calls "the dangerous prevalence of the imagination." Swift, in his later years, went mad; Johnson came dangerously close to it. The poets of the age of sensibility—say 1740 through 1770—reacted against Pope and Johnson and sought to return to the intellectual and aesthetic daring of Milton, with results in their lives, at least, which bore out Johnson's melancholy warnings. Chatterton killed himself at seventeen; Cowper, Collins, Christopher Smart, and others spent years in asylums for the insane, as the Romantic poet John Clare was to do after them; while poets like Gray and Burns ended in deep melancholy or profound social alienation. The spectre haunting these generations was the fear of psychic energy, and the conviction that death-in-life awaited any poet who indulged his imagination.

As a phenomenon, this mid-eighteenth-century prevalence and fear of creative madness, or "perilous balance" as one critic has called it, has still not been solved, and what we cannot understand we need not attempt to judge. But we need to keep this phenomenon in mind if we are to understand William Blake, the sanest of all poets, who by the dubious irony of literary history was considered mad by some of his contemporaries, and is still considered so by some of ours, who have no excuse for not knowing better. In Blake the satirical theme of a willful intellectual madness becoming an involuntary spiritual disorder is sounded as early as the youthful *Mad Song* in *Poetical Sketches*. In *The Book of Urizen*, Blake gives his definitive analysis of the phenomenon of eighteenth-century imaginative madness, one that I suspect we are not likely to improve upon, even if we wince at the rigor of the intellectual satire by which it is presented. The contrary to the Johnsonian fear of imagination is the Romantic apocalyptic hope to be achieved through and in imagination. It is here, in the astonishingly fecund and bewilderingly varied concept of imagination, that Romantic poetic theory finds its center.

The neoclassic theory of poetry was a refined and coherent version of the ancient mimetic theory, in which poetry is regarded as an imitation of human actions. In Romantic poetic theory, this is not so. We find it today the merest commonplace to speak of the "creative" power of the artist or poet, forgetting that the very considerable metaphor involved in the word "creative" in this context is a great departure from the more primary notion of art as imitation. A colorless or dead metaphor or stock term is, as M. H. Abrams says, the residue of a figure of speech "which only four centuries ago was new, vital, and—because it equated the poet with God in his unique and most characteristic function—on the verge, perhaps, of blasphemy." The ancient history of this aesthetic metaphor, one should add, contains no consciousness that blasphemy could ever be involved. The metaphor appears in premonitory hints in first-century Christian writings and second-century Greek aestheticians. In the third century, the metaphor emerges clearly in the founder of Neoplatonism, Plotinus. In the Italian Renaissance, the Neoplatonists of the Florentine Academy expand the metaphor into a theory, until it reaches the bald statement of the critic Scaliger, for whom the poet is one who "maketh a new Nature and so maketh himself as it were a new God." Scaliger is the source for Sir Philip Sidney's similar declaration in his *Apologie for Poetrie*. We reach the end of this account with Sidney's contemporary George Puttenham, who joined to the idea he found in Sidney's *Apologie* the crucial word "create," based on the ecclesiastical Latin common word that connoted the orthodox concept that God made the world out of nothing. If poets, said Puttenham, "be able to devise and make all these things of themselves, without any subject or veritie," then "they be (by manner of speech) as creating gods."

This nutshell history, if taken too literally, would make it sound as if Sidney and his contemporaries already had a Romantic theory of imagination, but this is one of the curious illusions that the relative flatness of intellectual history is liable to give us. Sidney states the aesthetic metaphor of creation, and then instantly abandons it for a definition of poetry as imitation, "that the truth" of the poet's role, as he says, "may be the more palpable." Sidney's rapid passage from the theological to the more traditional metaphor of art as a mirror held up to nature is the precise point at which Romanticism both derives from and separates itself from its Renaissance forebear.

Before the Romantics, literature and the arts had somewhat the same educational and cultural status that they now possess, but they were generally judged to be dependent for their meanings on theology, philosophy, and history; that is, they allegorically were reduced to truths that were held to be stated more plainly in more privileged fields of learning. If a poem possessed truth, it was an elaborated or ornamented truth that could be met more directly in a religious or moral context. When the Romantics, from Blake on to Shelley and Keats, talk about the relation of poetry to other areas of culture, they make the direct claim that poetry is prior to theology or moral philosophy, and by "prior" they mean both more original and more intellectually powerful.

As an assertion, this Romantic self-exaltation can be viewed as mere megalomania of course, and it has been so viewed by a series of modern critics from Irving Babbitt and T. E. Hulme through T. S. Eliot down to the American academic critics called "New" in the decades just past. But the Romantic assertion is not just an assertion; it is a metaphysic, a theory of history, and much more important than either of these, it is what all of the Romantics—but Blake in particular—called a vision, a way of seeing, and of living, a more human life. Northrop Frye notes that even in the dissenting Protestant vision, all the traditions of civilization that were held worthy of preservation were believed to have been instituted by God himself. But by the early nineteenth century, as Frye adds, the idea that much of civilization was of human institution had begun to appear, however uncertainly, in radical Protestant writing. It is present, for example, in the Unitarians Price and Priestley, and it plays a central role in the thought of William Godwin, who began as a Dissenter and then converted himself into a curious blend of idealistic anarchist and materialistic humanist. In Blake it appears as a new myth, that is, a new and comprehensive story of how man got to be what he is now, and how he is again to become what once he was. If all deities, as Blake said, reside in the human breast, then all traditions of knowledge are human also, and it followed that the most human and complete knowledge was that of poetry.

Milton is the fountainhead of this kind of belief, and yet would have rejected it, in the conviction that it led to a Satanic idolatry of self. It is one of the great characteristics of the Romantic period that each major poet in turn sought to rival and surpass Milton, while also renewing his vision. To surpass Milton in this context could only mean to correct his vision by humanizing it, which is a secular analogue to the entire process by which Calvinist Protestantism became the radical dissent of the later eighteenth century. The immense hope of Blake and of the early Wordsworth, of Shelley and of Keats, was that poetry, by expressing the whole man, could either liberate him from his fallen condition or, more compellingly, make him see that condition as unnecessary, as an unimaginative fiction that an awakened spirit could slough off. So Blake's Milton, in the brief epic of which he is the hero, comes to cast off the rags of decayed conceptions, to strip himself of the nonhuman. And so, in the poetry of our own time which is the direct legacy of Romanticism, Yeats cries out:

> Thought is a garment, and the soul's a bride
> That cannot in that trash and tinsel hide.

So also with the vision of Wordsworth, in which we are to be saved by words which speak of nothing more than what we are, a vision that finds its highest honorific words in "simple" and "common," and human felicity in the moving line "the simple produce of the common day," in which we are told our lives are perpetually renewed by that ordinary process of hallowing the commonplace that Wordsworth had first described in poetry. This vision is renewed for us in the poetry of Wallace Stevens, the most authentic and relevant I think of our time. Romanticism opposed to supernatural religion the natural passion that Wallace Stevens has so eloquently expressed:

> The greatest poverty is not to live
> In a physical world, to feel that one's desire
> Is too difficult to tell from despair.

The central desire of Blake and Wordsworth, and of Keats and Shelley, was to find a final good in human existence itself. It is these poets who came closest to answering the question that Wallace Stevens, following after them, propounds:

> And out of what one sees and hears and out
> Of what one feels, who could have thought to make
> So many selves, so many sensuous worlds,
> As if the air, the mid-day air, was swarming
> With the metaphysical changes that occur,
> Merely in living as and where we live.

THE VISIONARY COMPANY

A READING OF ENGLISH ROMANTIC POETRY

PROLOGUE

BLAKE died in the evening of Sunday, August 12, 1827, and the firm belief in the autonomy of a poet's imagination died with him. Just four months before death he affirmed again the faith in which he had lived: "I have been very near the gates of death, and have returned very weak and an old man, feeble and tottering, but not in spirit and life, not in the real man, the imagination, which liveth for ever." [1]

We strive to admire, yet this is remote from us; we want to know what Blake means. Similarly, we are moved by Shelley's statement that "the great instrument of moral good is the imagination," but we scarcely believe that "a man, to be greatly good, must imagine intensely and comprehensively." Matthew Arnold said of the Romantics that they failed for not knowing enough, yet a careful study of Blake or Shelley or Wordsworth will not convince a disinterested reader that these formidable energies wasted themselves in ignorance. What separates us from the Romantics is our loss of their faithless faith, which few among them could sustain even in their own lives and poems. Blake's Milton comes "to wash off the Not Human," to take the rags of decayed conceptions from man, "and clothe him with Imagination." Wordsworth says of his own function as poet that he desires to "arouse the sensual from their sleep of Death," and makes it clear that he would do this "by words which speak of nothing more than what we are." In the accents of our own voice Wallace Stevens, the legitimate heir of these aspirations, says of poetry that it is "a present perfecting, a satisfaction in the irremediable poverty of life." If we take from Stevens two more statements, we have our way back to understanding the enormous desire and eloquent hope of the Romantics. "To live in the world but outside of existing conceptions of it," Stevens writes, and also: "In the presence of extraordinary actuality, consciousness takes the place of imagination." [2] The world of actuality faced first by Blake, Coleridge, and Wordsworth, and by Shelley, Byron, and Keats after them, afforded no existing conceptions fully acceptable to the imagination, and presented a provocation for a heightening of consciousness so intense that a true awareness of reality inevitably sought for itself the identifying sanction of imagination. The outward form of the inward grace of Romantic imagination was the French Revolution, and the Revolution failed. Desire, too long restrained, burst forth as what Blake called the Prolific, and the Prolific choked, as Blake said, in "the excess of his delights." Milton, after the failure of his Revolution, turned inward like Oedipus, making of his blindness a judgment upon the light. Wordsworth's movement to the interior was more gradual, and ended in defeat, with the light of imagination dying into the light of another day, in which existing conceptions of the world seemed acceptable. Coleridge found the blinding light of theology, and forgot that "a whole Essay might be written on the Danger of *thinking* without Images," and so left the essay unwritten.

Blake's response, like that of Shelley after him, was to strengthen the myth or self-made account of reality given by his own poetry. This has been called a pattern of retreat, but Blake was a dialectician of the imagination. He understood his own quest as being a displacement of antinomian desire from an outer actuality that had ceased to be very extraordinary, to the intense warfare of consciousness against itself within a psyche whose burden of reality remained both extraordinary and representative.

In the next generation the three major poets met the age of Metternich and Castlereagh with very different but related accounts of self-realization accomplished against the spirit of society. Shelley made an attempt to live in the world but failed, and moved instead within his own conceptions of it, until at last the humanly desperate consequences of his vision wore out even his tenacious strength of desire. He remains, like Blake and Keats, a hero of the imagination in his unwavering insistence that an increase in consciousness need not be an increase in the despair of actuality, and in his stubborn identification of imagination with the potential of consciousness. His final cry affirms the vision, but denies the efficacy of himself as seer. Like D. H. Lawrence, he would have still repeated the ancient truth of the vatic poet: not I, but the wind that blows through me.

Byron never left the world, nor could he ever abandon any of the existing conceptions of it. His is therefore the most social of Romantic imaginations and so the least Romantic. Few poets had less trust in their own consciousness, and no great English poet had less faith in the validity of his own powers than Byron. The powers were exuberant, but Byron's Devourer was very nearly as strong as the Prolific portion of his being, and this conflict of contraries could rarely be accepted by the poet as a value in itself, which in *Don Juan* it finally proved to be. Byron's imagination found its escape from self-consciousness in the social ideal of "mobility," but "mobility" did not always find a way back to an identity with imagination, as the heightened awareness of both actuality and human possibility.

That Keats had the healthiest of imaginations, balanced at last in a harmony of its own impulses, is now generally and rightly believed. The world of Keats is our world as Shakespeare's is, at once actual and visionary, sensuous, probable, yet open to possibility. From the *Ode to Psyche* on, it is accurate to say of Keats that his consciousness and imagination were one, and his sense of actuality absolute. He was refreshingly free of existing conceptions of the world, and free also of apocalyptic desire, the inner necessity that compelled Blake and Shelley to create their radical but open conceptions of possible worlds. The presence of death heightened Keats's imaginative naturalism by giving it relentless urgency, without persuading Keats that the earth was less than enough.

What allies six great poets so different in their reactions to the common theme of imagination is a quality of passion and largeness, in speech and in response to life. All of them knew increasingly well what Stevens seems to have known best among the poets of our time, that the theory of poetry is the theory of life. As they would not yield the first to historical convention, so they could not surrender the second to religion or philosophy or the tired resignations of society. They failed of their temporal prophecy, but they failed as the Titans did, massive in ruin and more human than their successors.

CHAPTER ONE

WILLIAM BLAKE

Thought is a garment and the soul's a bride
That cannot in that trash and tinsel hide.

W. B. YEATS

BLAKE is a poet in the tradition of Spenser and Milton, and ought to be read as one of their company. He is not a mystic or an esoteric philosopher. Like Wordsworth, he sought to emulate and surpass *Paradise Lost*. Wordsworth's strength and glory are to have gone naked to that hard task, and to have stayed so long at it before resorting again to the received myth that sustained Milton. Blake made his own myth almost from the start, and died sustained still by a story entirely of his own telling.

Spenser and Milton were Christian poets. The Romantics were not. Wordsworth and Coleridge died as Christians, but only after they had died as poets. Byron rejected no belief, and accepted none. Shelley lived and died agnostic, and Keats never wavered in believing religion an imposture. Blake thought himself a Christian, but was not a theist in any orthodox sense. If the divine is the human released from every limitation that impedes desire, then Blake is a believer in the divine reality. Yet this is not the divine of any orthodox theology in the West, for Blake wishes to take away from our vision of divinity everything that would make God a "wholly other":

Thou art a Man. God is no more;
Thine own Humanity learn to adore.

Blake's God possesses no powers that differ in kind from the highest human gifts, for Blake's God is "the real man, the imagination, which liveth for ever." This anthropocentric view is the basis for Blake's apocalyptic humanism, a stance that rejects naturalism and supernaturalism alike. Blake's position has much in common with Shelley's, a similarity owing to both poets valuing poetry over all other human speech.

Blake was painter as well as poet and the inventor of a new art form, in which a sequence of engraved plates mixes design and text in varied combinations, so that design and text illuminate one another. Blake's mature poetry falls into two large groups: an engraved canon, and poems abandoned in manuscript, sometimes with sketches worked out for the projected designs. Of the longer poems that will be described here, only one is outside the canon, *The Four Zoas*. Some attempt will be made to present the canonical work in its proper context, with the designs studied in relation to the texts.

Blake preceded the other Romantics, and never identified himself with them. Yet this is hardly unique among them; Wordsworth and Coleridge published the *Lyrical Ballads* together, and were close for a long time, yet neither identified himself with the other's poetry. Byron claimed to have little use for Wordsworth's poetry, though he did not escape its influence. Shelley and Keats acknowledged Wordsworth's poetic ancestry, but both repudiated the later poetry of their great original. All this aside, Blake and these others can be read more richly in each other's company, for their problem, theme, and central resource are nearly as one. Though he began earlier, in the time of Cowper and Gray, the poetry of Blake reaches further into the present than that of Wordsworth, and may be more prophetic of the future. As an introduction to Blake's emergence, I will begin by studying a poem published eleven years before Blake's birth, William Collins' marvelous *Ode on the Poetical Character,* an index to the time of Sensibility into which Blake was born, and a prophecy of the Romanticism that was to come.

1 *The Heritage of Sensibility*

COLLINS' *Ode on the Poetical Character*

. . . if we say that the idea of God is merely a poetic idea, and
that our notions of heaven and hell are merely poetry not so
called, even if poetry that involves us vitally, the feeling of
deliverance, of a release, of a perfection touched, of a vocation
so that all men may know the truth and that the truth may set
them free—if we say these things and if we are able to see the
poet who achieved God and placed Him in His seat in heaven
in all His glory, the poet himself, still in the ecstasy of the poem
that completely accomplished his purpose, would have seemed,
whether young or old, whether in rags or ceremonial robe, a
man who needed what he had created, uttering the hymns of
joy that followed his creation.

WALLACE STEVENS, *The Figure of the Youth as Virile Poet* [3]

TO MAKE a myth is to tell a story of your own invention, to speak a
word that is your word alone, and yet the story is so told, the word
so spoken, that they mean also the supernal things and transcend
the glory of the ego able to explain itself to others. We say of Blake
and Wordsworth that they are the greatest of the Romantic poets,
and indeed the first poets fully to enter into the abyss of their own
selves, and we mean that they perform for us the work of the ideal
metaphysician, which is the role our need has assigned to the modern poet.

William Collins is a poet of the Age of Sensibility and enthusiasm, of the conscious return to Spenser, Shakespeare, and Milton.
We have progressed beyond studying Collins as a fitful prelude to
Keats, or Blake as a freakish premanifestation of Romanticism.
What does ally Collins and Keats, Blake and Wordsworth, is one of
the great traditions of English poetry, the prophetic and Protestant
line of Spenser and Milton, which reaches its radical limits in the

generation after Wordsworth. The characteristic concern of this line is with the double transformation of the individual and of nature; the apocalyptic ambition involved is to humanize nature, and to naturalize the imagination. The *Ode on the Poetical Character* shares this concern and, with great intensity, manifests this ambition.

The poem belongs to the class of the allegorical ode, which moves in the Romantic period from personification to mythopoeic confrontation, from subject-object experience to the organized or deliberate innocence of a confrontation of life by life, in which all natural objects come to be seen as animate with the one life within us and abroad.[4] The inherent values of eighteenth-century personification were undoubtedly very real, but the values of Collins' mythical confrontations are rather different from those of traditional personification. What distinguishes Collins from the Wartons, or Christopher Smart from Gray, is that Collins and Smart sometimes (as in the *Ode on the Poetical Character* and *Jubilate Agno*) attain a transfiguration of the matter of common perception. They do this, usually, by consciously simplifying, as Blake and Wordsworth do after them. They reduce the manifold of sensation to a number of objects that can actually be contemplated, which F. A. Pottle sets forth as *the* mark of the poetic imagination in Wordsworth.[5] Having created worlds with fewer and more animate objects, they proceed to dissolve the objects into one another, even as Blake will later view natural objects as "men seen afar" and as Wordsworth, in his supreme acts of imagination, will have "the edges of things begin to waver and fade out." The "fade-out" or fluid dissolving of the imagination is more familiar to us in Wordsworth and Keats and most radically evident in Shelley, but its presence in Collins is crucial, and constitutes much of the "confusion" of the *Ode on the Poetical Character*. The confusion of Collins' *Ode* is thematically deliberate, for in it Collins' soul, God, and nature are brought together in what Northrop Frye has called "a white-hot fusion of identity, an imaginative fiery furnace in which the reader may, if he chooses, make a fourth." [6] This fusion of identity, the highest imaginative moment in the poetry of Collins, establishes the *Ode on the Poetical Character* as one of the group of lyrics that Frye has usefully classified as "recognition poems," in which the usual association of dream and waking are reversed, "So

that it is experience that seems to be the nightmare and the vision
that seems to be reality." [7] Within this larger group are the "poems
of self-recognition, where the poet himself is involved in the awakening from experience into a visionary reality." Frye gives the *Ode
on the Poetical Character, Kubla Khan,* and *Sailing to Byzantium*
as examples, to which one can add the *Hymn to Intellectual Beauty*
as a major Romantic representative of the type. Collins' *Ode,* like
Kubla Khan, is on the borderline of another group of lyrics, the
rhapsodic poems of iconic response, "where the poet feels taken
possession of by some internal and quasi-personal force" as in the
Ode to the West Wind, Robert Bridges' *Low Barometer,* or Hart
Crane's Shelleyan masterpiece, *The Broken Tower.*

The fullest reading of the *Ode on the Poetical Character* is that
of A. S. P. Woodhouse, who terms it "an allegory whose subject
is the *creative imagination* and the poet's passionate desire for its
power." [8] Woodhouse's reading is perhaps imaginatively less daring
than Collins' poem, for the *Ode* goes beyond the poet's desire for
the power, and suggests that a poet is born from a quasi-sexual
union of God and Imagination. The celebrated bluestocking Mrs.
Barbauld said of this allegory that it was "neither luminous nor
decent," but Woodhouse calls it only a "repetition of the fact already simply stated: God imagined the world, and it sprang into
being." But this central myth of the poem is both luminous and
nonrepetitive, though as unorthodox as any myth-making is likely
to be.

Collins begins the ode by repeating the central polemic of his
literary generation. Spenser's school, the line of late Drayton, Milton, of Collins himself, is the one most blessed by the Faerie
Queene, who by implication is the Muse herself. The polemic is
not renewed until the close of the ode, when Collins will see himself "from Waller's myrtle shades retreating," in full flight from the
school of Pope. The urbane "with light regard" in the first line of
the ode is a probable indication that Collins is aware of his two
"mistakes" in reading Book IV, Canto V, of *The Faerie Queene.*
The magic girdle is Florimel's, but can be worn by whoever has
"the vertue of chast love and wifehood true." At the solemn tour-
ney it is Amoret who alone can wear it, as Florimel is not present,
and the other ladies who are lack the prescribed "vertue." Collins
is compounding Florimel and Amoret so as to get a creative con-

trary to his own idea of Fancy. Florimel and Amoret together represent the natural beauty of the world adorned by an inherent chastity. Fancy represents a beauty more enthusiastic than that of nature, and this more exuberant beauty is distinguished by an inherent sexuality. As Woodhouse says, to Collins "poetry is not primarily concerned with nature, but with a bright world of ideal forms." [9] But in Collins as in Blake this bright world is attained through an increase in sensual fulfillment. We have here almost a prelude to Wordsworth's myth of nature's marriage or Blake's myth of Beulah as the married land. The beauty of Florimel becomes transformed into the bright world of Fancy by a consummation analogous to sexual completion.

The girdle of Florimel is better not worn at all than applied to a "loath'd, dishonour'd side." The implication is that it is more horrible to assume unworthily "the cest of amplest pow'r" which is in young Fancy's gift. That gift is godlike; they who wear it, once they "gird their blest, prophetic loins," are able to "gaze her visions wild, and feel unmix'd her flame!" That the gift has a sexual element is made finely obvious by the diction.

The epode is a creation myth, and a startling rhapsody in the context of its literary age. Coleridge said of the epode that it had "inspired and whirled *me* along with greater agitations of enthusiasm than any but the most 'impassioned' scene in Schiller or Shakespeare." Coleridge modified the value of his rapture by saying that the "impassioned" (he meant ordinary human passions) kind of poetry is more generally valuable, but *Kubla Khan,* with its echo of Collins' ode on the Passions and its youthful poet with flashing eyes and floating hair, indicates why the *Ode on the Poetical Character* had so strong an effect on Coleridge.

The concept of an all-creative and yet strictly male Deity has always been very satisfying to the moralizing temper of orthodox Judaism and Christianity, but it is imaginatively rather puzzling. The poem of creation can do very little with anything *ab nihilo,* for the imagination wishes to be indulged, as Wallace Stevens remarked, and opaque mysteries are not gratifying to it. Poets, even those as devout as Spenser and Wordsworth, have a tendency to parallel unorthodox speculations on the role of a female element in the creation. These speculations rise from the swamps of Neoplatonism, gnosticism, occultism, and that richest and dankest of morasses, the cabala. Collins' "lov'd enthusiast," young Fancy, who has long wooed the Creator, and who retires with Him behind a veiling cloud while seraphic wires sound His "sublimest triumph swelling," has her place in that long arcane tradition that stems from the cabalistic *Shekhina,* and that may include the Sapience of Spenser's *Hymne of Heavenly Beautie.*

There are no scholarly reasons for supposing that Collins was deep in the *esoterica* of theosophy, as we know Christopher Smart to have been. But while the passage from Proverbs 8: 23–30, on Wisdom having been daily God's delight, rejoicing always before Him, when He appointed the foundations of the earth, is an adequate source for Milton, it is not for Collins' ode. Source study is not likely to help us here, any more than it has helped much in the comprehension of Spenser's *Hymnes.* Collins' Goddess Fancy is enigmatic enough in her function to make us probe further into the difficulty of the ode.

Collins saw himself as a poet separated by the school of Waller from a main tradition of the English Renaissance, the creation of a British mythology: the Faery Land of Spenser, the green world of Shakespeare's romances, the Biblical and prophetic self-identification of Milton. This reading of English poetic history, with Waller and Pope in the Satanic role, is itself of course a poetic myth, and a very productive one, in Blake and the Romantics as much as in Collins and the Wartons. We need not worry as to whether Collins is being fair or accurate in his reading of history; it is enough that he is telling us and himself a story, and that he at least believes the story to be true.

To emulate Spenser and Milton, Collins must first see man, nature, and poetry in their perspective, not that of Pope. Their perspective, at its limits, is that of the rugged sublime, in which the poet is an original, whose inventive capacity is divinely inspired. The poet is an "enthusiast" or possessed man, and what possesses him is Fancy, which itself is a "kindred power" to Heaven. So inspired, the enthusiast moves into nature to form out of it an imaged paradise of his heart's desires. His ambition is enormous, but is founded on his claim to potential divinity. This is the background of Blake's astonishing ambitions, and particularly of his myth of Orc, which I invoke now as a context in which to read Collins. Northrop Frye, in tracing the orgins of Blake's Orc, considers the large claims of the poets of the Age of Sensibility and writes:

> It is in Collins' *Ode on the Poetical Character* that the most daring claim is made. There, not only does the poet in his creation imitate the creative power of God, but is himself a son of God and Fancy, a "rich-hair'd youth of morn" associated with the sun-god, like the Greek Apollo, a prophet and visionary of whom the last exemplar was Milton. This youth is the direct ancestor of Blake's Orc.[10]

Orc is the most complex and suggestive of Blake's symbolic figures. His name is based on his prime identity, which is that of the recurrent energy of human desire, frequently assigned by orthodox timidity to the realm of Orcus, or hell. Orc is the human imagination trying to burst out of the confines of nature, but this creative thrust in him is undifferentiated from merely organic energy. He is thus a very comprehensive myth, for he is Blake's Adonis and Blake's Prometheus, Blake's Apollo and Blake's Christ, and he is manifested in Blake's time by figures as diverse as Napoleon and Blake himself. This apparently bewildering range of identifications is possible because Orc is a cyclic figure; he is the babe of Blake's poem, *The Mental Traveller,* who goes around on the wheel of birth, youth, manhood, old age, and rebirth.

His relevant aspect here is that in which he resembles the Apollo of Keats's two *Hyperions,* the story of a poet's incarnation as a god of the sun. Blake's dialectic concerns man and nature, but is also a dialectic of poetry itself. Orc represents not only the sun in its dawn and spring but in their human analogies as well. He means new life and sexual renewal, which appear in the periodic overthrow of literary conventions as well as of restrictive social and religious forms. When we encounter a youth of the sun who incarnates a rebirth of poetry, and whose early existence is in an earthly paradise, then we encounter a myth of the birth of Orc, or rebirth of Apollo, whether we find him in Collins or Coleridge or Blake or Keats or Shelley.

What makes Collins' "rich-hair'd Youth of Morn" a direct ancestor of Blake's and Coleridge's youths is his attendant iconography, which is derived from the Bible and Spenser, the sources we should expect.

Blake's best and most famous portrait of Orc or the Romantic Apollo is his line engraving called traditionally "Glad Day" after the lines in *Romeo and Juliet:*

> Night's candles are burnt out, and jocund day
> Stands tiptoe on the misty mountain tops.

Blake's Orc dances on tiptoe, a superbly Renaissance figure, with both arms flung out and the light bursting from him. His eyes are flashing, and his floating hair is rich with light. He both reflects the sunlight and radiates light to it, and he treads underfoot the serpent and the bat as he dances. Blake's vision here goes back to the same source in Spenser that Collins' lines echo:

> And Phoebus, fresh as brydegrome to his mate,
> Came dauncing forth, shaking his deawie hayre,
> And hurld his glistring beams through gloomy ayre.

Spenser echoes Solomon's Song, with its visions of a great marriage in nature, an appropriate resonance for the Red Crosse Knight's great epiphany as he stands fully armed in the sun, both reflecting and radiating light from his "sunbright armes."

If we take this myth of the Romantic Apollo to Collins' *Ode,* we can suddenly see the startling unity of vision that Collins has achieved in the second strophe of his poem. The band of Fancy, which only the true poet dare assume, is analogous to the girdle of Florimel only in being a danger to the unworthy. For Fancy's cest, or girdle, was woven on the "creating day" when God rested from his labors, but in the company of his spouse, Fancy, who long had wooed him. On this day, "in some diviner mood," God takes her. Amidst the triumphal music, Fancy breathes her magic notes aloud, and the poet as Orc, or Apollo, is born. We can trace in the features of Blake's Glad Day the self-portrait of the young Blake. Collins here, unlike Blake, or Coleridge at the climax of *Kubla Khan,* is not audacious enough to claim this full identification. Indeed, Collins' fear of such a claim dominates the last strophe of his poem. Yet Collins indicates the significance of this sudden incarnation for him by excitedly breaking into the second-person invocatory address, which usually accompanies mythopoeic confrontation:

> And *thou,* thou rich-hair'd Youth of Morn,
> And all thy subject life, was born!

Everything in the ode before and after these lines is in the first or third person; Collins shows extraordinary artistry and a firm grasp of his subject by this moment of direct address, as in a supreme act of imagination he shares a meeting with a self he longs to become.

From this height of startled apprehension, in which the object world has dropped away, Collins as suddenly descends. If he were to entertain such "high presuming hopes" it would be "with rapture blind." For to incarnate the poet within oneself is to be a resident of that poet's paradise, inaccessible to Collins, which he pictures in the antistrophe.

An earthly paradise on an inaccessible mountain top suggests the structure of the *Purgatorio,* and introduces into Collins' poem another of the great archetypes of literature, which Frye has termed the point of epiphany, where a cyclical order of nature and a higher eternal order come together.[11] The Romantic form of this point is the natural tower of consciousness, as Wallace Stevens calls it, or the dread watchtower of man's absolute self, as Coleridge calls it in his poem *To William Wordsworth.*[12] Keats, in the *Ode to Psyche,* builds this point of epiphany within his own mind as a refuge for the love of Eros and Psyche. From the point of epiphany we look down benevolently to the natural world, free of its cyclic variation, and up to the eternal world, but we are still more involved in nature than the apocalyptic world need be. Blake calls this point the upper limit of Beulah. Wordsworth reaches it on the side of Snowdon in the transfiguring climax of *The Prelude.* Keats's special accomplishment is to naturalize it, to locate it out of nature and within the poet's mind, as Stevens does after him. But Collins, like Smart or Cowper, is one of the doomed poets of an Age of Sensibility. His personal myth, which intimately allies his art and his life, is one of necessary historical defeat. The cliff on which Milton lay is "of rude access," and supernatural beings guard it. No manic seizure

will bring Collins there, nor has he yet learned the Wordsworthian
metaphysic of internalization that will be available to Keats. As the
ode closes, Collins looks upward in vain:

> such bliss to one alone
> Of all the sons of soul was known,
> And Heav'n and Fancy, kindred pow'rs,
> Have now o'erturn'd th' inspiring bow'rs,
> Or curtain'd close such scene from ev'ry future view.

The "inspiring bow'rs" are those of Spenser's Adonis and Milton's
Eden, and are righted again in Blake and Wordsworth.

Poetical Sketches

POETICAL SKETCHES was printed (1783) but not published, as no
copies were ever offered for sale. Blake seems not to have given away
many copies, and presumably the choice not to publish was his own.
Poetical Sketches manifests many influences, but these are homoge-
nous, and show Blake to be in the direct line of the poets of the Age
of Sensibility, particularly Collins. Had we only these youthful
poems of Blake (written between his twelfth and twentieth years),
it is likely we would place him as a second and greater Collins. As
with Collins, his early poems are haunted by the pastoral elements
in the King James Bible, Spenser, Shakespeare, and Milton. Coming
later than Collins, Blake shows the full effect of the Gothic Revival
—of Percy's *Reliques,* Chatterton, Ossian, and the Old Norse poetry,
probably this last through the medium of the poetry of Gray. The
movement from personification to mythical confrontation, evidenced
in the Revival, is nowhere clearer than in Blake's four poems on the
seasons, which open *Poetical Sketches.*

In *To Spring* the tone of the Song of Songs is heard. The lovesick
Earth has bound up her modest tresses in mourning for her absent
lover, Spring. He returns to deck her forth with his fair fingers, and
to put the crown of new growth upon her head. In this poem personification clearly still prevails.

To Summer is an address from the landscape to an Apollo figure
who resembles the Poetical Character of Collins' *Ode:*

> thou, O Summer,
> Oft pitched'st here thy golden tent, and oft
> Beneath our oaks hast slept, while we beheld
> With joy thy ruddy limbs and flourishing hair.

Here the abstraction and the figure are too fused for separate consideration; neither the season nor the god takes priority. In *To Autumn* the humanization of landscape and season is complete, as Earth and Autumn carry on a dialogue. Earth speaks:

> O Autumn, laden with fruit, and stained
> With the blood of the grape, pass not, but sit
> Beneath my shady roof; there thou may'st rest,
> And tune thy jolly voice to my fresh pipe;
> And all the daughters of the year shall dance!
> Sing now the lusty song of fruits and flowers.

It takes an effort to remember that "my shady roof" refers to foliage, and that the jolly singer who replies is a season. In *To Winter* the transition to myth-making is complete. Urizen, the withered limiter of desire, makes a premonitory appearance as the devouring season:

> Lo! now the direful monster, whose skin clings
> To his strong bones, strides o'er the groaning rocks:
> He withers all in silence, and his hand
> Unclothes the earth, and freezes up frail life.

The groaning rocks are nearly those of the barren realm of Ulro, where the self-absorbed consciousness will dwell in holy communion with itself. These hints of incipient myth are subtler elsewhere in *Poetical Sketches*. *To Morning*, a Spenserian lyric echoing the *Epithalamion*, salutes Morning as a "holy virgin" who unlocks the "golden gates" of heaven, and then hunts with the sun across the sky:

> O radiant morning, salute the sun,
> Rouz'd like a huntsman to the chace, and, with
> Thy buskin'd feet, appear upon our hills.

The "buskin'd feet" identify Morning as a huntress, and as she is a "holy virgin," a Diana association is inevitable. In Psalm 19, also

echoed by Blake, the sun is described "as a bridegroom coming out
of his chamber, and rejoiceth as a strong man to run a race." Blake
makes the race into a hunt, and the light ambiguous touches
("golden gates" is equivocal, and so are "purest white" and a reference to Eos or Aurora as a "holy virgin") reinforce the Diana
image to give the little poem a faintly sinister quality. The exquisite
To the Evening Star is the finest result in *Poetical Sketches* of
Blake's animating vision. The Spenserian coloring is again present,
but a new movement enters into the marriage imagery:

> Let thy west wind sleep on
> The lake; speak silence with thy glimmering eyes,
> And wash the dusk with silver.

Blake was always capable of putting sensuous apprehension into
euphonious form, but when mature he generally avoided it except
for special purposes, as in his Beulah imagery. Blake is one of the
technical masters of English poetry; whatever he wanted to do he
could do. The odd but popular notion that he wrote more harshly
as he grew older because he had lost his lyrical gifts is nonsense.

The poems so far described are in the tradition of landscape verse.
A larger group in *Poetical Sketches* are songs in the Elizabethan
manner. The most beautiful of them is also the most profoundly
deceptive. Perhaps inspired by a line from the Elizabethan Davies,
"Wives are as birds in golden cages kept," Blake writes a song
mingling Innocence and Experience:

> How sweet I roam'd from field to field,
> And tasted all the summer's pride,
> 'Till I the prince of love beheld,
> Who in the sunny beams did glide!
>
> He shew'd me lilies for my hair,
> And blushing roses for my brow;
> He led me through his gardens fair,
> Where all his golden pleasures grow.
>
> With sweet May dews my wings were wet,
> And Phoebus fir'd my vocal rage;
> He caught me in his silken net,
> And shut me in his golden cage.

> He loves to sit and hear me sing,
> Then, laughing, sports and plays with me;
> Then stretches out my golden wing,
> And mocks my loss of liberty.

Eros, Prince of Love, is here also Helius or Apollo, Prince of Light, and a male equivalent of Keats's Belle Dame. The silken net of courtship and the golden cage of sexual capture are related to Petrarchan convention, but by association with the sun they become nature's entrapments also. The gardens fair that grow the golden pleasures of sexuality grow also the fruits of deceit and sadism, jealous possessiveness, and the depravity of a natural heart. Apollo kindles the bird into song, and also shuts her in the cage that will mock the earlier sweetness of free roaming. The poem's last ironic touch is the gilding of the trapped bird's outstretched but ineffectual wing. Gold is becoming Blake's prime emblem of the tyranny of nature.

The *Mad Song* is the furthest reach of the *Poetical Sketches* toward the *Songs of Experience*. The tradition of mad songs goes from the Elizabethans to the Romantics, and thence to Yeats in his last phase. Blake is unique in evading both the line of pathos (Ophelia's songs, Madge Wildfire's in Scott, the afflicted mothers of Wordsworth and Tennyson) and that of wisdom (the Fool in *Lear*, the great *Tom-O-Bedlam's Song* "From the hag and hungry goblin," and the Crazy Jane of Yeats). Blake's *Mad Song* is a satire upon its singing protagonist, and through him upon all who choose to narrow their perceptions to a chink in the cavern of nature. The poem's madman welcomes sleep as an unfolder of griefs and is so attached to night that he crowds after it as it goes, and so is sleepless because of his own fear of half of the natural cycle. The grim humor of the poem is that he is not as mad as he wishes to be, but presumably will attain the state through perseverance. He accepts outer realities only insofar as they accord with his preferred inner state (wild winds, cold night) and turns his back on light and warmth, though he can still recognize them as comforts. His ideal is to be:

> Like a fiend in a cloud,
> With howling woe.

Thus amorphous, he could escape the consequences of shape even as he seeks to escape those of duration. For even his heaven is a paved vault, and therefore an image of the bounded. He is a potential visionary gone wrong by an inadequate because simplistic metaphysic. Oppressed by space and time he does not see through those conventions but merely flees them into the evasions of a willful madness. The poem may well be Blake's ironic commentary on the escape into melancholia and despair of the poets of the Age of Sensibility—Smart, Cowper, Chatterton, MacPherson, and Collins. Blake's sardonic reaction to being accused of madness was to read and annotate at least part of a work on insanity. He comments there on the relation between religious enthusiasm and madness: "Cowper came to me and said: 'O that I were insane always. I will never rest. Can you not make me truly insane? I will never rest till I am so.' "

This has in it a touch of the *Mad Song*, and the gallows humor is parallel, for Cowper goes on to say: "You retain health and yet are as mad as any of us all—over us all—mad as a refuge from unbelief —from Bacon, Newton and Locke."

The gathering ironies of *Poetical Sketches* culminate in *To the Muses*, Blake's charming mockery of the state of eighteenth-century poetry, in what had become its own frozen diction. Wherever the "fair Nine" are, they are not on the English earth, and have forsaken poetry:

> How have you left the antient love
> That bards of old enjoy'd in you!
> The languid strings do scarcely move!
> The sound is forc'd, the notes are few!

As Frye observes, this is the germ of Blake's myth which separates the "Daughters of Beulah," human inspiration, from the "Daughters of Memory," the Nine Muses, natural inspiration from the generative world. To understand this distinction, we need to leave *Poetical Sketches* and begin to explore Blake's somewhat technical concept of Beulah.

2   *The Individual Vision*

The Concept of Beulah

ISAIAH the prophet, having for a last time detailed the transgressions of the people, proclaims the acceptable year of the Lord. Comforting the people, he sings the glory of the state of being to come: "Thou shalt no more be termed Forsaken; neither shall thy land any more be termed Desolate: but thou shalt be called Hephzibah, and thy land Beulah: for the Lord delighteth in thee, and thy land shall be married" (62:4).

The married land, Beulah, is the world of Solomon's Song, where the contract between the Bride and the Bridegroom was renewed, as John Bunyan comments in his *Pilgrim's Progress*. There, the state of Beulah finds its place between the dangers of the Enchanted Ground and the radiance of the Celestial City. In Bunyan's Beulah the Pilgrim may solace himself for a season—not longer. For Beulah lies beyond both mortality and despair, nor can doubt be seen from it. And yet it is upon the borders of Heaven, not Heaven itself. It is not what the Pilgrims had sought for in all their Pilgrimages, though here they are within sight of the City they are going to.

Of Blake's four states of being—innocence, or Beulah; experience, or Generation; organized, higher innocence, or Eden; and the Hell of rational self-absorption or Ulro—it is the lower, unorganized innocence or Beulah, about which he has most to say. For Beulah is the most ambiguous state. Its innocence dwells dangerously near to ignorance, its creativity is allied to destructiveness, its beauty to terror. Blake's Beulah poems are the *Songs of Innocence, The Crystal Cabinet, The Book of Thel, Visions of the Daughters of Albion*, and the dominant parts of the brief epic, *Milton*. These are Blake's pastorals, and are mostly in the lyrical mood, even in the millenarian *Milton*. Beulah also figures in nearly all the rest of Blake's work, visual and literary. The overt horrors of our existence are in Ulro, our worldly struggles in the Experience of Generation, our visionary end in the city-state of Eden, of which Blake tells us rather less than we might have hoped from an imagination so dedicated to revelation by word and picture, and so predicated against the Harlot Mystery. The ideal within our sexual reach is Beulah, the land *we* attain through the marriage of the male and female contraries. It is the state we lived in as children, when that state was at its best. It is the state we re-enter in sexual intercourse, in sleep and dream, and in our reveries. A relaxed state, an Elysium for the tormented spirit that cannot consume its torment in the furnace of creativity that is Eden, in the world of a fully human, altogether realized art.

The sources of Blake's Beulah are not esoteric; indeed, no important aspect of Blake need be traced to those wastelands of literature, the occult and theosophic traditions. Blake's Beulah is Hebraic and Protestant, in the Left Wing Protestant tradition of the Inner Light; it is the married land of Isaiah and Bunyan, the Beulah land of the Nonconformist hymns. Equally important as literary source is a tradition of a lower or earthly paradise running through Classical, Medieval, and Renaissance poetry, a tradition that finds its seminal English example in Spenser's Gardens of Adonis.

Blake is, with Coleridge, the most profound theorist of the imagination yet to appear among the poets. By this comparison I do not mean the "official" Coleridge, for that Coleridge tended, as Frye remarks, to regard literary criticism as a kind of natural theology, but rather the visionary who wrote in *Anima Poetae:* "Idly talk they who speak of poets as mere indulgers of fancy, imagination, superstition, etc. They are the bridlers by delight, the purifiers; they that combine all these with reason and order—the true protoplasts—Gods of Love who tame the chaos." Despite the "reason and order" reference, the dominant notion here is the Blakean one of the poet's exuberance. The energy embodied in poetry finds only its outward boundary in reason and order: it makes that boundary where it will, at the limit of the poet's informing desire. With Blake the desire is exuberantly infinite, and the epic *Jerusalem* is an enlarging furnace of *mind,* where the principle of structure in poetry is identified with the canonical plan of organization of the King James Bible.

The progression sought by Blake's dialectic is to make the sensuous given of our everyday experience into the "Human Form Divine"; to unite the human perceiver with the object he creates, or, as Blake's myth would put it, to restore the primal unity of perception. Blake's image for this unity is the giant figure of a man who includes the cosmos, and whose preceptive activity is the constant re-creation of himself.

Blake, like the phenomenologists, studies man in four principal relationships: man and his world, man and his body, man and his fellow men, and man and his own past and future. In Blake, man either creates his world, or else is passively brutalized by nature. Man *is* his body, when he raises his body to its full potential of sensual enjoyment, or, as Blake puts it, when he enlarges and expands all of his senses. If man fails, then he merely *has* his body, and is finally possessed and imprisoned by it. Man's relation to his fellow man is one of willed confrontation, not use. The most sublime act, Blake says, is to set another before you. When man fails, when he is used by or uses another, then the world—nature—becomes remote and hostile. In the presence of man and man confronting one another in love and mutual forgiveness, a redeemed nature is very close. Finally, a man's time in Blake is either imaginatively redeemed—as by the work of the poet-prophet Los—or else it becomes oppressive and restrictive, the clock time symbolized by the Spectre of Urthona, the shadow or dark Selfhood of Los, or the ruin that stalks Love's shadow, as Shelley puts it in *Prometheus*. For Blake the true past is always that which was *as it now appears to us,* and the future is *that which comes as it comes to meet us now.* The healthy or imaginative present, for Blake, true time, is a rushing forward beyond oneself, or a being already at and in the things that are to come. Time is thus of necessity a redemptive and prophetic agent. Blake writes:

Time is the mercy of Eternity; without Time's swiftness, Which is the swiftest of all things, all were eternal torment.

For Blake every moment is either an Eternal Moment—less than the pulsation of an artery, he says in *Milton*—or it is a dreary infinity. As in Shelley, it is the poem and the prophetic temper it embodies that must overcome the infinity of clock time. *What* it is that rushes forward *is* the poem as it becomes. To paraphrase both the *Defence of Poetry* and Blake's *Milton*, the poem's present time is a throwing forward of what was into what is to come.

Most poets who attempt cosmic and religious epics are forced by the nature of their themes to experiment with the presentation of radically different but coexistent states of being. Dante's Paradise, Purgatory, and Inferno are generally acknowledged to be the most technically perfect resolution of the problem, but in fact they evade it, as all are visions of the last things, taking place after death. Blake, after designing a diagram of the Circles of Hell for his illustrations to Dante, remarked: "This [the diagram] is Upside Down when view'd from Hell's gate, which ought to be at top, But right when View'd from Purgatory after they have passed the Center." Having followed Dante so far, Blake adds sardonically: "In Equivocal Worlds Up & Down are Equivocal."

The concept of four states of being existing simultaneously here and now in this life is Blake's answer to Dante's and Orthodoxy's allegorical abodes, those equivocal worlds of bliss, purgation, and agony, of light without heat, and heat without light. The Isaiah-Bunyan influence was probably decisive for Blake's Beulah, but the general concept of states seems to have been formed by Blake out of sources no more esoteric than Spenser and Milton, his two great originals, as they were to be for Shelley and Keats after him.

Milton's states of existence are rigorously severed, one from another. There are the two worlds of Man, before and after the Fall. There are the two worlds of the Angels, Heaven and Hell. Milton's Garden of Eden is Blake's Beulah; his post-lapsarian world, Blake's Generation. The razor of Blake's dialectic exposes both Milton's Heaven and his Hell as being merely negations of one another. Blake does not take Milton's Heaven for his Ulro and Milton's Hell for his Eden, though with a grim wit he plays rhetorically at merely inverting the Miltonic categories. Here, where Milton is imaginatively most inadequate, at least in his naming of parts, Blake turns to Spenser for a body of archetypes.

No literary world, no part of the verbal universe, has quite the beautiful ambiguity of Spenser's Faery Land, not even the metamorphic cosmos of Ovid, who was, in a certain sense, Spenser's original. There is a Chaos beneath Faery Land and a City, the Faerie Queene's Cleopolis, above it, but mingled within it are at least three states of being: a Hell in several distinct aspects, a lower paradise in the Gardens of Adonis, and a comprehensive vision of the fallen natural world. If we isolated Book I of *The Faerie Queene* from the complexity of the rest of the poem, we would still have all the essential states of being: the redeemed City of the Faerie Queene, the paradisal Garden of Una's parents, restored by St. George's triumphal dragon fights and his marriage to Una, the post-lapsarian generative universe in which the knight undergoes trials, deceptions, and unsanctified sexual experience, and the self-absorbed Ulro, or hell-within-nature, of Archimago's hermitage, Duessa's bowers, and Fradubio's vegetative prison. In this shifting world of phenomenal images, where appearance is either to be trusted absolutely or not at all, but rarely is seen as being intermediate between Good and Evil, it is natural for us, like the Knight of the Red-Cross, to be perpetually deceived. From Spenser, Blake takes this vision of the natural world as being multileveled. But Blake is categorical, whereas Spenser is suggestive. Milton is categorical too, but his categories are received, not self-created, or, as Blake would have said, enslaved, not seen.

Blake's account of Beulah is full and rather technical, but these are the main outlines. Beulah is the contrary of Eden, and so a successful exercise of the imagination must marry Beulah and Eden together, which is Blake's dominant point in *The Marriage of Heaven and Hell*. Beulah is female, Eden male; Beulah a state of rational repose, Eden of energetic creativity. In Blake's theory of the seasons Beulah is spring and Eden autumn; here Blake relies on the interesting fact that the Bible mentions no other seasons until after the flood, and the flood, in Blake's gnostic cosmology, was one and the same event with the fall of nature and man, and the creation of nature and man in their present form. So the unfallen or Divine Man, Blake's Albion, lived in a world without summer or winter, but in a perpetual alternation of the spring seeding of Beulah and the autumn harvesting of Eden, a constant cyclic movement between sexual fecundity and creative activity. The two seasons, spring and autumn, pass over into one another at a point of epiphany that Blake calls the upper limit of Beulah, which is his direct parallel to Spenser's Gardens of Adonis:

> There is continuall Spring, and harvest there
> Continuall, both meeting at one tyme.

If Beulah is spring and Eden autumn, then we may expect Generation to be summer and Ulro winter, which is the case. This cycle has certain important implications for Blake's poetry. With the event of the Creation-Fall-Deluge, the cycle of history begins, and Generation and the Ulro lying within and below it are created. No longer can one move directly from spring to harvest. The only road from innocence to creativity and apocalypse lies through the realm of summer, through Generation, the hard world of experience. Thel, the virgin, in the book that bears her name, refuses to learn this lesson and will not move forward beyond spring and Innocence. If you will not move voluntarily in the cycle (and Thel's name means "will" or "wish"), then you will move back involuntarily into the Winter of Ulro, into the Spenserian Bower of Bliss which yawns waiting beneath the lower limit of Beulah. Conversely, if you are in the Hell of the Ulro, rationalistically and solipsistically absorbed in yourself, then your only hope is to move up from Winter into Spring, to pass on through an increase in sensual enjoyment and sexual fulfillment until you find yourself in Beulah again.

Beulah, according to Blake, is the emanation of Eden—that is, its outer and feminine or created form. Beulah is therefore temporal and illusory; in it the Imagination sleeps, but does not die, provided it does not sleep too long. If it does it awakens in the tomb of the Ulro. Energy struggling to get out of Ulro is Generation. So the ordinary forms of nature are mostly Ulro, but the sexual element is defined as being higher than the rest of nature. Wordsworth provides an analogy when he speaks of the marriage between the discerning intellect of man and the goodly universe of nature which will produce a joy which in turn will liberate the sensual and the proud from the sleep of death. The great consummation of which Wordsworth promises to write the spousal hymn is precisely what Blake composes epithalamia for in his Songs of Beulah. Phenomenal nature is therefore threefold in both Wordsworth and Blake, and contains Ulro, Generation, and Beulah. Blake breaks from Wordsworth because he cannot approve of a myth that is content with the illusory earthly Paradise of a Beulah. Wordsworth, like Keats, is too naturalistic for Blake. For Wordsworth, generation and creation are very nearly an identity; for Blake they are altogether different. Wordsworth and Freud in their theories of artistic creation can be assimilated to one another; Blake and Freud cannot.

Why does Blake posit Beulah as being at all necessary or desirable if he believes so strongly that the Earth is not enough? Blake's vision of Eden or theory of the Imagination is not mystical, nor is it dependent upon rejecting the world of Coleridge's Primary Imagination, the realm of phenomenal appearance. Eden is inner and primal and subsists in itself, but how is it to be made available to us?

Beulah is constantly created, says Blake, by the Lamb of God out of mercy for those that sleep. As the Lamb of God is in Blake the faculty of organized innocence in man, Beulah is therefore *the* great work of Eden, or the imagination, and is meant as appearance to the imagination's reality. Rational beliefs of any kind are not yet fully imaginative, but they exist in Beulah with all other forms and creeds, for in Blake a belief is held by the mind only as a reposeful substitute for imaginative, creative apprehension. Therefore in Blake a rational belief has exactly the same status as sexual existence; indeed, to Blake all our beliefs are sexual in causation and our sexual preferences are embodied modes of belief. And all rational beliefs, creeds, and forms and all sexual preferences are equally true for Blake because Beulah is a land where all contrarieties, as Blake says, are equally true. This being so, genetic explanations do not work in Beulah. The rationally conceptual and the sexual underlie each other equally, as they do in Spenser's Gardens of Adonis.

If you look at Blake's flowers in the engraved illustrations to his Beulah works, particularly the *Songs of Innocence,* you quickly notice that these flowers are flames in their form and movement. This is because visually Eden is a flame and Beulah a flower. Milton Percival, who has the distinction of being Blake's most rigorous doctrinal expositor, in his book, *The Circle of Destiny,* to which I am indebted here, notes that Blake has four ways of picturing a flower. In Eden it is a pure flame; in Beulah the flame manifests itself to us as the appearance of a flower; in Generation the flowers tend to take on photographic realism (for instance, the flowers in the illustrations to the *Songs of Experience*); and finally, in Ulro, the flowers' tendrils take on the aspect of an imprisoning trap. Eden then is a city of Fire, surrounded by a flowery Garden, or Beulah. Around this are the forests of the night of the *Tyger* Song of Experience, or Generation, and things look as the passive eye of the camera records them, if you insist upon seeing them that way. Around this earth is the watery chaos of Ulro, where every natural growth is an imprisoning womb, a world of embowered forms and grasping tendrils. Essentially this is Blake's cosmology.

The ethical aspects of Beulah are the clear consequences of its structural peculiarities. Its emotions are all of the forgiving variety, emphasizing feminine self-sacrifice, in a Miltonic vision of the ideal human love relationship. Beulah is possible only because the Daughters of Beulah (who are Blake's Muses) are willing to sacrifice the Female Will. Like the Oothoon of the *Visions of the Daughters of Albion*, they are prepared to abstain from sexual jealousy. The active virtue of the Daughters of Beulah is pity; the condition producing this virtue is peace. In Eden the contraries are in a mode of union which seems to transcend marriage; they are united in essence and not just in act. In Beulah all meeting is sexual; the contraries remain separate but cease to war. There is Intellectual Warfare in Eden according to Blake, for creativity knows no peace, but it is a war that transcends separateness.

The sexual doctrine of Beulah is an exaltation of the natural heterosexual relation. Blake is both more sensual than Spenser or Milton and yet more aware even than they are of the dangers of seeking an apocalyptic release in sexual fulfillment. You can believe in Beulah, but you cannot know. That is, you can know something only by and in creating it. So, for Blake, carnal knowing and knowledge are only carnal believing and belief.

The Garden of Beulah at its upper limits becomes the Gates of Paradise. Before the Fall, according to Blake, the gate to Eden from Beulah was always open. Among other things, this approximates the Miltonic belief that the sexual entrance was wider, was in fact an entire body entering into an entire body. The Blakean difference is of course that God and Man are one and the same and no intermediate orders of hierarchy therefore exist. In Eternity, Blake says, the sexual act was a mixing from head to toe, and not a priest entering in by a secret place. The startling association between the high priest entering the innermost recess of the temple and the act of fallen heterosexuality accounts for the ambiguity of the symbol of the veil in Blake. It is the golden net of the harlot Vala, the ultimate Belle Dame of Blake's system. But it is also the little curtain of flesh on the bed of our infinite desire that appalls Thel, and again it is the primal veil of Solomon's Temple, the first deception and Mystery of Priestcraft. For Blake, the Imagination must transcend any prevalent conceptualizations of it; so also the sexual must carry the possibility of surmounting our vision of its limits. Blake borders on contradiction here, and knows it; Beulah is in a paradoxical relationship to Generation, being above it technically but below it pragmatically. The youth who enters the crystal cabinet is able to see another England there, like his own but more visionary. Yet when he strives to grasp the inmost form of what he sees and makes love to, he only shatters the cabinet and finds himself in the psychotic second childhood of the Ulro. But if the youth could have accepted the forms for their own sake as appearances, they would have vanished to be replaced by others. It is the continuous cycle of substance in Spenser's Gardens of Adonis which keeps them from turning into their demonic parody in the static Bower of Bliss. The voluntary death of the feminine forms of Beulah assures both the renewal and continuity of the world of the imagination. The form dies, and the substance is liberated to find a fresh form. Creativity depends on a sublimation of sexuality which is curiously different from the kind of sublimation treated by Freud in this connection. In Blake, sexuality voluntarily dismisses it conceptual aspect as illusory in order that artistic creation can have freedom to function.

The virtues of Beulah are no greater than the dangers potential in it. Underneath Beulah lies the Ulro. Spenser accomplishes this structure by making the Bower of Bliss a parody of the Gardens of Adonis; Blake makes this inverted relationship a good deal more direct. The abyss of Ulro is Spenser's wide womb of the created world—as the rational mind falls over into the abyss it has a last vision of reality before it suffers the fate of Humpty Dumpty. It sees an external nature spreading forth out of Beulah on every side, and yet for the pulsation of an artery it sees as well a Beulah still momentarily emanative. This is Blake's equivalent of Wordsworth's intimation of immortality from memories of earliest childhood— the mind, in falling for a last time, sees the immortal sea lapping around every side of its consciousness, and sees behind it the garden it is abandoning. In the shock of its fall a gradually decaying resistance to nature is set up, but soon this unorganized innocence vanishes, and the child at length perceives it fade away and vanish into the light of common day.

With the loss of Beulah in Blake's myth, the flood of space and time sweeps over the sleeping Albion, and the paradox of merely natural creation has begun. The womb of nature is an abyss of death, and yet it brings life into being.

The infinity of Eden is for Blake a fully integrated entity. Though infinite and eternal, it is definite and bound. But Beulah is constantly expanding and contracting: its outlines are elusive. The daughters of Beulah are always at work, weaving spatial illusions meant to be an act of mercy, but always bordering on the delusive. Beulah is therefore crystalline. Its images are threefold or even ninefold as in the sinister Chinese box effect in the poem *The Crystal Cabinet*. The leading images of Beulah are the moon, love, silver, water, sleep, night, dew, eternal spring, and a relaxed drowsiness. The catalog, as Frye remarks, contains the entire pattern of symbols to be found in Keats's *Endymion,* to which one may add the imagery of Shelley's pastoral romances—*The Sensitive Plant, The Witch of Atlas,* and the climactic canto of *The Revolt of Islam.* The themes of Beulah are those of the elusive but beckoning virgin, the poet as young shepherd-king, of fabrics crystalline presided over by Circe- or Acrasia-like figures, of kingdoms of lost innocence within the depths of ocean, or embowered in the skies.[13]

Beulah's dominant symbol is what Blake, in a compound of irony and pity, calls "a little tender moon," which lights the night of marriage with a love whose radiant power is only a pale reflection of the creative sun of Eden.

Frye, commenting on Blake's account of the rival transformations of love and art, sees it as a distinction between an act that transforms the object into the beloved and one that transforms it into the created. The characteristic movement in Shelley's poetry is a wavering between these rival modes—between the epipsyche or emanative beloved and the deliberating dying metaphor, whose vanishing liberates the object from its fallen status.

The crisis of vision in Beulah is the most crucial aspect of that state, and the dominant influence on Frye's theory of myths. There are two gates to Beulah, two limits: the upper and the lower. The upper limit of Beulah, on one level of its allegory, is that place existent in every religion (according to Blake) where it has a chance to become the true faith of the Imagination—the vision of Eden, where the universal human and divine creator exists as a composite unity. Put another way, in the world of Eden there is only energy incorporating itself in form, creator and creature, which means that somewhere (and that is on the upper limit of Beulah) this permanent objective body which nourishes and incubates the imaginative form drops out. What takes its place there is Mother Nature, or the homely nurse Nature, as Wordsworth with great precision calls her. The frequent symbol for the upper limit of Beulah is a ring of fire, cutting off the natural and emanative from the self-creative world. This symbol in Isaiah, as Frye points out, appears as the apocalyptic entry into Canaan by the Messiah from the South, moving through Edom, which Blake tells us is another name for the Upper Limit. Blake also intimates that the sense of hearing drops out at the upper level and is subsumed by a more intense sense of sight. Frye does not note the archetypal analogue in Coleridge and Wordsworth, but his theory encourages us to do so, and one can trace the pattern of the organic sense of seeing-hearing as an apocalyptic foreboding, as indeed the mark of the joy of imagination, in both Coleridge's *Dejection* and Wordsworth's *Intimations* odes.

Any account of a Fall from one state of existence to another, whether scriptural or poetic, tends to confine its vision to Beulah. This is because of Beulah's double aspect. For us in Generation it is the dawn of day and the Spring of the year, the place of natural and of imaginative seed, whence both children and poem proceed, insofar as a poem makes use of natural imagery. But from a fully creative point of view Beulah is a state of only dormant life. The consequence is that there are two entrances to Beulah. The way out of natural cycle in Blake, the opening in the womb of nature, is the upper limit or entrance of Beulah. If the individual does not go out by this gate, and also refuses to take the way into Generation through the lower limit, then he is doomed to the vision of eternal recurrence and Beulah becomes the static state of Ulro.

Next to this composite state and symbol we have Blake's theory of Beulah's limited but essential role in artistic creativity, and his further theory of the crisis of vision that finally occurs at its uppermost point, when the individual must choose to leave Beulah or accept it as what it is but no more, or else abide in it, expecting what it does not have to give, an ultimate form of reality, a joy without fluctuation, and a final truth. *The Book of Thel* and *The Crystal Cabinet* illustrate the self-surrender to the temptations of Beulah, as Thel flees back to it after viewing the price of generative experience and as the youth of the cabinet, grasping his threefold temptress, attempts to seize her inmost form and thus smashes the cabinet and finds himself out in the wilds of Ulro. We can illustrate this point by Wordsworth's career: *Tintern Abbey,* the *Intimations* ode, and *Peele Castle* trace the stages by which the bard of Beulah, desperately trying to maintain a vision of a married land against the lengthening shadow of organic mortality, gradually gives way to orthodoxy and timidity and at last falls into the Ulro of the *Ecclesiastical Sonnets,* and beyond that, the final abyss of the sonnets favoring capital punishment. This cycle from the poet of "possible sublimity" and "something evermore about to be" to the Urizen who could write of "Fit retribution, by the moral code," *is* the natural cycle that Beulah alone as a vision must at the last come to.

The Giant Forms

COLERIDGE, translating Schiller in 1799, pleaded the heart's necessity for myth, and insisted on the relevance of the imagination's instinctual thrust toward making natural forms intelligible:

> The intelligible forms of ancient poets,
> The fair humanities of old religion,
> The Power, the Beauty, and the Majesty,
> That had their haunts in dale, or piny mountain,
> Or forest by slow stream, or pebbly spring,
> Or chasms and wat'ry depths: all these have vanished.
> They live no longer in the faith of reason!
> But still the heart doth need a language, still
> Doth the old instinct bring back the old names. . . .

For Blake, the old instinct of myth-making no longer brought back the old names. With Coleridge, he believed that in Greek religious poetry all natural objects were dead, but that in the Hebrew poets everything had a life of its own, and yet was part of the one life within man.

Such a belief prevented Blake from anticipating Shelley and Keats in writing poems about Prometheus and Apollo, for to Blake these figures were hollow statues, and the study of the Classics only the study of death. In Blake the old instinct brought forward new names and gave the heart and head their proper language by a new grouping of intelligible forms.

He speaks of these, on the third plate of *Jerusalem,* as his "Giant

Forms," and we are not likely to find a better term for them. They are figures of myth and cannot be interpreted aside from their speeches and activities within Blake's poems. A myth is a story, and a mythic figure moves and has his being only within the meaningfulness of his story.

Blake's poems do not tell one story only, but they do try to tell as complete a story as can be told. The story's hero is Man, and Blake as an English poet calls him Albion. Fully integrated, Blake's Man is all Imagination, an extraordinary actuality whose consciousness is a final apprehension of human potential, and who is therefore God as well as Man, a vision of all that is. What this Man creates Blake calls his Emanation; when the creation assumes an object status the creator becomes only a shadow of himself, an isolated self Blake calls the Spectre. As Blake's religious heritage was nonconformist Protestant, he calls Albion's Emanation Jerusalem, and his Spectre Satan.

Blake is neither naturalist nor supernaturalist, for he refuses to accept the given human body as reality, yet he insists that the body is the path back to the real. The soul, for Blake, is the real or unfallen body; the body is all of the soul that fallen Man possesses. Man's body has heart, head, loins, and a working unity containing them, and so therefore must the human soul. The soul, or imaginative body, has a head called Urizen, while the loins are called Urthona, the heart Luvah, and the function that unifies them in the image of the human is named Tharmas. The fallen body's functions take different names. Urizen appears as Satan or the Spectre, Luvah as Orc, Urthona as Los and also as a detached Spectre of Urthona. Tharmas disappears, to be replaced by the chaos of nature that covers the former shape of the human. The Emanations of each primal power appear in nature as separate female beings. The head's creation is manifested as Ahania, a wisdom goddess. The form beloved by the heart appears as Vala, the ethos of nature, a vegetation goddess. The loins produce their Emanation in Enitharmon, a goddess associated with everything least attainable in nature. The power of unity, Tharmas, becomes separated from his Emanation who appears in nature as the earth mother, Enion.

The principal figures in Blake's stories of the fall, struggle, and redemption of Man and nature are Los, Orc, and Urizen-Satan. Orc has been introduced in the consideration of Collins' *Ode*. Urizen, the binder and circumscriber of the fallen world, is prayed to in this world as God, under the names of Jesus and Jehovah, and is identified by Blake with various accounts of fallen human reason. Los, with whom Blake finally will identify both himself and the true Jesus, is forced in the world of time and space to assume the imaginative function that rightly belongs to the whole Man, the Human Form Divine. The Spectre of Urthona is the dark shadow of Los, the ordinary fearful selfhood in every poet.

The central strife of Blake's poems is for the fate of Orc, the natural Man, the human energy warred over by the contraries of Los and the opposing Spectres of Urizen and Urthona: art against the doctrines and the circumstances that restrict.

3   *The Contraries*

Songs of Innocence and of Experience

BLAKE's songs within the canon of his engraved poetry need to be read with their full and accurate title clearly in mind. They are an integrated work, not *Songs of Innocence* and *Songs of Experience,* but *Songs of Innocence and of Experience, Shewing the Two Contrary States of the Human Soul* (1794). Without the simultaneous presence of both states, human existence would cease. The states are contraries because they cannot be reconciled within the limitations of a human existence. But their simultaneous reality demonstrates that neither merely negates the other. Rather, they expose one another in an interplay as various as existence itself.

Innocence is the married land Blake called Beulah; Experience is the harsh but vital world of Generation, in which the sexual strives with all that denies it. There is a double irony in play between Innocence and Experience as states of being. You progress, both organically and imaginatively, in moving from Innocence to Experience, and yet you fall back as well, again both naturalistically and creatively. Blake resolves the paradox by positing two modes of innocence: "unorganized," which is merely ignorance, and "organized," which can withstand the test of experience. On the manuscript of *The Four Zoas* he scribbled, *"Unorganiz'd Innocence: An Impossibility.* Innocence dwells with Wisdom, but never with Ignorance."

Therefore Blake does not prefer Innocence *or* Experience, Beulah or Generation, one or the other. The desirable state is that in which the artist creates, called Eden. The nadir is the Ulro or solipsistic self-reflection. But Innocence and Experience, though both inadequate, are neither of them a total loss, and need the correction of satire. In seeing that the states *are* satires upon one another, Blake showed enormous insight regarding his own symbolism. Experience exposes the precarious unreality of Innocence; Innocence censures the duplicity of Experience's realities.

In Experience, even though contraries continue to have each their own truth, one must always be more true than the other, else Experience collapses into the static condition of Ulro. But in the state of Innocence all contrary statements *are* equally true, and no progression is in any case possible. The interpretative problems of the *Songs* of both states will find their clarifications readily and accurately if these principles are kept in mind. In the world of Innocence it is equally true to hold that God is a loving father and Nature a benevolent mother, and also that God is nobody's father, Nobodaddy, and Nature a cruel and deceptive foster nurse. In Experience, the latter contraries tend to be the truer. The *Songs of Innocence* are therefore the more ambiguous, and the *Songs of Experience* the more frankly bitter. But this is not a bitterness born of mere disillusion, for the ambiguities of Innocence are the most genuine aspect of that wavering state. The darker contraries find their demonstration in Experience; the child's brighter vision finds its justification at the upper level of Beulah that lies beyond Experience, in the organized Innocence that enables one to dwell with Wisdom.

The *Introduction* to Innocence establishes the *Songs* as relating themselves to pastoral convention; the singer plays the shepherd's pipe. But the design in the frontispiece is of a shepherd dropping his pipe at the appearance of the child upon a cloud. So the *Songs* are not piped, but at the child's command are written down with a rural pen. For ink, the shepherd says, "I stain'd the water clear," and a slight shadow falls in the double meaning of "stain'd." The title page shows Mother Nature instructing her children from a book in her lap. Confronting her is a fruit-bearing apple tree, but the tree is diseased or broken, and its clinging vine is bound closely round it.

The Shepherd is a simple variant upon the Twenty-third Psalm, except for the implied question at its close. Does the Shepherd know that *his* Shepherd is nigh? *The Ecchoing Green* introduces another shadow, organic decay, in the movement from sound to the closing sight of "the darkening Green." *The Lamb,* usually considered a fine example of namby-pamby, is a poem of profound and perilous ambiguity, and raises for us the crucial problem of the *Songs of Innocence and of Experience,* the pairing of matched poems, here *The Lamb* and *The Tyger.*

The Lamb's design shows a naked child holding out his hands to the lamb. The design of *The Tyger* shows a shabby pawn-shop sort of stuffed tiger, more an overgrown house cat, with a confused and rather worried smile on what the text would hold is the fearful symmetry of his countenance. The Tyger of the text burns brightly "in the forests of the night." The tiger of the design exists in the clear spaces of day; in organized innocence and imaginative vision he is hardly an object of awe. The lamb is emblematic of both reality and deception in the ambiguities of merely natural innocence. In the world of experience within *The Tyger* he would be an object of pity. Read properly, *The Tyger* will reveal a state of being beyond either Innocence or Experience, a state where the lamb can lie down with the tiger.

A reading of *The Tyger* at some length is justified if it can reveal the traps that Blake prepares for the unwary reader. Blake differs from most other poets in the deliberation with which he sets rhetorical and conceptual traps. If the reader persists, he is rewarded by an awakened sense of what is possible in poetry and in poetry's effect upon existence.

The poem begins with the startled outcry "Tyger! Tyger!" But in what tone is this uttered? To know that, conclusively, is to understand the poem.

The organization of *The Tyger* is that of a series of fourteen increasingly rhetorical questions, in which the questioner who speaks the poem becomes more and more sure of the answer, and concurrently further and further away from the true answer. This questioner is of course not Blake; he is merely the Bard of Experience, and is trapped by the limitations of Experience. But Blake is not, and the purpose of his poem is to liberate us from such limitations.

The rhetorical web spun about himself by the questioner results in his moving within the poem from the state of Generation into that of Ulro; at the close he is alone with himself and with his own awe at a mystery he has imposed upon himself. The best commentary is Blake's own in *Auguries of Innocence:*

> We are led to Believe a Lie
> When we see not Thro the Eye
> Which was Born in a Night to perish in a Night
> When the Soul Slept in Beams of Light
> God Appears & God is Light
> To those poor Souls who dwell in Night
> But does a Human Form Display
> To those who Dwell in Realms of day

The speaker of *The Tyger* has been led to believe a lie because he sees his Tyger not through his eye but with it, and so he sees the Tyger as a fearful symmetry framed by darkness. The eye in its shrunken perception was born in the night of our fall from Imaginative vision and will perish in that same night. The bodily eye was born in the soul's self-deluding sleep. And to those poor souls who dwell in the voluntary darkness of minimal sense perception, if God appears at all He must appear as a light shining into the darkness. But He shows a human form to those who choose to live in light. So in *The Tyger*; the animal is burning bright and its symmetry is fearful to those who choose to see it in darkness, for the forest is not *in* the night, but "of the night," and does not exist apart from it. The man who sees the fearful symmetry may see also God's Love as light, and His Wrath as fire, and may identify the Tyger with the latter, and say that God made both tiger and lamb. Or he may choose the darkness and be a kind of Gnostic, and believe that two gods are in question, and assign one beast to each. But Blake wants neither answer; God is human in the clear light, and the fierce Tyger only the poor creature of the design. Blake wants us to question the questioner, rather than to attempt an answer to a question that already seeks merely to answer itself.

In the first stanza the speaker excludes a mortal hand or eye in the third line, without basis, and overlooks the double meaning of his own word "frame," for his own mortal eye *is* framing the Tyger with darkness, and making its ordering a fearful one. The distant deeps of some hell or the skies of some heaven are not the only possible workshops; the speaker excludes the world he stands in. The orthodox timidity that creates hell and heaven forms also the movement from "could frame" (immortal assumption) to "dare he aspire" (Icarus) and "dare seize the fire" (Prometheus). The hand or eye must be immortal, the speaker implies, for mere man would suffer the fate of Icarus or Prometheus if he dared frame the Tyger. It begins to be clear that the Tyger is a precise equivalent of the Leviathan and Behemoth of Job. In Blake's view, between Job and visionary emancipation lay the tyranny of the order of nature, the "War by Sea Everlasting" of the great Dragon-Serpent-Crocodile figure, and the "War by Land Everlasting" of the almost-as-dreadful primeval shore beast. Hobbes, Blake believed, had read his Bible properly, and Blake would have believed the same for Melville. The Tyger is Blake's Leviathan, and Blake does not want us to be frightened out of our imaginative wits by it. The questioner in Experience may wonder in what furnace was the brain of his Tyger, but Blake would have it that in Eden we know the framing furnace to be the fires of our own intellect. Blake must have recited *The Tyger,* as we know Kafka read aloud to his friends from *The Metamorphosis* or *The Trial,* with a laughter that seems inexplicable only to the Urizenic reader. The tone of the initial "Tyger! Tyger!" is one of affrighted and startled awe only if you dramatically attempt to project the poem's speaker as the self-duped creature he assuredly is; read aloud with understanding, the tone has a fierce and ironic joy. The satiric aspect of the poem reaches its height as the Urizenic Bard of Experience stirs himself into a perfect frenzy of adoring fear:

> And what shoulder, & what art,
> Could twist the sinews of thy heart?
> And when thy heart began to beat,
> What dread hand? & what dread feet?

Blake carefully revised so as to produce that last line, with its frightened leap in grammar. What follows is a marvelous heightening of self-induced fear:

> What the hammer? what the chain?
> In what furnace was thy brain?
> What the anvil? what dread grasp
> Dare its deadly terrors clasp?

We miss the point of this anthropomorphic projection of a black-smith god unless we apprehend the mechanical operation of the spirit implicit in its speaker. And as the speaker is now identified as the orthodox religious mind (which to Blake meant one tinged by Deism), we expect, after the frightened reference to Icarus and Prometheus, a glance at the fallen star, Lucifer:

> When the stars threw down their spears,
> And water'd heaven with their tears,
> Did he smile his work to see?
> Did he who made the Lamb make thee?

In the beautiful lament of Urizen which closes Night the Fifth of *The Four Zoas,* that former Prince of Light (whose name in fallen time is Satan) tells the story of his downfall, which echoes the fall of Lucifer in the King James Book of Isaiah and carries overtones of the Ovidian story of Phaethon, another ill-fated shining one. When he makes his conspiracy, Urizen says:

> I call'd the stars around my feet in the night of councils dark;
> The stars threw down their spears & fled naked away.
> We fell.

The stars throwing down their spears may carry the image of a falling star or comet; more directly in this passage from the *Zoas* it refers to the failure of Urizen's realm to rise with him in revolt against the primal unity of reality before the Creation-Fall. So in *The Tyger,* the similar passage refers also to an abortive revolt of the angels. Unlike the Miltonic Angels, who fought well, the Angels of Experience cry like children and the poem's speaker asks if God smiled on this scene of repentance. Did God loose Lamb or Tyger upon the rebels? The speaker has worked himself into the dilemma of orthodox theology in regard to the problem of God's Mercy and His Wrath, and resorts to the orthodox resolution of bringing forth a Mystery. The poem closes on a reaffirmation of the framing dark-ness, with the significant "dare frame" its only mark of progression from the opening. The speaker has turned his rhetorical question into a testimony to Urizenic ineffable power, and the close is properly Jobean. This bard too could say "I abhor myself" and bow before the Creation.

The child's confident replies of *The Lamb*'s second stanza are thus exposed as simplistic evasions that gratuitously give only one of two equally true positions. The Lamb of Innocence *is* Christ, and so is the Child, but the contrary is true also, and they are only victims, marked for the slaughter of Generation. The equivocation is present not only in the dialectic of Blake's argument but in the subtle rhetoric of the text:

> Gave thee life, & bid thee feed
> By the stream & o'er the mead;
> Gave thee clothing of delight,
> Softest clothing, wooly, bright;
> Gave thee such a tender voice,
> Making all the vales rejoice?

From the perspective of Experience the lamb is meat and wool, and its tender bleat conveys the pathos of the sacrifice. The rhetorical questions of *The Lamb* drive toward the answer of God-in-man or Christ, but can simply be answered "Man," which puts a shudder into the humanism of "clothing of delight," the lamb dressed in infant's wool. The ultimate difference between the states (and songs) of Innocence and Experience is sharply revealed by the alternate replies and their effect. A reply of "Man" to *The Lamb* means horror; to *The Tyger* it means a triumphant and emancipated humanism. A reply of "God" to *The Lamb* means triumphant reassurance; to *The Tyger* it means an enslaving resignation. The Man of Innocence is Natural Man, prone to all the brutalities of Experience. The Man of Experience is Imaginative Man, creating a nature beyond brutality. Each Man, and each God, satirizes the other.

In some of the *Songs of Innocence,* Blake's rhetorical irony is more overt. In *The Little Black Boy,* both the little boy speaking the poem, and his mother, quoted by him within it, contradict themselves and one another, without awareness of the confusions between and within them. The boy begins by affirming a vicious dualism: his own soul, and angels, and English children are all of them white, but his body is black, as if *bereaved* of light.

The symbolic interplay that follows turns upon heat and light. The boy, born in the southern wild, is instructed by his mother beneath a tree and before the heat of day—the intimation is that the heat is to be avoided. The mother points to the morning sun, identifies it as God's home, and says that God's grace is both light and heat:

> "And flowers and trees and beasts and man receive
> Comfort in morning, joy in the noonday.
>
> "And we are put on earth a little space,
> That we may learn to bear the beams of love . . ."

God's love, our joy, is too strong for us; we must learn to bear it as easily as we find the morning light a comfort. Presumably, the more we bear it, the darker we become, and the darker we are, the more we can abide. But the mother does not reckon thus, and does not glory in her blackness:

> "And these black bodies and this sunburnt face
> Is but a cloud, and like a shady grove.
>
> "For when our souls have learn'd that heat to bear,
> The cloud will vanish; we shall hear his voice . . ."

What is being satirized here is not a racial attitude but Christian dualism, the white ghost of the soul in the black machine of the body, and, more particularly, the unhappy orthodox paradox that simultaneously deprecates the body in relation to the soul and yet celebrates the doctrine of its resurrection. The mother's metaphors are badly chosen; blackness is not a cloud or a shady grove if heat is love, as blackness absorbs love. Having learned so odd a lesson from his mother, the little black boy seizes both ends of the paradox, unknowingly defying his instruction:

> Thus did my mother say, and kissed me;
> And thus I say to little English boy:
> When I from black and he from white cloud free,
> And round the tent of God like lambs we joy,
>
> I'll shade him from the heat, till he can bear
> To lean in joy upon our father's knee.

The irony of "I from black and he from white cloud free" is not intended by the child, but it exposes the nonsense to which he so movingly assents. These are also clouds imposed upon the children's understanding by their parents' Urizenic confusions. The God who gives both His light and His heat away intends them as equal gifts, and those who accept light and reject heat receive neither grace. The poem's final irony is the dark child promising to shield his English friend from God's love until the less favored can bear with joy the blackening beam of divine energy and affection.

The Chimney Sweeper of Innocence achieves its subtle and terrible effect by similar rhetorical means. The child's voice appalls us with its forceful ironies:

> There's little Tom Dacre, who cried when his head,
> That curl'd like a lamb's back, was shav'd: so I said
> "Hush, Tom! never mind it, for when your head's bare
> You know that the soot cannot spoil your white hair."

The shorn lambs of Innocence cry out the more effectively for not understanding their own victimization. *The Chimney Sweeper* of Experience understands the restrictive contrary as a hideous truth, and supplies his oppressors' motives with the unanswerable logic of childhood:

> Because I was happy upon the heath,
> And smil'd among the winter's snow,
> They clothed me in the clothes of death,
> And taught me to sing the notes of woe.

The beautiful *Holy Thursday* of Innocence is equally effective in its ironies. On Holy Thursday, Ascension Day, the charity children are marched, "walking two & two," in their regimented rows into the high dome of St. Paul's. The children's innocent faces have been scrubbed clean. They are dressed in the colors of life, "in red & blue & green," but they are escorted by gray-headed beadles who carry wands as white as snow, these being simultaneously emblematic of aged ignorance, of the beadle's office, and of instruments of discipline as well.

The children flow into the cathedral with the natural movement of Thames water, and they seem to Blake so many flowers of London town. In the vision of Innocence they are multitudes of lambs, wisely guarded by the aged men, and as objects of holy charity they suggest the orthodox tag that ends the poem: "Then cherish pity, lest you drive an angel from your door." But in the ambiguities of Innocence the contrary is true as well. The aged men sit beneath them as they *are* beneath them, for only the children are holy, and the beadles are servants of Urizen. The hum of multitudes which will be heard in the dread valley of decision is heard now as the accusing voice of the oppressed children, as "they sit with radiance all their own" and raise to heaven the "harmonious thunderings" of the brutalized. Read thus, the final couplet is cruel in its irony, and menacing in its implications. The *Holy Thursday* of Experience makes the point without indirection:

> Is this a holy thing to see
> In a rich and fruitful land,
> Babes reduc'd to misery,
> Fed with cold and usurous hand?
>
> Is that trembling cry a song?
> Can it be a song of joy?
> And so many children poor?
> It is a land of poverty!

The contraries expose one another most fully in the matching pair of *The Divine Image* of Innocence and *The Human Abstract* of Experience. These titles deliberately mislead, as *The Divine Image* is a collection of abstractions while *The Human Abstract* develops an extended image, that of the Tree of Mystery. In the ambiguities of Innocence, *The Divine Image* can take a precariously straightforward reading, but can be read just as accurately with the counterpoint of its experiential parody continuously in mind. In that case the poem looks rather more like the Divine Abstract, and an unwritten third poem would represent the Human Image Blake seeks.

The surface meaning of *The Divine Image* is sentimental. This Divine Image is turned to in distress, but the seeker is confronted by a series of abstractions—Mercy, Pity, Peace, and Love—repeated mechanically as a kind of idiot refrain. These four abstractions are identified with "God our father" and "Man his child," the crisis of identity coming in a very equivocal stanza:

> For Mercy has a human heart,
> Pity a human face,
> And Love, the human form divine,
> And Peace, the human dress.

This makes little sense. If Mercy's *heart* is human, what face, form, and dress has it got? Similar questions need to be put to the other abstractions. The poem's speaker does not expect to be questioned, and could not reply. What keeps the poem from dissolving into a tiresome refrain of abstractions is the striking phrase that is crucial for all of Blake: "the human form divine," the figure of risen man, of the imagination. Yet Blake jeopardizes what is closest to him by placing it into a namby-pamby singsong. What can be made explicit to the idiot, Blake said, was not worth his care. As *The Divine Image* is a little too explicit to the idiot, it promises to be worth the responsible reader's care.

The Human Abstract of Experience begins by standing *The Divine Image* on its head:

> Pity would be no more
> If we did not make somebody Poor;
> And Mercy no more could be
> If all were as happy as we.
>
> And mutual fear brings peace,
> Till the selfish loves increase.

So much for the virtues of Innocence. The remainder of the poem deals with the experiential virtue of religious Humility. Having created the poor and unhappy as objects for Pity and Mercy, and having established the Hobbesian peace of mutual fear with its attendant possessive love, the Selfhood goes on to its triumph. The net of religion is woven as a snare, and nature is then watered by the holy tears of the cruel weaver. Humility grows from the moisture of self-righteousness and blossoms into the tree of the ultimate abstraction, religious Mystery, which bears the fruit of Deceit. The mysterious tree upon which the god Odin impaled himself, to hang nine days and nights, sacrificed to his own glory that he might learn the mystery of the runes, is a likely ancestor for Blake's tree, but the Cross of orthodoxy will do as well. The Raven nests in the thickest shade of the tree, for it is dead nature, upon which man crucifies himself and so provides carrion for the Devourer.[14] The poem ends by reminding us that the Tree grows not in nature but in the human brain, where nature is created. The natural virtues of Innocence are thus a Divine Abstract, a mask for the Mystery worshiped as the god of Experience.

The *Introduction* to *Songs of Experience* starts with this realization and summons the reader to progress with the aid of the contraries, to carry Innocence over into Experience and Experience into a more organized Innocence. The Bard of Experience calls upon Earth to return to her original human form:

> O Earth, O Earth, return!
> Arise from out the dewy grass;
> Night is worn,
> And the morn
> Rises from the slumberous mass.

Literally, Earth must arise from her own form, but, like the Earth at the start of *Prometheus Unbound,* she lacks the courage so to rise:

> "Turn away no more;
> Why wilt thou turn away?
> The starry floor,
> The wat'ry shore,
> Is giv'n thee till the break of day."

In *Earth's Answer,* she blames her turning away on "Starry Jealousy," whom Blake will later call Urizen, the circumscriber who draws horizons for man so as to bind his energies. Her answer makes plain that continued bondage is sexual in its origins:

> Does the sower
> Sow by night,
> Or the plowman in darkness plow?

Yet lovers meet in the forests of the night and not in the radiance of day. This theme finds perfect expression in *The Sick Rose,* thirty-four words forming a marvelously compressed poem. As with *The Tyger,* this poem's difficulty inheres in the problematical tone of the exclamatory opening:

O Rose, thou art sick!

The emphasis is on the word "art," and the tone is grim with the assurance of a prophet who has seen his prophecy of calamity fulfilled:

> The invisible worm
> That flies in the night,
> In the howling storm,
>
> Has found out thy bed
> Of crimson joy,
> And his dark secret love
> Does thy life destroy.

The bed has to be "found out" because it is concealed, and it is already a bed "of crimson joy" before the worm comes to it. The elements of deliberate concealment and of sexual self-gratification make it clear that the poem attacks the myth of female flight and male pursuit, with its sinister pattern of sexual refusal and consequent destructiveness. The worm's love is a dark, secret love and hence destroys life, yet the worm comes invisibly in the night and by agency of the howling storm because a bright open love would not be received. Neither worm nor rose is truly at fault, for Nature has concealed the rose bed and so set the male and female generative contraries against one another. The poem's force is in its hinted human parallel, where concealment is more elaborate and the destructive rape-marriage a social ritual.

A similar power and deceptiveness are crystallized in the little poem *Ah! Sun-flower*. The pity Blake feels for "my Sun-flower" transcends pity in any accepted sense, and the lyric's tone can be characterized as a kind of apocalyptic sardonicism. The poem is so precise and economical, its beauty so involved in deliberately invoked longings and nostalgias, that it nearly slips its toughness and censure past even the wary reader. The curious irony is that Blake, so masterful in playing upon our quasi-imaginative self-indulgings, is so frequently and wrongly accused of losing himself in his own. The mind of Blake is so subtle and formidable that one learns not to condescend to him:

Ah, Sun-flower! weary of time,
Who countest the steps of the Sun,
Seeking after that sweet golden clime
Where the traveller's journey is done:

Where the Youth pined away with desire,
And the pale Virgin shrouded in snow
Arise from their graves, and aspire
Where my Sun-flower wishes to go.

That sweet golden clime is both the daily sunset and the timeless heaven where the Sun-flower, weary of the mechanics of its natural cycle, wishes to follow the sun. The poem's leading irony is in the absolute identity of the three illusory "wheres" of lines 4, 5, and 8. The Youth and the Virgin have denied their sexuality to win the allegorical abode of the conventionally visualized heaven. Arriving there, they arise from their graves to be trapped in the same cruel cycle of longings; they are merely at the sunset and aspire to go where the Sun-flower seeks his rest, which is precisely where they already are. The Sun-flower must live a merely vegetative existence, being bound into nature, but the lovers trap themselves in the limitations of the natural world by refusing the generative aspects of their state. By an increase in sensual fulfillment they could break out of cycle, but their minds are bound as the Sun-flower is literally bound. Blake's dialectical thrust at asceticism is more than adroit. You do not surmount nature by denying its prime claim of sexuality. Instead you fall utterly into the dull round of its cyclic aspirations.

That nature is largely responsible for the cruel deceptions of Experience becomes clearer as one reads through the cycle of songs. Even in *London,* generally interpreted as a poem of political protest, the "mind-forg'd manacles" are not entirely self-made or forged with the aid of government informers, and the bans are not merely Pitt's proclamations against the people's liberties. The Thames is "charter'd" in mockery of the chartered rights of Englishmen, and for commercial purposes as well, but also it is bound down by natural restriction. The marks of weakness and of woe in every face manifest the tyranny of the natural world as much as of the British government. The Chimney Sweeper's cry (" 'weep! 'weep!" in notes

of woe) appalls the forever blackening church in the literal sense of
"appall"; it makes the church pale and so exposes the church as a
whited sepulcher. The hapless Soldier's sign runs down palace walls
in the blood of the victims he is compelled to slaughter. But this
blood presages the king's blood, as David Erdman observes, and
indeed the blood of all men when the apocalypse tears down nature
as well as society. As the breath released in word or sigh whitens
and reddens church and palace respectively, so the Harlot's breath
released as a curse

> Blasts the new born Infant's tear,
> And blights with plagues the Marriage hearse.

In natural fact newborn infants have no tears, as their tear ducts
are closed. To blast a tear would be to scatter it out of existence,
and so Blake is attributing a natural fact to the Harlot's curse. The
Harlot is therefore both a literal figure and Nature herself, and the
plagues blighting the Marriage hearse stem literally both from a
youthful whore self-righteously accused by a Urizenic society, and
from the natural world itself, triumphing over life in the apotheosis
of natural morality that the social institution of marriage constitutes. Reason, Nature, and Society, the triple crown of eighteenth-
century culture, are for Blake a triple goddess of destruction ultimately to be identified with Rahab, the Harlot Mystery, herself a
demonic parody of the classical triple goddess Diana.

The most difficult of the *Songs of Experience* is written in defiance
of one manifestation of the Harlot. *To Tirzah* is an address to
Nature as the cruel Mother of Blake's mortal part, here repudiated
by his immortal parts of imagination and touch, for this last sense
is in Blake's myth the least fallen of the human senses. Tirzah was
the capital of the northern kingdom of Israel when Jerusalem was
opposed to it as capital of the southern kingdom of Judah. The ten
northern tribes were lost, and four senses, in this poem's reading,
were largely lost with them. Blake chooses Jerusalem as his intimation of imaginative immortality, the spiritual freedom given him as
a poet:

> Whate'er is Born of Mortal Birth
> Must be consumed with the Earth
> To rise from Generation free:
> Then what have I to do with thee?

In a note written about 1822 Blake wrote: "The Pope supposes Nature & the Virgin Mary to be the same allegorical personages, but the Protestant considers Nature as incapable of bearing a Child."

Blake says, "Then what have I to do with thee?" to Tirzah as Jesus said it to his mother, in a declaration that establishes the visionary's freedom from the bondage of the natural world. But as Blake's Jesus is antinomian, giving precedence to imagination over the morality of Reason, Nature, and Society, and thus declaring that he is his own son, so Blake tells Tirzah that she was incapable of bearing him. The Earth will be consumed if it heeds the prayer of the Bard of Experience, and will rise free of Generation into the expanded perceptions of Beulah. Tirzah molded with cruelty Blake's human heart:

> And with false self-deceiving tears
> Didst bind my Nostrils, Eyes, & Ears:
>
> Didst close my Tongue in senseless clay,
> And me to Mortal Life betray.

Only four senses are mentioned here, for the fifth gate to Paradise is still open, and through sexual touch the way back to Beulah can be found. Yet even touch has been altered by Tirzah. The divided Sexes, their division in Blake's myth a consequence of man's fall from imaginative integration, rise to work and weep in the generative struggle back toward primal reality. The poem ends in a realization that takes Blake out of Experience into the self-liberation of his visionary art:

> The Death of Jesus set me free:
> Then what have I to do with thee?

We see now that Tirzah is the goddess not only of Experience but of the unorganized Innocence or ignorance of the entire song cycle. The doctrine of the Vicarious Atonement has become a declaration of freedom not from Adam's sin but from the nature of eighteenth-century empirical observation, and from any beliefs founded upon what seemed to Blake to be minimal sensory perception. The *Songs of Innocence and of Experience* merely *show* the two contrary states of the soul. Blake's more ambitious engraved poems attempt the story of how these contraries are to be made into a progression rather than a cycle.

4   *Negations*

The Book of Thel

THE beautiful engraved poem *The Book of Thel* (1789) was written at the same time as the *Songs of Innocence* and it begins where they begin, in the garden that is Beulah, the Paradise of Adam and Eve in Milton and the Gardens of Adonis in Spenser. The poem opens with a motto:

> Does the Eagle know what is in the pit?
> Or wilt thou go ask the Mole:
> Can Wisdom be put in a silver rod?
> Or Love in a golden bowl?

The first two lines imply the necessity of descending into the pit. The silver rod is a phallic variant of the silver cord in *Ecclesiastes* 12:6; the golden bowl is an emblem of the virgin womb. But silver and gold, opaque and dedicated to Mammon, are ambiguous substances in Blake, as they were in the Bible. Love, put in a golden bowl, must mar the bowl or cease to be love. Wisdom is in the rod, but only if the rod ceases to be altogether silver. At a deeper level of Blake's symbolism both Eagle and silver rod belong to Tharmas the Shepherd, the Zoa, or Titan, whose element is water and whose power consists in the potential of life. The Mole (an emblem of Man as miner) belongs to Urthona, who appears in time as Los the black-smith, whose element is earth and special attribute the imagination. The golden bowl is Urizen's golden head, fitting the Zoa of wisdom, whose element is air. The motto, to Blake, must have signified the conceptual scheme of *The Book of Thel*, which is the failure to move from Innocence to Experience, from Beulah the realm of Tharmas to Generation the world of Luvah, the fourth and last of

the Zoas, whose element is fire and quality is love. By failing to make
the passage to Generation and fallen sexuality, Thel is condemned
to fall into the Ulro of Urthona.

Thel's name means "wish" or "will" (from the Greek), and the
movement into life that she fails to make is a voluntary one. Thel
lives in the "vales of Har," a lower paradise and seed bed of potential life which undergoes its own cycles but never dies into the life of
human existence and so never becomes altogether real. The title
plate of the poem shows Thel standing beneath a young and helpless tree while she watches the infant love of two blossoms. She holds
a shepherd's crook, signifying her functionless status in a pastoral
world where flocks can come to no harm and require little care:

> The daughters of the Seraphim led round their sunny flocks,
> All but the youngest: she in paleness sought the secret air,
> To fade away like morning beauty from her mortal day:
> Down by the river of Adona her soft voice is heard,
> And thus her gentle lamentation falls like morning dew.

Blake is writing in the fourteeners of Chapman's version of
Homer. This long, flowing line is the medium in which *The Four
Zoas, Milton,* and *Jerusalem* are written, and Blake, who is every-
where its master, has received very little recognition for his technical
achievement with this difficult line. The use of the line is more likely
to have been suggested to Blake by William Warner's *Albion's England* (1586) than by Chapman, for Warner's poem attempts the
synthesis between Biblical and British history which Blake came to
favor.

The first line of *The Book of Thel* identifies the heroine as one
of the daughters of the seraphim, traditionally the highest order of
angels and frequently depicted as having the heads of children.
Thel is the youngest of these shepherdesses, and therefore is in a
better position to notice the gradual fading of her sisters as they
grow older. Her soft voice is heard by the river of Adona, possibly
a Spenserian hint. Her lovely lament, with its deliberately wavering
imagery, is closer to Shelley than to Spenser as an outcry against
mutability:

> "O life of this our spring! why fades the lotus of the water?
> Why fade these children of the spring? born but to smile & fall.

Ah! Thel is like a wat'ry bow, and like a parting cloud;
Like a reflection in a glass; like shadows in the water;
Like dreams of infants, like a smile upon an infant's face;
Like the dove's voice; like transient day; like music in the air.
Ah! gentle may I lay me down, and gentle rest my head,
And gentle sleep the sleep of death, and gentle hear the voice
Of him that walketh in the garden in the evening time."

The reference to Genesis 3:8 in the last line of this passage reminds us that Thel's garden is identical with Adam's, and is a place
from which we must fall. Thel is as transient as the images she
creates, but cannot accept so precarious a reality. The "Lilly of the
valley," which toils not nor spins but is arrayed in greater glory
than Solomon's, answers Thel's lament by assuring her that transience has its Divine use. Summer's heat will melt the flower until
it dissolves to flourish again in eternal vales. Thel is not prepared to
accept this as comfort, for the flower has the assurance of its present
use, but Thel's beauty seems as gratuitous as the momentary kindling of a faint cloud at the rising sun. A cloud's comforting is no
better, for Thel lacks its cyclic use. She is close to despair as she
turns aside from the beauty of her innocent world:

But Thel delights in these no more because I fade away;
And all shall say, "Without a use this shining woman liv'd,
Or did she only live to be at death the food of worms?"

When she confronts the "image of weakness" of the feared Worm,
Thel is astonished at her previous repugnance. A Clod of Clay
speaks for the voiceless Worm, inviting Thel to enter into the house
of Clay and to return, if she so desires. The Worm is a phallic em-
blem of Generation, pathetic and helpless in Beulah but with the
double efficacy of creation and destruction in its own realm. The
Clay is the red earth of which Adam was formed, and so "the matron
Clay" is inviting the virgin Thel to accept incarnation. Even before
Thel descends from her garden through its northern, or lower, gate,
Blake has hinted at the ambiguities of the experiential world. The
Clod of Clay, assured by her deity that he has given her a crown that
none can take away, confesses her inability to understand this as-
surance:

"But how this is, sweet maid, I know not, and I cannot know;
    I ponder, and I cannot ponder; yet I live and love."

This is the Urizenic faith of Experience, content to abide in a
Mystery. As Thel wanders in Experience she sees the terrible world
Blake had shown in its songs, until at last she comes "to her own
grave plot," at once the natural seed ground in which she must be
planted if she is to grow into use, and also the grave in which she
will be buried when that generative use is done. This second aspect
affrights her, as she hears what would be her own posthumous voice
breathe a lament from out of the hollow pit of natural destruction:

"Why cannot the Ear be closed to its own destruction?
 Or the glist'ning Eye to the poison of a smile!
 Why are Eyelids stor'd with arrows ready drawn,
 Where a thousand fighting men in ambush lie?
 Or an Eye of gifts & graces show'ring fruits & coined gold!
 Why a Tongue impress'd with honey from every wind?
 Why an Ear, a whirlpool fierce to draw creations in?
 Why a Nostril wide inhaling terror trembling & affright?
 Why a tender curb upon the youthful burning boy!
 Why a little curtain of flesh on the bed of our desire?"

This lament should be juxtaposed with Thel's first lament in the
poem, for the two are a matching pair like the pairs in *Songs of Innocence and of Experience*. In her first lament, Thel regretted the
transience of what the senses apprehended, for her senses were the
expanded and alerted senses of Innocence. In the chant from her
grave the senses become the cause of lament, but in a complex pattern. Eye, tongue, ear, and nostril were too enlarged for their own
or Thel's good, but were anything but alert. The imagery of deception here is drawn ironically from the rhetorical conventions of
Elizabethan love poetry. After deploring the excessive ferocity and
strength of four senses that lead one on to the culminating sense of
sexual touch, the voice suddenly reverses its lament to wish that the
last sense had no natural impediments to overcome:

Why a tender curb upon the youthful burning boy!
Why a little curtain of flesh on the bed of our desire?

This is a protest against natural virginity itself, with its Urizenic
curtain and curb, however little, however tender. The voice's im-

plication is that Thel's timidity has never ceased, and that she has remained a virgin unto the experiential death. Confronted by the evidence of her having carried the cycle of denial over into a terrible world offering no compensations for such denial, Thel can bear reality no longer and with a shriek flees back "unhinder'd" into her paradise. It will turn in time into a dungeon of Ulro for her, by the law of Blake's dialectic, for "where man is not, nature is barren" and Thel has refused to become man.

The pleasures of reading *The Book of Thel,* once the poem is understood, are very nearly unique among the pleasures of literature. Though the poem ends in voluntary negation, its tone until the vehement last section is a technical triumph over the problem of depicting a Beulah world in which all contraries are equally true. Thel's world is precariously beautiful; one false phrase and its looking-glass reality would be shattered, yet Blake's diction remains firm even as he sets forth a vision of fragility. Had Thel been able to maintain herself in Experience, she might have recovered Innocence within it. The poem's last plate shows a serpent guided by three children who ride upon him, as a final emblem of sexual Generation tamed by the Innocent vision. The mood of the poem culminates in regret, which the poem's earlier tone prophesied.

Visions of the Daughters of Albion

THE heroine of *Visions of the Daughters of Albion* (1793), Oothoon, is the redemption of the timid virgin Thel. Thel's final grief was only pathetic, and her failure of will a doom to vegetative self-absorption. Oothoon's fate has the dignity of the tragic. She attempts to carry Innocence over into Experience, but fails because her tormented lover cannot accept the gift.

The motto of *Visions* is "The Eye sees more than the Heart knows," and so the poem concerns not a failure in perception but an inadequacy in the knowledge and understanding of the heart. Oothoon sings hymns to the hope of free love which were not to be matched until the Shelley of *Epipsychidion* dared to venture those rocks on which high hearts are wrecked. If the *Visions* ends hopelessly, its heroine yet maintains her protest and passion, and her final cry hints at an awakening still to come:

Arise, and drink your bliss, for every thing that lives is holy!

Except for the names given its tortured characters—Oothoon, Theotormon, and Bromion—the *Visions* has little to do with Ossian, or any other bard of the age of Sensibility. The atmosphere of the *Visions* depends upon the Revolution's ethics of release, and the poem's exuberant diction expresses a libertarian hope that sexual slavery will cease with all other forms of repression. Albion, in Blake, is the fallen archetypal Man, from whose fragmented form the existent world takes its being. Blake, commenting on his own painting of "The Ancient Britons," identified Albion with Atlas, and Atlas with the ruler of the lost continent Atlantis: "The giant Albion was Patriarch of the Atlantic; he is the Atlas of the Greeks, one of those the Greeks called Titans."

Heracles, in his eleventh labor, sailed into the ocean of the far west to obtain the golden apples of the Garden of the Hesperides (the "daughters of evening," identified also as daughters of Atlas, and therefore Blake's Daughters of Albion). At the opening of Blake's poem the Daughters of Albion weep, and their lamentation sighs toward America, where their sister, "the soft soul of America, Oothoon," wanders in unhappy isolation seeking a flower to comfort her loneliness. She plucks not a golden apple but a golden flower, a bright Marygold of Leutha's vale. At this point in Blake's work, Leutha is only a representative of sexual potentiality. Like the apples of the Hesperides, the Marygold represents an Innocence to be recovered through sensual fulfillment. Placing the flower between her breasts, the virgin Oothoon flies east across the Atlantic, which is the realm of her lover, Theotormon, hoping to find him and present him with her love. But Theotormon, an ocean Titan, is an agent of division. As the Atlantic he separates Oothoon from her sisters. Within himself he is a sick and divided soul, tormented by his conception of God (hence his name). Before the awakened Oothoon can reach this unworthy lover, she is evidently raped by a thunder Titan, Bromion (whose name is Greek for "roaring"). Bromion has not the moral courage of his own lust, and proceeds to classify his victim as a harlot. As befits a thunder deity he is a slave-driver, and ironically offers Oothoon to Theotormon as a more valuable property now that she carries a thunderer's child.

The remainder of the poem consists in a fierce dialectical interplay among the three demigods. Theotormon, consumed by jealousy, is too divided either to accept Oothoon's love or to reject her entirely. Bromion is desperately concerned to demonstrate that his mad morality is a natural necessity, by insisting that Experience must be either uniform or chaotic. He is, as Frye observes, more a Deist or natural religionist than he is a Puritan, for he associates morality and nature as binding codes.[15] But Oothoon, though she has entered into sexual reality through the wrong agent, has been liberated by it from the negations of natural morality. She denounces Urizen, the god of restraint worshiped by both her ravisher and her beloved, and asserts against the oppression of his reasonable uniformity the holy individuality of each moment of desire:

"The moment of desire! the moment of desire! The virgin
   That pines for man shall awaken her womb to enormous joys
   In the secret shadows of her chamber: the youth shut up from
   The lustful joy shall forget to generate & create an amorous
      image
   In the shadows of his curtains and in the folds of his silent
      pillow.
   Are not these the places of religion? the rewards of continence?
   The self enjoyings of self denial? why dost thou seek religion?
   Is it because acts are not lovely that thou seekest solitude
   Where the horrible darkness is impressed with reflections of
      desire."

This remarkable passage is more than an anticipation of contemporary theories of psychic repression. Oothoon states the dark dialectic that makes man fall from a divine image to a human abstract. Sexual hindrance of oneself leads to imaginative crippling, and at last to the Ulro of solipsism, "the self enjoyings of self denial," here equated both with masturbation and Urizenic, that is, conventionally orthodox religion. Supreme embodiment of energy as she now is, the exultant Oothoon is all but trapped among the negations of her profoundly stupid males. The frontispiece of *Visions* shows Oothoon and Bromion chained back to back in a cave, while the oceanic Theotormon weeps outside. The binding is what Theotormon sees, not what is, for Oothoon cries out that love is as free as the mountain wind. To find the path past negation in Blake, we need to turn back from *Visions* to the poet's greatest polemical work, *The Marriage of Heaven and Hell,* etched about 1793 but written in 1790. The rhetoric of antinomian desire, splendidly but vainly employed by Oothoon, is combined in the *Marriage* with Blake's definitive account of the contrary laws of human process.

The Crystal Cabinet

THE CRYSTAL CABINET (manuscript lyric, 1803) opens with a youth dancing merrily in the Wild of unorganized Innocence. The Maiden catches him, puts him into her Cabinet, and locks him up with a golden key; probably this is an account of initial sexual experience. The youth is passive; no resistance or even surprise is mentioned. He gives an ambiguous description of the Cabinet:

> This Cabinet is form'd of Gold
> And Pearl & Crystal shining bright,
> And within it opens into a World
> And a little lovely Moony Night.

The exterior is precious or semiprecious in substance; the pearls are those "of a lovesick eye," and the gold "of the akeing heart," to quote *The Mental Traveller,* a poem in the same notebook. The crystal, judging by the title, dominates the façade, so that the Cabinet appears "shining bright." Within, the Cabinet opens into the "little lovely Moony Night" of Blake's sexual state of Beulah. Everything in the outer Wild has its counterpart in this inner world. The movement of the inward vision is centripetal, from another England to another London to another pleasant Surrey Bower dominated by another Maiden, each *like* its prototype in the outward air:

> Another Maiden like herself,
> Translucent, lovely, shining clear,
> Threefold each in the other clos'd—
> O, what a pleasant trembling fear!
>
> O, what a smile! a threefold Smile
> Fill'd me, that like a flame I burn'd;
> I bent to Kiss the lovely Maid,
> And found a Threefold Kiss return'd.

The youth now sees a threefold boxed image or triple mirror outline, which inspires sexual fear and desire. The threefold smile becomes his own as well as the Maiden's, but when he bends to kiss the smile's source he is confronted by a triple image, each within the other, and desires the inmost as the real form:

> I strove to sieze the inmost Form
> With ardor fierce & hands of flame,
> But burst the Crystal Cabinet,
> And like a Weeping Babe became.

But "the inmost Form" cannot be seized in Beulah; as Thel lamented, there is no unwavering or ultimate form there. The youth has attempted finality in the sexual, which cannot sustain it. As the Cabinet's precarious reality bursts, the youth and former maiden are thrown "upon the wild" of Ulro; they are no longer "in the Wild" of untried Innocence or lost Experience. The youth is reduced to the schizoid second infancy or idiocy of Ulro, and the Maiden who initiated the act seems to regret the experience that made her a woman:

> A weeping Babe upon the wild,
> And Weeping Woman pale reclin'd,
> And in the outward air again
> I fill'd with woes the passing Wind.

The seventieth plate of *Jerusalem* shows three women walking under a giant dolmen or Druid monument (as Blake took Stonehenge to be), with a full moon of Beulah shining down upon them (in the Stirling copy of the poem). Druidism was for Blake the sacrificial religion of nature, which immolated male victims for the glory of the Female Will. The three women are three forms of the Great Whore Rahab, a triple goddess of heaven, earth, and the underworld:

A Three-fold Wonder: feminine: most beautiful: Three-fold
Each within other. On her white marble & even Neck, her Heart,
Inorb'd and bonified: with locks of shadowing modesty, shining
Over her beautiful Female features, soft flourishing in beauty
Beams mild, all love and all perfection, that when the lips
Receive a kiss from Gods or Men, a threefold kiss returns

From the press'd loveliness: so her whole immortal form three-
   fold
Three-fold embrace returns: consuming lives of Gods & Men
In fires of beauty melting them as gold & silver in the furnace.

The Maiden in *The Crystal Cabinet* is not Rahab, a Belle Dame
Sans Merci, but she clearly has attributes associated with Rahab,
who at this point is "the whole order of nature," as Frye comments.
As in *London,* a poem with which *The Crystal Cabinet* has affinities,
Blake identifies apocalyptic whoredom with the tyranny of the natural world over the human imagination. In the light of *Jerusalem,*
the enigmatic structure of *The Crystal Cabinet* becomes perfectly
clear. Though an improvement in sensual fulfillment is the first step
in man's renovation, it cannot be the last. The image of sexual completion, so eloquent in D. H. Lawrence, is inadequate and finally
dangerous to Blake. Finality is not in the onefold Self of Ulro, the
twofold subject-object world of Generation, or the threefold world
of lovers and their love of Beulah. The inmost form is reserved for
art, and achieved art for Blake is a harmony of the fourfold man, in
whom the living creatures of imagination, wisdom, love, and power
have found again their human form.

The Mental Traveller

THE lunar cycle of man in nature is the story of misplaced energy
for Blake, the story of Orc, the youth who begins in desire and ages
into restraint and death, the Devil who becomes an Angel, and so
accedes to what C. S. Lewis has genially termed "the Great Divorce"
between Heaven and Hell.

The Mental Traveller, an astonishingly condensed poem, is well
characterized by Frye as an ironic encyclopaedic form, like Yeats's
A Vision or Graves's *The White Goddess,* "visions of a cycle of experience, often presided over by a female figure with lunar and
femme fatale affiliations." [16] What Blake worked out at great length
and beauty in his epics receives gnomic expression in *The Mental
Traveller,* a cruel and powerful poem in itself, and an excellent
entrance into Blake's more complex mythopoeic poems.

The ballad's title seems to refer to a wandering Eternal, who has

visited the fallen world and is able so to stand back from it as to see
its horrific cycle:

> I travel'd thro' a Land of Men,
> A Land of Men & Women too,
> And heard & saw such dreadful things
> As cold Earth wanderers never knew.

> For there the Babe is born in joy
> That was begotten in dire woe;
> Just as we Reap in joy the fruit
> Which we in bitter tears did sow.

Like his fellow Eternals in *The Book of Urizen,* the Mental
Traveller shudders when he sees man begetting his likeness on his
own divided image, and so he sees the Babe as "begotten in dire
woe." The first stanza indicates again that in Eternity men and
women have no separate identities. Also echoed is the motto of
Visions of the Daughters of Albion; the Mental Traveller's heart is
able to know what his eye sees, unlike cold Earth wanderers. The
Traveller disappears from the poem with his reminder that, as Blake
told Crabb Robinson, "there is suffering in Heaven; for where there
is the capacity of enjoyment, there is the capacity of pain." So the
Eternals sow the bitter tears of the warfare of contraries, and reap in
joy the fruit of contrary progression.

In the third stanza the rhythm becomes more tense, the Traveller
ceases to refer to himself, and Blake begins his incredible intensification of a vision of the whole of reality into less than a hundred lines:

> And if the Babe is born a Boy
> He's given to a Woman Old,
> Who nails him down upon a rock,
> Catches his shrieks in cups of gold.

> She binds iron thorns around his head,
> She pierces both his hands & feet,
> She cuts his heart out at his side
> To make it feel both cold & heat.

> Her fingers number every Nerve,
> Just as a Miser counts his gold;

> She lives upon his shrieks & cries,
> And she grows young as he grows old.

The Babe is fresh human life, the Old Woman the natural world into which human life is born. The Babe receives the martyrdom of the Norse Titan Loki (Stanza III) and of Jesus and Prometheus (Stanza IV), all of them crucified by religions of mystery founded upon nature, and offered up as sacrifices to Urizen, under the names of Odin, Jehovah, Zeus. The Old Woman is Rahab, Enitharmon, Vala depending upon the phase of the cycle; the Babe moves from Orc to Urizen and then back to Orc again. The poem records two cycles, then, one of man and one of nature, each out of phase with the other and each moving in a direction opposite to and feeding upon the other.

The Old Woman, the Babe's tormenting nurse, grows young as he grows old, for she is renovated by feeding upon his growth pangs:

> Till he becomes a bleeding youth,
> And she becomes a Virgin bright;
> Then he rends up his Manacles
> And binds her down for his delight.
>
> He plants himself in all her Nerves,
> Just as a Husbandman his mould;
> And she becomes his dwelling place
> And Garden fruitful seventy fold.

In this next phase, they meet in their rival cycles, but the result is a demonic parody of the married-land image of Beulah. As he ages into a Shadow, he accumulates riches, but as the only wealth for Blake, as for Ruskin, is life, the precious stones and gold are morbid secretions of "the martyr's groan & the lover's sign." We are in the situation of *The Human Abstract* again. In one of Blake's fiercest ironies the Shadow's wealth is seen both as his vampire nourishment and the means of his charity:

> They are his meat, they are his drink;
> He feeds the Beggar & the Poor
> And the wayfaring Traveller:
> For ever open is his door.

As he has aged, Nature has become younger, and she reappears as a changeling little Female Babe emerging from the hearth fire:

> And she is all of solid fire
> And gems & gold, that none his hand
> Dares stretch to touch her Baby form,
> Or wrap her in his swaddling-band.

This terrible child grows older and seeks a form of man in her own sexual phase. With an earlier version of himself secured, she drives out the now aged host. The allegory constitutes Blake's most anti-Wordsworthian moment, for it demonstrates the dark end of Wordsworth's vision of nature. When in the *Intimations* ode or *Tintern Abbey* the poet loses or fears to lose the glory of nature, he is consoled by memory of an earlier self that shared in the glory. Here in *The Mental Traveller "they* soon drive out the aged Host," and so one's earlier self is nature's ally against one in the darkening years.

For the man who has been failed as son and father, and failed himself as husband, only the Emanation remains as a female form through whom renovation can be found. The last half of the poem deals with the ruinous cycle of Spectre and Emanation, until things roll round again virtually to where they were at the start, with the only change a worsening one. Where the first half of the poem described the mutual betrayals between man and nature, the second is concerned with man's failure to transmute nature into art, but again the guilt is double. The Poor Man, as he has become, finds a Maiden again, in an earlier phase than that of the one who rejected him for an earlier version of himself. But he has learned nothing from his defeats, and this embrace costs him the remnants of his imaginative vision:

> And to allay his freezing Age
> The Poor Man takes her in his arms;
> The Cottage fades before his sight,
> The Garden & its lovely Charms.
>
> The Guests are scatter'd thro' the land,
> For the Eye altering alters all;
> The Senses roll themselves in fear,
> And the flat Earth becomes a Ball;

The stars, sun, Moon, all shrink away,
A desert vast without a bound,
And nothing left to eat or drink,
And a dark desert all around.

As he becomes Urizen, he undergoes the sensory limitations imposed upon Urizen by Los in the Creation-Fall. The flat Earth is here an image of infinity; the Ball, of the finite bounded universe. The stars, sun, moon shrink away and become the remote, mocking heaven of the separate Eternals. In the "dark desert" of the Ulro, man and his beloved natural form play their love game of teasing elusiveness. He reverses in cycle and starts back to a second infancy, while she grows forward as she learns the arts of natural deception:

The honey of her Infant lips,
The bread & wine of her sweet smile,
The wild game of her roving Eye,
Does him to Infancy beguile;

For as he eats & drinks he grows
Younger & younger every day;
And on the desert wild they both
Wander in terror & dismay.

Like the wild Stag she flees away,
Her fear plants many a thicket wild;
While he pursues her night & day,
By various arts of Love beguil'd.

This process culminates in a phase directly before the one that opens the poem. He becomes a *wayward* Babe, and she a *weeping* Woman Old; at the poem's opening and conclusion he is newborn and she in condition to nail a Babe upon a rock. In this next-to-the-last phase, a possibility is open that the cycle can be broken and man's freedom from nature asserted:

Then many a Lover wanders here;
The Sun & Stars are nearer roll'd.

The trees bring forth sweet Extacy
To all who in the desert roam;

> Till many a City there is Built,
> And many a pleasant Shepherd's home.

Love can provide the imaginative foundation for such a revelation, as it heightens perception and brings the Sun and Stars nearer again. In the magnificent twenty-seventh stanza, Blake brings together all four of his states of being, to indicate that chance and choice are momentarily one. Those who roam in Ulro's desert are saved by the "sweet Extacy" of Generation, until the Eden of art can be built as an abiding City and the pastoral Beulah again become a pleasant Shepherd's home. But the possibility of freedom, presented through the rebirth of Orc as a kind of Christ child, strikes man with terror:

> But when they find the frowning Babe,
> Terror strikes thro' the region wide:
> They cry "The Babe! the Babe is Born!"
> And flee away on Every side.
>
> For who dare touch the frowning form,
> His arm is wither'd to its root;
> Lions, Boars, Wolves, all howling flee,
> And every Tree does shed its fruit.

As in Yeats's *The Second Coming*, the new revelation comes to man as an abomination of desolation, whose frown withers. Yet the cycle of history, though it repeats, has itself become more terrible. The Babe of the poem's beginning could simply be *given* to a Woman Old; the Babe reborn can be touched only by the Woman herself:

> And none can touch that frowning form,
> Except it be a Woman Old;
> She nails him down upon the Rock,
> And all is done as I have told.

With the grim irony of that last line, the poem ends. There is an implication that this cyclic evolution will become more fearsome each time it rolls around, which for Blake argues the necessity of apocalypse, a breaking of the cycle by an uncovering of the reality of both nature and man. In that merciless but comforting vision,

Blake attempted to shape an epic poem that would comprehend nature, man, and history from creation to apocalypse. The first attempt, *Vala*, Blake judged a failure, and revised into *The Four Zoas*. But the revised poem pleased him no better, and he left it in manuscript, though he used material from it in his final pair of poems, *Milton* and *Jerusalem*, which constitute his definitive achievement, his vision and his word, difficult but rewarding, and worthy of the line of Spenser and Milton.

5 Bible of Energy

The Marriage of Heaven and Hell

As THE Book of Isaiah gathers to its judging climax, a red figure comes out of Edom, moving in the greatness of his strength. His garments are like those of one who treads in the wine vat, the day of vengeance is in his heart, and the year of his redeemed is come. This apocalyptic figure is the red Orc of Blake's symbolism, an upsurge of the Hell of desire against the Heaven of restraint. In 1790, Edom is France and Orc the spirit of revolt which has moved first from America to France and now threatens to cross into England.

The Marriage of Heaven and Hell is an apocalyptic satire, created in response to the threatened dominion of Edom. Blake is thirty-three, the Christological age, and in this greatest of his polemical works he enters fully into the kingdom of his own thought and art. He has been reading the theology of Swedenborg (who died in 1772) and he likes less and less what may once have seem to him an imaginative protest against orthodoxy. Swedenborg is another minor Orc aged into Urizen, another Devil become an Angel. Annotating Swedenborg, Blake observes that the contraries of Good and Evil can be married together, and finally asserts: "Heaven & Hell are born together." So it is in the *Marriage*. Swedenborg, in his *True Christian Religion*, had placed the Last Judgment in the spiritual world in 1757, the year that William Blake was born. Christ rose in the body in his thirty-third year. The Marys, come to his tomb, find the stone rolled from its door and an angel sitting upon it, who tells them that the dead has awakened. Blake, in his thirty-third year, now rises in the body, preaching the consuming of finite creation "by an improvement of sensual enjoyment." Swedenborg is only the angel sitting at the tomb. His writings are but the linen clothes folded up, for Blake has thrown off the winding-sheet of imaginative death.

In form, the *Marriage* is a condensed version of what Frye has termed an "anatomy," a mixture of verse and prose, characterized by a satiric tone, variety in subject matter, and an intense concern with intellectual error.[17] This anatomy opens with a verse "Argument." Rintrah, an angry prophet like John the Baptist, prepares Blake's way before him by hinting at the political and natural destruction that threatens. A cycle is turning over, the Eternal Hell is reviving, and a voice in the wilderness cries aloud the burden of surging energy and desire.

The "Argument" is an oblique and very effective poem. The truly "just man" or "Devil" rages in the wilds, having been cast out of "perilous paths" by the "villain" or "Angel." Yet this is not the reversal it seems, for

> Roses are planted where thorns grow,
> And on the barren heath
> Sing the honey bees.

The present tense establishes the coexistence of contraries. The just man is a river, a spring, red clay (Adam), while the villain finds his natural forms in cliff, tomb, and bleached bones. Cliff and river, tomb and spring, bones and Adam's red flesh alternate in nature, and so do the just man and villain in the history of society. As the cycle turns, a merely ironic progression is always taking place. The perilous generative path that leads at last to death is always being planted, and the just man is always being driven out. The villain usurps, over and again, this path of life-in-death. The just man always returns, and drives the villain again into "paths of ease," the roads that lead to Ulro. To this cycle, there can be no end until nature in its present form is cast out by the visionary eye. As the cycle keeps turning, the categories of "just man" and "villain" begin to merge into one another, and the more deliberately equivocal "Devil" and "Angel" come into being as the *Marriage*'s contraries.

As the villain comes upon the perilous path in 1790, a new "heaven" or "mild humility" of angelic restraint begins. Blake is thinking of Pitt's bans, of the entire repressive apparatus of British society as it self-righteously attempts to put down the popular unrest that begins to respond to the hope of revolution. But Heaven and Hell are born together, and so "the Eternal Hell revives": "Without Contraries is no progression. Attraction and Repulsion, Reason and Energy, Love and Hate, are necessary to Human existence."

Contraries are creative oppositions, necessary if existence is to be Human, which for Blake means "Poetic or Prophetic" as much as "Philosophic & Experimental." The Human, standing still, becomes the wholly natural "unable to do other than repeat the same dull round over again." Progression means to become more Human, and the final mark of such development is to marry all contraries together without reconciling them. Blake's dialectic has no synthesis or transcending of contraries, but seeks a mutual immanence of creative strife, an exuberant becoming. Marriage means so placing the contraries of Reason and Energy that they cannot absorb and yet do not reject one another.

But *The Marriage of Heaven and Hell* is a work written to its time, an age that fears energy as if the energetic and the demonic were one. Blake therefore resorts to antinomian rhetoric, and declares himself as one of the possessed, celebrating the active springing from Energy and thus embracing "what the religious call Evil" and assign to Hell. When the contraries are next stated, in "The Voice of the Devil" passage, they have ceased strictly to be contraries, for Blake declares one set to be error and the other to be true. Christian dualism is now seen as a negation, which hinders action and prevents movement toward the Human, while the identity of body and soul is a truth both pragmatic and imaginative:

> Man has no Body distinct from his Soul for that call'd Body is a portion of Soul discern'd by the five Senses, the chief inlets of Soul in this age.
>
> Energy is the only life and is from the Body and Reason is the bound or outward circumference of Energy.
>
> Energy is Eternal Delight.

Reason is the horizon or bounding circle of energy, and is not the same that it will be when our energy has expanded our conscious-

ness. Urizen, the fallen Prince of Light in Blake's pantheon, takes
his name from the same root as "horizon." Energy is Eternal Delight, or Joy, as Coleridge and Wordsworth more simply call it. This
delighted exuberance is the outward mark of a healthy imagination,
and is definitive of beauty and identifiable with it. Though he declares for diabolical wisdom, and sees the *Marriage* as a Bible of
Energy, Blake does not forget the dialectics of his theory of existence. Reason, the bound, is not Eternal Torment, though Reason's
story claims unbounded Energy to be such torment. "For this history," Blake ironically observes, "has been adopted by both parties,"
Angels and Devils. *Paradise Lost* is an Angel's version of the story;
Blake now gives a contrary account:

> Those who restrain desire, do so because theirs is weak
> enough to be restrained; and the restrainer or reason usurps its
> place & governs the unwilling.
> And being restrain'd it by degrees becomes passive till it is
> only the shadow of desire.
> The history of this is written in Paradise Lost, & the Gov-
> ernor or Reason is call'd Messiah.
> And the original Archangel or possessor of the command of
> the heavenly host, is call'd the Devil or Satan and his children
> are call'd Sin & Death.
> But in the Book of Job Milton's Messiah is call'd Satan.

In the Book of Job, Satan is God's accusing agent, and with
heavenly permission subjects Job to an external Hell of maximum
tribulation, complete with soreboils and imputations of sin. In
Paradise Lost the Messiah, with chariot of fire, drives the rebel
angels out of Heaven and thrusts them forth into Chaos. Eternal
wrath burns after them to the bottomless pit. Messiah is thus the
agent who creates an external Hell, a torture chamber for punish-
ments, and so in Blake's view is one with Job's Satan, the restrainer
of desire. Milton's Satan begins as desire, but, being restrained, he
by degrees becomes passive, until he is only a Spectre, a shadow of
desire. Yet Satan's lost substance is the stuff of life, which Milton's
God and Messiah can only bind and order, in the present time of
Paradise Lost, when all divine creation is in the past. The abyss of
the five senses, chaotic substance, undifferentiated energy, is stolen
by the Messiah, who undergoes a Satanic fall that he may perform

his Promethean act of stealth. From this stolen substance, the orthodox bound of Heaven, the horizon of *Ah! Sun-flower* is formed. Milton, according to Blake, wrote in fetters when he wrote of Angels and God, and at liberty when of Devils and Hell. As literary criticism this is true, for Satan is certainly more aesthetically satisfying than Milton's God, and Hell is livelier than Heaven. Milton, without knowing it, was of the Devil's or Energy's party, because he was a true poet. "The Poet," Blake said in his annotations to Dante's *Inferno*, "is Independent & Wicked; the Philosopher is Dependent & Good." And so "the grandest Poetry is Immoral, the Grandest characters Wicked, Very Satan." It follows that the grandest proverbs will be the Proverbs of Hell, seventy gnomic reflections and admonitions on the theme of diabolic wisdom, where Blake's antinomian rhetoric and more comprehensive dialectic meet in combat.

Blake's proverbs take their meaning from his dialectical definitions of "desire" and "act," though their overt force depends upon a rhetoric of disassociation which transvalues conventional beliefs. Desire leads to an action that is not the hindrance of another and that is therefore positive. Act is positive and is virtue. Blake, commenting on the moralist Lavater, defines the contrary of act as "accident":

> Accident is the omission of act in self & the hindering of act in another; This is Vice, but all Act is Virtue. To hinder another is not an act; it is the contrary; it is a restraint on action both in ourselves & in the person hinder'd, for he who hinders another omits his own duty at the same time.

The Proverbs of Hell laud active Evil as being better than passive Good, but Blake's vocabulary is ironic, and to take the Proverbs as approving sadism is to misread them utterly. The organization of the Proverbs is complex, being based on delayed association after preconceived response has been altered by apparent disassociation. The Proverbs resolve themselves into four overlapping groups, defined by dominant patterns of imagery. One is apocalyptic and largely sexual in emphasis, and includes images of plowing and harvest, water and wine, prayer and praise, baptism and intercourse. Another deals with excess and frustration, and includes proverbs dealing with strength and weakness, desire and restraint, body and soul, wisdom and foolishness. A third group, more overtly antinomian, emphasizes animal powers, and organizes itself about the themes of violence, revenge, law, and religion. The fourth and largest category is dominated by images of perception, and finds its subject matter in problems of time and eternity, space and form, art and nature, cycles and divisions, and in comparisons between the elements and man's body. The four groups can be brought together in a single diabolical formula: sexual excess leads to antinomian perception. By it, the whole creation is consumed and appears infinite and holy. The doors of perception are to be cleansed by an improvement of sensual enjoyment. The risen body becomes the expanding imagination, and finite and corrupt nature becomes an infinite and redeemed Human Form Divine.

Yet Blake does not forget his dialectic of immanence, the necessity of coexistent contraries. Both portions of being, the Prolific Energy of Desire, and the Devouring Reason of Restraint, are finally to be held in strenuous and warring balance:

> Thus one portion of being is the Prolific, the other the Devouring: to the Devourer it seems as if the producer was in his chains; but it is not so, he only takes portions of existence and fancies that the whole.

> But the Prolific would cease to be Prolific unless the Devourer as a sea received the excess of his delights.

> Some will say: "Is not God alone the Prolific?" I answer: "God only Acts & Is, in existing beings or Men."

> These two classes of men are always upon earth, & they should be enemies: whoever tries to reconcile them seeks to destroy existence.

> Religion is an endeavour to reconcile the two.

The Angel, or Devourer, has taken all the negative force of Blake's rhetoric, but the Prolific needs constraint, and flourishes on the battle against confinement. The Devourer is a sea, a bounding moat without which the fountain of creativity would be choked in the excess of its own delight, by an invention so extravagant that it could find no coherence. The enmity between Prolific and Devourer is the foundation of human existence, and whoever seeks to end such enmity would destroy the human aspect of existence. Such a destruction is religion's purpose, when orthodoxy attempts to inflict upon us the greatest poverty of not living in a physical world.

Blake's dialectical stance, with its apotheosis of the physical and its simultaneous rejection of the merely natural, is most frequently misunderstood at just this point. Against the supernaturalist, Blake asserts the reality of the body as being all of the soul that the five senses can perceive. Against the naturalists, he asserts the greater reality of the imaginative over the given body. The naturalist or vitalist, in Blake's view, teaches heat without light; the orthodox theist wants light without heat. Blake insists upon both, and finds his image of consummated marriage between the two in poetic genius or imagination.

The humanistic satire of the *Marriage* is concentrated in a sequence of emblematic stories that Blake (in mockery of a phrase in Swedenborg) calls Memorable Fancies. The Fancies illustrate the central polemical truth that serves as the *Marriage*'s last sentence: "One Law for the Lion & Ox is Oppression." The maker of that oppressive law is Urizen, the true Satan, who is worshiped as God of this World under the names of Jehovah and Jesus. The penultimate sentence of the *Marriage* promises the world the Bible of Hell, the imaginative reading of creation and apocalypse. Blake's Bible of Hell begins with *The Book of Urizen*, and goes on to the much-revised complexities of the epic poem called first *Vala* and then *The Four Zoas*. The *Marriage* is the prelude to that Bible, and a richer work than my brief description can suggest.

The last plate of the *Marriage* shows King Nebuchadnezzar crouching on all fours, reduced to the state of nature, as Daniel had prophesied. This is Man, of whom one of the Proverbs of Hell says: "The head Sublime, the heart Pathos, the genitals Beauty, the hands & feet Proportion." The distance between Nebuchadnezzar and the Proverb is the hideous gap that Blake's major poems exist to explain, and hope to close.

6   Bible of Hell

The Book of Urizen

THE BOOK OF URIZEN (1794) is Blake's most powerful illuminated poem before the great abandoned *Four Zoas* and the epics that followed it. On the title page of Urizen the protagonist crouches, a hideous emblem of Ulro. We see an immensely old man, of godly appearance, sitting against the double tombstone of the tables of the law. His position puts him out of human shape. He is a creature who rises in four symmetrical mounds (shoulders and knees) with flowing white beard cutting him in two and trailing off on the ground. What keeps him from perfection in his fearful symmetry is that his left foot protrudes clawlike from his snowy beard. Each hand writes on slablike tablets, which contain his wisdom. He sits on his own writings as well, and fibrous roots extend beneath him. Behind the tombstones arches the bower of Ulro and over all bend the encircling branches of a Tree of Mystery. Urizen's eyes are closed, and his countenance shows profound and contented self-absorption.

The Book of Urizen is Blake's version of the Fall of Man, which is also the Fall of God, and is the same event with the creation of both mankind and the universe in their present forms. *Urizen* parodies Genesis and *Paradise Lost,* and attempts to correct what Blake considers the imaginative errors of those myths of creation.

In the Human society that was Eternity, an event of division takes place. Urizen rises as a mysterious shadow intent upon itself. From this solipsistic isolation a self-closed void creates itself in the midst of Eternity.

Urizen broods until he begins to divide himself, separating off part from part. The divisions become shapes with whom he obscurely struggles:

> For he strove in battles dire
> In unseen conflictions with shapes
> Bred from his forsaken wilderness,
> Of beast, bird, fish, serpent & element
> Combustion, blast, vapour and cloud.

We are not told what initially persuaded Urizen to draw apart and so begin this inward torment that will finally result in the appearance of the phenomenal world of Experience, the universe of Newton and natural religion. At the end of Urizen's terrible labors is the lamenting Earth of Experience, "prison'd on wat'ry shore," and kept in her den by Starry Jealousy, the god that Urizen is at last to become.

In Milton, Satan falls first. From pride and disobedience, is the traditional explanation, but Blake insisted that Satan, being repressed, had become only the shadow of desire, just as Urizen is a rising shadow in Eternity. In *The Four Zoas*, Blake begins with a primal Man, Albion, who falls by betraying his own imaginative power in seeking a single form for it. *The Book of Urizen* does not mention Albion, and starts with the power in the human mind which can philosophize in the sense of abstracting ideals and principles from the minute particulars of the observed world. Urizen is to Albion as

> a Shadow from his wearied intellect,
> Of living gold, pure, perfect, holy; in white linen pure he hover'd,
> A sweet entrancing self-delusion, a wat'ry vision of Albion,
> Soft exulting in existence, all the Man absorbing.

This passage is from the twenty-ninth plate of *Jerusalem* (Blake quarried it from the *Zoas* manuscript), but its vision of Urizen as a Spectre of man is consonant with the earlier *Book of Urizen*. The Spectre Blake defined in an unfinished poem also left in manuscript:

> My Spectre around me night & day
> Like a Wild beast guards my way.
> My Emanation far within
> Weeps incessantly for my Sin.

> A Fathomless & boundless deep,
> There we wander, there we weep;
> On the hungry craving wind
> My Spectre follows thee behind.

The Spectre is the isolated abstraction of any human self, withering gloriously in the air of monologue. The Emanation is a confronted other with whom reality is shared, without self-appropriation. In Eden and Beulah, the Emanation is within a unity, or condition of dialogue, whether as the artist's creation or the lover's desired and attained vision. In the world of Experience the Emanation hovers outside, and the Spectre shadows the mocked and questing self, as in Shelley's *Alastor*. The abstract world of Ulro, the state of being Urizen creates for himself, is shown in Blake's verses *My Spectre around me night & day*. Ulro is the fathomless and boundless deep of the inchoate, where the Spectre stalks a demonic and illusory Emanation, while the true form of creation and love weeps incessantly far within the self, unable to emanate.

As Urizen becomes "a self-contemplating shadow," his baffled fellow Eternals stand watch to see what will emerge from "the petrific, abominable chaos." At last Urizen speaks out, articulating himself in thunders, like the oppressive sky god he is to become:

> From the depths of dark solitude. From
> The eternal abode in my holiness,
> Hidden set apart in my stern counsels
> Reserv'd for the days of futurity,
> I have sought for a joy without pain,
> For a solid without fluctuation
> Why will you die O Eternals?
> Why live in unquenchable burnings?

Blake has shifted from a seven-beat to a three-beat line, seeking a nervous and abrupt utterance. The speeches of Urizen are marvelously effective in their dramatic appropriateness. The blind self-righteousness and self-regard of a cosmic demiurge who is also the first moralist is felt in the tone of every line Urizen speaks. He has identified his self-seclusion with his new idea of the holy, and in its name he rejects the contraries of eternal existence. The passionate desires of eternity seem to him a series of dyings. He is majestic in his horrible sincerity, as he longs for a repose that ever is the same. Like Milton's Satan, he has journeyed through the chaos of the self:

> Where nothing was: Nature's wide womb;
> And self balanc'd stretch'd o'er the void
> I alone, even I!

From his conflicts with what he now names as the seven deadly sins of his own soul, he has discovered the secrets of dark contemplation, and he records this wisdom in the Book of eternal brass. The doctrine is already familiar to us:

> Laws of peace, of love, of unity,
> Of pity, compassion, forgiveness;
> Let each chuse one habitation:
> His ancient infinite mansion:
> One command, one joy, one desire,
> One curse, one weight, one measure
> One King, one God, one Law.

These are the laws of *The Human Abstract,* and no flesh can keep them, lest it become itself brass or stone. Urizen's doctrine is a Deistic blend of the Mosaic and the Newtonian formulations, and the combination emphasizes that both views enforce uniformity.

When he expanded his myth, in *The Four Zoas,* Blake accounted for the fall of all the Zoas or "living creatures," Giant Forms who represented the various faculties of unfallen Man, and thus were "Sons of Eden." Blake took the name "Zoas" from Revelation 4, where four Zoas or living creatures surround God's throne. Revelation's source is Ezekiel 1, which makes Blake's vision clearer. "Also out of the midst thereof came the likeness of four living creatures. And this was their appearance; they had the likeness of a man."

These four cherubim make up a chariot, "the wheels and their work," and the chariot bears the flaming likeness of a man. This is Blake's Man, Albion, who comprises both God and Adam within himself. In *The Book of Urizen,* Albion and two of his supporting cherubim are uninvolved, as the poem attempts what is for Blake only a limited theme. How did the present world and man reach their shrunken physical form? Urizen, the leading mental power of Man before the Fall, is only a minimal kind of reason when things settle into their current material dimensions. Yet even in this poem, rationalism is no solitary demon. The other Eternals take the active part in the downward swerve, stirred by indignation at Urizen's passive withdrawal from the life of Eternity. In Blake's ironical reading, the other Eternals are parallel to Milton's God and Messiah, who expelled Satan and his host by fire:

> The roaring fires ran o'er the heav'ns
> In whirlwinds & cataracts of blood
> And o'er the dark desarts of Urizen
> Fires pour thro' the void on all sides
> On Urizen's self-begotten armies.
> But no light from the fires: all was darkness
> In the flames of Eternal fury.

Blake's cosmic irony is too little appreciated. Urizen introspected until he passively found the "Seven deadly Sins of the soul." But it takes the rage of the Eternals to bring about the appearance of the sins "in living creations." The creative fire of the Eternals becomes heat without light, and so Hell is actively created by the Wrath of God, not by the Satanic Urizen. The difference is that Blake's Eternals do not intend their rage as punishment; passive rejection of fire has led to the active suffering of it.

Against this torment the deteriorating Urizen frames a petrific roof and falls into a stony sleep "unorganiz'd, rent from Eternity." Another Zoa enters into the story of Fall: Los, the shaper in fire, the divine smith like Thor or Vulcan, who until now has been closely joined with Urizen, is set to keep watch "to confine the obscure separation alone." The source of Los's name is not known; Frye suggests that it may be derived from a Chaucerian synonym for fame.[18] Los is the eternal prophet as Urizen is the eternal priest. History belongs to Urizen, yet "the mediator and redeemer, Time" is finally an attribute of his prophetic antagonist.

Blake's crucial separation from the Romantics who followed him is centered on his increasing identification with Los, the only Romantic hero whose primary role is activity rather than passive suffering. Wordsworth speaks for every other Romantic poet in a speech from his early drama, *The Borderers:*

> Action is transitory—a step, a blow,
> The motion of a muscle—this way or that—

'Tis done, and in the after-vacancy
We wonder at ourselves like men betrayed:
Suffering is permanent, obscure and dark,
And shares the nature of infinity.

The sufferings of Wordsworth's solitaries, and of the poet himself in the crisis of mind recorded by *The Prelude,* are more intense than any actions in the same poems. Passivity is the mark of Shelley's Prometheus, Coleridge's Mariner, Keats's Apollo in *Hyperion,* all of whom undergo purgations in which they govern only their receptivities to altered states of being. Even the Titanic Byron finds no action proper for his heroes. Manfred defies, Childe Harold observes, Juan is seduced or refuses seduction. Cain acts, after long and confused inner sufferings, and characteristically his act exceeds his intentions, and becomes merely hindrance, in Blake's sense. The Los of *The Book of Urizen* is as yet no agent of apocalypse; he does rather more harm than good. But he acts and forms, laboring too feverishly against chaos, or whatever he judges to separate him off from Eternity. In the *Marriage* Blake had already identified his own engraving technique and poetic art with the therapy of the prophet:

But first the notion that man has a body distinct from his soul is to be expunged; this I shall do by printing in the infernal method, by corrosives, which in Hell are salutary and medicinal, melting apparent surfaces away, and displaying the infinite which was hid.

The hammer and furnace of Los are prophesied also in the ironies of *The Tyger,* where the speaker fails to identify the titanic creative power with anything within himself. The Los of *Urizen* hardly knows what he is doing as yet, and the poem satirizes man's imaginative as well as his intellectual errors. But as Blake works through to the terrible clarity of his masterpiece *Jerusalem,* Los gains progressively both in self-consciousness and in the dangers involved in consciousness of self.

At first Los, separated from the abstracted Urizen, curses his lot, for he finds he has

a fathomless void for his feet,
And intense fires for his dwelling.

Yet the moving fires must be his salvation, the element in which
he will forge a new form out of the fathomless void. As Urizen
boils through the sleep of seven ages of dismal woe, an evolution
down to the level of matter, the furious and desperate Los labors
mightily to put some regularity into the evolving forms:

> And Urizen (so his eternal name)
> His prolific delight obscur'd more & more
> In dark secresy hiding in surgeing
> Sulphureous fluid his phantasies.
> The Eternal Prophet heav'd the dark bellows,
> And turn'd restless the tongs, and the hammer
> Incessant beat, forging chains new & new
> Numb'ring with links: hours, days & years.

Even time becomes a liberating form against the irregular self-
devourings of the crumbling eternal mind. Under the cyclic beat-
ings of Los's hammer, Urizen falls into the present human shape,
and becomes something close to mortality. Appalled, Los ceases to
labor, suffers his fires to decay, and falls into the same dark void as
his artifact, and so falls victim to pity, which "divides the soul."
Forgiveness is Blake's great virtue, pity a vice, for pity is founded
on self-deception and is hindrance, not action. Blake's "pity" is like
Shelley's "self-contempt" or Yeats's "remorse," an unimaginative
abstraction masking as a human quality, which must be cast out if
the poet is to create. Crippled by his pity, Los is "divided before
the death image of Urizen," and his Emanation splits off as "the
first female now separate," in parody of Eve's creation. The Eternals, still joined to their Emanations (Milton portrayed the angels
as being each one both male and female), are frightened by this
evidence of change and move to separate themselves from the fallen:

> They began to weave curtains of darkness,
> They erected large pillars round the Void,
> With golden hooks fasten'd in the pillars;
> With infinite labour the Eternals
> A woof wove, and called it Science.

This selfish act creates the "heaven" of orthodoxy, and the woof
of the universe becomes the "Science" of Newton and his contem-

poraries. Los's Emanation is called Enitharmon because "she bore an enormous race," and evidently her name is derived from the Greek for "without number." She begins the reign of what Blake was to call the Female Will, with its elaborate courtly love conventions of "perverse and cruel delight." Enitharmon wantonly flees, Los follows, and sexual procreation begins:

> Eternity shudder'd when they saw,
> Man begetting his likeness,
> On his own divided image.

The birth of Orc results, and the appearance of that fierce child affrights the now timidly orthodox Eternals, who close down the tent of the universe, and so complete Los's separation from Eternity. Afflicted by resentment and jealousy of his portentous son, Los binds Orc down on a mountain top, in an analogue to both the binding of Prometheus and Abraham's attempted sacrifice of Isaac. The "Orc cycle," as Frye calls it, thus commences, as a cyclic pattern of natural tyranny which is traced most vividly in *The Mental Traveller*.

Yet the voice of the child is heard in the world of sleeping matter, and things begin to waken to life. Urizen himself, in whose deathful shadow the child is bound, is "stung with the odours of Nature" and begins to explore his dens, to achieve again an ordered cosmos in the chaotic watery shore for which he is primarily responsible. But his horror at the diversity and grief of phenomenal Experience awakens his most sinister quality—"And he wept & he called it Pity." Pity divides him from his Spectre, and the Spectre follows him behind:

> And wherever he wander'd in sorrows
> Upon the aged heavens
> A cold shadow follow'd behind him
> Like a spider's web, moist, cold & dim,
> Drawing out from his sorrowing soul
> The dungeon-like heaven dividing
> Where ever the footsteps of Urizen
> Walked over the cities in sorrow.

This is the Net of Religion, and those enmeshed in it shrink by its contact:

Six days they shrunk up from existence
And on the seventh day they rested
And they bless'd the seventh day, in sick hope:
And forgot their eternal life

The parody of the sabbath is typical of Blake's intellectual satire, which depends for its force on sudden transvaluations of accepted concepts. Under the influence of the worship of Urizen, man completes his fall by inventing natural death:

No more could they rise at will
In the infinite void, but bound down
To earth by their narrowing perceptions
They lived a period of years
Then left a noisom body
To the jaws of devouring darkness

This completes the Genesis aspect of *The Book of Urizen,* which passes next to an Exodus account in the sequel *The Book of Ahania,* so entitled by the name of Urizen's discarded Emanation. *Ahania* introduces themes that attain more vital visualization in *The Four Zoas,* so that consideration of it can be deferred until a description of the *Zoas* is attempted. The last plate of *Urizen* shows the Old Man, melancholy and resigned, trapped in the net of his own religion. The same illustration was used by Blake for *The Human Abstract,* but there, as Damon points out, Urizen still struggled with his own net.[19] Blake has shown the birth and growth of error, and its gradual acceptance of itself. To separate the human from its abstract becomes the heroic quest of his major poetry, which replaces the satire of the *Marriage* and *Urizen* with the visionary romance of a fully formulated and comprehensive myth.

7   *States of Being*

The Four Zoas

Few poets of the highest class have chosen to exhibit the beauty of their conceptions in its naked truth and splendour; and it is doubtful whether the alloy of costume, habit, &c., be not necessary to temper this planetary music for mortal ears.

SHELLEY, *A Defence of Poetry*

THE difficulty of Blake's major poems, which has caused impatient readers to call them failures, is the difficulty of the beauty of Blake's conceptions in its naked truth and splendor. Frye, the most Blakean commentator on Blake we are likely to get, says of these poems that "they are difficult because it was impossible to make them simpler." [20]

The motto of *The Four Zoas*, from Ephesians, characterizes the tone of the work: "For our contention is not with the blood and the flesh, but with dominion, with authority, with the blind world-rulers of this life, with the spirit of evil in things heavenly." The Zoas, the Four Mighty Ones who are in every Man, are now the blind world rulers of this life, and their fallen status makes them also the spirit of evil in things heavenly, for when united they had formed "the Universal Brotherhood of Eden." How they came to fall, the manner of their present warfare, and the ways in which they must regenerate form the subject of the poem.

The first and greatest problem presented by *The Four Zoas* is that it is neither complete in itself nor even one poem, but rather at least two poems intermingled, with many late additions and corrections in the manuscript. We cannot even date its versions confidently, except to say that Blake began it in 1795 and finally abandoned it in 1804. Yet he gave the manuscript to his disciple, the painter Linnell, just before he died, apparently in the hope that it would be preserved, so we cannot assume that Blake was altogether willing to see the poem die. In its first version the epic was entitled *Vala, or the Death and Judgement of the Ancient Man, a Dream of Nine Nights.* The hypothetical text of *Vala* was edited from the manuscript by H. M. Margoliouth, and can now be read and studied more or less in its own right. Here I will give a brief description of the second version, *The Four Zoas,* subtitled *The Torments of Love & Jealousy in the Death and Judgement of Albion the Ancient Man.* Though harder to hold together than *Vala, The Four Zoas* is much the richer poem, with an ampler rhetoric than the relatively chastened *Milton* or the somewhat astringent *Jerusalem.* It may even be that as Blake's poems become more widely read and accurately studied, our response to them will follow the now familiar pattern of response to Dante, where youth seems to prefer the *Inferno,* middle age the *Purgatorio,* and later years the *Paradiso.* The spectacular *Four Zoas,* with its dazzling *Night the Ninth, Being the Last Judgment,* is the most energetic and inventive of Blake's poems, while the rewards of *Milton* and *Jerusalem* become progressively subtler. The rhetorical movement is from the urgency of "The stars consum'd like a lamp blown out" to the quiet clairvoyance of "All Human Forms identified, even Tree, Metal, Earth & Stone." In action, the poems progress toward ever deeper internalization, until at last we can never forget that "all deities reside in the human breast."

The account of the fall, in Blake's more comprehensive version, begins not with Urizen but "with Tharmas, Parent power, dark'ning in the West," and lamenting the loss of his Emanations. Tharmas, in Eternity, was the particular representative of unity, man's attribute of the power of harmony between love, intellect, and imagination. Man's unified sense of taste and touch, which still come together in sexual experience, is in the domain of Tharmas. The origins of the name "Tharmas" are obscure, but this is really just as well, as it is usually misleading to interpret one of Blake's creatures by its name's supposed etymology. The names are arbitrary, but the functions and qualities are not. Blake's entire purpose in breaking with names like Venus and Apollo was to eliminate irrelevant associations, and we serve him badly by the more irrelevant of our pedantries.

Tharmas is the unfallen link between the potential and the actual, what Man wants and what he can get. Before the fall into division, every desire is carried over into realization by Tharmas. As Albion, or primal Man, was all Imagination for Blake, Tharmas must therefore be what Wallace Stevens means by "a figure of capable imagination." Urizen was the firm outline of Imagination, Urthona (who becomes Los in fallen time) its shaping spirit, and Luvah (who becomes Orc) the passion that imparted desire to the forming and shaping inventiveness of Man. When the human ceased to be divine, and our world came into being, then Tharmas necessarily fell first, which is the story of Night I of *The Four Zoas.*

Fall for Tharmas means separation from his outer female aspect, Enion, who becomes the earth mother of the generative world, and who resembles the fearful Earth, mother of Prometheus, in Shelley's lyrical drama. The poem's action begins with a pathetic dialogue of misunderstanding between Tharmas and Enion. Innocence has been lost, for Tharmas was the presiding genius of Beulah, where the Zoas rested in renovating passion, and where a fresh tide of life never ceased to pulsate. Split off from his emanation, Tharmas has lost Beulah and is in danger of becoming a shadow or spectral self of his shepherd's reality. He is now the western or Atlantic ocean to Enion's isolated British earth, and so Blake reminds us again of the myth of destroyed Atlantis, and the great deluge that overwhelmed it. Tharmas was, in a sense, Thel's river of Adona, the life of the Gardens of Adonis. When the other Zoas split the unity of Albion, Tharmas raged until he became an oceanic flood, which drowned out the married land and produced what and where we are.

The separated Enion, as a female will, both desired Tharmas and yet in him "found Sin & cannot return." His eloquent lament refuses reunion on her analytical and self-righteous terms:

> "Why wilt thou Examine every little fibre of my soul
>   Spreading them out before the Sun like Stalks of flax to dry
>   The infant Joy is beautiful but its anatomy
>   Horrible Ghast & Deadly nought shalt thou find in it
>   But Death Despair & Everlasting brooding Melancholy
>
> "Thou wilt go mad with horror if thou dost Examine thus
>   Every moment of my secret hours Yea I know
>   That I have sinn'd & that my Emanations are become harlots

I am already distracted at their deeds & if I look
Upon them more Despair will bring self-murder on my soul
O Enion thou are thyself a root growing in hell
Tho' thus heavenly beautiful to draw me to destruction"

Enion weaves the garment of phenomenal nature, until she has
perfected a cycle or "Circle of Destiny" which is the monument and
tombstone of her separation from Tharmas. The Daughters of
Beulah, Blake's Muses, are terrified by the chaos their deity has become, and reject the now completed Circle of human destiny:

The Circle of Destiny complete they gave to it a Space
And nam'd the Space Ulro & brooded over it in care & love
They said: "The Spectre is in every man insane & most
Deform'd. Thro' the three heavens descending in fury & fire
We meet it with our Songs & loving blandishments & give
To it a form of vegetation. But this Spectre of Tharmas
Is Eternal Death. What shall we do O God, pity & help!"
So spoke they & clos'd the Gate of the tongue in trembling fear.

To close the Gate of the tongue is to restrict the natural entrance
into Beulah, and limits the imaginative possibilities of human sexual experience. Enion now beomes "a bright wonder, Nature, Half
Woman & half Spectre." From her intercourse with the raging
Spectre of Tharmas she brings forth the weeping infants of the
Songs of Experience, now identified as Los and Enitharmon, time
and space, restricted imagination and confining form. These infants
soon become fierce, reject their mother, and wander through the
painful world of Experience.

Meanwhile, Blake's narrative goes back to the events that caused
the ruin of Tharmas. The fall of man is no longer viewed as the
fault of Urizen alone, but of Luvah as well, and so the contraries of
reason and energy are equally capable of selfish plotting against the
full life of man. Luvah, like Phaethon, seizes the chariot of the sun,
which belongs to Urizen, Prince of Light. Yet desire cannot usurp
reason without disaster, even in Blake, and Luvah's desertion of
moon for sun is Albion's fall into a self-righteousness of emotional
pride, a glorification of the heart's impulses at the expense of man's
other legitimate powers.

The remaining Zoa, Urthona, is working at his anvil, preparing spades and colters for the heavenly plowing, when he feels the effects of the strife between Eternals. In this crisis of imagination, the inventive faculty experiences a failure in nerve, in which Enitharmon, his emanation, flees from him to the comforting Tharmas. In a first act of possessiveness, "Enion in jealous fear / Murder'd her, & hid her in her bosom." Left a specter, Urthona also collapses into Enion, from whose form he is to reappear in the world below as the prophetic and poetic principle, Los.

Albion's emanation is Jerusalem. Blake said that he knew no other Christianity "than the liberty both of body and mind to exercise the divine arts of imagination," and Jerusalem is identified by him as this "liberty," which is in every man insofar as he possesses the Inner Light of the Protestant tradition. Night I closes with the darkening of this Light, as Jerusalem is "scatter'd into the indefinite," and man falls "downwards & outwards" into chaos.

Night II centers on the fall of Luvah and his emanation Vala, who becomes the deceptive beauty of nature after she has won primacy over Albion. The wandering children of Experience, Los and Enitharmon, whom we now know to be only foster children of Tharmas and Enion, rehearse in song the story of Luvah's fall. The complexity of Blake's art has largely escaped notice here. As Enitharmon and Los repeat the fall in song, they enact the torments of love and jealousy between themselves as well, and their nuptial song recapitulates both the terror of their own ambiguous passion and the strife of Eternity. Their tribulations are the direct consequence of Urthona's self-separating fear and doubt in Night I of the poem.

As Los and Enitharmon torment one another, they become the proper prey of Urizen, who descends as god of this world and offers the quarreling children dominion over the realm of the emotions, and the right of judgment upon Luvah and Vala. They accept, and so lose their last heritage of Innocence, the refusal to judge or be judged. Their powerful Nuptial Song places the blame for the fall entirely upon the emotional life, and so prepares them for a marriage of mutual envy and jealousy, a Urizenic compact between two grim children determined to perform again the cruelties and deceptions that disintegrated Eternity. As this dreadful union is celebrated, Enion wanders in chaos, lamenting the triumph of fallen morality to which she has contributed. At this point she is the Earth of the introductory poems of the *Songs of Experience*.

Hearing the voice of the wailing earth mother, the sick-unto-death Albion rises "upon his Couch of Death" and calls Urizen to take the scepter of control, so as to impose some order upon chaos. It was at this point that the poem *Vala* seems to have commenced.

Urizen now becomes "the great Work master," a demiurge who will build the Mundane Shell of present-day reality around the Rock of Albion. While Urizen prepares his instruments of measurement and restriction, the poem moves its focus to the fall of Luvah, now melted down by Vala in the Furnaces of affliction. Albion, like Urizen, has now equated chaos and emotion, and so man is delivered to Urizenic religion, with its hatred and repression of human sexual love. Such love is now self-divided and tormented, with its emanative portion become a separate, mocking, elusive creation. Inspired by the example of Vala, Enitharmon sings a courtly love hymn that proclaims the triumph of the female will:

"The joy of woman is the Death of her most best belovèd
Who dies for Love of her
In torments of fierce jealousy & pangs of adoration.
The Lovers' night bears on my song
And the nine Spheres rejoice beneath my powerful controll."

Night II concludes with what may be the finest of Blake's Biblical chants, the lament of Enion. The context of this song is complex; all of the Zoas are now separated from their Emanations, but Enion has been separated the longest. As she contemplates the active errors of Vala and Enitharmon, and grieves over her own outcast fate, Enion also excites Ahania, the wife of Urizen, to an awareness of the fallen state. Enitharmon is an Eve figure who will become a courtly-love Queen of Heaven. Vala is the beauty of outward nature, becoming progressively more deceptive as history continues. Enion herself is only a wandering Demeter, but Ahania is a more crucial figure in Blake's myth. As in *The Book of Ahania,* Urizen's Emanation is a total form of intellectual desire, which must express itself as sexual in the fallen world. Most particularly, then, Ahania is the kind of desire which a repressive Urizenic ethic dismisses as sin, but which Divine Wisdom nevertheless requires. Ahania is precisely the "lov'd enthusiast, young Fancy," of Collins' *Ode on the Poetical Character,* who must participate in any of the mind's acts of creation, lest those acts become merely the hindrances of sterility.

In the lament of Enion we hear for the first time in *The Four Zoas* the true voice of Blake himself:

"What is the price of Experience do men buy it for a song
Or wisdom for a dance in the street? No! it is bought with the
    price
Of all that a man hath his house his wife his children
Wisdom is sold in the desolate market where none come to buy
And in the wither'd field where the farmer plows for bread in
    vain"

The burden of Enion's song is a thought that, as Frye observes, can lead only to madness or apocalypse, for the song is a culminating lament for lost innocence, organized about the idea that human pleasure is based on a willful ignorance concerning the suffering of others.[21] Enion first "taught pale artifice to spread his nets upon the morning," when she accused Tharmas of sin. Now she understands the experiential price of such self-righteousness, but she has purchased wisdom at the expense of her being. Blake himself, in a passionate undersong, reminds us of the prophet's fate. Wisdom can be sold only where none will come to buy, and will be sought only where no harvest can come:

"It is an easy thing to triumph in the summer's sun
And in the vintage & to sing on the waggon loaded with corn
It is an easy thing to talk of patience to the afflicted
To speak the laws of prudence to the houseless wanderer
To listen to the hungry raven's cry in wintry season
When the red blood is fill'd with wine & with the marrow of
    lambs

"It is an easy thing to laugh at wrathful elements
To hear the dog howl at the wintry door, the ox in the slaughter
    house moan
To see a god on every wind & a blessing on every blast
To hear sounds of love in the thunder storm that destroys our
    enemies' house
To rejoice in the blight that covers his field, & the sickness that
    cuts off his children
While our olive & vine sing & laugh round our door & our chil-
    dren bring fruits & flowers

"Then the groan & the dolor are quite forgotten & the slave
    grinding at the mill
And the captive in chains & the poor in the prison, & the soldier
    in the field
When the shatter'd bone hath laid him groaning among the
    happier dead

It is an easy thing to rejoice in the tents of prosperity—
Thus could I sing & thus rejoice, but it is not so with me!"

The vision of Innocence is based upon ignorance, and the joy
of righteousness upon the prosperity of an untried Job. Enion's
warning, which forever ends Ahania's rest, preludes the blindness
of Urizen in Night III, where the fall of Urizen and Ahania leads
to a reappearance of Tharmas, a second deluge. Night III is dominated by images of light and darkness, as we would expect in a
Book of Urizen. The King of Light looks upon futurity, "dark'ning
present joy." He beholds a reborn Luvah, in the shape of the rebel
Orc, "that Prophetic boy," who will be "born of the dark Ocean"
that Tharmas has become. In anticipated revenge, Urizen curses the
passional life of man, asking that it die "a dark & furious death" in
the loins of Los before that shaper can bring it forth as an articulated antagonist. Ahania remonstrates with the now Satanic Urizen:

"O Prince! the Eternal One hath set thee leader of his hosts
    Leave all futurity to him Resume thy fields of Light
    Why didst thou listen to the voice of Luvah that dread morn
    To give the immortal steeds of light to his deceitful hands
    No longer now obedient to thy will thou art compell'd
    To forge the curbs of iron & brass to build the iron mangers
    To feed them with intoxication from the wine presses of Luvah
    Till the Divine Vision & Fruition is quite obliterated
    They call thy lions to the fields of blood they rowze thy tygers
    Out of the halls of justice, till these dens thy wisdom fram'd
    Golden & beautiful but O how unlike those sweet fields of bliss
    Where liberty was justice & eternal science was mercy"

The appeal leads to her expulsion, as Urizen suddenly sees her
as another Vala, prophesying for him the fallen fate of Luvah:

> He siez'd her by the hair
> And threw her from the steps of ice that froze around his throne
> Saying: "Art thou also become like Vala? Thus I cast thee out
> Shall the feminine indolent bliss, the indulgent self of weariness
> The passive idle sleep the enormous night & darkness of Death
> Set herself up to give her laws to the active masculine virtue?"

The fear of lapsing into passivity has begun to dominate Urizen. But to cast out one's desire is to become only the shadow of desire, and a Spectre must fall. Urizen crashes down, and his world of imposed reason and order with him. Noah's flood has come, and Tharmas with it as an instinctive principle of chaos, where once he was the spirit of unity. Emerging from the Smoke of Urizen, Tharmas stands on the affrighted Ocean:

> Crying: "Fury in my limbs, destruction in my bones & marrow
> My skull riven into filaments, my eyes into sea jellies
> Floating upon the tide wander bubbling and bubbling
> Uttering my lamentations & begetting little monsters
> Who sit mocking upon the little pebbles of the tide
> In all my rivers, & on dried shells that the fish
> Have quite forsaken O fool fool to lose my sweetest bliss
> Where art thou Enion ah too near to cunning too far off
> And yet too near Dash'd down I send thee into distant darkness
> Far as my strength can hurl thee wander there & laugh & play
> Among the frozen arrows they will tear thy tender flesh
> Fall off afar from Tharmas come not too near my strong fury
> Scream & fall off & laugh at Tharmas lovely summer beauty
> Till winter rends thee into Shivers as thou hast rended me"

One wonders how the voice of chaos could be better rendered. As always in his epics, Blake's rhetoric is wonderfully appropriate for each character, and in every context. Tharmas can barely articulate his watery longings, nor can he separate his desire for Enion from his wish to punish her in revenge. The confusions of fallen instinct are matched by the violent fluctuations of Tharmas' bellowing, as his voice thunders, sobs, and bursts over the ocean of space and time.

Night III climaxes in a desperate dialogue of misunderstandings and despairs. Enion, blind and bent by age, plunges into the cold

billows in terror at Tharmas' mixed curses and entreaties, and she
withers away in the cold waves of despair. Action and image are
fused, as is characteristic of Blake's epic style. Enion asks to be only
"a little showery form" near her "loved Terror," and she dissolves
into a tear even as she utters her prayer. Too late, Tharmas recoils
from his fierce rage into her semblance. He becomes a thundercloud
dissolving in tears, hoping thus to join her. But she is "vanished
from the wat'ry eyes of Tharmas," and her wandering place at the
verge of nonexistence is taken by Ahania.

Night IV is a night of raging flood, as the despairing Tharmas
pursues his lost "lineaments of ungratified desire." Luvah and
Urizen, who actively caused Tharmas to fall, are now without
power. The Spectre of Tharmas makes his instinctual attempt to
find a way out of his own inchoate rage. He commands Los to
"rebuild this Universe beneath my indignant power," but as "a
Universe of Death & Decay." Los is now in much the same position
that he held in *The Book of Urizen,* for he must hammer form out
of chaos, and set both a Limit of Opacity (Satan) and a Limit of
Contraction (Adam) beyond which man and the universe cannot
fall. The fate of the poetic visionary as he performs this grim task
is to take on the fallen form of what he beholds, to become what
he is doing. Night V opens with a frightening metamorphic dance
of destruction, as the creative imagination falls over into contraction. This, for Blake, is the true fall of man:

> Infected Mad he danc'd on his mountains high & dark as
>   heaven.
> Now fix'd into one stedfast bulk his features stonify
> From his mouth curses & from his eyes sparks of blighting
> Beside the anvil cold he danc'd with the hammer of Urthona
> Terrific pale. Enitharmon stretch'd on the dreary earth
> Felt her immortal limbs freeze stiffening pale inflexible
> His feet shrunk with'ring from the deep shrinking & withering;
> And Enitharmon shrunk up all their fibres with'ring beneath
> As plants wither'd by winter leaves & stems & roots decaying
> Melt into thin air while the seed driv'n by the furious wind
> Rests on the distant Mountain's top.

Night V recapitulates the story of the birth and binding of Orc
from *The Book of Urizen,* with the difference that the bound babe

of *Urizen* or *The Mental Traveller* is now understood to be a reborn
Luvah, one of a series of such reincarnations which will culminate
in the birth of Jesus. Urizen begins to explore his dens, as before,
in Night VI, which largely follows chapter 8 of *The Book of Urizen,*
down to the creation of the Web of Religion. Toward the end of
Night VI the exploring Urizen hears the howling of the bound Orc,
redoubles his immortal efforts, and is about to have Orc at his mercy
when he encounters Tharmas and a dreadful figure called the
Spectre of Urthona:

                                   & full before his path
    Striding across the narrow vale the Shadow of Urthona,
    A Spectre Vast appear'd whose feet & legs with iron scaled
    Stamp'd the hard rocks expectant of the unknown wanderer
    Whom he had seen wand'ring his nether world when distant far
    And watch'd his swift approach. Collected dark the Spectre
       stood
    Beside him Tharmas stay'd his flight & stood in stern defiance
    Communing with the Spectre who rejoic'd along the Vale
    Round his loins a girdle glow'd with many colour'd fires
    In his hand a knotted Club whose knots like mountains frown'd
    Desart among the Stars them withering with its ridges cold
    Black scales of iron arm the dread visage iron spikes instead
    Of hair shoot from his orbed scull; his glowing eyes
    Burn like two furnaces.

Faced by this double protector of man's imprisoned life force,
Urizen retires into his Web, which moves out to prepare his path
before him, and causes Tharmas and the Spectre of Urthona to
flee. Their flight and the descent of Urizen down to the Caves of
Orc begin Night VII of the poem, but this is a second Night VII.
In 1799–1800 Blake seems to have discarded his first version of
Night VII, and to have created a second that redetermined the
shape of his poem. One influential critic, Margoliouth, reads this
revision as a major change in Blake's mind, even calling it a "conversion" to a "new acceptance of Christianity." [22] As Margoliouth
concludes his useful book by saying that Blake "has much in common with St. Paul," his fanciful account of a conversion was clearly
part of a rather personal pattern-making. Whatever Blake was, he
believed to the end that "Energy is the only life, and is from the

Body," which is antithetical to the dualism of St. Paul. Yet there
is a crisis in Night VII of *The Four Zoas,* and it is possible that some
crisis in Blake's inner life is involved. Erdman finds a double crisis
embedded in the *Zoas* manuscript, the first being the Peace of
Amiens (first announced, autumn 1801) and the second a renewal of
war between France and England in the spring of 1803.[23] This may
be, but the problematical Spectre of Urthona seems to have more
to do with problems of poetic incarnation than with the external
warfare that undoubtedly provides the basis for Blake's historical
allegory.

If one reads *The Four Zoas* as a Freudian allegory, it would seem
clear that Urizen was a kind of superego, Tharmas an id, with Luvah-
Orc rising from him as libido; but Los, the fourth Zoa, is hardly a
representation of the Freudian ego. His dark brother, the dread
Spectre of Urthona, is closer to a function that meets external reality
and reacts to it by mediating between prevailing conceptions of it
and instinctual drives. Blake believed finally with the speculative
psychologist Meister Eckhart that "you are what you will to be,"
and his mature idea of Los identifies the fallen shaper-in-fire with
the active poetic will. Urizen is defied momentarily by ego and
id, the Spectre and Tharmas, but both yield to the Net of Religion,
and the bound energies of libido become vulnerable to the arts of
the superego. Los has no part in this scene, which is deterministic
and clearly indisputable as an act of psychic cartography.

Urizen proclaims that he has descended to view Orc out of pity,
but the fiery youth rejects his advances. As Urizen sits brooding
over Orc, the Tree of Mystery springs up around him. Though Orc
continues to resist, he is forced into the cycle of Mystery, to become
at length what he beholds. Urizen suddenly realizes that the terrible
being in front of him is a reappearance of his brother Luvah, with
whom he plotted to bring about the fall. Despising Urizen's light,
Orc turns it into flaming fire, and in the fury of his hatred "begins
to Organize a Serpent body." As the serpent, Orc goes up the mysterious tree and so represents a state of nature giving itself up to
mystery, and the religion of Urizen.

The remainder of the revised Night VII deals with the crisis of
the visionary will in Los. Beneath the Tree of Mystery are Los and
Enitharmon, absent from the poem since their binding of Orc in
Night V. Enitharmon, in the shadow of the tree, puts on the

Mystery of the possessive female will, and becomes the Shadow of Enitharmon, the "yardstick space" of the material world, as Frye calls her.[24] The Spectre of Urthona, in his manifestation as the "clock time" that governs the ego, comes to embrace her. He has a clear idea of his own nature:

> Thou knowest that the Spectre is in Every Man insane brutish
> Deform'd that I am thus a ravening devouring lust continually
> Craving & devouring but my Eyes are always upon thee O lovely
> Delusion & I cannot crave for any thing but thee not so
> The spectres of the Dead for I am as the Spectre of the Living
> For till these terrors planted round the Gates of Eternal life
> Are driven away & annihilated we never can repass the Gates

He takes her, knowing her for a "lovely delusion," hoping somehow that this act of possession will help him back into Eternity. But the product of dead time and dead space is "a wonder horrible," and the ego begets upon nature the image of a shadowy female, who in Night VIII is to be identified with Vala. The parents of this concentration of Mystery and delusion have courted one another with a story that is the most sinister version of the fall of Albion. In taking Luvah's emanation, Vala, as his mistress, and thus giving primacy to passive emotion, Man only prepared the way for his fall. The new element is that Urizen was born of that seduction, and finally conspired with Luvah to a joint revenge upon Man. That revenge attains its most ironic consequence in the dark event that has just taken place. The conspiracy of Urizen and Luvah led to the division of Urthona, which division in turn led to the fall of Tharmas. But the fall of one god is the collapse of all, and Luvah and Urizen followed Tharmas into the abyss. The falling Tharmas contained the divided components of Urthona, and we have summarized the complex story from that point on.

Everything that is material and negative culminates in Night VII with the birth of the Shadowy Female, which also climaxes the Orc cycle, as the serpent in the tree above the new Female is a final debased form of human energy and desire. But meanwhile another embrace leads to an apocalyptic prospect. Ego and will, clock and imaginative time, embrace in mutual forgiveness:

> Los Embrac'd the Spectre first as a brother
> Then as another Self; astonish'd humanizing & in tears

After a struggle, Enitharmon is reconciled to the work of creation that Los and the Spectre can perform together. Los summarizes the value of these labors:

> Stern desire
> I feel to fabricate embodied semblances in which the dead
> May live before us in our palaces & in our gardens of labour
> Which now open'd within the Center we behold spread abroad
> To form a world of Sacrifice of brothers & sons & daughters
> To comfort Orc in his dire sufferings. Look my fires enlume afresh
> Before my face ascending with delight as in ancient times

The palaces are of a City of Art, a New Jerusalem that Blake calls Golgonooza (evidently an anagram for New Golgotha, to replace the scene of the Crucifixion). The Center cannot hold, but opens this world into the firmness of Eternity, rather than into the vacuum of Ulro, where things fall apart to no definite end. The new creation that provides bodies for the impending Resurrection is intended as a comfort for Orc, the desire now at the end of its suffering endurance.

Night VII is more of a textual tangle than my description would suggest, but the remainder of the poem is very clear. Night VIII records the events, positive and negative, that carry the world to the verge of apocalypse. A saving remnant of Eternity meets in council and takes on the shape of One Man, Jesus. Los has fixed the limit of sensual Contraction as Adam, man in his present form, so the fall can go no further. The limit of opaque matter, of Opacity, has been fixed by Los as the Selfhood, now called Satan or the Accuser. As he can be in no worse condition, Albion begins to wake upon his rock. A conflict for the specters of this world begins between Los and Enitharmon, on the side of vision, and "the Shadowy female's sweet delusive cruelty." Jesus descends and puts on the robes of Luvah, thus consenting to be the last of the crucified vegetative gods in the Orc cycle. That cycle burns itself out in fierce wars, against which Los labors incessantly to build up his City of enduring imaginative forms. Vala seeks a reborn Luvah as Adonis to her Venus, but her quest becomes only another part of the Direful Web of Religion, of a nature unable to save itself and unwilling to be saved by a renovated Human.

The long labors of Los and Enitharmon climax in a reappearance of Albion's emanation, Jerusalem, "a City, yet a Woman," who carries within herself the image of lost Innocence, the Lamb of God. In a last blood sacrifice of natural religion, the Lamb suffers the dual fate of Jesus and Prometheus, crucified on the dead Tree of Mystery, and bound down to the rock of matter. The advent of Jesus is the start of the final Orc cycle, and though it ends in the irony of Jesus going up the dead tree to be worshiped as Jehovah, it also causes error to culminate in a new Babylon, identified by Blake with the Deism of his own day:

> For God put it into their heart to fulfill all his will
> The Ashes of Mystery began to animate they call'd it Deism
> And Natural Religion as of old so now anew began
> Babylon again in Infancy Call'd Natural Religion.

Something of the force of Blake's hatred of Deism has been lost with time. If we understand Deism only as a rejection of supernatural revelation, or as an exaltation of an indifferent and withdrawn God, we will think Blake to have been merely obsessed. To Blake, Deism was everything in his world that hindered humanization and then justified such hindrance by an appeal to reason, nature, or morality. We would not call our culture a Deist one today, but the relevance of Blake's passion and protest is a constant, as the thing, if not the name, survives.

The scheme of the Zoas had failed Blake's imagination, not because it explained too little, but because it explained so much as to be a determinism. It could account for the genesis of horrors, but itself becomes a machinery of apocalypse, not a human form of renewal. Night IX is the Last Judgment, and by itself is a uniquely powerful and complete poem. Read as the last section of *The Four Zoas,* it lacks all necessity. We can understand where it is going, but we rightly wonder where it comes from. Its dialectic is purely emotional and not imaginative, though its execution is a triumph of imagination. In a terrified reaction to the death of the Lamb, Los does what we might expect a liberated Orc to do: he stretches out his hands and attacks the starry heavens of Urizen:

> his right hand branching out in fibrous Strength
> Siez'd the Sun His left hand like dark roots cover'd the Moon

And tore them down cracking the heavens across from immense
    to immense
Then fell the fires of Eternity with loud & shrill
Sound of Loud Trumpet thundering along from heaven to
    heaven
A mighty sound articulate: "Awake ye dead & come
To Judgment from the four winds Awake & Come away"
Folding like scrolls of the Enormous volume of Heaven & Earth
With thunderous noise & dreadful shakings rocking to & fro
The heavens are shaken & the Earth removed from its place
The foundations of the Eternal hills discover'd

Revelation uncovers reality, but first the unreal vanishes in destruction:

      The tree of Mystery went up in folding flames
Blood issu'd out in mighty volumes pouring in whirlpools fierce
From out the flood gates of the Sky The Gates are burst down
    pour
The torrents black upon the Earth the blood pours down in-
    cessant.
Kings in their palaces lie drown'd Shepherds their flocks their
    tents
Roll down the mountains in black torrents Cities Villages
High spires & Castles drown'd in the black deluge Shoal on
    Shoal
Float the dead carcases of Men & Beasts driven to & fro on waves
Of foaming blood beneath the black incessant Sky, till all
Mystery's tyrants are cut off & not one left on Earth

Albion, bowing his head over the consuming Universe, cries out
against the "war within my members" but in a very different spirit
from the cry of St. Paul. He summons Urizen, warning him that
the "deceit so detestable" of Urizenic religion is past forgiveness.
In a tremendous (and inexplicable) effort of will, Urizen reassumes
the human:

    Then Go O dark futurity I will cast thee forth from these
    Heavens of my brain nor will I look upon futurity more
    I cast futurity away & turn my back upon that void
    Which I have made for lo futurity is in this moment

The effect of these lines depends upon *The Book of Urizen* as well as upon *The Four Zoas*. The fall of Urizen was from the beginning based upon his failure to see that "futurity is in this moment," in the timelessness of imaginative choice. Alive again in the moment, he rises again into the heavens in radiant youth, to be rejoined there by Ahania. Yet she seems to die, in excess of joy, but sleeps again until the final spring shall revive her. First comes a final cycle of plowing and sowing (the work of Urizen) in which the seeds of life are planted for a last time. Orc having burned up in the fires of judgment, Luvah and Vala return to where they belong, and the reign of what D. H. Lawrence called "sex in the head" is over:

> Return O Love in peace
> Into your place the place of seed not in the brain or heart
> If Gods combine against Man Setting their Dominion above
> The Human form Divine. Thrown down from their high Station
> In the Eternal heavens of Human Imagination: buried beneath
> In dark oblivion with incessant pangs ages on ages
> In Enmity & war first weaken'd then in stern repentance
> They must renew their brightness & their disorganiz'd functions
> Again reorganize till they resume the image of the human
> Co-operating in the bliss of Man obeying his Will
> Servants to the infinite & Eternal of the Human form

These lines summarize the themes of the epic. Luvah and Vala, Tharmas and Enion, are reborn into Beulah, to the accompaniment of Blake's most rapturous hymns of innocence—nervous, intense and vivid, and unique in literature as effective projections of paradise.

The last harvest begins with Urizen threshing out all nations, and with "the stars thresh'd from their husks." Tharmas wields the winnowing fan, until Luvah begins the fearful but necessary labor of the "Wine-press," and the vintage is trampled out. Urthona appears as the crippled heavenly smith of tradition, "limping from his fall," but able now to lean upon Tharmas. The two most primal Zoas, restored as imagination and intuition unhindered by negations, take on the task of loading "the waggons of heaven," and

take away "the wine of ages with solemn songs and joy." The climax
is in the fires that will not singe a sleeve:

> How is it we have walk'd thro' fires & yet are not consum'd
> How is it that all things are chang'd even as in ancient times

It is continuously inventive and beautiful, but Blake came to
trust it less and less. The Last Judgment, he began to sense, was
not so dramatic, and hardly so external a phenomenon. By 1804,
at the latest, he had decided to put *The Four Zoas* aside forever,
and to transfer his vision to the struggle within himself. A Last
Judgment, as he came to understand, began within each man, and
not in the outer cosmos: "Whenever any Individual Rejects Error
& Embraces Truth, a Last Judgment passes upon that Individual."

The brief epic *Milton* (1800–1808) shows an individual poet
prophet, Milton, rejecting Error in Eternity, and descending to
earth again to embrace Truth, thus passing a Last Judgment upon
himself. When Milton enters Blake, to be joined with him, a Last
Judgment is passed upon Blake as well, and an approach is made to
an apocalypse shaped by the imagination out of strength as well as
need, and without the necessity of natural fear.

8   *The Recovery of Innocence*

Milton

> Up led by thee
> Into the Heav'n of Heav'ns I have presum'd,
> An Earthlie Guest, and drawn Empyreal Aire,
> Thy tempring; with like safetie guided down
> Return me to my Native Element.
>   *Paradise Lost*, VII, 12–16

THE title plate of *Milton* shows the poet striding into the flames
of creative desire, right hand and right foot forward. Beneath is the

legend "To Justify the Ways of God to Men," the twenty-sixth line of *Paradise Lost*. So *Milton*, like *Paradise Lost* and the Book of Job, is intended as a theodicy, a treatment of the problem of evil. Originally in twelve books, like *Paradise Lost*, Milton was concentrated by Blake in only two books, with the result that the poem may be overorganized.

Milton begins with the famous dedicatory hymn "And did those feet in ancient time," in which Blake sees himself as inheriting the Miltonic chariot of fire, the prophetic vehicle that first appears in Ezekiel's vision. Beneath the lyric is the outcry of Moses against Joshua: "Would to God that all the Lord's people were prophets."

John Milton died in 1674. One hundred years later the young Blake began to write the later poems in *Poetical Sketches*, and the prophetic Protestant and radical vision of Milton revived in English poetry. What moved Milton to descend again, to incarnate himself once more in an English poet?

> Say first! what mov'd Milton, who walk'd about in Eternity
> One hundred years, pond'ring the intricate mazes of Providence
> Unhappy tho' in heav'n, he obey'd he murmur'd not; he was
> silent
> Viewing his Sixfold Emanation scatter'd thro' the deep
> In torment! To go into the deep her to redeem & himself perish?
> What cause at length mov'd Milton to this unexampled deed?

For one hundred years Milton has continued in error, "pond'ring the intricate mazes of Providence," even as his fallen angels sat in Hell

> and reason'd high
> Of Providence, Foreknowledge, Will, and Fate,
> Fixt Fate, free will, foreknowledge absolute,
> And found no end, in wand'ring mazes lost.

Like them, Milton has been Urizenic, but his imagination does not let him rest in that moralistic labyrinth. His Sixfold Emanation, his three wives and three daughters, is still separated from him, and so he realizes that he must perish as a selfhood to redeem it (which he had not done in his own poetry). The direct cause of Milton's resolve is a "Bard's Song" that he hears in Eternity. This Song, which continues through Plate 11, is both an extraordinary trans-

formation of a vital part of Blake's biography and a theory of
psychological types.

For three years (September 1800–October 1803) Blake and his
wife lived at Felpham in Sussex, under the kindly patronage of
William Hayley, a minor poet and gentleman of taste, friend and
biographer of Cowper. As Blake prepared to leave for Felpham, he
wrote a doggerel poem in which Hayley is seen as a "bless'd
Hermit," dispensing hospitality:

> The Bread of sweet Thought & the Wine of Delight
> Feeds the Village of Felpham by day & by night;
> And at his own door the bless'd Hermit does stand,
> Dispensing, Unceasing, to all the whole Land.

There is no irony here, though the aging man of *The Mental
Traveller* dispensed food in a similar way, and thus distributed
the martyr's groan and the lover's sigh. Blake went off to Felpham
hoping to find there a Beulah presided over by Hayley as a friend
to Genius. He found, eventually, Ulro and Hayley as a well-mean-
ing Satan. Blake's notebook doggerel at Hayley's expense has survived poor Hayley:

> To forgive Enemies Hayley does pretend,
> Who never in his Life forgave a friend.
>
> Thy Friendship oft has made my heart to ake:
> Do be my Enemy for Friendship's sake.
>
> Thus Hayley on his Toilette seeing the sope,
> Cries, "Homer is very much improv'd by Pope."

This is all good fun, but some of the verses move into the sinister:

> When Hayley finds out what you cannot do,
> That is the very thing he'll set you to.
> If you break not your Neck, 'tis not his fault,
> But pecks of poison are not pecks of salt.
> And when he could not act upon my wife
> Hired a Villain to bereave my Life.

That "Villain" is the dragoon Schofield, who accused Blake of
sedition after a scuffle, on August 12, 1803. Blake had determined

by then to leave Hayley, and the incident with Schofield came to be associated by him with Hayley's secret and unconscious enmity. Though Hayley aided Blake throughout the subsequent trial, which saw Blake acquitted, and assisted him later as well, Blake never ceased to suspect Hayley as an enemy of his imagination.

In Blake's terms, Hayley was his "Corporeal Friend," but "Spiritual Enemy," which seems true enough. This brief excursion into biography is justified only because the Satan of the "Bard's Song" is clearly founded upon Hayley, just as much in *Jerusalem* refers to the ordeal of Blake's trial.

The "Bard's Song," very briefly summarized, deals with the three classes of men created as his sons by Los:

> The first, The Elect from before the foundation of the World;
> The second, The Redeem'd; The Third, The Reprobate, & form'd
> To destruction from the mother's womb

Blake's vocabulary here is again ironic. The reasonable Satan-Hayley is like the Calvinist Elect in his equation of his worldly status with the supposed favor of heaven, though unlike any Calvinist in his Panglossian insistence that the way things are is as they ought to be. The Redeemed (Palamabron-Blake) is the class of men who can abide by their vision despite worldly pressure and Satanic reasoning. The Reprobate are the wrathful prophets, like Rintrah in *Milton,* who cry out as solitary voices in the wilderness, Elijah-figures. The "Bard's Song," in Frye's words, "does not relate a sequence of events, but tells the story of the dispute of Palamabron and Satan and then brings out its larger significance by a series of lifting backdrops." [25] The story of the dispute is in itself not important, except as it illustrates the unending struggle of the artist with the elements of morality, reason, and nature which would subvert him for his own supposed good:

> Of the first class was Satan: with incomparable mildness;
> His primitive tyrannical attempts on Los: with most endearing love
> He soft intreated Los to give to him Palamabron's station;
> For Palamabron return'd with labour wearied every evening
> Palamabron oft refus'd; and as often Satan offer'd

His service till by repeated offers and repeated intreaties
Los gave to him the Harrow of the Almighty; alas blamable
Palamabron fear'd to be angry lest Satan should accuse him of
Ingratitude, & Los believe the accusation thro' Satan's extreme
Mildness.

Los, as in *The Four Zoas,* is the father of any civilizing impulse,
of every attempt to build the City of Art. As Hayley had Blake
painting miniatures while Hayley translated Klopstock into English,
there is a likely biographical source for this usurpation of the cultivating Harrow by Satan. Probably we are better off for not knowing
more about the Blake-Hayley episode than we do, as it is better to
read Blake's myth in its own invented terms. Soft embraces between
Palamabron and Satan are a mistake, according to Blake, as they
produced Augustan culture, and would have inhibited a Milton
had he not had the wisdom to go over to the cleansing wrath of
Rintrah. The central issue of *Milton* is whether Blake can follow
Milton into the desert of prophecy, and whether Milton, in giving
Blake visionary courage, can himself eliminate the last part in his
own story which still belongs to Satan.

Satan's labors in place of Palamabron drive the horses of the
Harrow to a "tormenting fury." They "rag'd with thick flames
redundant" just as Wordsworth's thwarted inspiration at the opening of *The Prelude* becomes "a tempest, a redundant energy,
vexing its own creation." Poor Palamabron has only the "Science of
Pity," which divides the soul. He needs Rintrah's "Science of
Wrath," which understands how to cast out the things of this world
which impede prophecy. Palamabron serves the Mills of Satan
which grind down creation, when he should be cultivating a new
creation. When the judgment of Eden is made between Palamabron
and Satan, it is no surprise that Satan is condemned, though Leutha,
his Emanation, offers to take on his sin. In the *Visions of the
Daughters of Albion,* Leutha was only a spirit of potential sexuality.
Now she is a self-sacrificing Rahab figure, attempting to save Satan,
in a parody of the darker function of Sin as Satan's daughter in
Paradise Lost. For once we have Hell offering to redeem another
state, by self-immolation. Leutha insists that her passion for Palamabron, put off by his Emanation, Elynittria, was transferred to Satan
as an insane possessiveness:

This to prevent, entering the doors of Satan's brain night after
  night
Like sweet perfumes I stupified the masculine perceptions
And kept only the feminine awake; hence rose his soft
Delusory love to Palamabron: admiration join'd with envy
Cupidity unconquerable! My fault, when at noon of day
The Horses of Palamabron call'd for rest and pleasant death:
I sprang out of the breast of Satan, over the Harrow beaming
In all my beauty! that I might unloose the flaming steeds
As Elynittria used to do; but too well those living creatures
Knew that I was not Elynittria, and they brake the traces.

Blake is making it clear that neither Palamabron's Pity nor
Satan's love is a virtue. When the Bard ends his Song, many in
Heaven condemn it, saying: "Pity and Love are too venerable for
the imputation of Guilt." But Milton has heard enough. The
necessity for a new Rintrah is clear to him, and the behavior of
Leutha suggests that he has undervalued the female capacity for
self-sacrifice, and was wrong therefore to abandon his Emanation in
the deep. He states the purpose of his descent:

I will go down to self annihilation and eternal death,
Lest the Last Judgment come & find me unannihilate
And I be seiz'd & giv'n into the hands of my own Selfhood.
The Lamb of God is seen thro' mists & shadows, hov'ring
Over the sepulchers in clouds of Jehovah & winds of Elohim
A disk of blood, distant; & heav'ns & earth's roll dark between
What do I here before the Judgment? without my Emanation?
With the daughters of memory, & not with the daughters of
  inspiration?
I in my Selfhood am that Satan: I am that Evil One!
He is my Spectre! in my obedience to loose him from my Hells
To claim the Hells, my Furnaces, I go to Eternal Death.

In this brilliant passage Milton identifies himself with his own
Satan, whom he thrust into Hell in *Paradist Lost*. Now, taking "off
the robe of the promise" and ungirding himself "from the oath of
God," Milton throws off the bondage of Urizenic religion and goes
naked to his Hells of Eternal Death, to remake himself there into
the image of Eternal Life. Heaven and Hell are to be married to-

gether, and the fires of wrath are to be the furnaces of Los, in which
the human is shaped.

Milton leaves Eternity and takes on his mortal Shadow as his
own again. His vision becomes that of fallen man once more as
he enters a vortex, like the Mental Traveller of Blake's ballad, and
so again accepts nature as his wide womb. He sees Albion in a
sleep of death upon his rock, and then falls further, into the "Sea
of Time & Space":

> Then first I saw him in the Zenith as a falling star,
> Descending perpendicular, swift as the swallow or swift;
> And on my left foot falling on the tarsus, enter'd there;
> But from my left foot a black cloud redounding spread over
>   Europe.

The return of Milton is signaled by the portent of a falling star,
and by a cloud of prophetic menace over Europe. Milton seeks his
Sixfold Emanation, which is divided in the dark Ulro, but his coming frightens not only Urizen but Los as well, who believes he is
the fallen star Satan.

The crucial contest for the incarnated Milton is with Urizen, who
meets the poet in a desperate wrestling match on the shores of a
river of error, the Arnon. The story of wrestling Jacob finds its
parody in this struggle:

> Silent they met, and silent strove among the streams, of Arnon
> Even to Mahanaim, when with cold hand Urizen stoop'd down
> And took up water from the river Jordan: pouring on
> To Milton's brain the icy fluid from his broad cold palm.
> But Milton took the red clay of Succoth, moulding it with care
> Between his palms; and filling up the furrows of many years
> Beginning at the feet of Urizen, and on the bones
> Creating new flesh on the Demon cold, and building him,
> As with new clay a Human form in the Valley of Beth Peor.

Urizen is like Jehovah at Peniel, but Milton is more than a Jacob
desiring a blessing. The Valley of Beth Peor is the burial ground of
Moses in the land of Moab, and to build a Human form there is
to replace the grave of the moral law of Urizen by a new Adam,
a man of "red clay," associated with the harvest festival of booths,
in which four plants represent the four classes of men who unite as

one man in the cooperation of worship. Milton is renovating Urizen and defying his icy intellectual baptism even as he does so.

As Milton works on in this heroic contest, Albion's sleeping Humanity begins to turn upon his couch. Los, in despair at Milton's descent until now, remembers an old prophecy:

> That Milton of the Land of Albion should up ascend
> Forwards from Ulro from the Vale of Felpham; and set free
> Orc from his Chain of Jealousy

In the spirit of this prophecy, a great illumination comes to Blake:

> But Milton entering my Foot; I saw in the nether
> Regions of the Imagination; also all men on Earth,
> And all in Heaven, saw in the nether regions of the Imagination
> In Ulro beneath Beulah, the vast breach of Milton's descent.
> But I knew not that it was Milton, for man cannot know
> What passes in his members till periods of Space & Time
> Reveal the secrets of Eternity: for more extensive
> Than any other earthly things, are Man's earthly lineaments.
>
> And all this Vegetable World appear'd on my left Foot,
> As a bright sandal form'd immortal of precious stones & gold:
> I stooped down & bound it on to walk forward thro' Eternity.

This giant metaphor can best be read together with that other moment of vision soon after, when Los joins himself to Milton and Blake:

> While Los heard indistinct in fear, what time I bound my
>   sandals
> On; to walk forward thro' Eternity, Los descended to me:
> And Los behind me stood; a terrible flaming Sun: just close
> Behind my back; I turned round in terror, and behold,
> Los stood in that fierce glowing fire; & he also stoop'd down
> And bound my sandals on in Udan-Adan; trembling I stood
> Exceedingly with fear and terror, standing in the Vale
> Of Lambeth: but he kissed me and wish'd me health
> And I became One Man with him, arising in my strength:
> 'Twas too late now to recede. Los had enter'd into my soul:
> His terrors now possess'd me whole; I arose in fury & strength.

Both these passages are full-scale incarnations of the Poetical Character, in the tradition of Collins' *Ode*. Udan-Adan, the lake of the indefinite, symbolizes the Ulro, while the bright sandal of the Vegetable World represents Generation. Milton entering into Blake redeems Blake from Generation; Los's similar entering into him redeems him from Ulro. The errors of Experience and of Self-hood leave Blake, and he is free to write of the re-entry into Beulah which will precede the apocalyptic thrust into Eden in *Jerusalem*.

The agent of Milton's restoration into Beulah is Ololon, the Emanation who is the goal of his quest. She is already in Eden as "a sweet River of milk & liquid pearl," but she too descends, to seek her poet even as he seeks her.

The rest of Book I describes the world of Blake's own day, which is overripe for apocalypse, like the world of Night VIII of *The Four Zoas*. The function of Milton-Blake-Los is to achieve a vision of this world which is the transcending contrary of its vision of itself.

Book II begins with Blake's fullest account of Beulah, as the first state into which Ololon descends. As this is the world of Thel, the exquisite rhetoric of Innocence returns:

> First e'er the morning breaks joy opens in the flowery bosoms
> Joy even to tears, which the Sun rising dries; first the Wild
>   Thyme
> And Meadow-sweet downy & soft, waving among the reeds
> Light springing on the air, lead the sweet Dance: they wake
> The Honeysuckle sleeping on the Oak: the flaunting beauty
> Revels along upon the wind; the White-thorn lovely May
> Opens her many lovely eyes: listening the Rose still sleeps
> None dare to wake her: soon she bursts her crimson curtain'd
>   bed
> And comes forth in the majesty of beauty; every Flower:
> The Pink, the Jessamine, the Wall-flower, the Carnation
> The Jonquil, the mild Lilly opes her heavens! every Tree,
> And Flower & Herb soon fill the air with an innumerable Dance
> Yet all in order sweet & lovely, Men are sick with Love!
> Such is a Vision of the lamentation of Beulah over Ololon

Beulah is sexual, Eden human; the first is the emanation of the second. A passage like the one above is technically interesting as a vision of Beulah, but also reminds us that Blake's rejection of nature has nothing to do with any supposed blindness toward the beauty of the natural world. The human form is Blake's index of delight, as it is Wordsworth's, but where Wordsworth found that love of nature led to love of man, Blake feared that love of nature more frequently led to the sacrifice of man on a natural altar.

Yet Ololon's descent is accepted by the inhabitants of Beulah as a sign that the Female Will of nature can "pity & forgive." More than Oothoon, who desired to carry Innocence into Experience but failed for want of an imaginative male will, Ololon is the final redemption of poor Thel. From Beulah Thel descended, but fled back shrieking. Ololon goes down as multitudes, in a descent into every possible depth, like Asia's descent to the cave of Demogorgon in *Prometheus Unbound*. In a supreme Moment of renovation, "when the morning odours rise abroad / And first from the Wild Thyme," and to the music of a Lark, Ololon

> Appear'd: a Virgin of twelve years nor time nor space was
> To the perception of the Virgin Ololon but as the
> Flash of lightning but more quick the Virgin in my Garden
> Before my Cottage stood

With Blake observing, Milton and Ololon confront one another in the garden at Felpham. Milton takes the lead in the mutual purgation by annihilating his negating Selfhood, the Satan that is within him:

> The Negation is the Spectre; the Reasoning Power in Man
> This is a false Body: an Incrustation over my Immortal
> Spirit; a Selfhood, which must be put off & annihilated alway
> To cleanse the Face of my Spirit by Self-examination.
> To bathe in the waters of Life; to wash off the Not Human
> I come in Self-annihilation & the grandeur of Inspiration
> To cast off Rational Demonstration by Faith in the Saviour
> To cast off the rotten rags of Memory by Inspiration
> To cast off Bacon, Locke & Newton from Albion's covering
> To take off his filthy garments, & clothe him with Imagination
> To cast aside from Poetry, all that is not Inspiration
> That it no longer shall dare to mock with the aspersion of
>   Madness
> Cast on the Inspired by the tame high finisher of paltry Blots,

Indefinite, or paltry Rhymes; or paltry Harmonies.
Who creeps into State Government like a catterpiller to destroy
To cast off the idiot Questioner who is always questioning,
But never capable of answering

When Milton is done with this declaration, everything that hides
the Human Lineaments has been purged away with fire. The Virgin
Ololon, so long as she remains virgin, cannot understand Milton,
and replies in despair:

> Altho' our Human Power can sustain the severe contentions
> Of Friendship, our Sexual cannot: but flies into the Ulro.
> Hence arose all our terrors in Eternity! & now remembrance
> Returns upon us! Are we Contraries O Milton, Thou & I
> O Immortal! how were we lead to War the Wars of Death
> Is this the Void Outside of Existence, which if enter'd into
> Becomes a Womb? & is this the Death Couch of Albion
> Thou goest to Eternal Death & all must go with thee.

The image of the vortex, which becomes nature's wide womb,
dominates these lines, that are the last the separate Female Will,
which is Ololon's virginity, ever speaks. With a shriek, the Shadow
of Ololon separates from her and leaves her as the poet's bride. The
forty-first plate, one of Blake's finest, shows the redeemed Milton
tenderly comforting the repentant Ololon. The Four Zoas appear in
Blake's Vale of Felpham to sound the four trumpets that herald
apocalypse:

> Terror struck in the Vale I stood at that immortal sound
> My bones trembled. I fell outstretch'd upon the path
> A moment, & my Soul return'd into its mortal state
> To Resurrection & Judgment in the Vegetable Body
> And my sweet Shadow of Delight stood trembling by my side

With his wife Catherine by his side, and Milton and Ololon
vanished, Blake is reminded of his vision's reality by the messengers
of Los, the Lark's trill, and the odor of the Wild Thyme:

> Immediately the Lark mounted with a loud trill from Felpham's
>   Vale
> And the Wild Thyme from Wimbleton's green & impurpled
>   Hills

And Los & Enitharmon rose over the Hills of Surrey
Their clouds roll over London with a south wind, soft Oothoon
Pants in the Vales of Lambeth weeping o'er her Human
    Harvest
Los listens to the Cry of the Poor Man: his Cloud
Over London in volume terrific, low bended in anger.

Oothoon, who received so little in the *Visions,* now gathers her
Human Harvest. Los the prophet returns to the tradition of social
justice, the line of Amos, as the Poor Man's cry comes up from the
streets of the London of *Songs of Experience.* Rintrah and Palamabron, Reprobate and Redeemed, prophet of Wrath and artist of
Pity, can return to their cultivation of a Human Harvest, as the
poem comes to its conclusion with an image of immediate potentiality:

Rintrah & Palamabron view the Human Harvest beneath
Their Wine-presses & Barns stand open; the Ovens are prepar'd
The Waggons ready: terrific Lions & Tygers sport & play
All Animals upon the Earth, are prepar'd in all their strength

To go forth to the Great Harvest & Vintage of the Nations

Milton is Blake's last *Song of Innocence,* and is incomplete without its matching contrary. To go from *Milton* to *Jerusalem* is to
pass from the Divine Image to the Human Abstract, but the passage
is necessary if all Human Forms are to be identified, and if we are
to converse "with Eternal Realities as they Exist in the Human
Imagination."

9   *Blake's Apocalypse*

Jerusalem

THE Strong Man represents the human sublime. The Beautiful Man represents the human pathetic, which was in the wars
of Eden divided into male and female. The Ugly Man repre-

sents the human reason. They were originally one man, who
was fourfold; he was self-divided, and his real humanity slain
on the stems of generation, and the form of the fourth was like
the Son of God. How he became divided is a subject of great
sublimity and pathos. The Artist has written it under inspiration, and will, if God please, publish it; it is voluminous, and
contains the ancient history of Britain, and the world of Satan
and of Adam.

BLAKE, describing his painting
"The Ancient Britons"

JERUSALEM is that voluminous work, a poem in one hundred engraved plates and more than four thousand lines. *Jerusalem* is twice
as long as its prelude, *Milton,* and very much more difficult, so much
so that I will not give a full summary of it. A brief introduction to
the poem, with some indication of its structure, and a few apprecia-
tions of its splendor, must serve here to round out my description of
Blake's poetic achievement.

Jerusalem is subtitled *The Emanation of the Giant Albion,* and
begins with an address "To The Public," which divides Blake's
potential audience into the categories of "Sheep" and "Goats," a
rather less complimentary division than that in the *Marriage* between "Angels" and "Devils." The date on the title page, 1804,
cannot be the date of the poem's completion, and is certainly not
that of its engraving, which may be as late as 1818. Probably the
writing of the basic text was over by 1809, though Blake may have
revised for another decade.

The poem is divided into four chapters, three of which concern
a strife of contraries progressing toward a humanizing solution.
Chapter 1 presents the contraries of the self-divided giant, Albion,
and his fourth component, Los, whose form is now like the Son of
God. Chapter 2 opposes the Orc cycle and Los's attempt to achieve
a form out of the cycle which shall liberate man. Chapter 3 shows
the human vision as represented by Blake's Jesus, conflicting with
the natural vision of reality as maintained by Deism. Chapter 4
gives us the final confrontation, in which contraries cease and
imaginative truth is set against a culmination of Satanic error. Blake
does not carry the poem into apocalypse but stops with the uncovering of all phenomena in their human forms.

The poem opens with both Albion and Blake asleep, but Albion is in the deathly sleep of Ulro, Blake in the creative repose of Beulah. The voice of the Savior awakens Blake, warning him that "a black water accumulates." This is the dark Atlantic, the blood of the fallen Albion, or Atlas, which will vanish in the apocalypse, when there shall be no more sea. Albion, hearing the Savior's voice, "away turns down the valleys dark," rejecting the vision as a "phantom of the over heated brain." Possessed by jealous fears, Albion has hid his Emanation "upon the Thames and Medway, rivers of Beulah." Spenser had pictured a marriage of the Thames and Medway as an image of concord in the natural world, an extension of the state of being described in the married land of the Gardens of Adonis. The hiding of Jerusalem signifies the fall of the Thames and Medway from human to natural status, a collapse of the phenomenal world into the system of nature.

Certain of Blake's major conceptions have evolved into a change in emphasis when we meet them again in *Jerusalem*. The most important concern Los, who in *The Book of Urizen* was as culpable as Urizen himself. In *The Four Zoas*, Los is still deeply immersed in error, but in *Milton* he merges into an identity with Blake and Milton, who are themselves in error but fighting toward truth. In *Jerusalem*, Los is closely involved with Jesus, and the furnaces of inspired art become identical with the machinery of salvation.

In Albion's continued (and willful) fallen condition, all human perfections "of mountain & river & city, are small & wither'd & darken'd." Against this shrinking of human lineaments, Blake offers himself as prophet:

Trembling I sit day and night, my friends are astonish'd at me.
Yet they forgive my wanderings, I rest not from my great task!
To open the Eternal Worlds, to open the immortal Eyes
Of Man inwards into the Worlds of Thought: into Eternity
Ever expanding in the Bosom of God, the Human Imagination
O Saviour pour upon me thy Spirit of meekness & love:
Annihilate the Selfhood in me, be thou all my life!
Guide thou my hand which trembles exceedingly upon the rock
    of ages,
While I write of the building of Golgonooza, & of the terrors of
Entuthon:

Of Hand & Hyle & Coban, of Kwantok, Peachey, Brereton,
  Slayd & Hutton:
Of the terrible sons & daughters of Albion, and their Genera-
  tions.
Scofield! Kox, Kotope and Bowen, revolve most mightily upon
The Furnace of Los: before the eastern gate bending their fury.
They war, to destroy the Furnaces, to desolate Golgonooza:
And to devour the Sleeping Humanity of Albion in rage &
  hunger.

Golgonooza we have met before as the New Jerusalem or City of
Eden, a city of redemption like Spenser's Cleopolis or Yeats's Byzantium, or a "Fourfold Spiritual London," in Blake's vocabulary.
Entuthon is the wasteland outside the city, at once a garden become
a forest and a road to Eternity become a maze, like Spenser's Faery
Land in Book I of his romance. Hand and his eleven brothers (down
to Bowen) are the sons of Albion, and several fairly congested para-
graphs are necessary to introduce their identity and function.

Zechariah the prophet mentions seven "eyes of the Lord, which
run to and fro through the whole earth" (4:10). In Blake these Eyes
of God become seven Orc cycles, seven attempts by which the God
in Man tries to reverse his fall. The first two Eyes, Lucifer and
Moloch, are pre-Hebraic, Druidic cycles, leaving behind giant monuments like Stonehenge. The third Blake calls Elohim, and sees as
fixing the limit of contraction, or the creation of Adam and Eve.
The fourth, Shaddai, is the age of Abraham, in which human sacrifice ends and so the limit of opacity is established: that is, Satan is
identified and cast out. The fifth Eye, Pachad, or the "fear" of
Isaac, finishes the first twenty "churches," or epicycles, into which
the third, fourth, and fifth cycles are divided. The sixth Eye, that
of Jehovah, is the cycle coming to an end in Blake's own time,
where the last phase, or twenty-seventh church, is called Luther,
the final orthodoxy into which the Protestant Orc aged. The twenty-
eighth phase is the seventh Eye, or church of Jesus, the inaugura-
tion of which will be the act of apocalypse.

Blake lives toward the end of the sixth Eye whose god, Jehovah-
Urizen, made a covenant with Jacob under the name of Israel. We
have seen Milton struggling with Urizen on the banks of the Arnon,
seeking to abrogate that covenant by molding Urizen into human

form. Jacob, or Israel, is Albion, the fallen Man of the sixth Eye of God, and so Albion, like Israel, must have twelve sons. Orc first came in Israel's cycle as Moses, who, Palamabron-like, was caught between a Rintrah (Elijah, the pillar of fire, Los) and a Satan (Aaron, the pillar of cloud, Urizen). Moses yielded to Satan, and so the Jehovah cycle was bound over to natural morality, not the imagination of the prophets. When the Israelite host crossed into Canaan across the Jordan from the East, they accomplished another fall, identical in Blake's myth with the collapse of Atlantis and the isolating of Britain from America. In *Milton,* the Female Will tries to tempt Milton to a similar error in entry, but the renovated poet refuses. The imaginative entrance into Palestine, for Blake, is through Edom from the South, the upper gate of Beulah through which *The Marriage of Heaven and Hell* expects the Savior to come.

As Albion-Israel sleeps, the struggle around him is transferred to his sons against Los. Albion's twelve sons are both a human Zodiac (as they worship the Starry Wheels, which they credit Urizen with having created) and an accusing jury, like the one Blake sat before in his treason trial.

Kwantok, Peachey, and Brereton were judges at Blake's ordeal. Kox was a confederate of Scofield, the accusing dragoon. The origin of the other names is shadowy, but this does not matter. Only four of Albion's sons are of importance in the structure of Jerusalem. They are first, Hand, a death principle, probably based on the three Hunt brothers who published the literary review *The Examiner,* which made two hideous attacks upon Blake's work as an artist. Hand is the Satanic Selfhood of Israel's oldest son, Reuben, who is the particular symbol in *Jerusalem* of the natural or vegetative man, separated by Hand from Merlin, his immortal part or imagination. The next two brothers are Hyle (Hayley, or the Greek word for "matter") and Coban (possibly an anagram for Sir Francis Bacon, who with Newton and Locke is Blake's symbol of fallen reason and its empirical exaltation of nature). Simeon and Levi, the murderous twins, soldier and priest, correspond to Hyle and Coban. Scofield, the cause of Blake's bondage, is a Joseph figure, for he is responsible for Albion's fall as Joseph caused the descent of Israel into Egypt. The first three sons of Albion—Hand, Hyle, and Coban—are a

Triple Accuser and represent Reason, Nature, and Mystery respectively.

The poem next introduces the other antagonists of Los and Jerusalem, the sinister Daughters of Albion, whose names are drawn from accounts of early British history, who together form Tirzah, Mother Nature, and Rahab, the Whore of Babylon, who, as the Covering Cherub, blocks our way back into Eden.

With its new personages introduced, the poem turns to intense conflicts. Los hears Jerusalem lamenting for her children, the murderous sons and daughters of Albion. He knows that to save her he must revive Albion, and he can do that only by laboring to turn nature into art. But his Spectre, the selfish ego of Urthona we have met before in *The Four Zoas,* tries to lure Los away from the furnaces, reminding him that Albion's friendship for him has been deceitful. Blake's Spectre is reminding him that he is an unwanted and unheard prophet, rather like Shelley's selfhood turning on him in the fourth stanza of the *Ode to the West Wind,* when the other English prophet of the age is faced by the ordeal of despair. As Shelley rises into life in the great last stanza of the *West Wind,* so Blake-Los denies and subdues his Spectre:

> Thou art my Pride & Self-righteousness: I have found thee out:
> Thou art reveal'd before me in all thy magnitude & power
> Thy Uncircumcised pretences to Chastity must be cut in sunder!
> Thy holy wrath & deep deceit cannot avail against me
> Nor shalt thou ever assume the triple-form of Albion's Spectre
> For I am one of the living: dare not to mock my inspired fury
> If thou wast cast forth from my life! if I was dead upon the
>   mountains
> Thou mightest be pitied & lov'd: but now I am living; unless
> Thou abstain ravening I will create an eternal Hell for thee.
> Take thou this Hammer & in patience heave the thundering
>   Bellows
> Take thou these Tongs: strike thou alternate with me: labour
>   obedient.

As Los labors at his furnaces he creates "the Spaces of Erin," the bulwark that the poetic vision sets against the raging Atlantic of Time and Space (Erin because Ireland is a geographic buffer for

England against the Atlantic). The Spectre weeps, but the unmoved Los states the guiding law of Blake's work:

> I must Create a System, or be enslav'd by another Man's
> I will not Reason & Compare: my business is to Create.

The Spectre despairs, refusing to believe that the God in Man deserves Los's labors. But even in despair, the divided Blake works on, driven by the visionary will of Los, who compels the Spectre in Blake to work with him:

> So spoke the Spectre shudd'ring, & dark tears ran down his
>   shadowy face
> Which Los wiped off, but comfort none could give! or beam of
>   hope
> Yet ceas'd he not from labouring at the roarings of his Forge
> With iron & brass Building Golgonooza in great contendings
> Till his Sons & Daughters came forth from the Furnaces
> At the sublime Labours for Los, compell'd the invisible Spectre
> To labours mighty, with vast strength, with his mighty chains,
> In pulsations of time, & extensions of space, like Urns of
>   Beulah
> With great labour upon his anvils; & in his ladles the Ore
> He lifted, pouring it into the clay ground prepar'd with art;
> Striving with Systems to deliver Individuals from those Systems;
> That whenever any Spectre began to devour the Dead,
> He might feel the pain as if a man gnaw'd his own tender
>   nerves.

The striving with systems liberates the Daughters of Beulah, Blake's Muses, and in the power of that liberation Golgonooza is built. Outside the city is the desolate world of Ulro:

> There is the Cave; the Rock; the Tree; the Lake of Udan
>   Adan;
> The Forest, and the Marsh, and the Pits of bitumen deadly:
> The Rocks of solid fire: The Ice valleys: the Plains
> Of burning sand: the rivers, cataract & Lakes of Fire:
> The Islands of the fiery Lakes: the Tree of Malice: Revenge:
> And black Anxiety; and the Cities of the Salamandrine men:
> (But whatever is visible to the Generated Man,
> Is a Creation of mercy & love, from the Satanic Void.)

The land of darkness flamed but no light, & no repose:
The land of snows of trembling, & iron hail incessant:
The land of earthquakes: and the land of woven labyrinths:
The land of snares & traps & wheels & pit-falls & fire mills:
The Voids, the Solids, & the land of clouds & regions of waters:

Night and day Los walks round the walls of his city, viewing
the fallen state of the Zoas, and the rooting of the twelve sons of
Albion into every nation as the Polypus, the undifferentiated mass
of vegetative life. As Los looks out at the world through Blake's
eyes, he sees Albion cased over by the "iron scourges" of the natural
philosophy of Bacon and Newton:

Reasonings like vast Serpents
Infold around my limbs, bruising my minute articulations

All things that he sees acted on Earth have already been created
by Los as bright sculptures in the Halls of his city. But these inspired prophecies do not save Jerusalem from being accused of sin
by the twelve sons of Albion, and by Vala, Albion's mistress. The
fallen giant speaks out of his sleep, accusing himself, and so suffers
the fate of Job: "Every boil upon my body is a separate & deadly
sin." The first chapter closes with the Daughters of Beulah lamenting Albion's departure from self-forgiveness and the forgiveness of
others.

Chapter 2 is addressed "To the Jews," and begins with a lyric
that identifies ancient Jerusalem and modern London. Plate 26,
just before this lyric, shows Jerusalem, the woman, appalled by
Hand the Accuser, who stalks by her, left foot forward, a serpent
intertwined in his arms, a dark vision of reason identified with
death. Hand is the vision Blake calls upon the Jews to repudiate,
that their humility may be liberated from self-righteousness. As the
second chapter will concern the attempt to form history into vision,
Blake directs it to the Jews whose writings record the struggles
between contraries in a nation's spiritual history.

Chapter 2 begins with Albion's acceptance of Urizen as God,
under the cold shadows of the Tree of Mystery. After this, he creates a Female Will in Vala, and worships it as well. Reuben now
takes Albion's place as the man of ordinary perceptive powers, the
Adam who has reached the limit of contraction. As such, Reuben
is in the dreadful position of a creature who invents his own un-

necessary death and then grows forward toward it, but this perverseness is the pattern of ordinary generative life.

Los makes a series of resolutions to save Albion, and so deliver Reuben over to the Merlin within himself, but Albion is now interested only in justice and righteousness, like a Job's comforter, and will not allow himself to be saved by works of forgiveness. Instead, he orders Hand and Hyle to seize Los to be brought to justice. Los prays for the "Divine Saviour" to arise "upon the Mountains of Albion as in ancient time," and takes action by entering into Albion to search the tempters out of the giant's Minute Particulars. But he finds every Particular of Albion, every individual component of vision, hardened into grains of sand. Unable to save the degenerated Albion, Los as Savior builds a couch of repose for him to rest upon, the materials of the couch being composed of the books of the Bible. Jerusalem goes into the kind arms of the Daughters of Beulah, to await her lord's awakening. Erin, the spirit of myth-making or individual vision, ends the chapter with a speech of great complexity, addressed to the Daughters in their role as sources of a poet's inspiration. Beginning with a sense of horror at the collapse of Atlantis and the withering away of the human form, she passes to the paradox of fallen vision:

> The Visions of Eternity, by reason of narrowed perceptions,
> Are become weak Visions of Time & Space, fix'd into furrows
>   of death;
> Till deep dissimulation is the only defence an honest man has
>   left.

Certainly this is Blake chastising his own life, and lamenting the limits of his existence:

> The Eye of Man, a little narrow orb, clos'd up & dark,
> Scarcely beholding the Great Light; conversing with the Void:
> The Ear, a little shell, in small volutions shutting out
> True Harmonies, & comprehending great, as very small:
> The Nostrils, bent down to the earth & clos'd with senseless
>   flesh,
> That odours cannot them expand, nor joy on them exult:
> The Tongue, a little moisture fills, a little food it cloys,
> A little sound it utters, & its cries are faintly heard.

This is the contrary to Thel's lament over the senses. Yet Erin's speech centers as much on hope as on despair, for

The Lord
Jehovah is before, behind, above, beneath, around.

The work of this Jehovah makes it clear that he is the Jehovah of Blake's Jesus, not of Satan-Urizen, for he shows his forgiveness by "building the Body of Moses in the valley of Peor: the Body of Divine Analogy." We have met this valley where Moses is buried before, in *Milton*, for Urizen and Milton struggle there until Urizen puts on the human form and abandons the law of morality with its stone tablets. The fallen body of man is therefore also "the Body of Divine Analogy," made in the image of the unfallen Man-God. Frye sums up the central meaning of *Jerusalem* when he calls this use of analogy a "conception of the world of experience as a parody or inverted form of the imaginative world." [26] Blake's dialectical position in *The Marriage of Heaven and Hell* depended upon just such a conception of nature and experience. The naturalist or vitalist does not realize that nature can be turned inside out, as it were, without being repudiated, just as the ascetic cannot understand that inverted as nature is, it remains a form, however distorted, of the truth. For Blake, to hold a mirror up to man is to see nature.

Erin closes her speech by vowing to remain as a shield against the Starry Wheels of Albion's sons, while the Daughters of Beulah end the chapter by calling upon the Lamb of God to descend.

That Blake addressed chapter 3 "To the Deists" marks it as the part of the poem which seeks to consolidate error. Deism Blake now defines explicitly as "the Worship of the God of this World," and its morality as "Self-Righteousness, the Selfish Virtues of the Natural Heart."

When the poem begins again we see the grief of the imaginative heart as Los "wept vehemently over Albion." The Eternals elect the Seven Eyes of God, but the Daughters of Albion continue their wild cruelties, while the Sons maintain their battle against the hammer of Los. Urizen creates Druid temples for human sacrifice, while Los goes on with the perpetual work of making his city.

The cycles move on until we reach the story of Joseph and Mary. Blake had little use for any myth of a virgin birth; to him such an event could only occur as a demonic act in Ulro. His mother of Jesus is a Magdalen, like Oothoon. But Joseph is no Theotormon, and Mary becomes a form of Jerusalem:

> O Forgiveness & Pity & Compassion! If I were Pure I should never
> Have known Thee; If I were Unpolluted I should never have
> Glorified thy Holiness, or rejoiced in thy great Salvation.

The larger part of chapter 3 sharpens the opposition between Vala and Jerusalem, Satan and Jesus, until:

> The Human form began to be alter'd by the Daughters of Albion
> And the perceptions to be dissipated into the Indefinite. Becoming
> A mighty Polypus nam'd Albion's Tree: they tie the Veins
> And Nerves into two knots: & the Seed into a double knot:
> They look forth: the Sun is shrunk: the Heavens are shrunk
> Away into the far remote: and the Trees & Mountains wither'd
> Into indefinite cloudy shadows in darkness & separation.

This decay of nature is simultaneous with the union of the Daughters of Albion into "Rahab & Tirzah, A Double Female," who torture the human form and inspire their admirers to the sexual aberration of war. The twenty-seven churches now pass into the group of "the Male Females: the Dragon forms," stretching from Abraham to Luther, "and where Luther ends Adam begins again in Eternal Circle." But before the Circle can go round again, prophecy finally succeeds and breaks into history:

> But Jesus breaking thro' the Central Zones of Death & Hell
> Opens Eternity in Time & Space; triumphant in Mercy

With this event, the third chapter closes. The fourth begins with an address "To the Christians," for Blake is approaching his revelation and

> A man's worst enemies are those
> Of his own house & family;
> And he who makes his law a curse,
> By his own law shall surely die.

"Is the Holy Ghost any other than an Intellectual Fountain?"
Blake asks, and by that question separates himself from the insti-
tutional Christianity of his own day or of any other. A blank-verse
introductory poem goes further in separating Jesus from the Wheel
of fire that moves religion in his name:

> I stood among my valleys of the south
> And saw a flame of fire, even as a Wheel
> Of fire surrounding all the heavens: it went
> From west to east against the current of
> Creation and devour'd all things in its loud
> Fury & thundering course round heaven & earth
> By it the Sun was roll'd into an orb:
> By it the Moon faded into a globe,
> Travelling thro' the night: for from its dire
> And restless fury, Man himself shrunk up
> Into a little root a fathom long.
> And I asked a Watcher & a Holy-One
> Its Name? he answered: It is the Wheel of Religion

Jesus died, according to Blake, because he strove against the current of this Wheel. But as the institutions of religion have subsumed the first visionary, so they begin in our time to subsume
Blake also, whose doctrinal orthodoxy has been proclaimed by assorted divines.

The action of chapter 4 begins again with the incessant labors
of Los against the Spectres of Albion's Twelve Sons. These have
crowned Vala as queen of earth and heaven. Hand and Hyle have
been seduced by their Emanations, and only their Satanic Spectres,
ghosts of reason and nature, remain to battle Los. Los himself
wearies, for he is "the labourer of ages in the Valleys of Despair."
Yet he has resolution enough to take Reuben from his wanderings
and set him into the Divine Analogy of the six thousand years of
Biblical and post-Biblical history. A vision of Jerusalem within
Albion revives Los and he returns with fresh courage to his furnaces, but is betrayed into wearying strife again by Enitharmon,
who begins to recede into the Female Will.

The remainder of the poem is dominated by a full epiphany of
Antichrist and a gradually mounting consciousness of redemption.
On the eighty-ninth plate the Antichrist is revealed as "a Human

Dragon terrible and bright," who is also Ezekiel's "anointed cherub that covereth," a Leviathan who devours in three nights "the rejected corse of death" that the last Luvah had shed. In the final line of the eighty-ninth plate a Double Female who has mustered multitudes of the fallen becomes absorbed through those multitudes in Antichrist, and so becomes a Satanic One with him.

In reaction to this intensified horror, Los reaches the heights of his prophetic power on the wonderful ninety-first plate, which gathers together the hard-won wisdom of Blake's heroic life:

Go, tell them that the Worship of God, is honouring his gifts
In other men: & loving the greatest men best, each according
To his Genius: which is the Holy Ghost in Man; there is no other
God, than that God who is the intellectual fountain of Humanity;
He who envies or calumniates: which is murder & cruelty,
Murders the Holy-one: Go tell them this & overthrow their cup,
Their bread, their altar-table, their incense & their oath:
Their marriage & their baptism, their burial & consecration:
I have tried to make friends by corporeal gifts but have only
Made enemies: I never made friends but by spiritual gifts;
By severe contentions of friendship & the burning fire of thought.
He who would see the Divinity must see him in his Children,
One first, in friendship & love; then a Divine Family, & in the midst
Jesus will appear; so he who wishes to see a Vision; a perfect Whole
Must see it in its Minute Particulars

Milton had invoked the Holy Spirit as one that preferred "Before all Temples th' upright heart and pure." Now Blake overthrows all that is outward in worship as a distraction from the human. Los, with a tremendous effort, at last subdues his Spectre:

I care not whether a Man is Good or Evil; all that I care
Is whether he is a Wise Man or a Fool. Go! put off Holiness
And put on Intellect: or my thund'rous Hammer shall drive thee
To wrath which thou condemnest: till thou obey my voice

In the furnaces of Los the nations begin to fuse together. Albion
revives:

> The Breath Divine went forth upon the morning hills, Albion
>   mov'd
> Upon the Rock, he open'd his eyelids in pain; in pain he
>   mov'd
> His stony members, he saw England. Ah! shall the Dead live
>   again

The Four Zoas go to their apocalyptic tasks: "Urizen to his furrow, & Tharmas to his Sheepfold, and Luvah to his Loom." The
integrated Urthona labors at his Anvil, with Los within him "la-
bouring & weeping," for though unwearied, the prophet has labored
long, "because he kept the Divine Vision in time of trouble."
Jesus, in "the likeness & similitude of Los," appears before Albion, as the Good Shepherd before "the lost Sheep that he hath
found." They converse, "as Man with Man," the dialogical image
of mutual confrontation excluding any notion of subject-object experience between them. Jesus has died and must die for Albion,
but only the death of the Selfhood. In a clairvoyant moment of
humanist affirmation, Blake's Jesus, who is "the likeness & similitude" of Blake as both are of Los, states *Jerusalem*'s version of the
Atonement: "This is Friendship & Brotherhood: without it Man
is Not." Nothing in Blake is finer than those last five words, inevitable in their simplicity.
The Covering Cherub comes on in darkness and overshadows
them, and appears to "divide them asunder." Terrified for Jesus,
Albion throws himself into Los's furnaces of affliction, seeking to
lose himself in saving Jesus, but

> All was a Vision, all a Dream: the Furnaces became
> Fountains of Living Waters flowing from the Humanity Divine
> And all the Cities of Albion rose from their Slumbers, and All
> The Sons & Daughters of Albion on soft clouds Waking from
>   Sleep
> Soon all around remote the Heavens burnt with flaming fires
> And Urizen & Luvah & Tharmas & Urthona arose into
> Albion's Bosom: Then Albion stood before Jesus in the Clouds
> Of Heaven Fourfold among the Visions of God in Eternity

In this crucial moment, in and out of time, the workshop of the artist has become the Living Waters of Humanity's Intellectual Fountain, and "a pure river of water of life" as well, in reference to the last chapter of Revelation. The lineaments of Man are revealed, and the Four Zoas take their places in a wonderfully active Eden, very unlike Milton's static Heaven:

> And they conversed together in Visionary forms dramatic which bright
> Redounded from their Tongues in thunderous majesty, in Visions
> In new Expanses, creating exemplars of Memory and of Intellect
> Creating Space, Creating Time according to the wonders Divine
> Of Human Imagination, throughout all the Three Regions immense
> Of Childhood, Manhood & Old Age; & the all tremendous unfathomable Non Ens
> Of Death was seen in regenerations terrific or complacent varying
> According to the subject of discourse & every Word & every Character
> Was Human according to the Expansion or Contraction, the Translucence or
> Opakeness of Nervous fibres such was the variation of Time & Space
> Which vary according as the Organs of Perception vary & they walked
> To & fro in Eternity as One Man reflecting each in each & clearly seen
> And seeing: according to fitness & order.

The ninety-ninth plate shows Albion and Jerusalem in a sexual embrace, surrounded by fire on every side. The text is very quiet, and very sure:

> All Human Forms identified even Tree Metal Earth & Stone, all
> Human Forms identified, living going forth & returning wearied

Into the Planetary lives of Years Months Days & Hours re-
   posing
And then Awaking into his Bosom in the Life of Immortality.

And I heard the Name of their Emanations they are named
   Jerusalem

In this most definitive of Blake's visions, nothing is excluded.
Among the innumerable Chariots of the Almighty appearing in
heaven are not only "Milton & Shakspear & Chaucer," but "Bacon
& Newton & Locke," for contraries are necessary in Eden. Blake was
free even of his own apparent obsessions, for the imagination cannot
be obsessed, even as it cannot be contained. "The clearer the
organ the more distinct the object," Blake wrote, and the organ of
his imagination was the whole man.

WILLIAM WORDSWORTH

There is a human loneliness,
A part of space and solitude,
In which knowledge cannot be denied.
In which nothing of knowledge fails,
The luminous companion, the hand,
The fortifying arm, the profound
Response, the completely answering voice. . . .

WALLACE STEVENS

1   *The Great Marriage*

The Recluse

THE PRELUDE was to be only the antechapel to the Gothic church of *The Recluse*, but the poet Wordsworth knew better than the man, and *The Prelude* is a complete and climactic work. The key to *The Prelude* as an internalized epic written in creative competition to Milton is to be found in those lines (754–860) of the *Recluse* fragment that Wordsworth prefaced

to *The Excursion* (1814). Wordsworth's invocation, like Blake's to
the Daughters of Beulah in his epic *Milton,* is a deliberate address
to powers higher than those that inspired *Paradise Lost:*

> Urania, I shall need
> Thy guidance, or a greater Muse, if such
> Descend to earth or dwell in highest heaven!
> For I must tread on shadowy ground, must sink
> Deep—and, aloft ascending, breathe in worlds
> To which the heaven of heavens is but a veil.

The shadowy ground, the depths beneath, and the heights aloft
are all in the mind of man, and Milton's heaven is only a veil,
separating an allegorical unreality from the human paradise of the
happiest and best regions of a poet's mind. Awe of the personal
Godhead fades before the poet's reverence for his own imaginative
powers:

> All strength—all terror, single or in bands,
> That ever was put forth in personal form—
> Jehovah—with his thunder, and the choir
> Of shouting Angels, and the empyreal thrones—
> I pass them unalarmed.

Blake, more ultimately unorthodox than Wordsworth as he was,
had yet too strong a sense of the Bible's power to accept this dismissal of Jehovah. After reading this passage, he remarked sardonically:

> Solomon, when he Married Pharaoh's daughter & became a
> Convert to the Heathen Mythology, Talked exactly in this way
> of Jehovah as a Very inferior object of Man's Contemplations;
> he also passed him by unalarm'd & was permitted. Jehovah
> dropped a tear & follow'd him by his Spirit into the Abstract
> Void; it is called the Divine Mercy.

To marry Pharaoh's daughter is to marry Nature, the Goddess
of the Heathen Mythology, and indeed Wordsworth will go on to
speak of a marriage between the Mind of Man and the goodly universe of Nature. Wordsworth is permitted his effrontery, as Solomon the Wise was before him, and, like Solomon, Wordsworth
wanders into the Ulro or Abstract Void of general reasoning from

Nature, pursued by the ambiguous pity of the Divine Mercy. But this (though powerful) is a dark view to take of Wordsworth's reciprocal dealings with Nature. Courageously but calmly Wordsworth puts himself forward as a renovated spirit, a new Adam upon whom fear and awe fall as he looks into his own Mind, the Mind of Man. As befits a new Adam, a new world with a greater beauty waits upon his steps. The most defiant humanism in Wordsworth salutes the immediate possibility of this earthly paradise naturalizing itself in the here and now:

> Paradise, and groves
> Elysian, Fortunate Fields—like those of old
> Sought in the Atlantic Main—why should they be
> A history only of departed things,
> Or a mere fiction of what never was?
> For the discerning intellect of Man,
> When wedded to this goodly universe
> In love and holy passion, shall find these
> A simple produce of the common day.

No words are more honorific for Wordsworth than "simple" and "common." The marriage metaphor here has the same Hebraic sources as Blake had for his Beulah, or "married land." The true Eden is the child of the common day, when that day dawns upon the great consummation of the reciprocal passion of Man and Nature. What Wordsworth desires to write is "the spousal verse" in celebration of this fulfillment:

> and, by words
> Which speak of nothing more than what we are,
> Would I arouse the sensual from their sleep
> Of Death, and win the vacant and the vain
> To noble raptures.

This parallels Blake's singing in *Jerusalem:*

> Of the sleep of Ulro! and of the passage through
> Eternal Death! and of the awaking to Eternal Life.

But Wordsworth would arouse us by speaking of nothing more than what we already are; a more naturalistic humanism than Blake could endure. Wordsworth celebrates the *given*—what we already possess, and for him it is as for Wallace Stevens

> As if the air, the mid-day air, was swarming
> With the metaphysical changes that occur,
> Merely in living as and where we live.

For Wordsworth, as for Stevens, the earth is enough; for Blake it was less than that all without which man cannot be satisfied. We need to distinguish this argument between the two greatest of the Romantics from the simplistic dissension with which too many readers have confounded it, that between the doctrines of innate goodness and original sin. Wordsworth is not Rousseau, and Blake is not St. Paul; they have more in common with one another than they have with either the natural religionist or the orthodox Christian.

Wordsworth's Imagination is like Wallace Stevens' *Angel Surrounded by Paysans:* not an angel of heaven, but the necessary angel of earth, as, in its sight, we see the earth again, but cleared; and in its hearing we hear the still sad music of humanity, its tragic drone, rise liquidly, not harsh or grating, but like watery words awash, to chasten and subdue us. But the Imagination of Wordsworth and of Stevens is "a figure half seen, or seen for a moment." It rises with the sudden mountain mists, and as suddenly departs. Blake, a literalist of the Imagination, wished for its more habitual sway. To marry Mind and Nature is to enter Beulah; there Wordsworth and Blake are at one. Blake insisted that a man more fully redeemed by Imagination would not need Nature, would regard the external world as hindrance. The split between Wordsworth and Blake is not theological at all, though Blake expresses it in his deliberately displaced Protestant vocabulary by using the metaphor of the Fall where Wordsworth rejects it. For Wordsworth the individual Mind and the external World are exquisitely fitted, each to the other, even as man and wife, and with blended might they accomplish a creation the meaning of which is fully dependent upon the sexual analogy; they give to us a new heaven and a new earth blended into an apocalyptic unity that is simply the matter of common perception and common sexuality raised to the freedom of its natural power. Wordsworthian Man is Freudian Man, but Blake's Human

Form Divine is not. "You shall not bring me down to believe such fitting & fitted" is his reaction to Wordsworth's exquisite adjustings of the Universe and Mind. To accept Nature as man's equal is for Blake the ineradicable error. Blake's doctrine is that either the Imagination totally destroys Nature and puts a thoroughly Human form in its place, or else Nature destroys the Imagination. Wordsworth says of his task that he is forced to hear "Humanity in fields and groves / Pipe solitary anguish" and Blake reacts with ferocity:

> "Does not this Fit, & is it not Fitting most Exquisitely too, but to what?—not to Mind, but to the Vile Body only & to its Laws of Good & Evil & its Enmities against Mind."

This is not the comment of an embittered Gnostic. Blake constructs his poetry as a commentary upon Scripture; Wordsworth writes his poetry as a commentary upon Nature. Wordsworth, while not so Bible-haunted as Blake, is himself a poet in the Hebraic prophetic line. The visible body of Nature is more than an outer testimony of the Spirit of God to him; it is our only way to God. For Blake it is the barrier between us and the God within ourselves. Ordinary perception is then a mode of salvation for Wordsworth, provided that we are awake fully to what we see. The common earth is to be hallowed by the human heart's and mind's holy union with it, and by that union the heart and mind in concert are to receive their bride's gift of phenomenal beauty, a glory in the grass, a splendor in the flower. Until at last the Great Consummation will be achieved, and renovated Man will stand in Eden once again. The human glory of Wordsworth, which he bequeathed to Keats, is in this naturalistic celebration of the possibilities inherent in our condition, here and now. That Wordsworth himself, in the second half of his long life, could not sustain this vision is a criticism of neither the vision nor the man, but merely his loss—and ours.

Nutting

THE fragment *Nutting* (1798–1799) was originally intended for *The Prelude.* I place it here in my discussion for the contrast it affords with the poet's passionate spousal verse heralding the Great

Marriage. *Nutting* hints at the darker side of the sexual myth relating Man and Nature, for it describes an incident in which the
boy Wordsworth offended against the gathering covenant by ravishing a corner of Nature.

Nutting is strong in latent content. On "one of those heavenly
days that cannot die" the boy goes forth on a solitary nutting
expedition:

> O'er pathless rocks,
> Through beds of matted fern, and tangled thickets,
> Forcing my way, I came to one dear nook
> Unvisited, where not a broken bough
> Drooped with its withered leaves, ungracious sign
> Of devastation; but the hazels rose
> Tall and erect, with tempting clusters hung,
> A virgin scene!

The difficulty of approach, pathless, matted, tangled, is a feature
of many myths of quest that move toward a cynosure, a bower of
delight that serves as a center of centripetal vision. The rough analogy is with the human female body. Faced by this tempting scene,
the boy pauses to enjoy the luxury of the expectant eye:

> —A little while I stood,
> Breathing with such suppression of the heart
> As joy delights in; and with wise restraint
> Voluptuous, fearless of a rival, eyed
> The banquet.

This is the glance of potential possession and use, not that of
wise passivity and the shared initiative. Yet this is only a boy, and
his innocence is almost radical:

> —or beneath the trees I sate
> Among the flowers, and with the flowers I played;
> A temper known to those who, after long
> And weary expectation, have been blest
> With sudden happiness beyond all hope.

This is already true love of Nature, but rude love, without wisdom. The boy indulges in the youthful faculty of Fancy, and sets
himself to think of the natural place as being one where "fairy

water-breaks" murmur on endlessly. He sees the "sparkling foam" of his Fancy, and luxuriates in a sweet mood of pleasure until suddenly the strength of his passion for the bower overcomes his dreamings:

> Then up I rose,
> And dragged to earth both branch and bough,
>   with crash
> And merciless ravage: and the shady nook
> Of hazels, and the green and mossy bower,
> Deformed and sullied, patiently gave up
> Their quiet being.

The morality of observation here ("deformed and sullied") is presented as being that of the boy himself, though Wordsworth enters the reservation: "unless I now / Confound my present feelings with the past." The boy at first feels the wealth of possession of a ravisher, but his exclusion from unity with Nature rapidly afflicts him:

> Ere from the mutilated bower I turned
> Exulting, rich beyond the wealth of kings,
> I felt a sense of pain when I beheld
> The silent trees, and saw the intruding sky.

He has disturbed, and momentarily shattered, the peace of Nature. In the scene of perfect harmony which begins *Tintern Abbey,* the landscape is connected to the quiet of the sky. Here, because of the boy's action, there is no reciprocal giving between earth and sky. The trees are silent, and the sky is an intruder. The dialectic of generosity between Man and Nature must operate before there can be a mutual giving within Nature herself. In a touching displacement of responsibility for his act, Wordsworth transcends the directly sexual element in his poem by adjuring a gentle Maiden to move among the same shades, and so restore the spirit he has driven away:

> Then, dearest Maiden, move along these shades
> In gentleness of heart; with gentle hand
> Touch—for there is a Spirit in the woods.

Wordsworth lost his mother early, was extremely close to his sister, gave up his passionate love for Annette Vallon, and married moderately late. Very little of his best poetry has its roots in his years of marriage (1802 on), and the misgivings of *Resolution and Independence* relate to the anxieties that preceded his wedding. His bride was Nature, but many of his encounters with her are so presented as to provoke Shelley's satire in *Peter Bell the Third,* where Peter is Wordsworth:

> But from the first 'twas Peter's drift
> To be a kind of moral eunuch,
> He touched the hem of Nature's shift,
> Felt faint—and never dared uplift
> The closest, all-concealing tunic.

This has enough truth to make it a palpable hit, but not enough to let us accept it as a final statement on Wordsworth's attempt to hymn a naturalistic consummation. In Wordsworth's best poetry, there is no equivalent of Blake's Oothoon, Shelley's Emily, or Keats's Madeline. But there is the enigmatic mistress, Nature, and her complex dealings with the poet generally take subtler forms than do his with her in the fragment *Nutting.*

2   *Myth of Memory*

Tintern Abbey

TINTERN ABBEY (July 1798) is a miniature of the long poem Wordsworth never quite wrote, the philosophical and autobiographical epic of which *The Prelude,* the *Recluse* fragment, and *The Excursion* would have been only parts. As such, *Tintern Abbey* is a history in little of Wordsworth's imagination. The procedure and kind of the poem are both determined by Coleridge's influence, for *The Eolian Harp* (1795) and *Frost at Midnight* (February 1798) are its immediate ancestors, with the eighteenth-century sublime ode in the farther background. Yet we speak justly of the form of *Tintern Abbey* as being Wordsworth's, for he turns this kind of poem to its destined theme, the nature of a poet's imagination and that imagination's relation to external Nature. Coleridge begins the theme in his "conversation poems," but allows himself to be distracted from it by theological misgivings and self-abnegation. *Tintern Abbey*, and not *The Eolian Harp*, is the father of Shelley's *Mont Blanc* and Keats's *Sleep and Poetry*.

In the renewed presence of a remembered scene, Wordsworth comes to a full understanding of his poetic self. This revelation, though it touches on infinity, is extraordinarily simple. All that Wordsworth learns by it is a principle of reciprocity between the external world and his own mind, but the story of that reciprocity becomes the central story of Wordsworth's best poetry. The poet loves Nature for its own sake alone, and the presences of Nature give beauty to the poet's mind, again only for that mind's sake. Even the initiative is mutual; neither Nature nor poet gives in hope of recompense, but out of this mutual generosity an identity is established between one giver's love and the other's beauty. The process of reciprocity is like a conversation that never stops, and cannot therefore be summed up discursively or analyzed into static elements. The most immediate consequence of this process is a certain "wide quietness," as Keats was to call it in his *Ode to Psyche*. As the dialogue of love and beauty ensues, love does not try to find an object, nor beauty an expression in direct emotion, but a likeness between man and Nature is suggested. The suggestion is made through an intensification of the dominant aspect of the given landscape, its seclusion, which implies also a deepening of the mood of seclusion in the poet's mind:

> —Once again
> Do I behold these steep and lofty cliffs,
> That on a wild secluded scene impress
> Thoughts of more deep seclusion; and connect
> The landscape with the quiet of the sky.

The further connection is with the quiet of Wordsworth's mind, for the thoughts of more deep seclusion are impressed simultaneously on the landscape and on its human perceiver.

We murder to dissect, Wordsworth wrote in another context, and to dissect the renewed relationship between the poet and this particular landscape ought not to be our concern. Wordsworth wants to understand the interplay between Mind and Nature without asking *how* such dialogue can be, and this deliberate refusal to seek explanation is itself part of the meaning of *Tintern Abbey*. The poet has reached a point where the thing seen

> yields to a clarity and we observe,

> And observing is completing and we are content,
> In a world that shrinks to an immediate whole,

> That we do not need to understand, complete
> Without secret arrangements of it in the mind.

This is Wallace Stevens, in *Description without Place*, a poem that tries to suggest that to seem is to be, so that seeming, as well as everything we say of the past, is description without place, "a cast of the imagination." Until *Peele Castle*, natural seeming and reality are one for Wordsworth, and so his theory of poetry is a theory of description also. The language of description is employed by him both for the external world and for himself; if he will not analyze Nature, still less will he care to analyze man. The peculiar *nakedness* of Wordsworth's poetry, its strong sense of being alone with the visible universe, with no myth or figure to mediate between ego and phenomea, is to a surprisingly large extent not so much a result of history as it is of Wordsworth's personal faith in the reality of the body of Nature.

Away from the landscape he now rejoins, the poet had not forgotten it, but indeed had owed to memories of it sensations sweet, felt in hours of urban weariness, and therapeutic of the lonely ills he has experienced. Such tranquil restoration is only one gift of memory. Another is of more sublime aspect:

> that blessed mood,
> In which the burthen of the mystery,
> In which the heavy and the weary weight
> Of all this unintelligible world,
> Is lightened:—that serene and blessed mood,
> In which the affections gently lead us on,—
> Until, the breath of this corporeal frame

> And even the motion of our human blood
> Almost suspended, we are laid asleep
> In body, and become a living soul:
> While with an eye made quiet by the power
> Of harmony, and the deep power of joy,
> We see into the life of things.

This is not mysticism but, rather, a state of aesthetic contemplation. All contemplation of objects except the aesthetic is essentially practical, and so directed toward personal ends. The poet's genius frees contemplation from the drive of the will, and consequently the poet is able to see with a quiet eye. To see into the life of things is to see things for themselves and not their potential use. The poet attains to this state through memories of Nature's presence, which give a quietness that is a blessed mood, one in which the object world becomes near and familiar, and ceases to be a burden. The best analogue is the difference we feel in the presence of a stranger or a good friend. From this serenity the affections lead us on to the highest kind of naturalistic contemplation, when we cease to *have* our bodies, but *are* our bodies, and so are "laid asleep / In body, and become a living soul."

Having made this declaration, Wordsworth gives his first intimation of doubt as to the efficacy of Nature's presences:

> And now, with gleams of half-extinguished thought,
> With many recognitions dim and faint,
> And somewhat of a sad perplexity,
> The picture of the mind revives again.

The "sad perplexity" concerns the future and the enigma of the imagination when transposed from past to future time. In this moment of renewed covenant with a remembered and beloved landscape, is there indeed life and food for future years?

> And so I dare to hope,
> Though changed, no doubt, from what I was when first
> I came among these hills.

The process of change is what troubles Wordsworth. He speaks of three stages of development already accomplished, and fears the onset of a fourth. The "glad animal movements" of his boyish days preceded any awareness of nature. Then came the time when his perception of natural objects brought an immediate joy, so that he speaks of the simultaneity of vision and emotion as

> An appetite; a feeling and a love,
> That had no need of a remoter charm,
> By thought supplied, nor any interest
> Unborrowed from the eye.

That time is past, and Wordsworth has lost its "aching joys" and "dizzy raptures." He has entered into a third time, and other gifts have recompensed him for such loss. In this mature stage he *looks* on Nature, and *hears* in it

> The still, sad music of humanity,
> Nor harsh nor grating, though of ample power
> To chasten and subdue.

The dialectic of the senses here is vital in Wordsworth. The young child has an organic sense that combines seeing and hearing. The older child, awakening to the phenomenal world, sees a gleam in it that the mature man cannot see again. But the man gains an intimation of immortality, of his renewed continuity with the young child, by hearing a still, sad music *as* he sees a soberer coloring in Nature. Here in *Tintern Abbey*, eight years before the completion of the Great Ode, Wordsworth anticipates the totality of its myth. As he listens to the sad music ("still" because it pipes to the spirit, not to the sensual ear of man) he hears evidence not only of man's mortality but of man's inseparable bond with Nature. But perception and response are no longer simultaneous, and it is an act of meditation that must bring the riven halves together. This meditation does not start in the mind, but is first felt as a presence that disturbs the mind with the joy of elevated thoughts:

> a sense sublime
> Of something far more deeply interfused,
> Whose dwelling is the light of setting suns,
> And the round ocean and the living air,
> And the blue sky, and in the mind of man:
> A motion and a spirit, that impels
> All thinking things, all objects of all thought
> And rolls through all things.

This is parallel to Coleridge's *The Eolian Harp:*

> O! the one Life within us and abroad,
> Which meets all motion and becomes its soul,
> A light in sound, a sound-like power in light,
> Rhythm in all thought, and joyance every where.

As a consecration or sacramental vision this becomes the main burden of Wordsworth's song, until in *Peele Castle* it is exposed as only a dream, and the great light pervading it is deprecated as "the light that never was, on sea or land." When Wordsworth still believed in that light, as in this crucial passage from *Tintern Abbey,* he was able to see and hear a primal unity manifested simultaneously in all subjects and all objects. Again, it is a laziness of our imaginations that tempts us to call this vision mystical, for the mystical is finally incommunicable and Wordsworth desires to be a man talking to men about matters of common experience. The emphasis in *Tintern Abbey* is on things seen and things remembered, on the light of sense, not on the invisible world. The presence of outer Nature disturbs the mind, sets it into motion, until it realizes that Nature and itself are not utterly distinct, that they are mixed together, interfused. They are more interfused than the reciprocal relation between the outer presence and the mind's inner elevation in response would seem to indicate, for in speaking of that relation the poet still uses the vocabulary of definiteness and fixity. But the imagination dissolves such separateness. Within both Nature and Wordsworth is something that moves and breathes, and that blends subject and object as it animates them. *Therefore* the poet, though he has lost the aching joy that is Nature's direct gift, still loves Nature as he can apprehend it by eye and ear:

> —both what they half create,
> And what perceive; well pleased to recognise
> In nature and the language of the sense
> The anchor of my purest thoughts, the nurse,
> The guide, the guardian of my heart, and soul
> Of all my moral being.

But why "half create"? Though the boundaries between man and Nature have wavered, Wordsworth wishes to avoid the suggestion of a total absorption of Nature into man. Man is almost totally absorbed in Nature in his childhood, and again in extreme old age, as in *The Old Cumberland Beggar* and the Leech Gatherer of *Resolution and Independence*. But for the mature man, outward Nature must be recognized as external. That is his freedom and his grief. His consolation is that he half creates as well as perceives "outward" Nature, for what is outward comes to him only through the gates of his own perception, and whatever cannot come to him is not relevant to his condition. Eyes and ears, the gates of perception, are not passive but selective. He cannot create the phenomena that present themselves to him; they are given. But his choice among them is a kind of creation, and his choice is guided by memory. Memory is the mother of poetry for Wordsworth because the poem's half of the act of creation cannot proceed without the catalyst of recollecting the poet's response to an earlier version of the outward presence of Nature. Nature's half of the act is mysterious, except that Wordsworth insists that it cannot proceed without the initiating expression of man's love for what is outside himself.

This mature love for Nature leads to love for other men, to hearing the still, sad music of *humanity*. The soul of a man's moral being, its inwardness, *is* Nature once the earlier relation between man and Nature, where no meditation was necessary betwen perception of natural beauty and the deep joy of the perceiver's response, is in the past. The meditation of the later stage, the time of mature imagination, brings vision and joy together again by linking both with the heart's generosity toward our fellow men.

This is the teaching that preserves Wordsworth's "genial spirits" from decay, but the teacher himself is uncertain of the efficacy of his doctrine in the fourth stage that is to come, when natural decay may dull his responsiveness to the presences of beauty. He turns therefore to his sister Dorothy as an incarnation of his earlier self, as one who still feels the dizzy joys of natural communion that he himself can only recollect. The curious element in this ritualistic substitution is that the poet is only twenty-eight, and his sister just a year younger. Wordsworth's troubled forebodings were nevertheless justified; his imagination aged very quickly, and Dorothy's remained young and perpetually receptive to the beauty of the natural world:

> and in thy voice I catch
> The language of my former heart, and read
> My former pleasures in the shooting lights
> Of thy wild eyes. Oh! yet a little while
> May I behold in thee what I was once,
> My dear, dear Sister!

There is an urgency in the tone of this which deepens almost to a desperation:

> and this prayer I make,
> Knowing that Nature never did betray
> The heart that loved her.

The prayer thus heralded is never quite expressed in the remainder of the poem. Its burden is more life, survival, imaginative immortality. More directly, it is a desire to be free of the fear that enters so early into the poet's life and his poem. When he bounded like a roe over the mountains, and followed wherever Nature led, he was

> more like a man
> Flying from something that he dreads than one
> Who sought the thing he loved.

He sped as if to out-distance time, and sought an immediacy he was doomed to lose. Only Nature has the privilege of leading us from joy to joy; we have to wait upon her, brood on past joys, and have faith that she will not abandon hearts that have loved her. Wordsworth uses the strong word "betray" with its sexual implications, which are certainly present in the opening lines of the poem, where the poet's renewed passion is a lover's return. The lover returns, not to the wild ecstasy he had known, but to the sober pleasure of a marriage with Nature.

The most beautiful lines in *Tintern Abbey* invoke the possibility of perpetual renewal for Dorothy:

> Therefore let the moon
> Shine on thee in thy solitary walk;
> And let the misty mountain-winds be free
> To blow against thee.

As in *Michael* and *The Prelude,* the freedom of mountain mist and wind, sudden in their comings and goings, is a natural type of the wild freedom of ecstatic human imagination, the deep joy of that time when Nature for us is all in all.

Wordsworth looks forward to Dorothy's return to the beloved landscape, and prophesies the healing power memories of it will have for her. The fear of mortality, which has been haunting the poem, finally becomes overt:

> Nor, perchance—
> If I should be where I no more can hear
> Thy voice, nor catch from thy wild eyes these gleams
> Of past existence—wilt thou then forget
> That on the banks of this delightful stream
> We stood together.

In her wild eyes he sees the gleam that he can no longer see in Nature, but that once he did see, so that he almost literally reads his former pleasures in the eyes of another. His survival will be in those eyes, even as his earlier self has already survived there. He will live in her memory, and his faith will have its historical record:

> and that I, so long
> A worshipper of Nature, hither came
> Unwearied in that service: rather say
> With warmer love—oh! with far deeper zeal
> Of holier love.

This is the vocabulary of religious devotion, displaced into a naturalistic mode. Certainly he protests too much; we feel a desperation in his insistence, another presage of waning faith, or faith affirmed more vehemently even as it ebbs. We begin to understand the prayer he intends but does not make explicit. It is "Do not forget, or the life in me, the creative joy, will die." The closing lines, with their immense music, are not complete:

> Nor wilt thou then forget
> That after many wanderings, many years
> Of absence, these steep woods and lofty cliffs,
> And this green pastoral landscape, were to me
> More dear, both for themselves and for thy sake!

He leaves out "for my sake," but the poem has made clear that his salvation, as man and poet, is dependent upon the renovation he celebrates. The parallels of *Tintern Abbey* exist in many kinds of experience, including sexual and religious, but we do best to hold to the poem's own central story, its account of aesthetic contemplation and its personal myth of memory as salvation.

The misgivings and the ultimate fear of mortality are part of the poem because of Wordsworth's insistence upon autobiographical honesty. They help to make *Tintern Abbey* the major testament it is, for through them the poem convinces us it has earned the heights upon which it moves. The consoling story of a natural growth that tests the soul, teaches it generosity, and accepts its love becomes finally what Wallace Stevens in *The Rock* calls "a cure of the ground and of ourselves, in the predicate that there is nothing else." This predicate of nakedness is a sublime act of honesty, and prepares us for the Wordsworth who is the first poet ever to present our human condition in its naturalistic truth, vulnerable and dignified, and irreducible, not to be explained away in any terms, theological or analytical, but to be accepted as what it is. The mind, knowing only itself and Nature, but remembering a time when Nature gave it direct joy, and having remoter memories of an earlier time when it knew itself only in union with Nature, is able to turn back through memory for a faith that at last gives courage and a love for others. Blake did not believe in the goodness of the natural heart, and Coleridge could neither believe in nor deny it, but Wordsworth brings its possibility as truth alive into our hearts, as he did into the heart of Keats. There are greater Romantic poems than *Tintern Abbey,* but they surpass it as vision or rhetoric, not as consolation. No poem, unless it be *The Old Cumberland Beggar,* humanizes us more.

The Prelude

THE PRELUDE, completed in 1805, was published after Wordsworth's death in 1850. The title was chosen by the poet's widow; for Wordsworth it was simply "the poem to Coleridge." The 1850 text both suffers and gains by nearly half a century of Wordsworth's revisions, for the poet of the decade 1798–1807 was not the Urizenic

bard of the *Ecclesiastical Sonnets,* and the attempts of the older
Wordsworth to correct the younger are not always fortunate. The
1850 text shows better craftsmanship, but it also sometimes manifests an orthodox censor at work, straining to correct a private myth
into an approach at Anglican dogma. As Wordsworth's modern edi-
tor, Ernest de Selincourt, has observed, nothing could be more significant than the change of

> I worshiped then among the depths of things
> As my soul bade me . . .
> I felt and nothing else . . .
> > [XI, 234–238; 1805]

to

> Worshipping then among the depths of things
> As piety ordained . . .
> I felt, observed, and pondered. . . .
> > [XII, 184–188; 1850]

In the transition between these two passages, Wordsworth loses
his Miltonic heritage, an insistence upon the creative autonomy of
the individual soul. With it he loses also an emphasis peculiar to
himself, a reliance upon the *felt* experience, as distinguished from
received piety or the abstraction that follows experience. In what
follows I shall cite the 1850 text, but with reference, where it seems
desirable, to the 1805 version.

The poem approximates epic structure, in that its fourteen books
gather to a climax after a historical series of progressively more vital
crisis and renovations. The first eight books form a single movement, summed up in the title of Book VIII, *Retrospect—Love of
Nature Leading to Love of Mankind.* Books IX, X, and XI carry
this Love of Mankind into its natural consequence, Wordsworth's
Residence in France, and his involvement with the Revolution.
Books XII and XIII deal with the subsequent crisis of Wordsworth's *Imagination, How Impaired and Restored.* The *Conclusion,* Book XIV, is the climax of Wordsworth's imaginative life
and takes the reader back, in a full cycle, to the very opening of
the poem. The *Conclusion* presents Wordsworth and Coleridge as
"Prophets of Nature," joint laborers in the work of man's redemption:

                    what we have loved,
          Others will love, and we will teach them how;
          Instruct them how the mind of man becomes
          A thousand times more beautiful than the earth
          On which he dwells.

Blake, had he read this, would have approved, though he might
have wondered where Wordsworth had accounted for that "thousand times more beautiful." Blake's distrust of Wordsworth's dialectics of Nature is to some extent confirmed by Wordsworth himself. "Natural objects always did and now do weaken, deaden, and
obliterate imagination in me," was Blake's comment on Wordsworth's fragment *Influence of Natural Objects* . . . , and Wordsworth does fall mute when the external stimulus is too clearly present. Geoffrey Hartman remarks that even in Wordsworth "poetry
is not an act of consecration and Nature not an immediate external
object to be consecrated." [27] A natural object liberates Wordsworth's imagination only when it both ceases to be purely external
and fades out of its object status.

The Romantic metaphor of the correspondent breeze has been
discussed earlier.[28] The wind of Beulah, creative and destructive,
rises in the opening lines of *The Prelude*. Wordsworth need not
call upon this spirit, for it precedes his invocation. It begins as a
gentle breeze, and a blessing, half-conscious of the joy it gives to
the new Moses who has escaped the Egypt that is London, and
new Adam who can say:

          The earth is all before me. With a heart
          Joyous, nor scared at its own liberty,
          I look about; and should the chosen guide
          Be nothing better than a wandering cloud,
          I cannot miss my way.

Adam and Eve, scarcely joyous, go out hand in hand as loving
children into all that is before them to choose a place of rest, with
the Divine Providence as their guide. Wordsworth seeks a place
where he will be lulled into the creative repose of epic composition,
and he picks his own guide; nor need it be a Mosaic pillar, for he
cannot miss his way. Nature, all before him, is generous, and his
choice can only be between varying modes of good. *The Prelude*

therefore opens without present anxiety: its crises are in the past. Unlike *Paradise Lost* and Blake's *Jerusalem, The Prelude* is a song of triumph rather than a song of experience. Wordsworth sings of what Blake called "organized innocence."

When the wind blows upon Wordsworth, he feels within a corresponding breeze, which rapidly becomes

> A tempest, a redundant energy,
> Vexing its own creation.

Wordsworth's account of this vexing redundancy is that he is

> not used to make
> A present joy the matter of a song.

Although he tries again, aided by aeolian visitations, his harmony disperses in straggling sounds and, lastly, utter silence. What matters is his reaction. There is no despair, no sense of loss, only a quiet confidence based upon the belief that his inspiration is henceforward to be perpetual:

> "Be it so;
> Why think of anything but present good?"

We mistake *The Prelude,* then, if we seek to find a crisis, rather than the history of a crisis, within it. *The Prelude* is not a tragic poem but an autobiographical myth-making. Dominating *The Prelude* is the natural miracle of memory as an instrumentality by which the self is saved. Supreme among Wordsworth's inventions is the myth of renovating "spots of time," crucial in the *Intimations* ode and *Tintern Abbey,* and the entire basis for the imaginative energy of *The Prelude.*

The story of *The Prelude* is mysterious only in that Wordsworthian Nature is now a mystery to most of us. For Wordsworth, Nature is first of all the sensuous *given*—what is freely offered for our discernment at all times. Like Blake, Wordsworth is pre-eminently a master of phenomenology, in the sense that he is able to read reality in appearances. Like Abraham, Wordsworth is the patriarch of a Covenant, made in the latter case between phenomenal appearance and the human heart. If the human heart, in its common, everyday condition, will love and trust the phenomenal world, then that world will never betray it. Betrayal here takes some of the force of its meaning from the context of sexuality and marriage. For man to betray Nature is to embrace one of the several modes in which the primacy of Imagination is denied. For Nature to betray man is to cease as a renovating virtue for man when he returns to it. Man turns from that loving embrace of Nature which *is* in fact the supreme act of the Imagination, and takes the cruel mistress of discursiveness in her place. Nature turns from man by ceasing to be a Beulah state, and becoming instead a hostile and external object. What Wordsworth never considers is the more sinister manifestation of Nature-as-temptress, Blake's Vala or Keats's Belle Dame. Shelley climaxes his heritage from the Wordsworth tradition in *The Triumph of Life* by introducing Wordsworthian Nature as the deceptive "Shape all light," who tramples the divine sparks of Rousseau's imagination into the dust of death. Wordsworth's symbol of the covenant between man and Nature, the rainbow, is employed by Shelley as the emblem that precedes the appearance of the beautiful but destructive Nature figure of *The Triumph of Life*.

The inner problem of *The Prelude,* and of all the poetry of Wordsworth's great decade, is that of the autonomy of the poet's creative imagination. Indeed, as we have seen, it is the single most crucial problem of all that is most vital in English Romantic poetry. Even Wordsworth, the prophet of Nature, is uneasy at the prospect of his spirit's continual dependence upon it. He insists, like all prophets in the Hebraic tradition, upon the mutual dependence of the spiritual world and its human champion. The correspondent breeze is necessary because of natural decay; our mortality insists upon being redeemed by our poetry. To serve Nature in his early years, Wordsworth needed only to be wisely passive. But to sustain himself (and Nature?) in his maturity, an initiative from within is required. And yet if the initative is too overt, as here at the opening of *The Prelude,* then Nature refuses to be so served, and the mutual creation that is the poem cannot go forward.

Hartman, analyzing this problem, says that "Nature keeps the initiative. The mind at its most free is still part of a deep mood of weathers." Wordsworth's problem is thus a dialectical one, for what he seeks is the proper first term that will yield itself readily to be transcended. The first term is not Poetry, for Nature at *The Prelude's* onset will not have it so. Nor can the first term be Nature, for it will not allow itself to be subsumed even by the naturalizing imagination, at least *not immediately*. Blake has no patience for the Primary Imagination, but the whole of the secret discipline of Wordsworth's art is to wait upon it, confident that it will at last consent to dissolve into a higher mode.

Hartman speaks of the difficult first term of Wordsworth's dialectic as being "neither Nature nor Poetry. It is, rather, Imagination in embryo—muted yet strengthened by Nature's inadequacies." This is certainly the best balance to keep, unless we consent to a more radical review of Wordsworth's doctrine of Nature. Gorky said of Tolstoy's dealings with God that they reminded him of the old proverb "two bears in one den," and one can say the same of Wordsworth's relations with Nature. After a time, there is not quite room for both of them in Wordsworth's poetry if either is to survive full-size, and clearly it is Nature that makes room for Wordsworth. Yet the struggle, while concealed, inhibits Wordsworth and limits his achievement. There are unresolved antagonisms between Poetry and Divinity in Milton, but nothing so prolonged as the hidden conflict between Poetry and Nature in Wordsworth. But for this conflict, Wordsworth might have attempted national epic. Because of it, he was compelled to work in the mode of Rousseau, the long confessional work that might clarify his relation both to Nature and his own poetic calling.

The Nature of *The Prelude* is what Wordsworth was to become, a great teacher. Nature is so strong a teacher that it first must teach itself the lesson of restraint, to convert its immediacy into a presence only lest it overpower its human receiver. Wordsworth desires it as a mediating presence, a motion and a spirit. When it *is* too powerful, it threatens to become first, an object of worship, and second, like all such objects, an exhaustible agent of reality, a life that can be drained. Wordsworth knows well the dangers of idolatry, the sinister dialectic of mutual use. He desires only a relationship, a moment-to-moment confrontation of life by life, a dialogue. In this respect he is the direct ancestor of Shelley's vision of Nature.

The Prelude tries to distinguish between the *immediate* and the *remembered* external worlds. It is the paradoxical freedom of the Wordsworthian Imagination that it must avoid bondage to the immediate but seek the reign of the remembered world. In Blake the Imagination strives to be totally free of both, externals and memory, and delights only in the final excellence, the imagined land. Blake has no quest; only a struggle against everything within and without himself that is not pure Imagination. But Wordsworth has the quest that Blake's marginalia upon him gave clear warning of, the search for the autonomy of his own imagination. Hartman suggests that Nature's particular grace toward Wordsworth is to unfold *gradually* his own freedom to him, as his quest is largely an unwilling one; he does not want to be free of Nature. This suggestion is a displaced form of the Christian reading of history; for Wordsworth's "Nature" read St. Augustine's "History," as both are varieties of mercy presented as gradualism.

The hidden tragedy running through *The Prelude* is Wordsworth's resistance to his own imaginative emancipation. Wordsworth has clues enough, but usually declines to read them. In the presence of too eloquent a natural image, he is speechless. Nor does he attempt, after *Tintern Abbey*, to particularize any local habitations for vision. He diffuses the secret strength of things over the widest possible landscape, in contrast to his disciple Shelley, who stands before Mont Blanc and cries, "The power is there." Again, unlike their operations in Shelley and in Blake, the epiphanies in Wordsworth are not really sudden; there are no raptures of prophecy, but rather a slowly mounting intensity of baffled vision until at last the illumination greatly comes.

For Blake, and finally for Shelley, the Imagination's freedom from Nature is a triumph. It makes Wordsworth profoundly uneasy; he does not believe that time and space ought to be abandoned quite so prematurely. For Blake, the matter of common perception, the world of Primary Imagination, is hindrance, not action, but for Wordsworth it is something better than action; it is contemplation, and to see something clearly is already to have made some sense out of the diffuse and chaotic world of sensation. To mold a few of these clear things into a simpler and still clearer unity is to have made imaginative sense out of sensation. Blake's protest is absolute. He saw both these operations as passive, as a surrender to the living death of a world too small to contain the expansive vision of a more human Man.

The world of *The Prelude* is exquisitely fitted to the individual mind of the young Wordsworth. Even when it works upon him by frustration or fear, it continues to teach the young poet. The pas-

sages at the opening of the poem concerning the frustrating of composition have been examined above. Though he puts aside these
failures, which are due to the immediacy of his inspiration, he is
more troubled by the greater frustration of seemingly finding no
subject for sustained epic. Even this vacant musing is redeemed by
Nature, for in reproving himself he is carried back into remembrances, and these not only give him his only proper subject but
begin the genuine forward movement of his poem. The growth of
a poet's mind, as fostered by the goodly universe around him, becomes the inevitable subject as he sustains a gentle self-chastise-
ment:

> Was it for this
> That one, the fairest of all rivers, loved
> To blend his murmurs with my nurse's song.

As the Derwent River once flowed along his dreams, now it stirs
a flow of memory, carrying the mature poet back into the salvation
of things past. The image of the coursing river runs through the
entire poem, and provides the analogue for the flowing progress of
the long work. Wordsworth speaks of "the river of my mind," and
warns that its portions cannot be traced to individual fountains, but
rather to the whole flow of the sensuous generosity of external
phenomena.

The first two books of the poem show the child as encountering
unknown modes of being, the life of Nature which is both one with
us and yet dwells apart in its tranquillity. The primordial strength
of Wordsworth's mind, its closeness to the myth-makings of early
cultures and of children, is revealed in the incident in which an
early wrongdoing is followed by hints of natural nemesis:

> and when the deed was done
> I heard among the solitary hills
> Low breathings coming after me, and sounds
> Of undistinguishable motion, steps
> Almost as silent as the turf they trod.

We make a mistake if we read this as a projection of the child's
conscience upon the external world. That he heard it is warrant
enough for its reality. Similarly, when he hangs above the raven's
nest, sustained by the grip of finger tips, he hears a strange utter-

ance in the wind, and perceives a motion unlike any ordinary one, in a sky that does not seem a sky of earth. At such a moment he belongs more to the universe of elemental forces, of motions and spirits, than he does to ours.

These early incidents of participation in other modes of being climax in the famous episode of the stolen boat, "an act of stealth and troubled pleasure." There is a muffled sexual element in this boyish escapade. The moon shines on the child as he lustily dips his oars into the silent lake. Suddenly, from behind a craggy steep that had been till then the horizon's bound,

> a huge peak, black and huge,
> As if with voluntary power instinct,
> Upreared its head.

The grim shape, with its own purpose and the measured motion of a living thing, comes striding after him. He flees, returns the boat, and for many days is haunted by a sense of "unknown modes of being":

> No familiar shapes
> Remained, no pleasant images of trees,
> Of sea or sky, no colours of green fields;
> But huge and mighty forms, that do not live
> Like living men, moved slowly through the mind
> By day, and were a trouble to my dreams.

This is a fundamental paganism, so primitive that it cannot yield to any more sophisticated description without distortion. It is like the Titanism of Blake, with its Giant Forms like the Zoas wandering a world substantially our own. Worth particular attention is the momentary withdrawal of the given world of Nature from the boy, for it hints that familiar natural beauty is a gift, not to be retained by the unnatural.

The theme of reciprocity is introduced in this passage and strengthened by the skating incident, where the giving of one's body to the wind is repaid by being allowed to see, in a sense, the motion of earth in her diurnal round.

Summing up the first book, Wordsworth sees his mind as revived, now that he has found "a theme / Single and of determined bounds." Yet the most vital passage of the second book breaks be-

yond bounds, and makes clear how ultimately ambitious the theme
is:

> and I would stand,
> If the night blackened with a coming storm,
> Beneath some rock, listening to notes that are
> The ghostly language of the ancient earth,
> Or make their dim abode in distant winds.
> Thence did I drink the visionary power.

Listening to the wind is a mode of primitive augury, but it is not
gross prophecy of the future that the boy aspires toward as he hears
the primordial language of earth. The exultation involved, Wordsworth goes on to say, is profitable, not because of its content,

> but that the soul,
> Remembering how she felt, but what she felt
> Remembering not, retains an obscure sense
> Of possible sublimity, whereto
> With growing faculties she doth aspire,
> With faculties still growing, feeling still
> That whatsoever point they gain, they yet
> Have something to pursue.

No passage in *The Prelude* is more central, and nothing is a
better description of Wordsworth's poetry. *What* his soul felt in
different encounters with Nature, he will not always remember.
How it felt is recalled, and this retains that obscure sense of possible sublimity that colors all of the poetry of the Great Decade. As
the soul's faculties grow, the soul is in danger of becoming content,
of ceasing to aspire, but is saved from such sleep by the sense of
possible sublimity. This sublimity, in its origins, has little to do
with love or sympathy for others, and has small relation to human
suffering. It is a sense of individual greatness, of a joy and a light
yet unknown even in the child's life. *The Prelude,* until the eighth
book, devotes itself largely to an inward world deeply affected only
by external Nature, but with a gradually intensifying sense of others
held just in abeyance.

The soul in solitude moves outward by encountering other solitaries. Solitude, Wordsworth writes in Book IV, is most potent when
impressed upon the mind with an appropriate human center.

Having escorted a wandering old soldier to shelter, Wordsworth
entreats him to linger no more on the roads, but instead to ask for
the help that his state requires. With a "ghastly mildness" on his
face the vagrant turns back the reproof:

> "My trust is in the God of Heaven,
> And in the eye of him who passes me!"

From this first lesson in human reciprocity, Wordsworth's narrative flows inward again, but this time to make clear the imaginative relation between Nature and literature (Book V), which centers
on a dream of apocalypse and survival. Sitting by the seaside, reading *Don Quixote,* he begins to muse on poetry and mathematics
as being the ultimate apprehenders of reality, and having the "high
privilege of lasting life." He falls asleep, and dreams. Around him is
a boundless, sandy, wild plain, and distress and fear afflict him, till
a Bedouin appears upon a dromedary. He bears a lance, and carries
a stone beneath one arm, and holds a shell of surpassing brightness
in the opposite hand. The Arab tells him that the stone is "Euclid's
Elements" and the shell "is something of more worth," poetry.
When Wordsworth puts the shell to his ear, as commanded he
hears

> A loud prophetic blast of harmony;
> An Ode, in passion uttered, which foretold
> Destruction to the children of the earth
> By deluge, now at hand.

The Arab's mission is to bury "these two books," stone and shell,
against the day when the flood shall recede. The poet attempts to
join him in this enterprise, but he hurries off. Wordsworth follows,
baffled because the Arab now looks like Don Quixote, then an
Arab again, and then "of these was neither, and was both at once."
The waters of the deep gather upon them, but in the aspect of "a
bed of glittering light." Wordsworth wakes in terror, to view the
sea before him and the book at his side.

The dream is beautifully suggestive, and invites the kind of
symbol-building that W. H. Auden performs with it in his lively
exercise in Romantic iconography, *The Enchafèd Flood.* Unlike
the use of water symbolism in most of Wordsworth, the deluge

here threatens both Imagination and abstract reason, and the semi-
Quixote flees the waters of judgment that Wordsworth, like the
prophet Amos, elsewhere welcomes. Wordsworth puts Imagination
at the water line in the marvelous passage about the children sport-
ing on the shore which provides the *Intimations* ode with its liberating epiphany. The seashell participates in both the land of
reasoning and the sea of apocalypse, of primal unity, which makes
it an ideal type of the poetic Imagination. Though the Arab says
that the shell is of more worth than the stone, the passage clearly
sets high value on geometric as well as instinctual truth. Yet the
stone as a symbol for mathematical reason is very close to Blake's
Urizenic symbolism; the Ulro is associated with slabs of stone. Wallace Stevens' use of "the Rock" as symbol is closer to Wordsworth
in spirit. The Rock, like the stone, is the gray particular of man's
life, which poetry must cause to flower.

One can either pursue an investigation of the dream properties
in this incident, which is endless, or else turn to Wordsworth's own
reading of it, which takes us closer again to the design of *The
Prelude*. The most important point is how close Wordsworth comes
to identifying himself with the Arab Quixote. He fancies him a
living man, "crazed by love and feeling, and internal thought pro-
tracted among endless solitudes." This is a fate that Wordsworth
feared for himself, had his sensibility taken too strong control of
his reason. For the Arab's mission, though the poet calls it mad,
"that maniac's fond anxiety," is very like Wordsworth's own in
The Prelude. Both desire to save Imagination from the abyss of
desert and ocean, man's solitary isolation from and utter absorption into Nature. But the Arab is quixotic; he pursues a quest that
is hopeless, for the deluge will cover all. Wordsworth hopes that his
own quest will bring the healing waters down, as he pursues his
slow, flowing course toward his present freedom.

The first of the major breakthroughs of the Imagination in *The
Prelude* comes soon after this dream. The poet, in Book VI, describes a summer expedition to the Alps. He desires to cross the
Alps for reasons obscure even to himself. It may be a desire to
emancipate his maturing Imagination from Nature by overcoming
the greatest natural barrier he can encounter. He draws an explicit
parallel between his Alpine expedition and the onset of the French
Revolution:

> But Nature then was sovereign in my mind,
> And mighty forms, seizing a youthful fancy,
> Had given a charter to irregular hopes.
> In any age of uneventful calm
> Among the nations, surely would my heart
> Have been possessed by similar desire;
> But Europe at that time was thrilled with joy,
> France standing on the top of golden hours,
> And human nature seeming born again.

The rebirth of human nature heralds Wordsworth's own "irregular hope." He does not seem conscious altogether of the personal revolution he seeks to effect for his own imagination. He speaks of it as "an underthirst," which is "seldom utterly allayed," and causes a sadness different in kind from any other. To illustrate it, he cites the incident of his actual crossing of the Alps. He misses his path, and frustrates his "hopes that pointed to the clouds," for a peasant informs him that he has crossed the Alps without even being aware of the supposed achievement. This moment of baffled aspiration is suddenly seen as the agent of a transfiguration:

> Imagination—here the Power so called
> Through sad incompetence of human speech,
> That awful Power rose from the mind's abyss
> Like an unfathered vapour that enwraps,
> At once, some lonely traveller.

The mind's thwarted expectation makes it a shapeless abyss; the Imagination *rises from it,* and is self-begotten, like the sudden vapor, "unfathered," that enwraps the lonely traveler. Yet the Imagination remains ours, even if at the time of crisis it seems alien to us:

> I was lost;
> Halted without an effort to break through;
> But to my conscious soul I now can say—
> "I recognise thy glory"

The vertigo resulting from the gap between expectation and fulfillment halts Wordsworth at the moment of his disappointment, and leaves him without the will to transcend his frustration. But *now,* in recollection, he recognizes the glory of the soul's triumphant faculty of expectation:

> in such strength
> Of usurpation, when the light of sense
> Goes out, but with a flash that has revealed
> The invisible world, doth greatness make abode,
> There harbours; whether we be young or old,
> Our destiny, our being's heart and home,
> Is with infinitude, and only there;
> With hope it is, hope that can never die,
> Effort, and expectation, and desire,
> And something evermore about to be.

Even here, in a passage bordering the realm of the mystical, the poet's emphasis is naturalistic. Imagination usurps the place of the baffled mind, and the light of sense momentarily goes out: that is, the object world is not perceived. *But,* and this proviso is the poet's, the flash of greater illumination that suddenly reveals the invisible world is itself due to the flickering light of sense. Nature is overcome by Nature, and the senses are transcended by a natural teaching. The transcendence is the vital element in this passage, for in the Imagination's strength to achieve transcendence is the abode and harbor of human greatness. "More! More! is the cry of a mistaken Soul. Less than All cannot satisfy Man," is Blake's parallel statement. Wordsworth stresses infinitude because he defines the imaginative as that which is conversant with or turns upon infinity. In a letter to the poet Landor (January 21, 1824) he defines an imaginative passage as one in which "things are lost in each other, and limits vanish, and aspirations are raised." To the earlier statement in *The Prelude* celebrating "an obscure sense of possible sublimity" (II, 317–318), we can add this passage's sense of "something evermore about to be." Such a sense constitutes for the soul its "banners militant," under which it seeks no trophies or spoils, no self-gratification, for it is

> blest in thoughts
> That are their own perfection and reward,
> Strong in herself and in beatitude
> That hides her, like the mighty flood of Nile

Poured from his fount of Abyssinian clouds
To fertilise the whole Egyptian plain.

This is a tribute to the autonomy of the creative soul, and to its
ultimate value as well. The soul in creation rises out of the unfathered vapor just as the flood of the Nile rises from its cloud-
shrouded heights. The waters of creation pour down and fertilize
the mind's abyss, giving to it something of the soul's strength of
effort, expectation, and desire.

Directly after this revelation, Wordsworth is free to trace the
"characters of the great Apocalypse." As he travels through a narrow chasm in the mountains, Nature reveals to him the unity between its constant outer appearances and the ultimate forms of
eternity:

The immeasurable height
Of woods decaying, never to be decayed,
The stationary blasts of waterfalls,
And in the narrow rent at every turn
Winds thwarting winds, bewildered and forlorn,
The torrents shooting from the clear blue sky,
The rocks that muttered close upon our ears,
Black drizzling crags that spake by the way-side
As if a voice were in them, the sick sight
And giddy prospect of the raving stream,
The unfettered clouds and region of the Heavens,
Tumult and peace, the darkness and the light—
Were all like workings of one mind, the features
Of the same face, blossoms upon one tree;
Characters of the great Apocalypse,
The types and symbols of Eternity,
Of first, and last, and midst, and without end.

So much is brought together so magnificently in this that we
can read it as a summary of what the poet has to say about the
final relation between phenomena and the invisible world. The
woods are constantly in process of decay, but the process will never
cease; it will continue into Apocalypse. The waterfalls descend, and
yet give the appearance of being stationed where they are, not to
be moved. The winds are antithetical, balancing one another in the

narrow chasm. Thwarted, bewildered, forlorn—they are humanized
by this description. Torrents, rocks, crags participate in this speaking with tongues, and the raving stream takes on attributes of human disorder. Above, the unbound Heavens contrast their peace to
this torment, their light to this darkness. The above and the below
are like the workings of one unified mind, and are seen as features
of the same face, blossoms upon one tree, either and both together.
For the human and the natural are alike characters of the great
unveiling of reality, equal types and symbols of the everlasting. The
power that moves Man is the power that impels Nature, and Man
and Nature, taken together, are the true form, not to be transcended
even by a last judgment. This intimation of survival is given to
Wordsworth under Nature's guidance, but the point of relevation
is more human than natural. What the poet describes here is not
Nature but the force for which he lacks a name, and which is at
one with that "something far more deeply interfused" celebrated in
Tintern Abbey.

After this height in Book VI, the poem descends into the abyss of
residence in London in Book VII.

Imagination rises for Wordsworth in solitude, and yet *Tintern
Abbey* puts a very high value upon "the still, sad music of humanity," a love of men that depends upon societies. F. A. Pottle remarks
of Wordsworth in this context that though the poet "had the best
of intentions, he could never handle close-packed, present, human
crowds in the mode of imagination. If he were to grasp the life of a
great city imaginatively, it had to be at night or early in the morning, while the streets were deserted; or at least in bad weather, when
few people were abroad." [29] As Wordsworth goes along the overflowing street, he is oppressed by a sense that the face of everyone he
passes is a mystery to him. Suddenly he is smitten with the view

> Of a blind Begger, who, with upright face,
> Stood, propped against a wall, upon his chest
> Wearing a written paper, to explain
> His story, whence he came, and who he was.
> Caught by the spectacle my mind turned round
> As with the might of waters.

The huge fermenting mass of humankind does not set the poet's
imagination in motion, but the sight of one solitary man among

them does. Wordsworth says that the pathetic label the Beggar wears is an apt type of the utmost we can know, either of the universe or of ourselves, but this is not the imaginative meaning of the Beggar's sudden manifestation. Like the old Leech Gatherer of *Resolution and Independence,* he causes the mind to assume the condition of the moving waters of Apocalypse, to receive a hint of the final communion between Man and Nature. The Leech Gatherer does this merely by being what he is, a reduced but still human form thoroughly at peace in a landscape reduced to naked desolation, but still natural. The blind Beggar's landscape is the noise of the crowd around him. He sits "with upright face"; the detail suggests the inner uprightness, the endurance of the outwardly bent Leech Gatherer. Amid the shock for eyes and ears of what surrounds him, his label affords a silent vision of human separateness, of the mystery of individual being.

From this bleak image, the poet retires with joy in Book VIII, which both heralds his return to Nature and chronicles the course of the first half of the poem, the stages by which love of Nature has led to love for Man. The figure linking the first love to the second is the shepherd, endowed by the boy Wordsworth with mythical powers and incarnating the virtues of Natural Man, an Adam who needs no dying into life, no second birth. The shepherd affects his own domain by intensifying its own characteristics:

> I felt his presence in his own domain,
> As of a lord and master, or a power,
> Or genius, under Nature, under God,
> Presiding; and severest solitude
> Had more commanding looks when he was there.

This figure gives Wordsworth the support he needs for his "trust in what we *may* become." The shepherd, like Michael, like even the Old Cumberland Beggar, is a figure of capable imagination, strong in the tie that binds him to the earth.

Natural love for Man leads Wordsworth where it led the French followers of the prophet Rousseau, to Revolution in the name of the Natural Man. His particular friend in that cause, Michel Beaupuy (or Beaupuis, as Wordsworth spells it, Book IX, line 419), fighting for the Revolution as a high officer, says to him on encountering a hunger-bitten girl, " 'Tis against *that* that we are fighting." As simply, Wordsworth says of him: "Man he loved as man."

The 1850 *Prelude* omits the tragic story of Wordsworth's love affair with Annette Vallon, told under the disguise of the names Vaudracour and Julia in the 1805 *Prelude*. It is not likely that Wordsworth excluded the affair for aesthetic reasons, though much of it makes rather painful reading. Yet parts of it have a rich, almost passionate tone of excited recollection, and all of it, even as disguised, is crucial for the growth of this poet's soul, little as he seems to have thought so. Nowhere else in his poetry does Wordsworth say of himself, viewing a woman and not Nature, that

> his present mind
> Was under fascination; he beheld
> A vision, and he lov'd the thing he saw.

Nor does one want to surrender the charm of the prophet of Nature accomplishing a stolen interview at night "with a ladder's help."

Wordsworth was separated from Annette by the war between England and France. In the poem, Vaudracour and Julia are parted by parental opposition. The effects of the parting in life were largely hidden. Wordsworth the man made a happy marriage; Wordsworth the poet did not do as well. Julia goes off to a convent, and Vaudracour goes mad. Either in *The Prelude* or out of it, by presence or by absence, the story is a gap in the poem. Memory curbed was dangerous for Wordsworth; memory falsified was an imaginative fatality.

From the veiled account of his crisis in passion Wordsworth passes, in Books X and XI, to the crisis in his ideological life, the supreme test of his moral nature. When England went to war against the France of the Revolution, Wordsworth experienced the profound shock of having to exult "when Englishmen by thousands were o'erthrown," and the dark sense,

> Death-like, of treacherous desertion, felt
> In the last place of refuge—my own soul.

The profounder shock of the Terror and of France's career as an external aggressor followed. Wordsworth was adrift, his faith in the Revolution betrayed, and he sought to replace that faith by abstract speculation, and a blind trust in the supreme efficacy of the analytical faculty. He fell, by his own account, into the Ulro of the mechanists and materialists, a rationalism utterly alien to his characteristic modes of thinking and feeling:

> now believing,
> Now disbelieving; endlessly perplexed
> With impulse, motive, right and wrong, the ground
> Of obligation, what the rule and whence
> The sanction; till, demanding formal *proof,*
> And seeking it in every thing, I lost
> All feeling of conviction, and, in fine,
> Sick, wearied out with contrarieties,
> Yielded up moral questions in despair.

Love of Nature had led to love of Man, love of Man to revolutionary hope for Man, and the thwarting of that hope to this unnatural abyss. From these depths the poet's sister was to rescue him, maintaining "a saving intercourse with my true self," as he prays her to do in *Tintern Abbey.* In an extraordinary outburst of love for Coleridge, to whom the poem is addressed, the poet invokes a parallel salvation for his friend, to restore him "to health and joy and pure contentedness." He then proceeds, in Books XII and XIII, to tell of the final stages of his crisis of dejection, the impairment of his Imagination and Taste, and their eventual restoration.

"A bigot to the new idolatry," he

> Zealously laboured to cut off my heart
> From all the sources of her former strength.

The final mark of his fall is to begin to scan the visible universe with the same analytical view he has applied to the moral world. In the aesthetic contemplation pictured in *Tintern Abbey,* we see into the life of things because the eye has learned a wise passivity. It has been made quiet by the power of harmony, and the deep power of joy. Bereft of these powers, the poet in his crisis yields to the tyranny of the eye:

> I speak in recollection of a time
> When the bodily eye, in every stage of life
> The most despotic of our senses, gained
> Such strength in *me* as often held my mind
> In absolute dominion.

This fear of visual appearance is at one with Wordsworth's worship of the outward world, though it presents itself as paradox. For the visual surfaces of natural reality are mutable, and Wordsworth desperately quests for a natural reality that can never pass away. That reality, for him, lies just within natural appearance, and the eye made generously passive by Nature's generosity is able to trace the lineaments of that final reality, and indeed "half create" it, as *Tintern Abbey* says. The eye must share, and not seek to appropriate for its own use, for where there is self-appropriation there can be no reality, no covenant of mutual giving. The apocalyptic sense therefore tends to be hearing, as it is in the *Intimations* ode, or that sense of organic fusion, seeing-hearing, which Wordsworth attributes to the infant in that poem. Hartman usefully sums this up as "a vision in which the mind knows itself almost without exterior cause or else as no less real, here, no less indestructible than the object of its perception."

Two agents rescue Wordsworth from the tyranny of the bodily eye, and the consequent impairment of his imagination. One, already spoken of, is Dorothy. The other is the creative doctrine or myth that the poet calls "spots of time":

> There are in our existence spots of time,
> That with distinct pre-eminence retain
> A renovating virtue, whence . . .
> > . . . our minds
> Are nourished and invisibly repaired.

This virtue lurks in those episodes of life which tell us precisely how and to what point the individual mind is master of reality, with outward sense merely the mind's servant. Wordsworth gives two incidents as examples, both from his own childhood, as we would expect. In the first he is learning to ride, in the hills, encouraged and guided by his father's servant. Separated by mischance, he dismounts in fear, and leads his horse down the rough and stony moor. He stumbles on a bottom, where once a murderer had hung on a gibbet. Most evidences of an execution place are gone, but local superstition continually clears away the grass, and marks the murderer's name in monumental characters upon the turf. The boy sees them and flees, faltering and faint, losing the road,

> Then, reascending the bare common, saw
> A naked pool that lay beneath the hills,
> The beacon on the summit, and, more near,
> A girl, who bore a pitcher on her head,
> And seemed with difficult steps to force her way
> Against the blowing wind. It was, in truth,
> An ordinary sight; but I should need
> Colours and words that are unknown to man,
> To paint the visionary dreariness
> Which, while I looked all round for my lost guide,
> Invested moorland waste and naked pool,
> The beacon crowning the lone eminence,
> The female and her garments vexed and tossed
> By the strong wind.

The boy's fear of the fresh characters in the turf, and of the moldered gibbet mast, is "natural," as we would say, in these circumstances. But the "visionary dreariness" is a more complex sensation. The common is bare, the pool naked beneath the hills, as open to the eye of heaven as is the pool by which Wordsworth will encounter the Leech Gatherer in *Resolution and Independence*, a poem built around a "spot of time." The girl bearing the pitcher struggles against the wind, as winds thwarted winds in the apocalyptic passage in Book VI. Everything that the boy beholds, waste moorland and naked pool, the solitary beacon on the lone eminence, the girl and her garments buffeted by the wind, is similarly dreary, but the nudity and vulnerability of these phenomena, their receptivity to the unchecked power of Nature, unite them in a unified imaginative vision. They blend into one another and into the power to which they offer themselves.

The boy finds no consolation in the scene of visionary dreariness at the time he views it, but he retains it in his memory. Later he returns to the same scene, in the happy hours of early love, his beloved at his side. Upon the scene there falls the gleam of Imagination, with radiance more sublime for the *power* these remembrances had left behind:

> So feeling comes in aid
> Of feeling, and diversity of strength
> Attends us, if but once we have been strong.

The soul, remembering *how* it felt, but what it felt remembering not, has retained the power of a sense of possible sublimity. Imagination, working through memory, appropriates the visionary power and purges the dreariness originally attached to it in this instance. The power is therefore an intimation of the indestructible, for it has survived both initial natural dreariness and the passage of time.

The power is indestructible, but can the poet retain it? We hear again the desperate forebodings of loss:

> The days gone by
> Return upon me almost from the dawn
> Of life: the hiding-places of man's power
> Open; I would approach them, but they close.
> I see by glimpses now; when age comes on,
> May scarcely see at all.

The function of the spots of time is to enshrine the spirit of the Past for future restoration. They are meant to be memorials in a lively sense, giving substance and life to what the poet can still feel. That they become memorials in the sepulchral sense also is a sadly unintentional irony.

The poet gives a second example of a spot of time, more complex than the first. Away from home with his brothers, he goes forth into the fields, impatient to see the led palfreys that will bear him back to his father's house. He goes to the summit of a crag overlooking both roads on which the palfreys can come:

> 'twas a day
> Tempestuous, dark, and wild, and on the grass
> I sate half-sheltered by a naked wall;
> Upon my right hand couched a single sheep,
> Upon my left a blasted hawthorn stood.

With these companions he watches, as the mist gives intermitting prospect of the plain beneath. Just after this episode, his father dies, and he thinks back to his vigil, with its anxiety of hope:

> And afterwards, the wind and sleety rain,
> And all the business of the elements,
> The single sheep, and the one blasted tree,
> And the bleak music from that old stone wall,

> The noise of wood and water, and the mist
> That on the line of each of those two roads
> Advanced in such indisputable shapes;
> All these were kindred spectacles and sounds
> To which I oft repaired, and thence would drink,
> As at a fountain.

What does he drink there? We recognize first in this episode the characteristic quality of the nakedness of the natural scene. The boy is only half-sheltered by the naked wall. Beside him, seeking this exposed shelter from the wind, is a single sheep, and on the other side a hawthorn, blasted by the elements. The mist rises all about, blending the landscape into a unity. What can be drunk from this fountain of vulnerable natural identity is, as before, the consciousness of immutable existence, of a life in Nature and in Man which cannot die. This one life within us and abroad must bear the weather, however tempestuous, dark, and wild, but it will not be destroyed if it holds itself open to the elements in loving trust.

Thus "moderated" and "composed" by the spots of time, his faith in Nature restored, the poet is able to say in triumph:

> I found
> Once more in Man an object of delight,
> Of pure imagination, and of love.

He is prepared now for his poem's apocalyptic conclusion, the ascent of Mount Snowdon and the vision vouchsafed him there, in Book XIV. The poem's structure comes to rest on a point of epiphany, located on a mountainside and associated with the moon and all the mutable world below it, but also with the immutable world above. Girt round by the mist of rising Imagination, the poet looks up to see the Moon hung naked in the azure firmament. The mist stretches in solid vapors, a still ocean as far as the eye can see. In the midst of this ocean, a rift appears, and through the gap

> Mounted the roar of waters, torrents, streams
> Innumerable, roaring with one voice!
> Heard over earth and sea, and, in that hour,
> For so it seemed, felt by the starry heavens.

The mist, which has for so long figured as an emblem of Imagination in Wordsworth's poetry, now moves to an identity with the emblem of apocalypse, the gathering waters of judgment. The voice of mighty waters makes its strength felt past the point of epiphany, and momentarily influences even the starry heavens. Of this vision the poet says:

> it appeared to me the type
> Of a majestic intellect, its acts
> And its possessions, what it has and craves,
> What in itself it is, and would become.
> There I beheld the emblem of a mind
> That feeds upon infinity, that broods
> Over the dark abyss, intent to hear
> Its voices issuing forth to silent light
> In one continuous stream; a mind sustained
> By recognitions of transcendent power.

The whole scene before him is the "type of a majestic intellect," while the moon is the emblem of a mind brooding over the dark abyss. The moon, governing all that is mutable beneath it, feeds upon the infinity of the larger vision to gain an intimation of what is beyond mutability. The moon is like the poet's aroused consciousness, looking up to the indestructible heavens and down at the sea of mist which intimates both the impermanence of the world as we know it (the hint is that it will be flooded again) and its final endurance, after the judgment of the waters. Caught at what Eliot calls "the still point of the turning world," Wordsworth attains to an apprehension of the relation between his moonlike consciousness and the majestic intellect, which now feels the human mind's reciprocal force but which transcends both the human and the natural. What Wordsworth is giving us here is his vision of God, akin to Dante's tremendous vision at the close of the *Paradiso,* except that the mode of this manifestation is still extraordinarily naturalistic. Though not Nature but the power that moves her is revealed, the power's showing forth is not miracle but rather intensification of natural process and visual appearance. Later, in *The Excursion,* Wordsworth will not trust the powers of poetry enough to make so autonomous a statement, to see so human a vision. Here, as he gathers *The Prelude's* many currents together, he shows a confidence both in his art and in his personal myth of natural salvation. In this confidence he has created a major poem that refreshes life, that is, as Wallace Stevens wrote,

> An elixir, an excitation, a pure power.
> The poem, through candor, brings back a power again
> That gives a candid kind to everything.

3   Spots of Time

Resolution and Independence

WORDSWORTH'S comment on *Resolution and Independence* (1802) emphasizes the naked simplicity by which the old Leech Gatherer is presented to the poem's Traveller and to the reader:

> A young Poet in the midst of the happiness of Nature is described as overwhelmed by the thought of the miserable reverses which have befallen the happiest of all men, viz Poets—I think of this till I am so deeply impressed by it, that I consider the manner in which I was rescued from my dejection and despair almost as an interposition of Providence. . . . "A lonely place, a Pond" "by which an old man *was*, far from all house or home"—not stood, not set, but "*was*"—the figure presented in the most naked simplicity possible. . . .

Even here, in a letter (June 24, 1802, to Sara Hutchinson), his wording is very careful. The manner of his rescue he considers "*almost* as an interposition" of the supernatural, and the old man simply *was* in that lonely place. As a poem of the Imagination, in Wordsworth's own classification, *Resolution and Independence* at its most crucial moment relies on the technique of the fade-out, but this dissolving of boundaries between objects is presented as a naturalistic phenomenon, as much a part of given reality as is the Leech Gatherer's presence at a time and place when a "spot of time" is so badly needed. The old man *was*, as a rock or a shrub simply *is,* another part of an ordinary landscape on an ordinary morning.

An ordinary morning, but of the best kind, clearing after a storm, begins the poem. There have been floods, but now the sun rises, the birds sing, "and all the air is filled with pleasant noise of waters," in contrast to the roaring of the past night.

In the second stanza, the pleasant natural scene is visualized under the aspect of reciprocity. The sky rejoices in the morning's birth, the grass sparkles with raindrops, and the happy hare raises a mist from the earth which glitters in the sun and runs companionably with the hare. Into this unity, Wordsworth enters as a traveler upon the moor, a man who is at first one with the jocund phenomena around him. But the union with joy does not last:

> But, as it sometimes chanceth, from the might
> Of joy in minds that can no further go,
> As high as we have mounted in delight
> In our dejection do we sink as low;
> To me that morning did it happen so;
> And fears and fancies thick upon me came;
> Dim sadness—and blind thoughts, I knew not,
>   nor could name.

The very strength of joy engenders its contrary. When delight reaches its limits, dejection replaces it. But the second line means also that the mind is at its creative limit, and exhaustedly falls over into dejection. This stanza may have a reference to Coleridge's state of mind that was to produce the great *Dejection* ode. What comes upon Wordsworth is a "dim sadness," a grief without a name, and fundamental fears that strike at his being. But while these unknown anxieties range wide, they rapidly begin to particularize themselves. They concern the special fate of poets, who ought to be the happiest of men, but who are too often accursed, immolated by their sensibility and art. We think of the title, and can see something of its meaning. Resolution here can be either an act that resolves a situation, or an act of determination. Both suit the inner conflict that Wordsworth needs to transcend. As he walks "far from the world" he compares himself to skylark and playful hare as "a happy child of earth." They cannot anticipate future sorrows. So he has lived, "as if life's business were a summer mood." Now the visions of autumn and the winter beyond come to him—"Solitude, pain of heart, distress, and poverty." Before him is the example of the dependent and irresolute poet, the desperate Coleridge, unhappy in marriage, health, work:

> But how can He expect that others should
> Build for him, sow for him, and at his call
> Love him, who for himself will take no heed at all?

Behind Coleridge's terrible need to be loved, his descent into despondency, are the dark memories of the Romantics' forerunners, the poets of Sensibility and Enthusiasm, Chatterton and Burns in particular. Wordsworth's poem mounts to its crisis in a stanza that magnificently celebrates and mourns the marvelous boy and the plowman poet:

> I thought of Chatterton, the marvellous Boy,
> The sleepless Soul that perished in his pride;
> Of Him who walked in glory and in joy
> Following his plough, along the mountain-side:
> By our own spirits are we deified:
> We Poets in our youth begin in gladness;
> But thereof come in the end despondency and madness.

There is a particular poignancy in calling Chatterton "the marvellous Boy," for *The Prelude* makes clear how much Wordsworth dreaded leaving his own marvelous boyhood forever behind him, and so abandoning the hiding places of his power. Chatterton could not achieve resolution and independence, and failed to make the transition from his glad springtime to a summer of mature poethood. He perished in his pride, the sleeplessness of his soul encompassing both his splendor and his doom. Burns also began in glory and joy, which the Great Ode makes the two great attributes of Imagination. But Burns ended in sorrow, ruined by his vocation. Wordsworth sums up the paradox of the poet's curse in the profoundly equivocal line "By our own spirits are we deified." The young poet *is* a god, a rebirth of Apollo, stimulating new life and representing the perpetual freshness of the earth, but only so long as his spirits remain glorious and joyful. When they fail, the sad irony of the line, its sense of illusion, becomes dominant; it is *only* by our own spirits that we are deified. We merely follow a fatal

cycle. As youths we begin in gladness, but thereof, from the gladness itself, come in the end derangement and melancholia. We pass
from Orc to Urizen, Beulah to Ulro, in Blakean terms. At this
point Wordsworth is in stasis, at the dead end of Imagination,
which can do nothing with the hopeless and deceptive natural cycle.
He badly needs what he now receives, a "peculiar grace," an emblem of resolution and independence:

> Now, whether it were by peculiar grace,
> A leading from above, a something given,
> Yet it befell that, in this lonely place,
> When I with these untoward thoughts had striven,
> Beside a pool bare to the eye of heaven
> I saw a Man before me unawares:
> The oldest man he seemed that ever wore grey hairs.

It is another scene of visionary dreariness, like that in *The Prelude,* Book XII, when Wordsworth sees a girl forcing her way
against the blowing wind near "a naked pool that lay beneath the
hills" on the bare common. Here "beside a pool bare to the eye of
heaven" Wordsworth receives again "a something given." The
nakedness of the pool and its surroundings is a key element in both
passages. These are scenes naked to the skies, vulnerable, open to
natural grace, receptive to all that natural process can bring. "I
saw a Man," Wordsworth begins, as he does with the Old Cumberland Beggar, but having granted human status, he resorts to images
of minimal consciousness to convey how outrageously past normal
decrepitude this apparition is. Not only does he seem to be the
oldest man who ever wore gray hairs, but he suggests the inexplicable life of rock, "the gray particular of man's self," as Stevens calls
it, and again the primeval quality of life itself, evolving out of the
sea into the sun that calls forth the human:

> As a huge stone is sometimes seen to lie
> Couched on the bald top of an eminence;
> Wonder to all who do the same espy,
> By what means it could thither come, and whence;
> So that it seems a thing endued with sense:
> Like a sea-beast crawled forth, that on a shelf
> Of rock or sand reposeth, there to sun itself;

> Such seemed this Man, not all alive nor dead,
> Nor all asleep.

He seems to have emerged from the pool whose edge he wanders. His uncanniness breaks down antitheses, between life and death, sleep and waking. Wordsworth does not stop short of making him a grotesque; he is bent double, his head nearing his feet. Yet in context he has enormous and mysterious dignity:

> Himself he propped, limbs, body, and pale face,
> Upon a long grey staff of shaven wood:
> And, still as I drew near with gentle pace,
> Upon the margin of that moorish flood
> Motionless as a cloud the old Man stood,
> That heareth not the loud winds when they call;
> And moveth all together, if it move at all.

The gray staff is very like the old Man's body, except that it is upright. The pool, in his presence, diffuses to a moorish flood, and the old Man's immobility is massive as a cloud's, and therefore unitary. If the old Man is very like the scene in which he stands, a part of the landscape, it is also true that his presence makes it more like himself. The failure of communication between him and Wordsworth, which is the substance of the remainder of the poem, is due to his being part of the solitude around him while Wordsworth, with his anxieties, is a trouble to the place.

When the poet remarks, "This is a lonesome place for one like you," the resolute and independent, but feeble old Man is too courteous to state his astonishment at the opinion, but a "flash of mild surprise" breaks from his still vivid eyes. He answers the poet's question as to his occupation, but the Imagination fades out his reply:

> The old Man still stood talking by my side;
> But now his voice to me was like a stream
> Scarce heard; nor word from word could I divide;
> And the whole body of the Man did seem
> Like one whom I had met with in a dream;
> Or like a man from some far region sent,
> To give me human strength, by apt admonishment.

We have seen how, in *The Prelude,* Wordsworth constantly associates the sudden onset of the Imagination with the sound of
rushing waters. When he saw the blind Beggar in the streets of London, his mind "turned round as with the might of waters" and he
gazed at the steadfast face and sightless eyes of the Beggar "as if
admonished from another world." So, here, the old Man's words
blend together, and Wordsworth hears only the muffled rush of
waters. The Leech Gatherer's body begins to fade into a dream
landscape. The Imagination is effecting its salvation in Wordsworth, by seizing on this phenomenon of *"human* strength," but for
a brief time longer his foolish and anxiety-ridden selfhood attempts
to refuse the gift:

> My former thoughts returned: the fear that kills;
> And hope that is unwilling to be fed;
> Cold, pain, and labour, and all fleshly ills;
> And mighty Poets in their misery dead.
> —Perplexed, and longing to be comforted,
> My question eagerly did I renew,
> "How is it that you live, and what is it you do?"

The poor old Man repeats his words quite patiently, and with
a smile, for he has already answered the question and it is clear
even to him that the Poet is not listening. Lewis Carroll and Edward
Lear, in their wonderful and cruel parodies of *Resolution and Independence,* seized upon this element of irrelevance in the poem, but
clearly Wordsworth intends it as a vital part of his design. He is of
course not asking the old Man the question genuinely on his mind:
how have you endured, where do you find the resolution to pursue
so hard an independence? For Wordsworth's is "hope that is unwilling to be fed." He is verging on the imaginatively fatal sin of
willful despair, of being sullen in Nature's sweet air.

The old Man is so resolute that he attributes to outward phenomena the decay within himself. Not he, but the leeches he seeks
"have dwindled long by slow decay," but he undauntedly perseveres.
As he speaks on, renewing the same discourse again as he notices
Wordsworth's inattentiveness, the old Man's words suddenly liberate
Wordsworth into the full freedom of the Imagination. Suddenly,
all the elements present blend together, and the Imagination rises
triumphantly from the mind's abyss:

> While he was talking thus, the lonely place,
> The old Man's shape, and speech—all troubled me:
> In my mind's eye I seemed to see him pace
> About the weary moors continually,
> Wandering about alone and silently.

After this flashing out of a final reality, the final stanza is necessarily unemphatic by contrast. Wordsworth has had a vision of Natural Man triumphantly in his rightful place, at home in the heart of a dreariness humanized. In the poet's mind's eye, as opposed to his corporeal eye, the old man *paces* (the word implies a deliberateness) continually and silently in his wandering solitude. But he is not spoken of as being weary. The moors with whom he is alone are weary—out of sympathy, in a reciprocity of love. He gives them his weariness, and they give him their endurance. Faced again with the dialectic of love between Man and Nature, here at a quiet limit of the human condition, Wordsworth is renovated, and given yet another intimation of the natural strength of the human heart. The therapy for the poet's tortured sensibility, the way out of dejection, is to think of the earth, and to seek no wonder but the human face.

Ode: Intimations of Immortality

RUSKIN, in *Praeterita*, remembered that at eighteen he had felt "for the last time, the pure childish love of nature which Wordsworth so idly takes for an intimation of immortality." In the violence of his memory, Ruskin negated his chastising "idly": "Wordsworth's 'haunted me like a passion' is no description of it, for it is not *like*, but *is*, a passion; the point is to define how it *differs* from other passions,—what sort of human, pre-eminently human, feeling it is that loves a stone for a stone's sake, and a cloud for a cloud's." But the Great Ode knows, and defines, Ruskin's "different" passion. This "difference" is the cause of the *Ode's* peculiar continuity, its passionate logic of questioning, despairing, and ultimately hoping response. This is derivative, ultimately, from the prophetic portions of the Hebrew Bible. In the *Ode* a prophetic rhythm of thought appears as a mode of dialectic antithetical to the logic of most English poetry before Wordsworth.

Analysis of the *Ode*'s dialectic must begin with its questionings:

> Whither is fled the visionary gleam?
> Where is it now, the glory and the dream?

One begins by noting that the two questions are not identical, and that their seeming to be so has significance. If the peculiar "splendour in the grass" and "glory in the flower" are not here, then whither have they "fled"? Not "faded," but actively gone, and the "whither" need not be the "where *now*." Between the two questions lies the possibility of a kind of return which can have taken or may yet take place.

In Stanza v the "fled" has become the passive fading:

> At length the man perceives it die away,
> And fade into the light of common day.

To "die away" is not to flee but, in this context, to abate. The abatement's optical manifestation is a fading *into* the realm of the everyday.

By the next stanza glories are known only in the past perfect; in Stanza vii even this remembering is jeopardized by the child's "endless imitation" of those who have intimations of mortality. The child's "earnest pains" hasten his own encumbrance:

> Full soon thy Soul shall have her earthly freight,
> And custom lie upon thee with a weight,
> Heavy as frost, and deep almost as life!

The questions at the end of Stanza iv end the first movement of the poem; these lines, the second. Questioning has not been joyously answered, for the replies would seem to be implicit in this emphatic despairing. And yet, the next and final movement of the poem is one of triumphant rejoicing.

Discursive logic can demonstrate an adequate relationship between the poem's first and second movements, and a more complicated one between the first and third, but nothing to link together the second and the third. The poem's initial four stanzas state the problem; the next four embody a negative reaction to it;

the final three a positive. Is Wordsworth's movement back into joy only a "qualitative progression," to borrow the vocabulary of Yvor Winters, or is there a logic of the imagination operative here? A "graduated progression of feeling" would hardly qualify as a dialectic, one should admit at the start.

Frank Kermode, in his *Romantic Image,* handles this problem in another context. His solution is "significant form," within the tradition of the Romantic Image and its creator's vital isolation. Thus he can both agree with Winters that the logic of poetry *must* be a discursive logic of concepts, and yet justify the Romantic tradition as a system of unities based on a clear imagistic structure. But Winters is in fact wrong, if applied to the best poems of the major Romantics, though right enough on Eliot, Pound, and most modern poetry (one can exclude the most characteristic work of Yeats, Stevens, and Hart Crane). The continuity of argument in the best Romantic poems is not dependent on imagistic development alone, nor need we on faith accept it as a specific rhetorical tradition. Romantic argument can be studied as we now study Romantic or any other imagery, once we dispense with the odd modern critical dogma that what poetry is *about* is irrelevant to its aesthetic value. Kermode's attempt to demonstrate T. E. Hulme as a Romantic in spite of himself is convincing, but Hulme with his "subject doesn't matter" must still be judged an inadequate theorist, a man who did not know enough, least of all enough poetry.

Image, far from being the primary pigment of all poetry, is irrelevant to much of the highest poetry, whether in the Romantic tradition or not. Wordsworth and Wallace Stevens are at one in forsaking the image when they wish to tell their truths, and it is precisely then that they write some of their finest poetry:

> Paradise, and groves
> Elysian, Fortunate Fields—like those of old
> Sought in the Atlantic Main—why should they be
> A history only of departed things,
> Or a mere fiction of what never was?

> The greatest poverty is not to live
> In a physical world, to feel that one's desire
> Is too difficult to tell from despair.

Wordsworth's passage relies on the evocative power of lost Edens, and on a skillful use of the rhetorical question in a disinterested humanist context. Stevens' as aggressive humanism (both poets have the same enemy here: the universal and enduring vulgarization of the myth of the Fall) plays strikingly on "poverty," and achieves its power by ethical precision. Image and metaphor are not wanted here; this kind of poetry *has* a palpable design upon us, and does not disguise it. Any image might cause us to suspect disguise.

The *Intimations* ode is, of course, replete with a much-studied imagery. But a further study of that imagery will not solve the problem of the poem's transitions. The logic of the *Ode* only *plays* at being a logic of concepts: we do it wrong, the *Ode* being so marvelous a creation, to treat it as thought dressed in images. Like Stevens' sequence, *The Rock,* or Yeats's *A Dialogue of Self and Soul,* it plays at discursiveness only to mock the limitations of the discursive.

Wordsworth himself calls the principle of continuity in his poem "natural piety," which binds days "each to each," in the ideal. He "could wish" this, and the triumphant rejoicing of the *Ode*'s concluding stanzas testifies to the granting (at least momentary) of his wish. The manifestation of the wish-being-realized is the liberating occasion of the poem. The binding agent of the poem, the mode of its continuity, is "natural piety," defined in turn by the declaration "The Child is father of the Man."

"Natural piety," in this sense, is not a form of Deism; it has little to do with seventeenth- and eighteenth-century English natural religion. Wordsworth's "natural piety" is a phenomenological reality; Wordsworth's account of it is *descriptive.* He does not attempt to get at it by more than two modes: sensuous observation, and memory of such observation. Wordsworth's poem is concerned, not with a tradition of conceptualization, but with the flowing *given* of our sensuous experience. The *given* of the natural world joys us; traps us; finally, if we trust it, saves us. This, reduced, is the peculiarly Wordsworthian myth.

The *given,* in the *Ode,* is presented, without images, as "the things which I have seen" (a certain light, a glory, a freshness); the initial joying; the things he "now can see" (a Tree, of many, one; a single field; both speaking of something gone); the entrapment; and a "sober coloring"—the saving recompense for the glory's loss.

Childlike joy → fall into Nature → salvation through Nature: in Blake's system of states of being that would read Beulah → Generation → Ulro. In Wordsworth it is meant to be read Beulah → Ulro → Generation, with Eden a possible state if the discerning intellect of man can be wedded to the goodly universe of Generation. To Blake (though he was, if we can trust Crabb Robinson, greatly moved by the *Ode*), Wordsworth's dialectic made no sense. "There is no such Thing as Natural Piety Because the Natural Man is at Enmity with God." For Blake, God is the Imaginative man, and the Natural and Imaginative men are negations, not contraries, and the *Ode* progresses by their attraction and repulsion in relation to the protagonist "I" in the poem.

The child is the Natural Man in the *Ode;* the mature poet whose humanistic eye imparts a sober coloring to nature is the Imaginative Man. In between is the momentarily Trapped Man, the dejected man who becomes the protagonist of Coleridge's great *Dejection: An Ode.* In Wordsworth's *Ode* this man-in-the-middle (in mortal danger of dejection, acedia, Ulro) speaks with two voices, natural and imaginative. When his naturalistic lament is full, i.e., imaginatively completed, then his poetic salvation is announced in his rival voice. The logic of this continuity is the logic of growth, maturity, fatherhood, childhood, growth—human cycle. Here, a logic, because the child fathers the Man; Nature fathers Imagination; and Continuity fathers a discursive paradox. "The words are wild," joked Hopkins. At just this point the dialectic of the *Ode* reverses. "Heavy as frost, and deep almost as life" cycles into "O joy! that in our embers / Is something that doth live." Some thing that Nature "remembers," some thing that was fugitive, that has *fled* and sojourned, and can now be recalled: that thing is crucial to the *Ode*'s final movement.

Yeats, in *A Vision,* says that he could never believe, with Hegel, that the spring vegetables were refuted because they were over. In the *Ode* the Natural Man or child is not refuted by the sober coloring, but the earlier coloring, the glory, is over forever. Forever because the glory *is* the intimation of immortality, and the loss of the glory is the first intimation of mortality. We have here a particular instance of what Northrop Frye, in his very useful theory of myths, refers to as the resolution of tragedy in the manifestation of natural law:

Merely to exist is to disturb the balance of nature. Every natural man is a Hegelian thesis, and implies a reaction: every new birth provokes the return of an avenging death. This fact, in itself ironic and now called *Angst,* becomes tragic when a sense of a lost and originally higher destiny is added to it.[30]

Ruskin, brooding on "the Moral of Landscape," has a habit of returning to the *Ode* and its "sober coloring." Thus, he invokes Wordsworth's resolution of the burden of mortality as a parallel to the "opalescent twilight" of Titian, in contrast to the natural sun of a Rubens. The sense of loss, despite the Titian example, is more intense in Ruskin than the sober gain he seeks to approve. Wordsworth is much more strenuous in identifying mature imagination with the sober coloring, but the *Ode,* luckily for its poetic power, does not altogether agree with its author's judicious balancings.

What is it that lives on in our embers, that Nature can yet recall? Wordsworth is very precise here; he begins by distinguishing what the thing is *not*—not "the simple creed of childhood": perpetual hope, eternal delight, liberty—but the "obstinate questionings" of the child as his sense of organic continuity with the universe is broken down. The commentary here of Lionel Trilling is of perpetual value; his citations of Freud and Ferenczi are exactly relevant to the naturalistic phenomena with which Wordsworth is preoccupied. But his own summary, for its humanistic groundings, is still more useful than his psychoanalytical references:

That there should be ambivalence in Wordsworth's response to this diminution is quite natural, and the two answers, that of stanzas V–VIII and that of Stanzas IX–XI, comprise both the resistance to and the acceptance of growth. Inevitably we resist change and turn back with passionate nostalgia to the stage we are leaving. Still, we fulfill ourselves by choosing what is painful and difficult and necessary, and we develop by moving toward death. In short, organic development is a hard paradox which Wordsworth is stating in the discrepant answers of the second part of the Ode.[31]

To this I seek only to add that "the discrepant answers" are not presented as the "hard paradox"; they seek to counter that paradox by making, from the hard phenomena of organic development, a personal myth with universal properties—a story of how memory "saves" us from the state of nature.

Wordsworth raises his "song of thanks" for the infant's doomed resistance to mortality. As the fallings and vanishings of the organic continuity take place; as sense is differentiated from sense, and the child is forced to learn his limits—even then, according to Wordsworth, the child fights back against mortality. He has, in place of the lost continuity, his "first affections" for what is outside his own self. Most astonishing, in this personal reading of a child's growth in awareness of self and selves, is Wordsworth's conviction that these first affections are indistinguishable from the child's "shadowy recollections" of original unity with the external world. From this identification comes the moment of crisis and vision, the great epiphany that closes the ninth stanza and binds together the logic of Wordsworth's poem. Memories of a composite seeing-hearing constitute the "something" that lives on in the entrapped man who suddenly awakens to what seems a universe of separateness and deadness.

The myth of the *Ode* demands that these chief organic senses be reunited in the Imaginative Man, as they were united for the child, and as they clearly are *not* united for the Man of Stanzas I to IV, who fails to see what he hears. But for the Imaginative Man, the powers of the child are available through recollections, which in themselves are indeed "a master-light of all our seeing." For the child *is* an "Eye among the blind," precisely because he is without consciousness of mortality, and what that Eye reads is "the eternal deep," which encompasses us in all its guises, variously as "eternal mind," "eternal Silence," and "immortal sea," and which can be translated again as that which cannot know its own separateness and is therefore not yet separate. For here we have arrived at what I think the *Ode* is "about"; it is about separateness and consequent mortality, and about the imaginative power that can bridge that separateness and so intimate an immortality that is, in turn, just and only, "primal sympathy" of one human with another.

> Hence in a season of calm weather
> Though inland far we be,
> Our Souls have sight of that immortal sea
> Which brought us hither,

> Can in a moment travel thither,
> And see the Children sport upon the shore,
> And hear the mighty waters rolling evermore.

The first surprise in the passage is in the word "sight" in line 164; we expect "hearing" because of the "though" in the previous line. Even though we are too far inland to hear the sea (you need not be very far from the ocean not to see it), nevertheless in a season of calm weather we can *see* it, not hear it. Why then the "though"? Because, as the passage goes on to say, we can "in a moment" travel back to it if we can see it, and once we have traveled back we can see the children who play on its shore, and being there, we can hear it. Even though, being far inland, we ordinarily could not.

The children's presence is the other surprise of the passage. The poem's success is that, if we have grasped its dialectic, their presence is the lesser of the two surprises. The voice of Stanzas I–VIII could not evoke these children for us; the second voice, of IX–XI, must. *The* intimation of immortality from recollections of early childhood in the poem is the sight of these children, for to be able to travel back to their shore is to intimate one's fusion with them. It is never to die, because once we did not know death, and we can find our way back to that not-knowing. The immortal sea is what laps around every side of our separateness.

This vision of the children is set in what Blake calls Beulah, and is the vision of the *Songs of Innocence* and *The Book of Thel.* As such, it has a precarious reality; it exists "in a moment," but not from moment to moment. Something more habitual is what the imagination requires, when it surrenders Beulah:

> I only have relinquished one delight
> To live beneath your more habitual sway.

The poet's imaginative eye may not be an eye among the blind, able to read the eternal deep, but it can impart a sober coloring to the sunset, for it has "kept watch o'er man's mortality": it knows mortality's limits. It reaffirms, not the child's misgivings and obstinate questionings, but his first affections, his primal sympathy.

4   *Natural Man*

The Old Cumberland Beggar

THE OLD CUMBERLAND BEGGAR (1797) is Wordsworth's finest vision of the irreducible natural man, the human stripped to the nakedness of primordial condition and exposed as still powerful in dignity, still infinite in value. The Beggar reminds us of the beggars, solitaries, wanderers throughout Wordsworth's poetry, particularly in *The Prelude* and *Resolution and Independence*. He differs from them in that he is not the agency of a revelation; he is not responsible for a sudden release of Wordsworth's imagination. He is not even of visionary utility; he is something finer, beyond use, a vision of reality in himself. I am not suggesting that *The Old Cumberland Beggar* is the best of Wordsworth's poems outside *The Prelude;* it is not in the sublime mode, as are *Tintern Abbey,* the Great Ode, *Resolution and Independence.* But it is the most Wordsworthian of poems, and profoundly moving.

Nothing could be simpler than the poem's opening: "I saw an aged Beggar in my walk." The Old Man (the capitalization is the poet's) has put down his staff, and takes his scraps and fragments out of a flour bag, one by one. He scans them, fixedly and seriously. The plain beginning yields to a music of love, the beauty of the real:

> In the sun,
> Upon the second step of that small pile,
> Surrounded by those wild unpeopled hills,
> He sat, and ate his food in solitude:
> And ever, scattered from his palsied hand,
> That, still attempting to prevent the waste,
> Was baffled still, the crumbs in little showers
> Fell on the ground; and the small mountain birds,

> Not venturing yet to peck their destined meal,
> Approached within the length of half his staff.

It is difficult to describe *how* this is beautiful, but we can make
a start by observing that it is beautiful both because it is so matter
of fact, and because the fact is itself a transfiguration. The Old Man
is in his own state, and he is radically innocent. The "wild unpeo-
pled hills" complement his own solitude; he is a phenomenon of
their kind. And he is no more sentimentalized than they are. His lot
is not even miserable; he is too absorbed into Nature for that, as
absorbed as he can be and still retain human identity.

He is even past further aging. The poet has known him since
his childhood, and even then "he was so old, he seems not older
now." The Old Man is so helpless in appearance that everyone—
sauntering horseman or toll-gate keeper or post boy—makes way
for him, taking special care to keep him from harm. For he cannot
be diverted, but moves on like a natural process. "He travels on, a
solitary Man," Wordsworth says, and then repeats it, making a refrain for that incessant movement whose only meaning is that it
remains human though at the edge of our condition:

> He travels on, a solitary Man;
> His age has no companion. On the ground
> His eyes are turned, and, as he moves along,
> They move along the ground; and, evermore,
> Instead of common and habitual sight
> Of fields with rural works, of hill and dale,
> And the blue sky, one little span of earth
> Is all his prospect.

He is bent double, like the Leech Gatherer, and his vision of one
little span of earth recalls the wandering old man of Chaucer's
Pardoner's Tale. But Chaucer's solitary longed for death, and on
the ground he called his mother's gate he knocked often with his
staff, crying, "Dear mother, let me in." Wordsworth's Old Man sees
only the ground, but he is tenaciously alive, and is beyond desire,
even that of death. He sees, and yet hardly sees. He moves constantly, but is so still in look and motion that he can hardly be

seen to move. He is all process, hardly character, and yet almost stasis.

It is so extreme a picture that we can be tempted to ask, "Is this life? Where is its use?" The temptation dehumanizes us, Wordsworth would have it, and the two questions are radically dissimilar, but his answer to the first is vehemently affirmative and to the second an absolute moral passion. There is

> a spirit and pulse of good,
> A life and soul, to every mode of being
> Inseparably linked.

The Old Man performs many functions. The most important is that of a binding agent for the memories of good impulses in all around him. Wherever he goes,

> The mild necessity of use compels
> To acts of love.

These acts of love, added one to another, at last insensibly dispose their performers to virtue and true goodness. We need to be careful in our reaction to this. Wordsworth is not preaching the vicious and mad doctrine that beggary is good because it makes charity possible. That would properly invoke Blake's blistering reply in *The Human Abstract:*

> Pity would be no more
> If we did not make somebody Poor;
> And Mercy no more could be
> If all were as happy as we.

Wordsworth has no reaction to the Old Man which we can categorize. He does not think of him in social or economic terms, but only as a human life, which necessarily has affected other lives, and always for the better. In particular, the Old Man has given occasions for kindness to the very poorest, who give to him from their scant store, and are the kinder for it. Again, you must read this in its own context. Wordsworth's best poetry has nothing directly to do with social justice, as Blake's or Shelley's frequently does. The old beggar is a free man, at home in the heart of the solitudes he wanders, and he does not intend the humanizing good he passively causes. Nor is his social aspect at the poem's vital center; only his freedom is:

> —Then let him pass, a blessing on his head!
> And, long as he can wander, let him breathe
> The freshness of the valleys; let his blood
> Struggle with frosty air and winter snows;
> And let the chartered wind that sweeps the heath
> Beat his grey locks against his withered face.

Pity for him is inappropriate; he is pathetic only if shut up. He is a "figure of capable imagination," in Stevens' phrase, a Man perfectly complete in Nature, reciprocating its gifts by being himself, a being at one with it:

> Let him be free of mountain solitudes;
> And have around him, whether heard or not,
> The pleasant melody of woodland birds.

Mountain solitudes and sudden winds are what suit him, whether he reacts to them or not. The failure of his senses does not cut him off from Nature; it does not matter whether he can hear the birds, but it is fitting that he have them around him. He has become utterly passive toward Nature. Let it be free, then, to come in upon him:

> if his eyes have now
> Been doomed so long to settle upon earth
> That not without some effort they behold
> The countenance of the horizontal sun,
> Rising or setting, let the light at least
> Find a free entrance to their languid orbs.

The Old Man is approaching that identity with Nature that the infant at first knows, when an organic continuity seems to exist between Nature and consciousness. Being so naturalized, he must die in the eye of Nature, that he may be absorbed again:

> And let him, *where* and *when* he will, sit down
> Beneath the trees, or on a grassy bank
> Of highway side, and with the little birds

> Share his chance-gathered meal; and, finally,
> As in the eye of Nature he has lived,
> So in the eye of Nature let him die!

The poem abounds in a temper of spirit that Wordsworth shares with Tolstoy, a reverence for the simplicities of *caritas*, the Christian love that is so allied to and yet is not pity. But Tolstoy might have shown the Old Cumberland Beggar as a sufferer; in Wordsworth he bears the mark of "animal tranquillity and decay," the title given by Wordsworth to a fragment closely connected to the longer poem. In the fragment the Old Man travels on and moves not with pain, but with thought:

> He is insensibly subdued
> To settled quiet . . .
> He is by nature led
> To peace so perfect that the young behold
> With envy, what the Old Man hardly feels.

We know today, better than his contemporaries could, what led Wordsworth to the subject of human decay, to depictions of idiocy, desertion, beggars, homeless wanderers. He sought images of alienated life, as we might judge them, which he could see and present as images of natural communion. The natural man, free of consciousness in any of our senses, yet demonstrates a mode of consciousness which both intends Nature for its object and at length blends into that object. The hiding places of man's power are in his past, in childhood. Only memory can take him there, but even memory fades, and at length fades away. The poet of naturalism, separated by organic growth from his own past, looks around him and sees the moving emblems of a childlike consciousness in the mad, the outcast, and the dreadfully old. From them he takes his most desperate consolation, intimations of a mortality that almost ceases to afflict.

Michael

MICHAEL is the most directly Biblical of Wordsworth's poems. It turns upon the symbol of a covenant between father and son, and its hero, though a poor shepherd, has a moral greatness that suggests the stories of the Patriarchs. Had Michael ever heard of his vanished son again, he might have said, with Jacob: "It is enough; Joseph my son is yet alive: I will go and see him before I die." But in Wordsworth's poem, the covenant is forever broken, and the old shepherd dies without the solace of a prodigal's return.

Michael's world is one of all but utter solitude. He leaves behind him a pathetic memorial, the sign of the covenant broken by his son, a straggling heap of unhewn stones. The man himself is not pathetic, for

> he had been alone
> Amid the heart of many thousand mists,
> That came to him, and left him, on the heights.

These are the mists of natural imagination, and the heights are figurative as much as literal. Michael is Wordsworthian Man, the solitary against the sky celebrated in Book VIII of *The Prelude:*

> as he stepped
> Beyond the boundary line of some hill-shadow,
> His form hath flashed upon me, glorified
> By the deep radiance of the setting sun:
> Or him have I descried in distant sky,
> A solitary object and sublime,
> Above all height!

This is an appearance of the "sanctity of Nature given to man." The same spirit is in Michael's desire that his son should inherit his patrimonial fields:

> the land
> Shall not go from us, and it shall be free;
> He shall possess it, free as is the wind
> That passes over it.

The man at the heart of many thousand mists is free; there is a binding covenant between him and Nature, symbolized by the rainbow of *My Heart Leaps Up* and the epigraph to the *Intimations* ode. But a covenant between him and another man, even the child of his old age, has little force against the world of experience. When his loss comes upon him, Michael is not diminished, but we feel the impotence of grief:

> Among the rocks
> He went, and still looked up to sun and cloud,
> And listened to the wind. . . .

To be a natural man, for Wordsworth, is a heroism, but it affords no consolation. Michael at the end is a passive image, a human sufferer. Wordsworth has no interest in the son, Luke (he is given no line to speak in the poem). The mechanism of grief, its cause and cure, have nothing to do with the poem. We are left with an image that is permanent, obscure, and dark; a suffering that shares the nature of infinity.

5   *The Myth Denied*

Peele Castle

ON February 6, 1805, the best-loved of Wordsworth's brothers, a captain in the merchant service, went down with his ship off Portland. For three months, Wordsworth stopped work on *The Prelude*. The loss of his brother is as major an event in Wordsworth's poetry as in his life. Directly due to it are the powerful lines that form Wordsworth's palinode on his gospel of Nature, the *Elegiac Stanzas*, better known as *Peele Castle*.

The *Elegiac Stanzas* occupy in Wordsworth's canon the position held in the other Romantics by Coleridge's *Dejection;* Byron's *Stanzas to the Po* and poem on his thirty-sixth birthday; *The Triumph of Life, The Fall of Hyperion;* and Clare's *I Am*. Blake, who never recanted any major emphasis, has no such point of crisis within his poetry.

The full title of Wordsworth's elegy for his brother is *Elegiac Stanzas, Suggested by a Picture of Peele Castle, in a Storm, Painted by Sir George Beaumont*. Beaumont, who was Wordsworth's patron, was an amateur painter, and his scene of Peele Castle clearly provoked the poem not by its excellence but by the subject itself, a castle on a cliff overhanging a stormy sea.

Wordsworth begins in his customary mode of recollection, but for the first time memory and reality conflict. Memory is only appearance:

> I was thy neighbor once, thou rugged Pile!
> Four summer weeks I dwelt in sight of thee:
> I saw thee every day; and all the while
> Thy Form was sleeping on a glassy sea.

Peele Castle, reflected in a calm sea, showed only its Form asleep. The peace of Nature made the sea a deceptive mirror:

> So pure the sky, so quiet was the air!
> So like, so very like, was day to day!
> Whene'er I looked, thy Image still was there;
> It trembled, but it never passed away.
>
> How perfect was the calm! it seemed no sleep;
> No mood, which season takes away, or brings:
> I could have fancied that the mighty Deep
> Was even the gentlest of all gentle Things.

These stanzas are beautifully weighted. Wordsworth emphasizes his deception by detailing the profoundity and unity of the natural deceptiveness that worked upon him. The sameness of peace creates an illusion of constancy, and converts appearance almost into reality. We come to feel that the effect is ominous; there is a foreboding that this gentleness of the mighty Deep cannot prevail. Yet this seemed Nature's gift to Wordsworth then, and so he would have painted it:

> Ah! then, if mine had been the Painter's hand,
> To express what then I saw; and add the gleam,
> The light that never was, on sea or land,
> The consecration, and the Poet's dream.

Quoted out of context, as they usually are, the last two lines mean just the reverse of what they signify within the poem. The poem says that the idealizing light of vision *never was,* and the Poet's consecration of Nature was but a dream. There is no lasting ease within Nature, and its quiet merely seems to be Elysian. The fond illusion of Wordsworth's heart had seen in Nature "a steadfast peace that might not be betrayed." In *Tintern Abbey* Wordsworth had prayed as "a worshipper of Nature," confident "that Nature never did betray the heart that loved her." This confidence falters in the *Elegiac Stanzas.* A new control, more constant than the covenant between man's intellect and heart and Nature's gift of herself, has won Wordsworth's submission:

> So once it would have been,—'tis so no more;
> I have submitted to a new control:
> A power is gone, which nothing can restore;
> A deep distress hath humanised my Soul.

This stanza is in the vocabulary of the three closing stanzas of the *Intimations* ode, where Wordsworth acknowledges that the power of seeing a certain glory in outward phenomena is forever lost to him, but where he also salutes a new power that is given him in recompense for his loss. Though nothing can bring back the "glory in the flower," the very "meanest flower that blows" can now give Wordsworth thoughts of sympathy with others, thoughts so primal that they are deeper than grief itself. For the power to receive this final gift of the sober coloring or mature imagination, Wordsworth gives thanks to "the human heart by which we live." Here in the *Elegiac Stanzas,* in the poem's most striking line, Wordsworth extends this sober humanization from heart to soul. His inwardness is more human, more common, less sublime. But is it more or less imaginative?

In the early books of *The Prelude* the young Wordsworth undergoes a movement of initiation by which his soul and heart are, progressively and simultaneously, both naturalized and humanized. The two processes are so very nearly one that only irrelevant analytical techniques could hope to disentangle them. But here in the *Elegiac Stanzas,* we cannot say that love of Nature leads on to love of one's fellow men. It would be more accurate to state what is very nearly the contrary: love of Nature is shown to be illusory, and the shock of this revelation leads to an intensified love for common humanity. In *The Prelude,* Wordsworth receives gifts from Nature,

and a sense of gain engenders the youth's humanization. In the
Elegiac Stanzas a sense of loss, a deep distress, humanizes Wordsworth's soul. The emphasis of the Great Ode is repeated, but for
the first time Wordsworth darkens his vision of Nature. He cannot
bear to indict Nature for the deception, as he remains her lover,
though betrayed. He turns therefore upon himself, and blames that
very bliss of solitude he once held essential for vision. Vision has
degenerated to a dream, and to this productive blindness Wordsworth bids farewell:

> Farewell, farewell the heart that lives alone,
> Housed in a dream, at distance from the Kind!
> Such happiness, wherever it be known,
> Is to be pitied; for 'tis surely blind.

This is not intended as a farewell to the powers of poetry, but
the strength of Wordsworth's imagination is in the abyss of his own
and solitary Self. The dreadful paradox of Wordsworth's creativity
is that it flourished "at distance from the Kind," and waned in the
presence of even the most exemplary humanitarian concern. In his
wanderer's solitude, Wordsworth was at one with Man and Nature.
In his overt desire to celebrate the later consequences of that early
oneness, he became as solitary as Blake's Urizen, a frozen spirit
communing only with himself. The *Elegiac Stanzas* intimate an
ironic naturalization of Wordsworth's soul, and presage the iron
age upon which his poetry was to enter.

Ode to Duty

THE *Ode to Duty*, composed in 1805, is one of the crucial poems
for an understanding of the crisis of Wordsworth's imagination. It
is a Horatian poem, like Thomas Gray's *Ode to Adversity*, and its
stern diction suits its theme of restraint. Blake would have called
it a poem written by Urizen, and certainly it is not the kind of ode
we would expect from the poet of *Tintern Abbey* and *The Prelude*.
The youth who moved with the wind's freedom, whose heart was
an impulse to itself and reciprocated Nature's promptings, now
supplicates for the control of "a rod to check the erring, and re-

prove." What Wordsworth seeks to abandon here is the autonomy of his own imagination, which is one with his freedom:

> Through no disturbance of my soul,
> Or strong compunction in me wrought,
> I supplicate for thy control;
> But in the quietness of thought:
> Me this unchartered freedom tires;
> I feel the weight of chance-desires:
> My hopes no more must change their name,
> I long for a repose that ever is the same.

It was Wordsworth's ill fortune to realize his longing, to enter into a bower of self-satisfaction. The most frequently praised lines in the *Ode to Duty* are the most antipoetical in their implications:

> Thou dost preserve the stars from wrong;
> And the most ancient heavens, through
> Thee, are fresh and strong.

As rhetoric, this is excellent. In the context of Wordsworthian Nature, the goddess Duty merely circumscribes and baffles our sense of possible sublimity, our faith in something evermore about to be. Wordsworth's heavens do not renovate themselves by the dictates of law, nor do his stars need preservation in their courses by any moral precepts. The Nature of *Tintern Abbey* and *The Prelude* is an unrestrained effluence from a fountain beyond the relevance of traditional morality. Strong and eloquent as it is, the *Ode to Duty* is a betrayal of Wordsworth's myth of Nature.

Laodamia

COLERIDGE first observed of Wordsworth that he had no feminine element in his mind, and it is true that Wordsworth is almost too masculine a poet. He has no equivalent of Blake's emanation, Shelley's epipsyche, and similar figures in the love poetry of Coleridge, Byron, Keats, and Clare. He does not quest for a female principle, or celebrate erotic love on any level immediately recognizable as such. Yet in a clear sense all the poetry of the Great Decade is erotic, in a tradition going back to the Song of Solomon, with Wordsworth as the Bridegroom, Nature as the Bride, and the Great Marriage between the two as something evermore about to be, a possible sublimity never altogether consummated.

Shelley, an overtly erotic poet, thought Wordsworth's poetry prudish, and certainly it offers no companion work to *Visions of the Daughters of Albion* or *Epipsychidion*. In his poems of naturalistic celebration, Wordsworth is sympathetic to every kind of human passion. Later, in the poetry of his early middle age, as his naturalism wanes, he becomes dubiously moralistic, in what is too frequently a tiresome and conventional mode of judgment. *Laodamia* (1814), a great poem totally distinct from Wordsworth's characteristic achievement, is a paradox. In it Wordsworth is caught in a struggle between a Virgilian tenderness for a victim of what has become a hopeless passion, and a vehement condemnation of unreasonable desire that suggests the attitude of Blake's Bromion. The struggle rescues the poem; Wordsworth could not resolve it, and was never quite sure of how he ought to end it. *Laodamia* therefore is enigmatic; we cannot say finally just what it is that the poem wishes us to believe about the rival claims of reason and passion.

The story of Laodamia and Protesilaus figures most notably in the sixth book of Virgil's *Aeneid*. Protesilaus, a Greek, ensured victory for his side in the Trojan War by being the first to leap ashore at Troy, with the foreknowledge that the first to land would die. He had left behind him a new bride, Laodamia, whose intense mourning persuaded the gods to allow her slain husband one brief visit to the world of the living. When he returns to the shades, she dies so as to follow him.

Wordsworth's *Laodamia* begins with the widowed bride supplicating Jove to restore her slain husband to her *sight*. She does not ask for more as yet, but her body is agitated by desire as she awaits Jove's gift. Mercury, escorting the shade of Protesilaus, warns her to accept the gift as it is offered: "behold him face to face." But she is impassioned, and attempts to embrace the shade's "unsubstantial Form."

Protesilaus is a puritan and a prig, but a marvelous rhetorician. He speaks of himself as a "a self-devoted chief—by Hector slain," and means that he devoted himself to his fellow Greeks by his sacrifice. But his reference to himself as "self-devoted" has ironic force as well; where was his devotion to his bride in his proud sacrifice? Laodamia gently hints that her heart would have given him different counsel:

> "Supreme of Heroes—bravest, noblest, best!
> Thy matchless courage I bewail no more,
> Which then, when tens of thousands were deprest
> By doubt, propelled thee to the fatal shore;
> Thou founds't—and I forgive thee—here thou art—
> A nobler counsellor than my poor heart."

Forgiving him because he is again with her and forgiving him for his very boast of "self-devotion" are excellent touches. She reminds him that he was "kind as resolute, and good as brave," and begs him for one nuptial kiss" and to make her "a second time thy bride." His reply is the sternest and most classical stanza in Wordsworth:

> "This visage tells thee that my doom is past:
> Nor should the change be mourned, even if the joys
> Of sense were able to return as fast
> And surely as they vanish. Earth destroys
> Those raptures duly—Erebus disdains:
> Calm pleasures there abide—majestic pains."

No lines could be more contrary to the myth of the Great Decade. The joys of sense are destroyed, fitly and in due season, by Earth itself. Erebus, abode of the shades, disdains either to destroy or preserve such raptures, for it is too dignified a realm to acknowledge them. Its pleasures and its pains are under a higher control. The stanza is phrased so majestically, so calmly exemplifies the mood it recommends, that we cannot censure Protesilaus. Unfortunately, he then goes rather too far in censuring his bereaved bride; one's flesh protests this kind of admonishment when it comes from the tomb:

> "Be taught, O faithful Consort, to control
> Rebellious passion: for the Gods approve
> The depth, and not the tumult, of the soul;
> A fervent, not ungovernable, love.

Thy transports moderate; and meekly mourn
When I depart, for brief is my sojourn."

The first four lines of this stanza, read out of context, are a magnificent statement of the classical doctrine of the inner check, of harmonious balance and self-constraint. But how are we to regard them when they are spoken to a mourning bride, in these extraordinary circumstances? One admires Wordsworth for his characteristic way of making things difficult for himself here. He has chosen a context for this spare, hard doctrine that causes much in us to rebel, and to deprecate the tact of the heroic shade. The poor lady is told to moderate her transports, and meekly mourn, but she is quick to reply that she has a good deal of classical precedent for refusing to do so. She cites the stories of Alcestis and Aeson, restored to life by Hercules and Medea respectively, and passionately insists that love is stronger than death. But if he must go back to death, she will follow him.

Though he silences her, she has softened him at least to the point that he modulates his rhetoric from its iron admonitions to a Virgilian grace and melancholy. She is calmed and cheered, momentarily, because his features now lose their deathly cast and take on an Elysian beauty. And his discourse at least attempts some consolation:

He spake of love, such love as Spirits feel
In worlds whose course is equable and pure;
No fears to beat away—no strife to heal—
The past unsighed for, and the future sure;
Spake of heroic arts in graver mood
Revived, with finer harmony pursued;

Of all that is most beauteous—imaged there
In happier beauty; more pellucid streams,
An ampler ether, a diviner air,
And fields invested with purpureal gleams;
Climes which the sun, who sheds the brightest day
Earth knows, is all unworthy to survey.

With Tennyson's *Tithonus*, these stanzas are the closest in English to the spirit and manner of Virgil, for they possess something of his troubled hope, gentle gravity, and elegiac intensity. They constitute the most sympathetic vision of reason and order, albeit deathly, that the poem has to give us. Had Protesilaus (and Wordsworth) been able to maintain this tone, Laodamia (and the reader) might have been moved to no more protest. But after a very pathetic expression of the pangs of memory, in which the latent sexual content is very strong, Protesilaus delivers a final reproof, more in the manner of Bromion than of the tender Virgil:

> "Learn, by a mortal yearning, to ascend—
> Seeking a higher object. Love was given,
> Encouraged, sanctioned, chiefly for that end;
> For this the passion to excess was driven—
> That self might be annulled: her bondage prove
> The fetters of a dream opposed to love."

This is an inhumane pseudo-Platonism, and undermines the dignity of human affection. The poet of *Tintern Abbey* and *The Prelude* is not the poet of these lines in more than a merely biographical sense.

Hermes comes to take the shade to his appointed place, and poor Laodamia shrieks and dies. Her fate after death bedeviled Wordsworth; he could not decide how to dispose her in the nether regions. He first judged her gently, as being without crime, and removed her to a realm where she could "gather flowers / Of blissful quiet 'mid unwading bowers." He next decided that "by no weak pity might the Gods be moved," and so doomed her "to wander in a grosser clime / Apart from happy Ghosts." Still uncertain, he wrote to his nephew for advice: ought punishment to follow the heroine's criminal refusal to moderate her passion? The nephew kindly mitigated her doom; in the final version she must "wear out her appointed time" before she can join her happy and ghostly husband in the unfading bowers. Fortunately, this outrageous judgment is not the poem's final point. Wordsworth makes a recovery that is indicative of the poem's barely hidden obsession, regret for a sexual pleasure, for an erotic love that is forever in the past:

> —Yet tears to human suffering are due;
> And mortal hopes defeated and o'erthrown
> Are mourned by man, and not by man alone,

As fondly he believes.—Upon the side
Of Hellespont (such faith was entertained)
A knot of spiry trees for ages grew
From out the tomb of him for whom she died;
And ever, when such stature they had gained
That Ilium's walls were subject to their view,
The trees' tall summits withered at the sight;
A constant interchange of growth and blight!

It is a very Wordsworthian ending, and does not suit the classical decorum of what has gone before. But it rights the sexual balance of the poem. The more abundant life that Protesilaus had denied for the sake of his heroic but selfish death now asserts itself in an emblem of growth and blight. The denied sexuality bursts forth from the tomb as natural growth, encounters the sight of that for which it was repudiated, and is blighted again, as it was before. We cannot know whether or not the poem has an oblique reference to the blighting of Wordsworth's love for Annette Vallon, but it does not seem unlikely. As such, it is at last an elegy for more than Laodamia herself.

6   *The Frozen Spirit*

The Excursion

BYRON, in *Don Juan* (Canto III, lines 847–848), expressed what has become the majority view on *The Excursion:*

A drowsy, frowsy poem called *The Excursion,*
Writ in a manner which is my aversion.

Hazlitt said of this, the longest of Wordsworth's poems, that in it "we are talked to death by an arrogant old proser, and buried in a heap of the most perilous stuff and the most dusty philosophy." Coleridge was unhappy about the poem, and many who love Wordsworth's best poetry have been unhappy about it since. Matthew Arnold finely celebrated Wordsworth's healing power, but found *The Excursion* "a tissue of elevated but abstract verbiage, alien to the very nature of poetry." Yet *The Excursion* was vital for the development of Shelley and Keats (neither of whom lived to read *The Prelude*), and Wordsworth himself expressed the proud Miltonic hope that future times would "not willingly let die" his most ambitious work. Much of it never lived; more has died; some of it seems permanent. Nearly all of it constitutes an involuntary epitaph for the poet of the Great Decade, the man who wrote *Tintern Abbey* and *The Prelude*.

The best parts of *The Excursion* were written between 1795 and 1804, and include the powerful story of Margaret (I, 434–970), and a number of passages on Man and Nature which could fit into *The Prelude* and originally were intended for it. The lesser parts of the poem are versified argument, directed against materialists, rationalists, and too quick despairers.

The fear of mortality haunts much of Wordsworth's best poetry, especially in regard to the premature mortality of the Imagination and the loss of its creative joy. In *The Excursion* a harsher element, akin to that in *Peele Castle,* enters the darkening landscape of the poet's vision, the sense of irreparable loss of loved ones. The myth of Man and Nature called for a naturalistic acceptance of death as an inevitable absorption back into Nature. But Wordsworth could not so accept his brother's death, or view the two children he lost in 1812 as two more Lucy Grays, living spirits of landscape. *The Prelude* shows the struggle with despondency and disillusion, and the struggle is triumphant; but the causes of dismay, while absolute, had not the finality of death. The failure of the French Revolution cost Wordsworth a great hope and the major sexual relationship of his life, but the hope was translated into the consolations of religious belief, and the relationship was replaced by the poet's marriage. Nothing transcended death. The powers of poetry, the autonomy of imaginative vision, could not reconcile Wordsworth to a natural reality so terrible, so little fitted to human desire.

Yet the impotence of grief is a humanistic fulfillment in the story of Margaret, in the beautiful poem of 1795, *The Ruined Cottage,* absorbed into *The Excursion* as part of Book I. Even a brief parallel study of Margaret's fate and the poet's reaction to it, with a typical later passage from *The Excursion,* can show clearly the decline of Wordsworth, the heavy frost that encrusted a spirit endowed by Nature with a vitality nearly the equal of Blake's.

Margaret is described as a woman "tender and deep in her excess of love," a being framed to live on earth a life of happiness. But her husband is ruined by poverty, and abandons her and their two children for a soldier's life. One child she is forced to give away, and in her affliction she wanders close to madness. Her remaining child dies, and she is left alone in her solitude, still hoping for her husband's return. She dies, still constant in her torturing hope. The poet's sublime reaction is an ultimate human image:

> I stood, and leaning o'er the garden wall
> Reviewed that Woman's sufferings; and it seemed
> To comfort me while with a brother's love
> I blessed her in the impotence of grief.

With this, contrast Wordsworth's idealized Pastor, at the close of Book V of *The Excursion*, expounding the consolations of the dogma of immortality, and praising

> the care prospective of our wise
> Forefathers, who, to guard against the shocks,
> The fluctuation and decay of things,
> Embodied and established these high truths
> In solemn institutions:—men convinced
> That life is love and immortality,
> The being one, and one the element.
> There lies the channel, and original bed,
> From the beginning, hollowed out and scooped
> For Man's affections—else betrayed and lost,
> And swallowed up 'mid deserts infinite!
> This is the genuine course, the aim, and end
> Of prescient reason; all conclusions else
> Are abject, vain, presumptuous, and perverse.
> The faith partaking of those holy times,
> Life, I repeat, is energy of love
> Divine or human; exercised in pain,
> In strife, in tribulation; and ordained,
> If so approved and sanctified, to pass,
> Through shades and silent rest, to endless joy.

The first passage is permanent, and shares the nature of infinity. The second is a weariness, and justifies Hazlitt's complaint at being "talked to death by an arrogant old proser." Dr. Samuel Johnson's doubts about devotional verse are relevant and definitive when applied to much of *The Excursion:*

> Of sentiments purely religious, it will be found that the most simple expression is the most sublime. Poetry loses its lustre and its power, because it is applied to the decoration of something more excellent than itself. All that pious verse can do is to help the memory, and delight the ear, and for these purposes it may be very useful; but it supplies nothing to the mind.

Dr. Johnson would hardly have admired *The Prelude* and its attendant poems, but he would have acknowledged their excellence as invention, as a fresh attempt in the sublime mode. He would have found little in *The Excursion* to upset his own dogmatic orthodoxy, but little also of "such invention as, by producing something unexpected, surprises and delights."

Extempore Effusion

WORDSWORTH'S own note on his *Extempore Effusion upon the Death of James Hogg* (composed in November 1835) is simply a grim list that tells us that the poets Walter Scott, Coleridge, Charles Lamb, George Crabbe, and the popular Mrs. Hemans have all died between September 1832 and December 1834. The Scottish poet Hogg, known as "the Ettrick Shepherd," has now joined this company, and the old Wordsworth is suddenly moved to lament the passing of his literary generation. He calls the poem an "extempore effusion" as though to emphasize the sudden expressive resolution of a long-gathering grief. Coleridge had died in July 1834. Though the two men had become reconciled and were moderately good friends, they had not sought to revive the relationship they once had shared. The death of Coleridge had brought forth no elegy from Wordsworth, but the death of Hogg set in motion the imagination of the surviving poet. The result is one of the handful of good poems that Wordsworth wrote in his last decades.

A good contrast to the *Extempore Effusion,* with its dignified, Roman acceptance of the finality of death, can be found in the elegiac piece on Charles Lamb which Wordsworth also composed in November 1835, and which is a fair example of his later poetry. Though this reads like a parody of his earlier manner, it is the best that the old Wordsworth generally could do:

> ye were taught
> That the remembrance of foregone distress,
> And the worse fear of future ill (which oft
> Doth hang around it, as a sickly child
> Upon its mother) may be both alike
> Disarmed of power to unsettle present good
> So prized, and things inward and outward held
> In such an even balance, that the heart
> Acknowledges God's grace, his mercy feels,
> And in its depth of gratitude is still.

In these prosy lines custom lies upon Wordsworth with a weight heavy as frost, and deep almost as life. He wants to speak of a religious hope, but the evidence of things not seen is a poor stimulus for an imagination nurtured upon the phenomenal world. Milton, singing the entrance of Lycidas into heaven, is genuinely ecstatic:

> There entertain him all the Saints above,
> In solemn troops, and sweet Societies
> That sing, and singing in their glory move,
> And wipe the tears for ever from his eyes.

Wordsworth ends his poem on Lamb with what is meant to be a parallel ecstasy:

> yet why grieve? for Time but holds
> His moiety in trust, till Joy shall lead
> To the blest world where parting is unknown.

The substance of things hoped for is a felt presence in Milton's lines, but hardly in Wordsworth's, which merely give assent to a received doctrine of consolation. Very probably Wordsworth could not convince himself of an abstract immortality; he had come too close to intimations of an immortality here and now in his direct relationship with Nature. The genuinely Wordsworthian attitude toward death is expressed in the *Extempore Effusion*, where the poet is at one with his own imaginative reaction, and the great style returns:

> Nor has the rolling year twice measured,
> From sign to sign, its steadfast course,
> Since every mortal power of Coleridge
> Was frozen at its marvellous source.

Coleridge's powers were mortal; they had their source in the marvelous fountain of his spirit, and they are frozen with the spirit, in earth. In a stanza of great tenderness, Wordsworth writes his finest tribute to Coleridge, and also a farewell to Lamb more moving than the whole of his previous poem on the great essayist:

> The rapt One, of the godlike forehead,
> The heaven-eyed creature sleeps in earth:
> And Lamb, the frolic and the gentle,
> Has vanished from his lonely hearth.

Coleridge's features are Divine, but they sleep in earth. A Virgilian tone, like that of *Laodamia*, begins to dominate the poem:

> Like clouds that rake the mountain-summits,
> Or waves that own no curbing hand,
> How fast has brother followed brother,
> From sunshine to the sunless land.

To pass into death is a natural process, and only stoic acceptance is a proper response. The poem climaxes in a stark image, hopeless and impressive:

> Our haughty life is crowned with darkness,
> Like London with its own black wreath.

This dark crown of mortality, identified with the advancing blight of industrialism, is a proper climax for Wordsworth's poetry. He had done more than any man to find a natural wreath for his generation. In his great decade he had personified a heroic mode of naturalism, which even he then proved unable to sustain. We cannot ask so much; no poet since has given us more.

CHAPTER THREE

SAMUEL TAYLOR COLERIDGE

Like a solitude of the sun, in which the mind
Acquired transparence and beheld itself
And beheld the source from which transparence came;
And there he heard the voices that were once
The confusion of men's voices, intricate
Made extricate by meanings, meanings made
Into a music never touched to sound.
There, too, he saw, since he must see, the domes
Of azure round an upper dome, brightest
Because it rose above them all, stippled
By waverings of stars, the joy of day
And its immaculate fire, the middle dome,
The temple of the altar where each man
Beheld the truth and knew it to be true.

WALLACE STEVENS

1   *The Conversation Poems*

The Eolian Harp

COLERIDGE'S "conversation poems" are the origin of the Wordsworthian mode, of *Tintern Abbey* and its attendant works in which we hear "a man talking to men." And through Wordsworth, they are therefore the ancestors of Shelley's *Mont Blanc* and Keats's *Sleep and Poetry*, though those poems use rhyme. The conversational idiom of Coleridge and Wordsworth is descended from Cowper's softening of Milton's style in his domestic epic, *The Task*. Coleridge mixes Cowper with the Shakespeare of *The Winter's Tale* and *The Tempest* in forming this style, which moves from a low pitch of informal affection to climactic apostrophes and invocations to nature.

The Eolian Harp (1795) is a honeymoon poem in which we encounter a dialectic between two Coleridges, the imaginative and intellectually daring poet, and the timidly orthodox young husband, glad to submit to the mildly reproving eye of his "Meek daughter in the family of Christ!"

Dominating the poem is the most prevalent of Romantic symbols, the aeolian harp itself:

> And that simplest Lute,
> Placed length-ways in the clasping casement, hark!
> How by the desultory breeze caress'd,
> Like some coy maid half yielding to her lover.

As the poem has begun with a reference to "my pensive Sara," the young husband is perhaps brooding on the difficulties of his early days of marriage. But the wind harp's music moves him to an exuberant apprehension:

> O! the one Life within us and abroad,
> Which meets all motion and becomes its soul,

> A light in sound, a sound-like power in light,
> Rhythm in all thought, and joyance every where.

We may have here the source of the extraordinary myth of an organic sense of seeing-hearing as the special mark of capable Imagination, a myth whose complexities we have explored in Wordsworth, a poet sometimes referred to as Coleridge's "greatest work." In Coleridge, this myth tends to be diffident, as it is here in *The Eolian Harp*. In Wordsworth the revelations of the sounding light are frequently hard and primitive, being involved as they are in the organic mysteries of decay and death. In Coleridge, they are softened, until they become an immediate principle of love:

> Methinks, it should have been impossible
> Not to love all things in a world so fill'd;
> Where the breeze warbles, and the mute still air
> Is Music slumbering on her instrument.

To see all the air as potential music is an extreme consequence of the sacramental vision of nature. Spurred by this image, the poet's "indolent and passive brain" allows itself to be traversed by "many idle flitting phantasies," until a really daring thought emerges:

> And what if all of animated nature
> Be but organic Harps diversely fram'd,
> That tremble into thought, as o'er them sweeps
> Plastic and vast, one intellectual breeze,
> At once the Soul of each, and God of all?

Shelley was to remember this passage in *Adonais*, where the one Spirit's plastic stress sweeps o'er the dull dense world, torturing the dull dross into newly awakening forms. But Shelley was an agnostic humanist, questing for the supernal, and doubting even as he sought. Half of Coleridge fears a descent into paganism, the religion of nature. If the intellectual breeze is at once the Soul of each organic phenomenon (including every man) and God of all, then a radical identity between man, nature, and God is being suggested. The "more serious eye" of the poet's bride darts a "mild reproof" and Coleridge casts off "these shapings of the unregenerate mind" in favor of an orthodox babbling about "the Incomprehensible," a mystery transcending nature and language. The poem collapses in a self-surrender that augurs badly for the Imagination. Coleridge will go on to write several "poems of pure Imagination," but he will liberate himself into his potential all too rarely. *The Eolian Harp* shows why. The Imagination wishes to be indulged, and Coleridge feared the moral consequences of such indulgence.

Frost at Midnight

WITH *Dejection, The Ancient Mariner,* and *Kubla Khan, Frost at Midnight* shows Coleridge at his most impressive. *Frost at Midnight* is the masterpiece of the "conversation poems"; it gathers the virtues of the group, without diffuseness, into one form, and it shares with *Tintern Abbey* the distinction of inaugurating the major Wordsworthian myth of the memory as salvation. Indeed, Coleridge precedes Wordsworth. *Frost at Midnight* is dated February 1798; *Tintern Abbey,* we know from its title, was composed on July 13, 1798. The closing paragraph of Coleridge's poem, directed to his infant son, beginning "Therefore all seasons shall be sweet to thee," is a prelude to the closing lines of *Tintern Abbey,* addressed to Dorothy Wordsworth, where the poet asks nature's blessings on his sister:

> Therefore let the moon
> Shine on thee in thy solitary walk;
> And let the misty mountain-winds be free
> To blow against thee.

Frost at Midnight begins with Coleridge addressing himself to "abstruser musings." His cradled infant slumbers near him. The calm around the poet is so profound that its silentness vexes meditation:

> the thin blue flame
> Lies on my low-burnt fire, and quivers not;
> Only that film, which fluttered on the grate,
> Still flutters there, the sole unquiet thing.

The film on the grate was called, in popular superstition, a *stranger,* and was supposed to portend the arrival of some absent friend. The motion of the film makes it a companionable form to

the poet, for only they stir in this hush of nature. The puny flaps
of the film are like the motions of the poet's idling Spirit, which
both deprecates itself and seeks fellowship by finding echo or
mirror in the fluttering *stranger*. By doing so, the poet says of his
abstracter musings that they are turned into a toy. Yet this play-
fulness becomes vital, for the mind travels back in memory as it
idly broods on an identity with the film:

> But O! how oft,
> How oft, at school, with most believing mind,
> Presageful, have I gazed upon the bars,
> To watch that fluttering *stranger!*

One memory of school days leads to another in the same vein.
The child watching the grate dreams of his birthplace, and

> the old church-tower,
> Whose bells, the poor man's only music, rang
> From morn to evening, all the hot Fair-day,
> So sweetly, that they stirred and haunted me
> With a wild pleasure, falling on mine ear
> Most like articulate sounds of things to come!

This is a memory within a memory, and the poem goes back to
the initial recall. The child sleeps that night, dreaming of his sweet
birthplace. The next morning he broods, his eye fixed on his book
but seeing nothing of it and looking up each time the door opens:

> For still I hoped to see the *stranger's* face,
> Townsman, or aunt, or sister more beloved.

Carried back to his own childhood, the poet by an associative
progression is prepared to brood on the future of his slumbering
infant.

Coleridge, like Wordsworth, was country-born, but, unlike Wordsworth, he passed his school years in London. As he looks at the
sleeping infant Hartley, he utters a wishful prophecy that was to
find ironic fulfillment. His son, he hopes, will learn far other lore,
and in more natural scenes:

> For I was reared
> In the great city, pent 'mid cloisters dim,

> And saw nought lovely but the sky and stars.
> But *thou,* my babe! shalt wander like a breeze
> By lakes and sandy shores.

So Hartley was to wander, a vagrant in the Wordsworth country, a Solitary prematurely decayed. In a happier sense, as a Wordsworthian minor poet, he fulfilled the other half of the prophecy:

> so shalt thou see and hear
> The lovely shapes and sounds intelligible
> Of that eternal language, which thy God
> Utters, who from eternity doth teach
> Himself in all, and all things in himself.
> Great universal Teacher! he shall mould
> Thy spirit, and by giving make it ask.

Again we recognize the doctrine and sound of *Tintern Abbey,* anticipated but with a tremulous intensity, very unlike the primitive confidence Wordsworth at his best was to bring to the Coleridgean formulation of the religion of nature. The fierce epiphanies of Wordsworth are declared with the trumpetings of the prophet Amos, for whom judgment could run down like waters, and righteousness as a mighty stream. But something of an eternal child is in Coleridge (and in Hartley Coleridge after him), and a naïve sweetness graces *Frost at Midnight.* The end of *Tintern Abbey* has a deeper music than that of *Frost at Midnight,* but is not more moving than this:

> Therefore all seasons shall be sweet to thee,
> Whether the summer clothe the general earth
> With greenness, or the redbreast sit and sing
> Betwixt the tufts of snow on the bare branch
> Of mossy apple-tree, while the nigh thatch
> Smokes in the sun-thaw; whether the eave-drops fall
> Heard only in the trances of the blast,
> Or if the secret ministry of frost
> Shall hang them up in silent icicles,
> Quietly shining to the quiet Moon.

The poem comes full circle, back to its opening. The secret ministry of frost is analogous to the secret ministry of memory, for both bind together apparently disparate phenomena in an imaginative unity. The frost creates a surface both to receive and reflect the shining of the winter moon. Memory, moving by its overtly arbitrary but deeply designed associations, creates an identity between the mature poet and the child who is his ancestor, as well as with his own child. In this identity the poem comes into full being, with its own receiving and reflecting surfaces that mold the poet's and (he hopes) his son's spirits, and, by giving, make them ask who is the author of the gift. Wordsworth, in his prime years, would have given a phenomenological answer, and have been content to say Nature herself. In the more traditionally balanced *Frost at Midnight,* the answer is ontological, but the eternal language the Great Being is compelled to use is that of Nature, with her "lovely shapes and sounds intelligible."

The Nightingale

OF the poems in which Coleridge develops his "conversational thinking," the beautiful *Nightingale* (April 1798) is the only one to take the specific descriptive subtitle *A Conversation Poem.* The poem's activity begins in line 12 as the bird starts to sing. The first eleven lines perform the function of establishing the mood in which Coleridge addresses the silent friends, William and Dorothy Wordsworth, who accompany him. The day has reluctantly departed ("sullen light") and the night is unusually still and balmy. Coleridge is very content, grateful for the night's peace, and determined to find pleasure in all observable phenomena:

> and though the stars be dim,
> Yet let us think upon the vernal showers
> That gladden the green earth, and we shall find
> A pleasure in the dimness of the stars.

The point of this last, very lovely line is generalized in the subsequent denial of the traditionally sorrowful associations of the nightingale's music:

> In Nature there is nothing melancholy.

Nature's sweet voices are always full of love and joyance, and so it is the merry nightingale to whom the friends now listen. The bird of love has the same relationship to the moon that the aeolian harp has to the wind. When the moon is lost behind a cloud, there is a pause of silence,

> till the moon
> Emerging, hath awakened earth and sky
> With one sensation, and those wakeful birds
> Have all burst forth in choral minstrelsy,
> As if some sudden gale had swept at once
> A hundred airy harps!

Coleridge contrasts the moon's effect on the nightingales with its influence on his infant son. Once, when the child awoke in distress from a bad dream,

> I hurried with him to our orchard-plot,
> And he beheld the moon, and, hushed at once,
> Suspends his sobs, and laughs most silently,
> While his fair eyes, that swam with undropped tears,
> Did glitter in the yellow-moon-beam!

The nightingales are as passive as the aeolian harp; they utter the moon's music of natural love. The child's reaction is precisely opposite, because his Imagination is already an active principle, as active as the moon itself. He both reflects the moonlight in his eyes and sends forth a light of his own. As at the close of *Frost at Midnight,* the interchange of light is a sign of the Imagination's potency, and prepares the reader for the natural magic of moonlight in *The Ancient Mariner.*

2 *Natural Magic*

The Ancient Mariner

POETRY (and potentially its criticism) alone of all human talk need not be reductive. Coleridge in *The Ancient Mariner* tells a story that relates itself clearly to a major Romantic archetype, the

Wanderer, the man with the mark of Cain, or the mocker of Christ, who must expiate in a perpetual cycle of guilt and suffering, and whose torment is in excess of its usually obscure object and source. This archetype figures in Blake and in Keats, but is more basic to Wordsworth and Clare and Beddoes. In Coleridge, Byron, and Shelley it becomes something more, a personal myth so consuming that we hardly know whether to seek it first in the life or in the work.

The Ancient Mariner is in the tradition of the stories of Cain and of the Wandering Jew, but it does not reduce to them. It is a late manifestation of the Gothic Revival, and its first version is clearly to be related to the ballad of *The Wandering Jew* in Percy's *Reliques,* but its historical sources also tend to mislead us when we attempt to describe it in its own terms, which is the business of criticism.

The ancient Mariner, bright-eyed and compulsive, is a haunter of wedding feasts, and in a grim way he is the chanter of a prothalamium. Yet he does not address himself to bride or groom but to a gallant who is the bridegroom's next of kin. His story means most, he implies, when it is juxtaposed with the special joy of the wedding celebration, but it is not relevant to those being joined by a sacrament. Its proper audience is an unwilling one; its function is monitory. The message can only be relayed from a lurker at the threshold to a prospective sharer of the feast.

The world of the Mariner's voyage is purely visionary; the ship is driven by a storm toward the South Pole and into a realm simpler and more drastic than the natural world of experience. Into a sea of ice, where no living thing was to be seen, through the snow fog there comes suddenly a great sea bird, the albatross. Whatever its source, and Coleridge leaves this mysterious, the poem's albatross comes to the mariners as a free gift. They hail it in God's name as if it were human; they domesticate it with their food, which it has never eaten before; they play with it as if it were child or pet. Very directly they associate it with their luck, for now the ice splits, a south wind springs up, and they start the journey northward back to the ordinary word. The poem's first great event is suddenly placed before us; without apparent premeditation or conscious motive, the narrator murders the albatross.

The murder is a gratuitous act, but then so is the initial appearance of the bird. There is a tradition of seemingly motiveless malevolence that goes from Shakespeare's Iago (whom Coleridge saw as a tragic poet, manipulating men rather than words) and Milton's Satan to the protagonists of Poe, Melville, and Dostoevsky, and that appears in Gide, Camus, and other recent writers. The tradition begins with the demonic (tinged with Prometheanism), moves (in the later nineteenth century) into a vitalism crossed by the social image of man in revolt, and climaxes (in our own time) in a violence that yet confirms individual existence and so averts an absolute despair of self. Coleridge's mariner belongs to this tradition whose dark ancestors include Cain, the Wandering Jew, and the Judas whose act of betrayal is portrayed as a desperate assertion of freedom by Wilde, Yeats, and D. H. Lawrence.

This tradition's common denominator is that of a desperate assertion of self and a craving for a heightened sense of identity. This is what the Mariner brings about for himself, in a death-in-life purgatorial fashion; for his companions he brings only a terrible death and a mechanical life-in-death following his own partial redemption.

Several influential modern readings of *The Ancient Mariner* have attempted to baptize the poem by importing into it the notion of Original Sin and the myth of the Fall. But the Mariner is neither disobedient in his dire action nor altered in nature by its first effects. There is nothing in him to suggest the depravity of the natural heart, nor is the slaying of an albatross at all an adequate symbol of a lapse that demands expression in the language of theology. Coleridge in his *Table Talk* (May 31, 1830) felt the poem was already too overtly moral (thinking of the pious conclusion) and said of it:

> It ought to have had no more moral than the Arabian Nights' tale of the merchant's sitting down to eat dates by the side of a well, and throwing the shells aside, and lo! a genie starts up, and says he *must* kill the aforesaid merchant *because* one of the date shells had, it seems, put out the eye of the genie's son.

The Ancient Mariner seems to have just this peculiar moral logic; you shoot an albatross quite casually, as you might throw

aside a date shell. The tradition of the gratuitous crime also characterizes itself by its emphasis on the casual as opposed to the
causal. Lafcadio in *Les Caves du Vatican,* just before performing
his crime without a motive, says, "It's not so much about events
that I'm curious, as about myself." Lafcadio and the Mariner are
not (in advance) concerned about what ensues from an act; the
act for each becomes a bracketed phenomenon, *pure act,* detached
from motivation or consequences, and existent in itself. But the
Mariner learns not to bracket, and the poem would have us learn,
not where to throw our date shells, nor to love all creatures great
and small, but to connect all phenomena, acts and things, in the
fluid dissolve of the imagination:

> O! the one Life within us and abroad,
> Which meets all motion and becomes its soul.

Frequently noted by critics is the extraordinary passivity of the
Mariner. Wordsworth first said that the Mariner "does not act, but
is continually acted upon." Not only does the Mariner rarely act
(he shoots once, drinks his own blood once, so as to cry out that
he has seen a sail, and blesses once), but usually he expresses no
reaction to events.[32] Most of the strong emotional and moral statements in the poem are in Coleridge's frequently beautiful marginal
prose. The Mariner is merely an accurate observer, not a man of
any sensibility. Despite the wonder and terror of what befalls him,
he does not reach a height of emotional expression until Part IV
of the poem, and then is driven to it, fittingly, by *solitude.* Alone
with the dead men, and surrounded by the slime of subhuman life,
he wakens first into agony of soul, then into a sense of contrast
between the human and what is "beneath" it in the scale of being,
and finally into a startled awareness of unexpected beauty. The
crisis comes with moonrise on the seventh night of his lonely ordeal. The marginal prose meets the crisis with a beauty of expression which seems to touch at the limits of art:

> In his loneliness and fixedness he yearneth towards the
> journeying Moon, and the stars that still sojourn, yet still move
> onward; and every where the blue sky belongs to them, and is
> their appointed rest, and their native country and their own
> natural homes, which they enter unannounced, as lords that

are certainly expected and yet there is a silent joy at their arrival.

He can be saved only by translating this yearning from the moon and stars to what envelops his own loneliness and fixedness, by naturalizing himself in his surroundings and finding a joy that will intimate the one life he shares with the creatures of the great deep. The finest stanzas in the poem trace his transference of love from the moon and stars to "God's creatures of the great calm":

> The moving Moon went up the sky,
> And no where did abide:
> Softly she was going up,
> And a star or two beside—

> Her beams bemocked the sultry main,
> Like April hoar-frost spread;
> But where the ship's huge shadow lay,
> The charmèd water burnt alway
> A still and awful red.

> Beyond the shadow of the ship,
> I watched the water-snakes:
> They moved in tracks of shining white,
> And when they reared, the elfish light
> Fell off in hoary flakes.

The moon's beams *bemock* the ocean, because upon that rotting and still torrid surface (the moon is just rising and the heat of the tropical sun yet abides) an appearance of "April hoar-frost" is now spread. The light given by the water snakes is called elfish and is said to fall off "in hoary flakes." Moonlight and hoarfrost are an imaginative unity at the close of *Frost at Midnight;* they give and take light, to and from one another, and the light, like *Dejection's* fair luminous mist, is emblematic both of creative joy and of the One Life of the phenomenal universe.

The Mariner now sees the beauty and happiness of what he had characterized, not inaccurately, as slime:

> O happy living things! no tongue
> Their beauty might declare:
> A spring of love gushed from my heart,

And I blessed them unaware:
Sure my kind saint took pity on me,
And I blessed them unaware.

The self-same moment I could pray;
And from my neck so free
The Albatross fell off, and sank
Like lead into the sea.

His consciousness remains passive; he blesses them "unaware."
As a sacramental moment this is unique, even in Romantic poetry.
A less than ordinary man, never before alive to the sacramental
vision of nature as life, joy, love, suddenly declares the most elemental forms of life in nature to be joyous and deserving of his
affection. The slimy sea serpents are nearly as formless as the chaos
Coleridge is to dread in his late poems of "positive Negation,"
Limbo and *Ne Plus Ultra*. Yet these creatures have color and
beauty, they are alive, and "everything that lives is holy," as Blake
insisted. At this, its climactic point, *The Ancient Mariner* is the
most vital and imaginative achievement of Coleridge's poetry.
Here, for once, he places complete trust in his Imagination, and it
cannot fail him.

The Ancient Mariner is not, like *Kubla Khan,* a poem about
poetry. The shaping spirit, or Secondary Imagination, is not its
theme, though recently critics have tried for such a reading. The
Mariner's failure, and his subsequent salvation, is one of the Primary Imagination, "the repetition in the finite mind of the eternal
act of creation in the infinite I AM." God looked upon His Creation and saw that it was good. The Mariner has now first learned
to repeat in his very finite mind this eternal act of perception and
creation. This awakening certainly does not bring the whole soul
of this man into activity; the Mariner does not learn to order his
experience so as first to balance and then be free of it. He falls victim to it, and its eternal verbal repetition becomes his obsession.
Had the Mariner been a poet, he could have written the Rime he
incarnates. He has seen the truth, but the truth does not set him
free. He returns to life as a mere fundamentalist of the Primary
Imagination, endlessly repeating the story of his own salvation and
the one moral in it that he can understand:

> He prayeth best, who loveth best
> All things both great and small;
> For the dear God who loveth us,
> He made and loveth all.

The other moral is less simple, but quite as elemental. Coleridge has written the poem as an alternative reaction to the Mariner's experience, for that experience of purgation through love of the One Life is his own. The higher Imagination shapes truth; the lower merely takes it, through nature, from the Shaping Spirit of God. The poem celebrates the continued power of creative joy in its creator. But the poem also foreshadows the eventual fate of its creator, when the activity of the whole soul will yield to torpor. Coleridge as theologian and philosopher found more willing auditors than the Mariner did, but his quest came to duplicate that of his creation.

Christabel

CHRISTABEL is more a series of poems than it is a single fragment. Part I opens on an April midnight, chilly and in the light of a full moon, but the light is shrouded, and the moon looks both small and full. Christabel, Sir Leoline's child, described as a lovely lady, goes into the midnight wood to pray for her distant betrothed. Christabel's mother is dead; some say that her ghost haunts the castle. As Christabel prays beneath a huge oak tree, she hears a moan. She goes to the oak's other side and sees

> a damsel bright,
> Drest in a silken robe of white,
> That shadowy in the moonlight shone:
> The neck that made that white robe wan,
> Her stately neck, and arms were bare;
> Her blue-veined feet unsandal'd were,
> And wildly glittered here and there
> The gems entangled in her hair.

This damsel, Geraldine, is later revealed by the poem to be both sexually ambiguous and a vampire, but she has the only vitality contained in the poem's world. The work of Imagination in *Christabel* is to transform the crudity of evil into something beautiful, and to present a nightmare as if it were a fulfillment of desire. Nature in *Christabel* is absent, or depraved, or lacks will. A denial of life has brought a rapacious and disordered sexuality into a world that can neither contain nor effectually combat it. The poem's vividness and energy belong to Geraldine; Christabel comes to life only in torment or when under the vampire's spell. The poem, like *The Ancient Mariner*, is a ballad of the Imagination's revenge, in this case upon a repressive atmosphere that has impeded its free and autonomous functioning. The night world rebels against the evasions of consciousness, and to the frightened consciousness it takes on the appearance of the demonic.

Christabel's mother died giving birth to her only child. The girl's name indicates that her beauty has a particular innocence about it, being associated with the beauty of Christ. The Virgin Mary's name sounds through the poem, as the narrator continually and vainly calls upon her to protect Christabel from violation. Hovering closer is the ghost of Christabel's mother, haunting Geraldine, and providing another ineffectual safeguard.

The denial of life in the poem begins with Sir Leoline. The baron, since the death of his wife in bearing Christabel, has willfully sought death in life:

> Each matin bell, the Baron saith,
> Knells us back to a world of death.
> These words Sir Leoline first said,
> When he rose and found his lady dead:
> These words Sir Leoline will say
> Many a morn to his dying day!

This is the framing border of Christabel's world, a deathly bound brought to being by the child's birth. Against this background we can see more clearly the pattern of seduction by which Geraldine entraps her half-willing victim. She begins by twice begging Christabel to "stretch forth thy hand," without fear, and thus comfort a supposedly distressed maiden.

Christabel herself makes the next advance, in absolute innocence yet pragmatically seductive:

> All our household are at rest,
> The hall as silent as the cell;
> Sir Leoline is weak in health,
> And may not well awakened be,
> But we will move as if in stealth,
> And I beseech your courtesy,
> This night, to share your couch with me.

The motive is overtly innocent charity, but in this context the
extremes of innocence and evil meet as one. "As if" qualifies but
does not negate the "move in stealth," as victim and ravisher find
a single purpose, latent in one, manifest in the other. Geraldine
cannot cross the threshold, which probably is charmed against her,
so it is Christabel who actively introduces evil into the castle by
lifting the vampire over.

As they pass through the castle, Christabel is already under the
spell of Geraldine's eyes, and neglects the presages of evil: Geraldine's failure to praise the Virgin, the howling of the old mastiff
in her sleep out in the cold moonshine, the sudden fit of flame
that darts out of a dying brand. Yet Christabel can still see one
other thing, and reacts curiously:

> And Christabel saw the lady's eye,
> And nothing else saw she thereby,
> Save the boss of the shield of Sir Leoline tall,
> Which hung in a murky old niche in the wall.
> O softly tread, said Christabel,
> My father seldom sleepeth well.

Christabel unrobes herself first, "and lay down in her loveliness."
What she sees when Geraldine reveals herself, Coleridge cannot
bring himself to say:

> Behold! her bosom and half her side—
> A sight to dream of, not to tell!

As Geraldine is both sorceress and serpent, and also is divided
against herself sexually, we can speculate fairly accurately upon
what Coleridge will not tell. At the least, what Geraldine calls
"this mark of my shame, this seal of my sorrow" must be the traditional affliction of the sorceress, a withered, lean bosom and side,

of ghastly hue and possibly scaly. Whatever she be, she does manifest a struggle with self before she embraces Christabel:

> Ah! what a stricken look was hers!
> Deep from within she seems half-way
> To lift some weight with sick assay,
> And eyes the maid and seeks delay;
> Then suddenly, as one defied,
> Collects herself in scorn and pride,
> And lay down by the Maiden's side!—
> And in her arms the maid she took.

Even as she takes Christabel, Geraldine casts a spell of partial
forgetfulness upon the girl. Christabel will remember only that she
found a distressed lady in the woods, and brought her home for
shelter.

The remainder of the fragmentary poem or poems is obscure in
direction. Geraldine has "had her will," yet as she slumbers with
Christabel, she seems "as a mother with her child." Christabel,
though she weeps on wakening from her trance, yet "seems to smile
as infants at a sudden light." Her awakening to an experience of
evil has brought both pleasure and pain.

Geraldine completes her conquest by a verbal seduction of Sir
Leoline, whose dormant friendship for her supposed father is re-
awakened by the spell of her eyes and speech. He is deceived despite
both Christabel's tortured and cryptic request that he send Geraldine away, and by the warning of his attendant bard. The bard,
Bracy, has dreamed that the dove, Christabel, has been attacked:

> I saw a bright green snake
> Coiled around its wings and neck.
> Green as the herbs on which it couched,
> Close by the dove's its head it crouched;
> And with the dove it heaves and stirs.
> Swelling its neck as she swelled hers!

The warnings are disregarded, and the baron, despite his daughter's appeal in the name of her dead mother, turns from his own
sweet maid, and leads forth the lady Geraldine. With this apparent
triumph of evil, the narrative proper ends. Coleridge added a very

significant passage to his unfinished poem a year later, in 1801. Though it has no immediately apparent relevance to the story, a thematic hint in it can take us to the heart of *Christabel*'s enigmatic meanings. The passage seems to be based upon the poet's little son, Hartley:

> A little child, a limber elf,
> Singing, dancing to itself,
> A fairy thing with red round cheeks,
> That always finds, and never seeks,
> Makes such a vision to the sight
> As fills a father's eyes with light;
> And pleasures flow in so thick and fast
> Upon his heart, that he at last
> Must needs express his love's excess
> With words of unmeant bitterness.
> Perhaps 'tis pretty to force together
> Thoughts so all unlike each other;
> To mutter and mock a broken charm,
> To dally with wrong that does no harm,
> Perhaps 'tis tender too and pretty
> At each wild word to feel within
> A sweet recoil of love and pity.
> And what, if in a world of sin
> (O sorrow and shame should this be true!)
> Such giddiness of heart and brain
> Comes seldom save from rage and pain,
> So talks as it's most used to do.

As psychological observation of a kind of natural perversity, this is acute. Its relation to *Christabel* is that this is Coleridge's apologia for writing that poem, for so nearly allying a sublime innocence and an obscene evil. The father, watching his dancing child, is so burdened with an excess of love that he involuntarily expresses his love by bitterness. This is the perversity of the natural heart, which delights also in blaspheming the recesses of the sacred. There is a "metaphysical" prettiness in forcing together thoughts so unlike each other (Coleridge may be thinking of Dr. Johnson's observations on the school of Donne in his *Life of Cowley*). To write a poem like *Christabel,* or unfairly reprove a child, is "to dally with wrong that does no harm," to work off a demonic impulse without resorting to real and active evil. The aesthetics of profanation are subtly allied to a kind of therapy. At each wild word, whether to the young Hartley, or written about the violation of Christabel, the poet feels "a sweet recoil of love and pity." In a world imperfect, with a fallen consciousness of sin, the ecstasy of such aesthetic emotions as love and pity may result only from rage and pain, as one strong emotion provokes its contrary.

This throws a strange light back upon the poem. *The Ancient Mariner* is a purgatorial work, but *Christabel* seems to offer no *catharsis,* no release from the intense suffering it so vividly depicts, the fear it seeks to arouse. Wordsworth and Blake take us into desolations, and in great moments of sudden release reveal realities that transform the dreariness and so give us intense intimations of our own freedom, of a liberation from all that impedes the human. The strong Imagination of Coleridge is hag-ridden by horrors, and "the night-mare and her ninefold" ride over his most luminous visions. Like Blake, Coleridge more than the other English Romantics explores the night world, and distrusts nature partly because of it. Where Blake defied the demonic and sought to use it for his apocalyptic ends, Coleridge indulged his Imagination by it and came to distrust Imagination in consequence.

Kubla Khan

KUBLA KHAN is a poem of self-recognition, in which the figure of the youth as virile poet is finally identified with the poem's speaker. Behind Coleridge's poem is Collins' masterpiece of a poet's incarnation, the *Ode on the Poetical Character,* and the dark fates of Collins himself, the young Chatterton, Smart, and the other doomed bards of sensibility. These are the rich-haired youths of Morn, Apollo sacrifices who precede Coleridge in his appearance with flashing eyes and floating hair in the last lines of *Kubla Khan.* In Blake's myth such a youth is a form of the rising Orc, the fiery dawn of a new Beulah or increase in sensual fulfillment, but an Adonis as well as an Apollo, a dawn that is merely cyclic in nature, an outburst of energy in which the organic and the creative are uneasily allied. The young poets of *Alastor* and *Endymion,* with their dark and glorious destinies, and their sense of both embodying nature and yet being imprisoned by it, are later forms of Coleridge's myth. The old poet of *Sailing to Byzantium* with his deliberate voyage out of nature is the fitting dying fall for the Romantic tradition of tragic poetic self-recognition.

Internally, *Kubla Khan* is no fragment but a vision of creation and destruction, each complete. It is not quite a "poem about the act of poetic creation," for it contains that theme as one element in a more varied unity, just as Yeats's *Byzantium* does.

Kubla Khan and Xanadu belong to the *given* of the poem; we need to accept them without asking why *this* potentate or *this* place. Kubla has power and can command magnificence; that is enough. He builds a dome of pleasure for himself, as the rulers of Byzantium built a greater dome to honor God. But the Byzantine dome, while apt for Yeats's purposes, is too theological for Coleridge's poem. Kubla builds the dome for himself, and the poet with his music will build a dome in air, matching and at length overgoing the mightiest of human material power. The orthodox censor in Coleridge gives him the remote dome in Xanadu, and avoids the issue of the poet's relative sanctity against more than natural verities.

Kubla and we can visualize the following phenomena intimately associated: the dome (with sunlight upon it), the dome's shadow floating midway upon the waves of the seething, forced-up river; the fountain geyser with its hurling rocks, just next to the dome; and the exposed icy caverns beneath, from which the fountain has momentarily removed the covering earth. The effect is apocalyptic, for what is revealed is a natural miracle:

> It was a miracle of rare device,
> A sunny pleasure-dome with caves of ice!

The river, now raised again, is sacred. The chasm is holy and enchanted, and is associated with waning moonlight. The river comes up as the fountain before it settles down again, and so the fountain is sacred too, and the fragments of earth flung up in it take on the orderly associations of the sacred; they are dancing rocks. The exposed caverns are icy; the dome is sunny. What is exposed is holy; what was built for exposure is representative of a perfect pleasure, the dome being necessarily a perfect hemisphere.

At the midpoint of the momentarily flung-up river we see and hear, together, the extraordinary sight of the shadow of the pleasure dome, and the mingled music of the bursting fountain and the exposed underground current. As the contraries of sun and moon, dome and cavern, light and dark, heat and ice meet, Kubla hears the voices of the dead speaking to the living within a scene of peace and prophesying war. The momentary upheaval itself is the contrary and answer of nature to Kubla's decree of the power of art. The fountain rises suddenly like Blake's wind of Beulah or Shelley's West Wind, to create and destroy, to bring sun and ice together. The very sign of the fountain's potential for destruction is also an emblem of "chaffy grain beneath the thresher's flail," and the sexual intimations of the poem are undeniable, though they are subordinated to and subsumed by the more general theme of creation and destruction.

Kubla had not sought the balance or reconciliation of opposites which Coleridge and Blake alike saw as the mark of the creative imagination, but momentarily his dome and the bursting fountain together do present a vision of such a balance; the landscape becomes a poem, and the imagination has its manifestation. The triumphal chant that follows is Coleridge's assertion that he as poet can build a finer dome and a more abiding paradise than Kubla's, and one that would have both convex heat and concave ice without the necessity of earthquake. Coleridge's music would be "loud and long"; Kubla's is momentary.

The earthly paradise traditionally takes one of its alternate placings in Abyssinia. The crucial passage here is in *Paradise Lost:*

> Mount *Amara,* though this by some suppos'd
> True Paradise under the *Ethiop* Line
> By *Nilus* head, enclos'd with shining Rock.   [IV, 281–283]

This is Coleridge's Mount Abora, and his Abyssinian maid, in singing of it, is celebrating Paradise. Once the poet saw her in vision; if he now revives *within* himself her song of Eden he will enter a state of such deep delight

> That with music loud and long,
> I would build that dome in air,
> That sunny dome! those caves of ice!

He would rival Kubla's decreed dome, and also produce the imaginative miracle of the juxtaposed contraries, and without the equivocal aid of the paradoxical upheaval that simultaneously creates and threatens the destruction of the "rare device." For this is the potential of the poetic imagination, to create more lastingly than even nature and Art can do together. And could he do this, he would be a reincarnation of the young Apollo. Those who heard his song would *see* his visionary creation, for that is the inventive power of poetry. And they would grant him the awe due to the youth who has eaten the fruit and drunk the milk of the Eden forbidden to them, or open only through vicarious participation in the poet's vision:

> And all who heard should see them there,
> And all should cry, Beware! Beware!
> His flashing eyes, his floating hair!
> Weave a circle round him thrice,
> And close your eyes with holy dread,
> For he on honey-dew hath fed,
> And drunk the milk of Paradise.

3   *Wisdom and Dejection*

France: An Ode

SHELLEY told Byron that the best modern ode was Coleridge's *France: An Ode,* and certainly he benefited by the poem when he surpassed it with his *Ode to the West Wind,* for Shelley's ode derives its fundamental pattern from Coleridge's. Coleridge begins with a direct invocation to clouds, waves, and woods. They are free, and the woods in particular make "a solemn music of the wind." Just as these phenomena of nature "yield homage only to eternal laws," so the poet, inspired by them, worships only "the spirit of divinest Liberty."

France: An Ode, after this vehement invocation, traces the course of Blake's Orc cycle from Prometheus to Satan, from Orc to Urizen, from France the enlightener to France the terror, and finally to a tyrant no longer to be called France. The Titaness, "in wrath her giant-limbs upreared," goes out of control in her compulsive, organic cycle. Coleridge, writing in February 1798, anticipates Blake and Wordsworth in bidding the sleepers awake, in warning that man in revolt is inadequate if he is bound by minimal sense perception:

> The Sensual and the Dark rebel in vain,
> Slaves by their own compulsion!

The poet himself confesses that he has pursued liberty many a weary hour, but profitlessly. For

> Thou speedest on thy subtle pinions,
> The guide of homeless winds, and playmate of the waves!
> And there I felt thee!—on that sea-cliff's verge,
>   Whose pines, scarce travelled by the breeze above,
> Had made one murmur with the distant surge!
> Yes, while I stood and gazed, my temples bare,
> And shot my being through earth, sea, and air,
>   Possessing all things with intensest love,
> O Liberty! my spirit felt thee there.

This passage is Byronic as well as Shelleyan, and as a picture suggests characteristic Romantic art, a John Martin or a Caspar David Friedrich. The poet stands, bareheaded, on a sea cliff's verge, fronting the rising wind of Liberty. The pines, barely touched as yet by the breeze, are already mingling their measure with the waves in sympathy. Like the pines, Coleridge transcends himself, and shoots his being through forest, waves, and clouds. So transcended, by ceasing to possess himself, he possesses all things, and in the intense love that he now shares without self-appropriation he is able to feel Liberty. The poem's final contrast is between his creative and self-denying imaginative energy, and the destructive, self-aggrandizing merely organic energy of the self-ruined France.

Dejection: An Ode

THERE is only one voice in *Dejection: An Ode*. In this poem Coleridge does not argue with himself, though he has need to do so. But the voice is turned against itself with an intensity that only the greatest poets have been able to bring over into language. The ode's continuity as argument presents no problems; *Dejection* overtly rejects the dialectic of Wordsworth's memory-as-salvation. The logic of *Dejection* is that human process is irreversible: imaginative loss is permanent, and nature intimates to us our own mortality always.

The puzzle of *Dejection* is why and how it rejects *as imaginative argument* the Wordsworthian myth. The myth was initially a Coleridgean creation, in the "conversation poems" of 1795–1798, where it is beautifully stated, though always with misgivings. The "why" of rejection belongs to a study of how Coleridge's poetry itself discourses on poetic limits. The "how" is a lesson in the Romantic uses of self-directed argument.

The epigraph to Wordsworth's *Intimations* ode is a motto of natural piety. Against its rainbow Coleridge sets the natural emblem most in opposition: the new moon, with the old moon in its arms. In *Dejection* the storm is predicted, comes on, and finally is "but a mountain-birth," sudden and soon over. The poem's new moon is the Wordsworth surrogate, "Dear Lady! friend devoutest of my choice"; its old moon, Coleridge himself. The principal difference, then, between the two odes is that Wordsworth uses one protagonist passing though several states of being while Coleridge undertakes the lesser imaginative task and risks pathos by doubling the human element yet keeping the voice single. The poem's speaker is doomed to imaginative death; all hope for joy devolves upon the "Lady."

By evading individual progression-through-contraries, Coleridge has no ostensible need for poetic logic. But this evasion could not in itself make a poem of any value; flat personal despair joined to altruism and benevolence is hardly a formula for poetic power. *Dejection* is imaginatively impressive because Coleridge does not succeed in altogether distinguishing himself from the Lady whose joy he celebrates. The curious and yet extraordinarily successful effect is like that of a saint seeking to disavow Christian doctrine by avowing its efficacy for others, less sinful than himself.

Study of *Dejection: An Ode* can well begin backwards, with a consideration of the lines that enable the poem to end on the word "rejoice":

> To her may all things live, from pole to pole,
> Their life the eddying of her living soul!

The image of the eddy is the summary figure of the poem: the flux of nature throughout has prepared for it. Joy, as the effluence of Life, overflows as sound, light, cloud, shower; as a composite luminous and melodic mist of the soul; now solid, now liquid, now vaporous, now pure light or pure sound. This is repetitious summary, but the poem's repetitiveness is meaningful here. The myth of Wordsworth's Child is being rejected; the glory comes and goes, without relation to infancy, childhood, youth, maturity. The progression is simply linear and it is irreversible:

> There was a time when, though my path was rough,
>   This joy within me dallied with distress,
> And all misfortunes were but as the stuff
>   Whence Fancy made me dreams of happiness:
> For hope grew round me, like the twining vine,
> And fruits, and foliage, not my own, seemed mine.
> But now afflictions bow me down to earth.

The eddy has stopped its pole-to-pole movement; the cycle of joy is over. Taken literally, Coleridge's myth of dejection is a bizarre reinforcement of a single stage in the poetic argument of *Resolution and Independence:*

> We poets in our youth begin in gladness,
> But thereof comes in the end despondency and madness.

If *Dejection* had only its Stanzas I to VI and its climactic in Stanza VIII, it could not be defended from the charge of pathos. The usually evaded Stanza VII, which is generally considered a transitional mood piece, controls the poem's logic and equips it to avoid self-indulgence. The structure of the poem is in two units: Stanzas I, VII, VIII, and Stanzas II–VI. The first group are respectively devoted to the pre-storm calm, the storm itself, and the subsequent calm, which is analogous to the peace at the end of a formalized tragedy. The middle stanzas are argument, between Coleridge-as-Wordsworthian and Coleridge-in-dejection, with the latter dialectically triumphant. The connecting unit between the groups opens Stanza vii, in which the "viper thoughts" of ii–vi are dismissed as "Reality's dark dream":

> I turn from you, and listen to the wind,
> Which long has raved unnoticed.

As he listens to the wind, he resolves his poem. The resolution is purely dialectical in that the stanza offers a set of assumptions that *include* the opposing Wordsworthian and Coleridgean views on the relationship between external nature and the poet's creative joy. Certainly the resolution is indirect, and perhaps too ingenious. But the curious seventh stanza cannot be ignored as an embarrassing digression; it is the crisis of the poem, akin to the silence between the eighth and ninth stanzas of the *Intimations* ode. There the dialectic rises to poetic finality because it is a dialectic of discourse itself. The conflict of discourse and silence is resolved in favor of silence, with the result that the discourse, when it begins again, can move in reverse and state the contrary of the preceding stanzas.

Part of the functional obscurity of Coleridge's Stanza vii is its reference to the child as Otway might present her, where we would expect one of the solitary creatures of Wordsworth's poetry. The problem here is merely a genetic one, related to the successive "Edmund" and "Lady" substitutions for Wordsworth in the *Dejection* ode. Originally Coleridge had written: "As William's self had made the tender Lay." This vanished together with "A boat becalm'd! dear William's Sky Canoe" after the present line 36 of the ode, identifying the crescent moon with the visionary sky-boat of *Peter Bell*. With this went Coleridge's "I too will crown me with a Coronal" in direct answer to Wordsworth's "My heart hath its coronal," also vanished from the final version. Otway, like Chatterton, was a figure of Romantic myth: the poet as hungry outcast in the storm of organized society. Any poet of the time who cited either Chatterton or Otway can be assumed to be speaking of himself in his exemplary role. The lost child of Stanza vii could easily be Wordsworth's Lucy Gray, or Blake's Little Girl Lost, without the natural piety of the one or the cyclic function of the other.

The tone of Stanza VII is complex, for it presents the Wind as a bad actor, overplaying, or a worse poet, raving bombast. The aeolian harp is not the fit instrument for this Wind, as the harp is needlessly subtle, in itself too bare of easily negative associations. The Wind's song is unnaturally terrible: "worse than wintry." But the analogue to the Wind's song is what has been spoken while the song "long has raved unnoticed," that is, Stanzas II–VI of Coleridge's ode, stanzas "perfect in all tragic sounds," written by a poet "e'en to frenzy bold."

The aeolian harp sends forth a diminishing series of unhappy ravings, toning down from torture to rout to losing one's way, "a Tale of less affright," a "tender lay," and one that is "tempered with delight." But where is the "delight" in Coleridge's citation of the tale?

> 'Tis of a little child
> Upon a lonesome wild,
> Not far from home, but she hath lost her way:
> And now moans low in bitter grief and fear,
> And now screams loud, and hopes to make her mother hear.

The child does not find its way home in Coleridge's poem. And yet this is the agency of resolution in the poem's emergence from conflict. The poet in his last stanza keeps vigil far from sleep, but his vigil is in some way not specified an atonement for his friend, who will awaken from a gentle sleep lifted in spirit and attuned in voice by joy. The descent of the saving and shaping Spirit in that blessed sleep is announced in the phrase "with wings of healing." Coleridge has rejected the myth of Wordsworth's salvation, and yet he avers that Wordsworth is saved. The puzzle can be summarized in the question: what is involved in the "thus" that opens the poem's last line?

> Thus mayest thou ever, evermore rejoice.

Our only evidence for a reply is either *in* the final stanza, or in that and its relationship to the preceding "lost child" stanza. As in the *Intimations* ode, the dialectic turns over *between* the stanzas; the overt continuity is a puzzle to the Corporeal Understanding but a challenge to the Intellectual Powers, to employ Blake's characterization of the nature of Vision, not Allegory. The Intellectual

Powers are the imagination, and the imagination, assuming the perfect unity of *Dejection* as a work of art, goes to work upon the problem of continuity here by pondering the implications of the perfect unity of Stanza VIII with the remainder of the poem.

That unity is necessarily imagistic as well as argumentative, but to separate unities so is to create only another cloven fiction. What we have in *Dejection* could be studied as an imagistic dialectic or a dialectical image, the eddy and its widely assorted components. The eddy is, in the poem, inseparably both image and argument. As image it comprehends (as Abrams demonstrates) all of the subordinate imagery of the poem. As argument, it *is* the poem, or, more precisely, the poem's partially concealed emblem. The eddying movement of joy in the flux of nature is a cyclic signature of all things, both in *Dejection* and in *Intimations*. But in Wordsworth the signature is distorted, with more powerful poetic results than Coleridge obtains by his clean comprehensiveness of imagistic presentation.

In Wordsworth, the eddy is broken twice, once at the pole of nature, and once at the pole of Man. After the first break, nature serves as a kindly nurse or foster mother, until the movement of joy can be (partially) restored. The second break, at Man's pole, takes place in the sleep of death that the sensual and proud, that poor, loveless, ever-anxious crowd, enjoy as best they can when the true joy of the creation of self is gone. The composing of the *Intimations* ode is the awakening from this sleep of death, the flowing-on again of the joyous waters of continuity.

Coleridge's imaginative severity, his heightened sense of poetic limits, gives us a stricter argument and a more confined image. The movement breaks at only one pole, man's, because the movement can emanate out only from man. For

> we receive but what we give,
> And in our life alone does Nature live.

Out of the soul alone eddies the mysterious element-of-elements, self-creating joy, to borrow John Clare's phrase. Joy, the Imagination itself, the great I Am, the word of primal creation, issues forth as a light, a glory, a fair, luminous cloud, an ultimate voice which is the strong music of the soul. The light, glory, and luminous cloud are what the child Wordsworth *saw;* the potent music is what he *heard.* The "fountain-light of all our day," a "master-light of all our seeing," is how the *Intimations* ode finally summarizes them.

In his sixth stanza Coleridge says that the visitations of his affliction, his acedia, suspend his shaping spirit of Imagination: suspend, not abolish. Suspension is reinforced by "almost" as a qualifier in the stanza's last line. Joy still moves out of Coleridge, but fitfully; the eddy is haphazard, has lost its perfection of movement.

In Stanza VII, when Coleridge sends these "viper thoughts" from him, he chooses the healing power of Wordsworth's *Lucy Gray* as being appropriate for his state. He accepts it as comfort, where he rejects the consolation of *Intimations.* But his Lucy is hardly Wordsworth's. Coleridge's follows the phrasing of one of his letters to Poole; Wordsworth's neither moans low nor screams loud. Before being lost, Lucy is as blithe as the mountain roe. After her absorption into nature (or, more accurately, her absorption of nature into her) we have a myth:

> —Yet some maintain that to this day
> She is a living child;
> That you may see sweet Lucy Gray
> Upon the lonesome wild.
> O'er rough and smooth she trips along,
> And never looks behind;
> And sings a solitary song
> That whistles in the wind.

The final touch is the poem's initial affirmation; Wordsworth himself has *seen* her. Coleridge's odd tribute is to supply the poem's missing middle, and then to accept the given of it, without incorporating any trace of the *textus receptus* in his final version of *Dejection.* But the reference is there, and the reference does its work. Lucy's absorption is a proof of the imaginative finality of the eddy. Joy survives, though some of us do not, not wholly. And yet we all of us survive, some only partially, in it. Which, by a "commodious vicus of recirculation," takes us back to *Dejection*'s final stanza again.

The *Intimations* ode ends by celebrating "the human heart by which we live." The Wordsworth Lady in *Dejection*'s climax is to rise "with light heart," lifted by joy, attuned by it in voice. All things will live "to her"; for their life literally will be the pole-to-pole eddying of her living and creative soul. The unspoken question, or reservation, is in the missing "but to me?" The grief of Lucy Gray is absorbed into the eddy of creativity as thoroughly as if it had never been. But the Coleridgean lost child and the ruined man, blasted at the roots, are not to be subsumed by poetry. Wordsworth is saved, not by his own myth, as he avers, but because he is a "simple spirit, guided from above." Coleridge's passionate undersong, poised dialectically against the serenity of his poem's resolution, evidences that his comparative damnation came because he lacked both Wordsworth's guidance (egotism, as we call it now) and Wordsworth's saving simplicity. Coleridge could not be a fanatic, even of the Imagination.

To William Wordsworth

THE conversation poem *To William Wordsworth* is Coleridge's immediate reply to having heard Wordsworth read the entire *Prelude* aloud to him during January 1807. On the night Wordsworth finished, January 7, Coleridge composed the greater part of his beautiful but ambiguous tribute to

> what within the mind
> By vital breathings secret as the soul
> Of vernal growth, oft quickens in the heart
> Thoughts all too deep for words.

The reference to the final line of the *Intimations* ode attaches this poem to the *Dejection* ode as well. Indeed, the debate of *Dejection* is carried on here again, five years after the earlier poem. Coleridge says that *The Prelude*'s theme is

> of moments awful,
> Now in thy inner life, and now abroad,
> When power streamed from thee, and thy soul received
> The light reflected, as a light bestowed.

We receive but what we give, is the way Coleridge previously had phrased this sad truth. But the tone is different now. Coleridge both praises Wordsworth's power and implies that Wordsworth is deluded in assigning the power to nature. This curious double emphasis is carried through the poem, but in varying and disguised forms.

Coleridge praises *The Prelude* as being "more than historic," a "prophetic" poem dealing with "the building up of a Human Spirit," a high theme that Wordsworth has the distinction of being the first to sing aright. He emphasizes, rather more than Wordsworth does, the mystery of the subject. Wordsworth sees overt manifestations, both in nature and in his own inner life. Coleridge speaks of "vital breathings secret as the soul of vernal growth"; nature and Man are parallel mysteries. The shift from Wordsworth's thoughts too deep for tears to Coleridge's thoughts too deep for words is part of the same pattern. It is as though Coleridge desires to replace the naturalist in Wordsworth by a premature mystic.

When Coleridge turns to Wordsworth and the Revolution, his emphasis again results in a subtle distortion of Wordsworth's doctrine and poem. *The Prelude*'s crisis is slighted in this account of it:

> —Of that dear Hope afflicted and struck down,
> So summoned homeward, thenceforth calm and sure
> From the dread watch-tower of man's absolute self,
> With light unwaning on her eyes, to look
> Far on—herself a glory to behold,
> The Angel of the vision.

Poor Hope begins as a revolutionary humanist in this passage, but is baptized in the course of it, and ends an Angel. Wordsworth's hope is revived by memory, by spots of time and their consequences. Coleridge completes his revision of *The Prelude* by deftly importing the *Ode to Duty* into it:

> Then (last strain)
> Of Duty, chosen Laws controlling choice,
> Action and joy.

The true glory of the 1805 *Prelude* is that the soul is still an impulse to herself as the poem closes. It was just afterwards that Wordsworth supplicated for a new control, and composed the palinode of *Peele Castle*. The chastened Coleridge, himself somewhat broken, is rather too quick to welcome deviations from the religion of nature.

More extraordinary is Coleridge's complex emotional reaction to his friend's achievement:

> Ah! as I listened with a heart forlorn,
> The pulses of my being beat anew:
> And even as Life returns upon the drowned,
> Life's joy rekindling roused a throng of pains.

The pains, not the joy, dominate the lines that follow. Coleridge feels keen pangs of love for Wordsworth, but they awaken in him with the turbulent outcry of a weeping babe. As Coleridge apprehends his friend's achievement (and his own part in it) he reproaches himself for his own failure:

> Sense of past Youth, and Manhood come in vain,
> And Genius given, and Knowledge won in vain;
> And all which I had culled in wood-walks wild,
> And all which patient toil had reared, and all,
> Commune with thee had opened out—but flowers
> Strewed on my corse, and borne upon my bier
> In the same coffin, for the self-same grave!

The decorum of including this in a poem of ostensible tribute is strange. Sense of past youth, the cullings of "wood-walks wild," the natural gift of genius, the liberation of communion with another: these are all the themes of *The Prelude*. The implication of Coleridge's lines is: where is *my* poem on the growth of my own mind?

Coleridge attempts to check his lament, but again his diction betrays his sense of being overthrown upon his own ground:

> That way no more! and ill beseems it me,
> Who came a welcomer in herald's guise,
> Singing of Glory, and Futurity,
> To wander back on such unhealthful road,
> Plucking the poisons of self-harm! And ill
> Such intertwine beseems triumphal wreaths
> Strew'd before thy advancing!

This must have been a very uncomfortable poem for Wordsworth to read. Coleridge wanders back as Wordsworth advances. The only two activities possible for Coleridge are either to pluck the poisons of self-harm on the now unhealthful road of memory, or else to

strew triumphal wreaths before his friend. Another three years were
to pass; then the inevitable quarrel came.

The final sections of *To William Wordsworth* are profoundly
moving, for in them Coleridge, with immense effort, breaks out of
his selfhood communings, and achieves a sense of another. Though
he still refers to his past mind as "nobler" than his present, and
speaks of himself as listening to Wordsworth's reading "like a devout child" with passive soul, he does begin to manifest a revival
of sensibility, an end to torpor and self-pity:

> by thy various strain
> Driven as in surges now beneath the stars,
> With momentary stars of my own birth,
> Fair constellated foam, still darting off
> Into the darkness; now a tranquil sea,
> Outspread and bright, yet swelling to the moon.

Coleridge, in this passage, is compared to the sea; Wordsworth's
poem to a wind. The poem drives Coleridge along at certain moments as the wind causes the ocean to surge. The aroused Coleridge
both moves beneath the stars, symbols here of creativity, and momentarily creates his own stars, which dart off into the oceanic
darkness. In a very brilliant phrase, "fair constellated foam," the
stars are seen as a direct effluence from Coleridge's own being, the
foam on the waves of his surging consciousness. Even when not so
active, he is still, under the influence of Wordsworth's oral delivery,
a tranquil sea, outspread and bright, receptive to natural influences
and swelling to the moon. The sexual element in the passage ought
not to be avoided; it is so manifestly there. Coleridge had always
insisted that Wordsworth's genius was more masculine than that of
any other poet, and Coleridge's own Imagination tends to be feminine, as a close reading of *Christabel* ought to make clear. Wordsworth's account of nature is that of a lover describing his mistress.
Coleridge's nature is less of a Muse, and blends at last into the male
Godhead of Hebraic and Christian tradition. In this poem, which
joins *Dejection* as a prophecy of the crisis between Wordsworth and
Coleridge, *Dejection*'s argument with the *Intimations* ode comes to
a climax. Wordsworth's is the male dream of a perpetually given
grace, a generous presence of love and beauty which cannot cease.
Coleridge's is a reduced vision of reality; we get back what we give,

and need more love than we can hope to get, for we need more than we can give.

For Coleridge, Wordsworth is still "my comforter and guide," strong in himself, and powerful enough to give his friend strength. When the reading is done, and Coleridge's tributary poem ends also, the dependent poet is lost in imaginative reverie:

> Scarce conscious, and yet conscious of its close
> I sate, my being blended in one thought
> (Thought was it? or aspiration? or resolve?)
> Absorbed, yet hanging still upon the sound—
> And when I rose, I found myself in prayer.

The one thought, probably only an aspiration, but hopefully a resolve, is the thought of emulation, and the prayer is for a release of imaginative power. But the closing line is tribute also; to have participated in *The Prelude* is to have found in poetry a more than superfluous means of grace.

4 *Positive Negation*

Limbo

THE poem responding to *The Prelude* is Coleridge's last meditation in the mode that his "conversation poems" had pioneered. After January 1807 he bade farewell to nature as a muse. The sonnet *To Nature* may be as late as 1820 in composition, but its tone is altogether defensive and nostalgic:

> It may indeed be phantasy, when I
>   Essay to draw from all created things
>   Deep, heartfelt, inward joy that closely clings;
> And trace in leaves and flowers that round me lie
> Lessons of love and earnest piety.

This is at a dead end of vision. The poet can be only mildly defiant, and seek to justify nature by attaching her for sanction to

God as a "poor sacrifice" to the higher sacramentalism. Sometime about 1817, Coleridge scribbled a nightmare-like fragment in a notebook, and called it *Limbo*. The flight from nature leads to an Ulro as frightening as Blake's state of negations:

> The sole true Something—This! In Limbo's Den
> It frightens Ghosts, as here Ghosts frighten men.
> Thence cross'd unseiz'd—and shall some fated hour
> Be pulveris'd by Demogorgon's power,
> And given as poison to annihilate souls.

The substance of substances, or "sole true Something" in *Dejection: An Ode* was still "this light, this glory, this fair luminous mist." Now Coleridge is on the other side of dejection, in a den of quietude which knows an essence of annihilation. Ghosts dwell in Limbo, a state whose very name (Latin *limbus*) means border or edge, and where no judgment is possible, and non-being reigns. "The sole true Something," the dread substanceless substance, frightens ghosts in Limbo, as ghosts frighten us here. The "Thence cross'd unseiz'd" refers to the Acheron, the river in Hades over which Charon the boatman ferries the dead. In lines crossed out of the fragment, Coleridge says that the dread thing skimmed in the wake of Charon's boat and mocked his demand for a farthing fare. It can cross the gulf between existence and non-existence, for it has attributes both of what is and of what is not. It is thus the essence or soulless soul of chaos, and shall at a darkly fated time be ground into a poison by Demogorgon, the god of the primordial abyss, and used to annihilate souls. Even now, the fragment goes on to affirm, it shrinks souls who dread "the natural alien of their negative eye," just as moles dread light.

So far these are the metaphysics of nightmare, and the rhetoric of the fragment is oppressive. Coleridge's horror of mere matter, his aversion to metaphysical materialism, so dominates these lines as to give them an undoubted but perhaps illicit power. They play upon our obsessive fear of formlessness, and it needs no Coleridge to do that; any director of a horror film can do more. The fragment becomes poetry when Coleridge recovers himself, and speculates upon Limbo:

> —where Time and weary Space
> Fettered from flight, with night-mare sense of fleeing,

Strive for their last crepuscular half-being;—
Lank Space, and scytheless Time with branny hands
Barren and soundless as the measuring sands.

Limbo cannot let Time and Space go, but keeps them in dim and twilight form, else it vanishes into a still farther abyss. But their stay is reluctant; as in a nightmare they strive to flee, but stand fast, just this side of existent being. They are unmeaning, "as moonlight on the dial of the day." The juxtaposed images of the moon and the sundial suddenly liberate Coleridge's imagination into a lovely vision of "Human Time" as opposed to the horror of Limbo's minimal clock time:

An Old Man with a steady look sublime,
That stops his earthly task to watch the skies;
But he is blind—a Statue hath such eyes;—
Yet having moonward turn'd his face by chance,
Gazes the orb with moon-like countenance,
With scant white hairs, with foretop bald and high,
He gazes still,—his eyeless face all eye;—
As 'twere an organ full of silent sight,
His whole face seemeth to rejoice in light!
Lip touching lip, all moveless, bust and limb—
He seems to gaze at that which seems to gaze on him!

This, with its rhapsodic ecstasy, is one of the great and genuinely difficult passages in Coleridge's poetry. Flanked on each side "by the mere horror of blank Naught-at-all," these lines both exemplify and celebrate the revival of poetic joy and creativity within the poet who utters them. They stand with the chant at the close of *Kubla Khan,* the beautiful movement that ends *Frost at Midnight,* and the vision of the infant gazing at the moon in *The Nightingale.* These, with the moonlight episodes in *Christabel* and *The Ancient Mariner,* are Coleridge's moments of pure Imagination. Of all these, the vision by moonlight in *Limbo* is the most desperate and poignant, and is equivalent to Keats's suffering vision of the unveiled face of Moneta in *The Fall of Hyperion.* What Coleridge sees, like Keats, is beyond tragedy, and past all pathos.

Human Time is measured here, as in Blake, by the intensity of apprehension and creation which goes into it, not by duration. The

Old Man who is Time's Human emblem is very like Rilke's Angel, blind and containing the forms of reality within himself. But Rilke's Angel gazes within. Coleridge's sublime Old Man watches the skies with a steady look. Yet he has a statue's blind eyes; the Byzantine suggestion anticipates Yeats. As he gazes moonward he is one moon reflecting light upon another, Human Time receiving and giving again to a symbolic Eternity. Coleridge finely says that the Old Man's eyeless face is all eye, full of silent sight. The sight of Eternity is presumably a speaking one, as in certain moments of awakened Imagination in Coleridge and Wordsworth. Finally, Human Time is transfigured in the joy of the light coming down upon the Old Man. Lip touches lip in response, but all is moveless, for this is a mouth that has, as Yeats was to say in a similar moonlit context, no moisture and no breath. And yet the statue is all but animate, as Coleridge breathlessly cries out the last line of his vision; the gaze between Old Man and moon seems mutual. Against the materialist and dim temporal form of Limbo, Coleridge has set an idealistic image of humanized temporality; against the nightmare, a dream of desire. The dream dissolves, and the poem ends, not in the Purgatory curse of growthless, dull Privation, the lurid thought haunting *Dejection: An Ode,* but in the Hell of a fear far worse, the future state of positive Negation. The myth of nature had failed Coleridge, or he it. The philosopher-theologian in him found what seemed a rock to build upon, but the poet found only a fear of blind matter, and the torments of the formless, a poet's true Hell.

Ne Plus Ultra

THE nature of that inferno Coleridge explored at least once more, in a fragment probably inscribed in 1826, after the notebook draft of *Limbo.* Positive Negation is an oxymoron requiring illustration. The apocalypse of the brief *Ne Plus Ultra* fragment is as vivid an exemplification as nightmare can achieve. I quote it entire, as it is all one indivisible movement:

> Sole Positive of Night!
> Antipathist of Light!
> Fate's only essence! primal scorpion rod—

> The one permitted opposite of God!—
> Condensed blackness and abysmal storm
> Compacted to one sceptre
> Arms the Grasp enorm—
> The Intercepter—
> The Substance that still casts the shadow Death!—
> The Dragon foul and fell—
> The unrevealable,
> And hidden one, whose breath
> Gives wind and fuel to the fires of Hell!
> Ah! sole despair
> Of both th' eternities in Heaven!
> Sole interdict of all-bedewing prayer,
> The all-compassionate!
> Save to the Lampads Seven
> Reveal'd to none of all th' Angelic State,
> Save to the Lampads Seven,
> That watch the throne of Heaven!

The Lampads Seven are seven lamps of fire burning before the Divine Throne in Revelation 4:5, where they are called the seven Spirits of God. The two Eternities in Heaven are probably Divine Love and Divine Knowledge. *Ne Plus Ultra* means the acme, usually the highest point of perfection, further than or beyond which one cannot go. Here it means the lowest point of imperfection, the nadir of positive Negation, the Dragon that is Death, Chaos, Satan. The poem is a startled apprehension revealing the names and nature of this great beast, which coils itself formlessly at the outer borders of the ordered world.

This Antagonist is the negation of all values. He is darkness against light, and fate's only reality against the Will of God. Yet he is part of that Will—its one permitted opposite. All natural blackness and storm are compactly condensed in him. He stands, eternally, between prayer and its compassionate fruition.

Coleridge died on July 25, 1834. Some eight months before, he had composed his own epitaph, pathetic and characteristic:

> Stop, Christian passer-by!—Stop, child of God,
> And read with gentle breast. Beneath this sod
> A poet lies, or that which once seem'd he.

O, lift one thought in prayer for S. T. C.;
That he who many a year with toil of breath
Found death in life, may here find life in death!

For Coleridge, the Intercepter found his chief formless form as death in life. Death in life defeated the poet, but for Coleridge the theory of poetry was at last not the theory of life. The Imagination in Blake and Wordsworth sought life in life, and prevailed in Blake until the end. Coleridge initiated what he himself could not approve, and wrote his own epitaph many times before his death. The poems live; the theology and philosophy have only a life in death.

CHAPTER FOUR

GEORGE GORDON, LORD BYRON

but man's life is thought,
And he, despite his terror, cannot cease
Ravening through century after century,
Ravening, raging, and uprooting that he may come
Into the desolation of reality.

W. B. YEATS

1   *Promethean Man*

Childe Harold's Pilgrimage

BYRON's pilgrimage as poet will be introduced here by a study of this series of poems, as we might regard them. Cantos I and II (1812) are merely a descriptive medley, mixing travel and history. Canto III (1816) is a poem in the confessional mode of Rousseau and Wordsworth, and marks Byron's first imaginative maturity. Canto IV (1818) attempts a synthesis of the two previous poems. In it, Byron and Italy are alternatively obsessive themes, and fail to balance, so that Canto III remains probably the best poem of the sequence.

The entire series Byron called *A Romaunt,* and both the title and the verse form (the Spenserian stanza) derive from the romance tradition. The quest-theme of romance previously internalized by Blake and Wordsworth appears again in Shelley's *Alastor* and Keats's *Endymion* under Wordsworth's influence. Canto III of *Childe Harold* manifests a more superficial Wordsworthian influence, probably owing both to Byron's relationship with Shelley in 1816 and to his own reading of *The Excursion.* The theme of a quest away from alienation and toward an unknown good is recurrent in the Romantics, and Byron would have come to it without Wordsworth and Shelley, though perhaps then only in the less interesting way of Cantos I and II.

The alienation of Harold in Canto I is hardly profound, though peculiarly relevant both to Byron's time and to ours:

> Worse than adversity the Childe befell;
> He felt the fulness of satiety.

He has run through Sin's long labyrinth, is sick at heart, and more than a little weary. So are we as we read Cantos I and II, though this is more the fault of his imitators than it is of Byron. Too many Byronic heroes have moved across too many screens, and Byron's rhetoric in Cantos I and II is not yet supple enough to keep us from making the association between the master and his disciples:

> Yet oft-times in his maddest mirthful mood
> Strange pangs would flash along Childe Harold's brow,
> As if the memory of some deadly feud
> Or disappointed passion lurk'd below:
> But this none knew, nor haply cared to know;
> For his was not that open, artless soul
> That feels relief by bidding sorrow flow,
> Nor sought he friend to counsel or condole,
> Whate'er this grief mote be, which he could not control.

Most of what follows, in these first two cantos, has been described, quite aptly, as "the rhymed diary of two years' travel." What counts in these cantos is the first emergence of Byron's Romantic hero, Promethean Man, who will reach his culmination as Manfred and

Cain, and then be replaced by Don Juan. Manfred and Cain are ravaged humanists, though they acquire some diabolical coloring. Childe Harold is scarcely even a vitalist until Canto III, and ends his quest in Canto IV by implying that the posture of pilgrimage is itself a value worth the affirming. We can agree, provided this pilgrimage has an imaginative element, an energy of vision and creation powerful enough to convert its spiritual emptiness into a deliberate theme. This is in fact Byron's great achievement in the third and fourth cantos; his faltering Prometheanism becomes the vehicle for myth. The myth concerns the condition of European man in the Age of Metternich, and is presented in and by the person of the Pilgrim, a complex wanderer who shares only a name with the Childe Harold of the Romantic guidebook that is Cantos I and II.

Canto III opens with Byron's departure into voluntary exile, as he regrets the loss of his child, left behind with the estranged Lady Byron. The poet gives himself to the ocean's guidance, and is content to go "wher'er the surge may sweep." As he is borne on by wind and water, he states the nature of his alienation. No wonder awaits him; his deeds have pierced the depth of life. His heart has grown hard, having endured too much love, sorrow, fame, ambition, strife. Most important, his thought is now turned away from ordinary reality and towards the refuge of "lone caves, yet rife with airy images," and the visionary shapes of "the soul's haunted cell." Fleeing England, he escapes into his poem, and affirms a therapeutic aesthetic idealism:

> 'Tis to create, and in creating live
> A being more intense, that we endow
> With form our fancy, gaining as we give
> The life we image, even as I do now.
> What am I? Nothing: but not so art thou,
> Soul of my thought! with whom I traverse earth,
> Invisible but gazing, as I glow
> Mix'd with thy spirit, blended with thy birth,
> And feeling still with thee in my crush'd feeling's dearth.

Thought seeks refuge in the creation of poetry, for by it we gain more life, even as Byron gains in the life he images. His own limitations are transcended as he blends himself with the birth of what he creates. Rousseau, in Shelley's *Triumph of Life,* returns from this transcendental illusion to the reality of natural limitation. Byron is so wavering in his own aspiration that he turns from it in his very next stanza:

> Yet must I think less wildly:—I *have* thought
> Too long and darkly, till my brain became,
> In its own eddy boiling and o'erwrought,
> A whirling gulf of phantasy and flame.

Yet to cease in this wild thinking is to submit one's thoughts to others, and Byron says of his Childe Harold *persona:*

> He would not yield dominion of his mind
> To spirits against whom his own rebell'd.

This might be Manfred speaking. And again like Manfred, Harold turns to the mountains for companionship, for "they spake a mutual language." But between the Pilgrim and the Alps lies "an Empire's dust," the legacy of the fallen Titan, Napoleon. The poem pauses to brood on the fate of Prometheanism, and to read in Napoleon the same spirit, "antithetically mixt," that reigns in the Pilgrim. Napoleon is either "more or less than man," yet falls through an aspiration beyond man's hope:

> But quiet to quick bosoms is a hell,
> And *there* hath been thy bane; there is a fire
> And motion of the soul which will not dwell
> In its own narrow being, but aspire
> Beyond the fitting medium of desire;
> And, but once kindled, quenchless evermore,
> Preys upon high adventure, nor can tire
> Of aught but rest; a fever at the core,
> Fatal to him who bears, to all who ever bore.

Blake or Shelley would not have acknowledged that desire had a fitting medium, though Shelley frequently emphasizes its fatality to him who bears it. Byron is already caught between admiration and disapproval of those whose "breath is agitation," of "all that expands the spirit, yet appals." Unlike Wordsworth but like Shelley, he seeks the summits of nature not for their own sake but because they show "how Earth may pierce to Heaven, yet leave vain man below." Nor does Byronic solitude much resemble the Wordsworthian kind. Wordsworth goes apart the better to hear humanity's still sad music emanate from nature. Byron desires to be alone that he may "love Earth only for its earthly sake." If he lives not in himself, it is only to become a portion of the nature around him, and so to evade the burden of being a man, "a link reluctant in a fleshly chain."

Rather unfairly, Byron attributes the same desire to Rousseau, a greater Promethean than Napoleon or Byron:

> His love was passion's essence:—as a tree
> On fire by lightning, with ethereal flame
> Kindled he was, and blasted; for to be
> Thus, and enamour'd, were in him the same.

The fire stolen from Heaven both kindles and blasts, and in Rousseau, human love is one with the stolen flame and in turn becomes existence itself. Byron praises Rousseau as inspired, but dismisses him as "phrensied by disease or woe," an anticipation of modern Babbitry toward Rousseau's genius. Byron's ambivalence is a necessary consequence of the extraordinary view of the natural world that *Childe Harold's Pilgrimage* develops. Every element given to man is simultaneously a way to moral greatness and divine blessing, and also a quicker way to self-deception and damnation. Every human act that widens consciousness increases both exaltation and despair. No other poet has insisted on maintaining both views with equal vigor, and one can wonder if Byron ever justifies his deliberate moral confusion by fully converting its aesthetic consequences into personal myth.

In Canto IV Byron reaches Rome, the goal of his Pilgrimage, and is moved by its aesthetic greatness to intensify his statement of negations. The mind is diseased by its own beauty, and this auto-intoxication fevers into false creation. So much for the Romantic Imagination. Disease, death, bondage become an obsessive litany:

> Our life is a false nature—'tis not in
> The harmony of things,—this hard decree,
> This uneradicable taint of sin,
> This boundless upas, this all-blasting tree
> Whose root is earth, whose leaves and branches be

The skies which rain their plagues on men like dew—
Disease, death, bondage—all the woes we see,
And worse, the woes we see not—which throb through
The immedicable soul, with heart-aches ever new.

As Mr. Flosky says in Peacock's *Nightmare Abbey*, after hearing
Mr. Cypress (Byron) paraphrase this stanza, we have here "a most
delightful speech, Mr. Cypress. A most amiable and instructive
philosophy. You have only to impress its truth on the minds of all
living men, and life will then, indeed, be the desert and the solitude." But this is to miss, however wittily, the direction of Byron's
rhetoric, which does not seek to persuade, but to expose. Mr. Cypress is a marvelous creation, and we are sad to see him depart
"to rake seas and rivers, lakes and canals, for the moon of ideal
beauty," but he is a better satire upon Childe Harold than he is on
Byron the Pilgrim. Mr. Cypress sings a song that ends as Childe
Harold might be pleased to end, knowing that "the soul is its own
monument." Byron as the Pilgrim of Eternity refuses to yield the
human value of his life even to his own vision of all-consuming
sin:

> But I have lived, and have not lived in vain:
> My mind may lose its force, my blood its fire,
> And my frame perish even in conquering pain;
> But there is that within me which shall tire
> Torture and Time, and breathe when I expire;
> Something unearthly, which they deem not of,
> Like the remember'd tone of a mute lyre,
> Shall on their soften'd spirits sink, and move
> In hearts all rocky now the late remorse of love.

What survives, as in Shelley, is "like the remember'd tone of a
mute lyre." In this case, that means the continued reverberation
of this stanza, which accurately predicts its own survival. Seeking
an image for such aesthetic immortality, Byron turns to the plastic
art around him in Rome. Gazing at the Apollo Belvedere, he sees
the statue with the approving eye of neoclassic aesthetics, a doctrine of stoic and firm control, of the selected moment or incident
that shall be both representative and exemplary:

> Or view the Lord of the unerring bow,
> The God of life, and poesy, and light—
> The Sun in human limbs array'd, and brow
> All radiant from his triumph in the fight;
> The shaft hath just been shot—the arrow bright
> With an immortal's vengeance; in his eye
> And nostril beautiful disdain, and might
> And majesty, flash their full lightnings by,
> Developing in that one glance the Deity.

In the next stanza this statue's informing conception is called "a ray of immortality." Just as Byron, in this poem, makes no attempt to reconcile his conviction of the value of human aspiration with his conviction of sin, so he does not try to bring into harmony this neoclassic aesthetic and Rousseau's vision of art as expressive therapy or Wordsworth's more active theory of a poet's creation. A subsequent stanza demonstrates Byron's awareness of the conflict within his own views:

> And if it be Prometheus stole from Heaven
> The fire which we endure, it was repaid
> By him to whom the energy was given
> Which this poetic marble hath array'd
> With an eternal glory—which, if made
> By human hands, is not of human thought;
> And Time himself hath hallow'd it, nor laid
> One ringlet in the dust—nor hath it caught
> A tinge of years, but breathes the flame with which
>   'twas wrought.

The Promethean fire we "endure" rather than enjoy, for its origin is illicit; it was stolen. We repay the Titan for the gift of creative energy by a work like this statue, but though the work is of human hands, it is not of human thought. Byron is enough of a Romantic to credit the artist with Promethean energy, but is also too uneasy about the autonomy of Imagination to credit timelessness to a merely human conception. The statue breathes the stolen flame that wrought it, but the aid of more than human inspiration vivifies it.[33]

The timelessness of art ends the wanderings of Byron's Pilgrim, for he comes to rest before the beauty of Rome, his search accomplished. Byron concludes the poem by offering his Pilgrim to the reader as a means of aesthetic grace of the kind the statue of Apollo has supplied to the Pilgrim himself:

> Ye! who have traced the Pilgrim to the scene
> Which is his last, if in your memories dwell
> A thought which once was his, if on ye swell
> A single recollection, not in vain
> He wore his sandal-shoon and scallop-shell;
> Farewell! with *him* alone may rest the pain,
> If such there were—with *you*, the moral of his strain.

The Pilgrim has been a catharsis for his creator, who has sought by his creation to transvalue exile and wandering into an essential good appropriate for a generation whose Titanic force is spent. In an age of reaction and repression the heroic spirit must roam, must indulge the residue of a Promethean endowment, but without yielding to it utterly. Somewhere in the endurance of human art an ultimate value must lie, but Byron cannot give a final assent to any view of human nature or art available to him. In this powerful skepticism that refuses to be a skepticism, but throws itself intensely at rival modes of feeling and thought, the peculiar moral and aesthetic value of Byron's poetry comes into initial being. *Childe Harold's Pilgrimage* has passion and conflict without balance. We turn elsewhere in Byron to find both a clearer exaltation of the Promethean and a firmer control of the critical attitude that seeks to chasten and correct this immense energy.

Prometheus

IN July 1816, in Switzerland, Byron wrote a short ode in three stropes, *Prometheus*. Composed at the same time as the third canto of *Childe Harold's Pilgrimage,* this ode gathers together the diffused Titanism of the romance, and emphasizes the heroic rather than the sinful aspect of Prometheus' achievement and fate. Yet even here there is a troubled undersong, and a refusal to neglect the darker implications of the fire stolen from Heaven. The overt celebration of human aspiration is properly dominant, but is all the more impressive for the juxtaposition of Byron's darker intimations. The gift of fire is the basis of Byron's art and theme, but the gift is unsanctioned by the withdrawn but responsible Power that has lawful possession of energy. Byron's entire poetic career at its most serious—here, in *Manfred, Cain, Don Juan, The Vision of Judgment*—can be understood as an attempt to justify the theft of fire by creating with its aid, while never forgetting that precisely such creation intensifies the original Promethean "Godlike crime." Byron, in this, writes in the line of Milton's prophetic fears, as do Blake in *The Marriage of Heaven and Hell* and Shelley in *Prometheus Unbound*. The fallen Angels in *Paradise Lost* compose poetic laments and celebrations for their Fall and of their deeds respectively, while Satan journeys through Chaos. Milton rises with immense relief from the abyss he so powerful creates, and the temptations of Prometheanism constitute the dangers he has escaped. The invocations in *Paradise Lost* exist to establish Milton's hope that his inspiration is Divine, and not Promethean and hence Satanic. Byron has no such hope; his inspiration is both glorious and sinful, and his creation glorifies human aspiration (and his own) and increases human culpability.

The ode *Prometheus* defies the sufferings consequent upon such guilt, though it recognizes their reality:

> Titan! to whose immortal eyes
>   The sufferings of mortality,
>   Seen in their sad reality,
> Were not as things that gods despise;
> What was thy pity's recompense?
> A silent suffering, and intense;
> The rock, the vulture, and the chain,
> All that the proud can feel of pain,
> The agony they do not show,
> The suffocating sense of woe,
>   Which speaks but in its loneliness,
> And then is jealous lest the sky
> Should have a listener, nor will sigh
>   Until its voice is echoless.

This begins as the Prometheus of Aeschylus, but the emphasis on the pride of silent suffering starts to blend the Titan into the

figure of Byron the Pilgrim of Eternity, who does not show his
agony, but whose sense of radical sin is suffocating, and who speaks
to the mountains in the glory of mutual solitude. This first strophe
commends Prometheus as an accurate as well as compassionate observer of human reality, the function Byron tries to fulfill in his
poetry. The start of the second strophe dares to attribute directly
to the Titan the Byronic conflict of negations:

> Titan! to thee the strife was given
>   Between the suffering and the will,
>   Which torture where they cannot kill.

Prometheus suffers most, like Byron, in the conflict between his
sympathy for and participation in human suffering, and the impious
drive of his will in gloriously but sinfully bringing relief to humanity. Byron's will cannot bring fire to us, but can create an art that
returns the Titanic gift with the human offering of a poem, itself
a mark of creative grace but also an agency of further suffering, as
it increases our guilt. This rather vicious circularity, a distinctive
feature of Byron's view of existence, is very evident in *Childe Harold's Pilgrimage* and enters into the final strophe of *Prometheus*.
Byron rises to his theme's power with a firmness of diction and
mastery of rhythm that his lyrical verse does not often manifest:

> Thy Godlike crime was to be kind,
>   To render with thy precepts less
>   The sum of human wretchedness,
> And strengthen Man with his own mind;
> But baffled as thou wert from high,
> Still in thy patient energy,
> In the endurance, and repulse
>   Of thine impenetrable Spirit,
> Which Earth and Heaven could not convulse,
>   A mighty lesson we inherit.

The Titan's kindness was "Godlike," yet remains a crime. The
Promethean gift would have strengthened Man by making the hu-
man mind immortal, but the gift's full efficacy was baffled by God.
The stolen fire, thus imperfectly received, is itself a torture to us.
What survives unmixed in our Titanic inheritance is the emblem
of "patient energy," the endurance that will make Manfred's Spirit

impenetrable. Prometheus and Man alike fall short of perfection, and so share one tragic fate, but they share also in a triumphant force:

> Thou art a symbol and a sign
>   To mortals of their fate and force;
> Like thee, Man is in part divine,
>   A troubled stream from a pure source;
> And Man in portions can foresee
> His own funereal destiny;
> His wretchedness, and his resistance,
> And his sad unallied existence:
> To which his Spirit may oppose
> Itself—and equal to all woes,
>   And a firm will, and a deep sense,
> Which even in torture can descry
>   Its own concenter'd recompense,
> Triumphant where it dares defy,
> And making Death a Victory.

What is confused, here and throughout Byron, is the attitude toward divinity. The "inexorable Heaven" of the second strophe, which creates for its own pleasure "the things it may annihilate," is nevertheless to be identified with the "pure source" from which Prometheus and Man are only troubled streams. Byron insists upon having it both ways, and he cannot overcome the imaginative difficulties created by his spiritual shuffling. Man's destiny is "funereal," for his "sad unallied existence" is detached from God; such are the consequences of Man's Promethean fall. Byron is like Blake's Rintrah, a voice presaging a new revelation but too passionate and confused to speak its own clear truth. The concentrated requital for Man's tortured striving is merely the glory of a defiant defeat. It is only by making Heaven altogether remote that Byron goes further in *Manfred*, where a defiant Titanism at last attains to its imaginative limits.

Manfred

MANFRED, Byron thought, was "of a very wild, metaphysical, and inexplicable kind." The kind is that of Goethe's *Faust* and Shelley's *Prometheus*, the Romantic drama of alienation and renewal, of the self purged by the self. *Faust* strives for the universal, and *Prometheus* is apocalyptic; *Manfred* is overtly personal, and is meant as a despairing triumph of self, and a denial of the efficacy of even a Titanic purgation. The crime of Manfred is that of Byron, incest deliberately and knowingly undertaken. Oedipus gropes in the dark, the light bursts upon him, and outwardly he allows the light to pass judgment upon him. Manfred, like Byron, claims the right of judging himself.

The Manfred we first encounter in the drama has elements in him of Faust and of Hamlet. The setting is in the Higher Alps, where he has his castle. The opening scene is as it must be: Manfred alone, in a Gothic gallery, and midnight the time. By his deep art he summons a condemned star, his own, and attendant spirits. He asks forgetfulness of self; they offer him only power, and suggest he seek his oblivion in death, but refuse to vouchsafe he will find it there. They serve him only with scorn for his mortality; he replies with Promethean pride. His star manifests itself as Astarte. his sister and mistress, but she vanishes when he attempts to embrace her, and he falls senseless. A spirit song is sung over him, which marks him of the brotherhood of Cain.

The second scene is the next morning out on the cliffs. Manfred, alone, soliloquizes like Milton's Satan on Mount Niphates. But Byron's reference here is a deliberate and critical parody. Satan on Niphates has his crisis of conscience and realizes the depth of his predicament, but refuses to believe that he can escape the self he has chosen, and so is driven at last to the frightening inversion "Evil, be thou my good." Manfred, like Satan, sees the beauty of the universe, but avers that he cannot feel it and declines therefore to love it. But he then proceeds to declare its felt beauty. Like Hamlet, and curiously like Satan, he proclaims his weariness of the human condition:

> Half dust, half deity, alike unfit
> To sink or soar.

He desires to sink to destruction, or soar to a still greater destruction, but either way to cease being human. His attempted suicide is frustrated by a kindly peasant, but the wine offered to revive

him has blood upon the brim, and his incestuous act is made directly equivalent to murder:

> I say 'tis blood—my blood! the pure warm stream
> Which ran in the veins of my fathers, and in ours
> When we were in our youth, and had one heart,
> And loved each other as we should not love,
> And this was shed: but still it rises up,
> Colouring the clouds, that shut me out from heaven.

With his crime established, Manfred descends to a lower valley
in the Alps, where he confronts a cataract that he identifies with
the steed of Death in the Apocalypse. In a marvelous invention,
he calls up the Witch of the Alps, a Shelleyan spirit of amoral
natural beauty. To her he speaks an idealized history of the outcast Romantic poet, the figure of the youth as natural quester for
what nature has not to give, akin to the idealized portraits of self
in Shelley's *Alastor* and Keats's *Endymion*. But the incest motif
transforms the quester myth into the main theme of *Manfred*, the
denial of immortality if it means yielding up the human glory of
our condition, yet accompanied by a longing to transcend that condition. The Witch stands for everything in *Manfred* that is at once
magical and preternatural. She scorns the Mage for not accepting
immortality, and offers him oblivion if he will serve her. With the
fine contempt that he displays throughout for all spirits that are not
human, Manfred dismisses her. At no time in the play is Manfred
anything but grave and courteous to his servants, the poor hunter,
and the meddling Abbot who comes to save his soul. To the machinery of the poem, which he himself continually evokes, he is
hostile always. This is most striking when he glides arrogantly into
the Hall of Arimanes, the chief of dark spirits, and a veil for the
Christian devil.

Arimanes is a Gnostic Satan; like Blake's Satan, he is the god of
the natural world, worshiped by the three Fates and by Nemesis,
who is a very rough version of the dialectical entity Shelley was to
call Demogorgon. Manfred refuses to worship Arimanes, but the
dark god nevertheless yields to the poet's request and the Phantom
of Astarte appears. Manfred asks her to forgive or condemn him,
but she declines, and cannot be compelled by Arimanes, as she belongs "to the other powers," the infinitely remote hidden god of

light. But at an appeal from Manfred which is both very human in
its pathos and essentially Calvinistic in its temper, she yields just
enough to speak her brother's name, to tell him "to-morrow ends
thy earthly ills," and to give a last farewell. She leaves a momentarily convulsed Manfred, who is first scorned and then grimly
valued in a fine dialogue of demonic spirits:

> *A Spirit.* He is convulsed—This is to be a mortal
> And seek the things beyond mortality.
> *Another Spirit.* Yet, see, he mastereth himself, and makes
> His torture tributary to his will.
> Had he been one of us, he would have made
> An awful spirit.

The final act rejects Christian comfort with an intensity that
comes from a ferocious quasi-Calvinism. The Abbot seeks to reconcile Manfred "with the true church, and through the church to
Heaven," but Manfred has no use for mediators. The last scene is
in the mountains again, within a lonely tower where Manfred awaits
his end. The Spirits of Arimanes come to claim him, as the Abbot
utters ineffectual exorcisms. In two remarkable speeches, Manfred's
Prometheanism manifests its glory. By power of will he thrusts the
demons back, in repudiation of the Faust legend, and dies his own
human death, yielding only to himself:

> The mind which is immortal makes itself
> Requital for its good or evil thoughts,—
> Is it owns origin of ill and end—
> And its own place and time: its innate sense,
> When stripp'd of this mortality, derives
> No colour from the fleeting things without,
> But is absorb'd in sufferance or in joy,
> Born from the knowledge of its own desert.

The ultimate model here is again Milton's Satan, who hails his
infernal world and urges it to receive its new possessor:

> One who brings
> A mind not to be chang'd by Place or Time.
> The mind is its own place, and in itself
> Can make a Heav'n of Hell, a Hell of Heav'n.

Marlowe's Mephistopheles tells his Faustus that "where we are is hell." The Devil is an inverted Stoic; we have an idea of ill, and from it we taste an ill savor. Iago with his blend of the Stoic and the Calvinist is closer to Manfred; both beings, like Webster's Lodovico, could say of their work that they had limned their night pieces and took pride in the result. Manfred is a Gothic poet who has written his own tragedy with himself as protagonist. The Machiavellian villain plots the destruction of others, whether he himself be man like Iago or demon like Mephistopheles. But, as Northrop Frye remarks in his theory of myths, "the sense of awfulness belonging to an agent of catastrophe can also make him something more like the high priest of a sacrifice." [34] Frye points to Webster's Bosola in *The Duchess of Malfi* as an example. In the Romantic period this figure becomes a high priest who sacrifices himself, like Manfred or Prometheus. The analogue to Christ hovers in the Romantic background. But to what god does Manfred give himself?

Manfred's last words are a proud, naturalistic farewell to the Abbot:

Old man! 'tis not so difficult to die.

Yet even the defiance here is gracious, for the dying Manfred has previously said to the Abbot, "Give my thy hand." Byron insisted that Manfred's last words contained "the whole effect and moral of the poem." The death of Manfred is clearly a release, not a damnation, for his burden of consciousness has long been his punishment. He drives off the demons, who are not so much seeking to drag him down to an inferno of punishment as trying to compel a human will to abandon itself as being inadequate. Manfred has no assurance of oblivion as he dies, but he has the Promethean satisfaction of having asserted the supremacy of the human will over everything natural or preternatural that would oppose it. The supernatural or spiritual world does not enter into the poem; Manfred's relations, if any, with heavenly grace are necessarily a mystery. His rejection of the Abbot is merely to deny a mediator's relevance.

Cain

BYRON went further, into mystery itself, in his dramatic piece *Cain* (1821). Manfred's crime of incest is paralleled by Cain's crime of murder, for Manfred's complete knowing of his sister destroyed her, and Cain's destruction of his brother completes an act of knowledge. Byron's radical conception makes Cain the direct ancestor of a tradition that has not yet exhausted itself, that of the artist not just as passive outcast but as deliberate criminal seeking the conditions for his art by violating the moral sanctions of his society.

For Byron, Cain is the first Romantic. Hazlitt best typifies the Romantic in his portrait of Rousseau: "He had the most intense consciousness of his own existence. No object that had once made an impression on him was ever effaced. Every feeling in his mind became a passion." [35]

This is true of Byron also, and of Cain. The tragedy of Cain is that he cannot accomplish his spiritual awakening without developing an intensity of consciousness which he is ill-prepared to sustain. His imaginativeness flowers into murderousness, as it will later in the terrible protagonists of Dostoevsky. The dialectic that entraps Byron's Cain is simplistic and inexorable. Cain suspects that Jehovah is malicious, and identifies his own exclusion from Paradise with the ultimate punishment of death, which he does not feel he deserves. Lucifer presents him with evidence that an age of innocence existed even before Adam. Cain fears death, but Lucifer hints that death leads to the highest knowledge. As Northrop Frye points out, this "links itself at once with Cain's own feeling that the understanding of death is his own ultimate victory—in other words, with the converse principle that the highest knowledge leads to death." [36] Cain is mistaken because he does not go far enough imaginatively; he moves to a mere negation of the moral law, a simple inversion of Jehovah's repressive ethic. And yet Byron gives him a capacity to have accomplished more than this. At the climactic moment, when Abel has offered up a lamb in sacrifice to Jehovah, and urges his brother to emulate him, Cain offers instead

the first fruits of the earth. Abel prays, abasing himself. Cain speaks
his defiance directly to Jehovah:

> If a shrine without victim,
> And altar without gore, may win thy favour,
> Look on it! and for him who dresseth it,
> He is—such as thou mad'st him; and seeks nothing
> Which must be won by kneeling: if he's evil,
> Strike him! thou art omnipotent, and may'st—
> For what can he oppose? If he be good,
> Strike him, or spare him, as thou wilt! since all
> Rests upon thee; and good and evil seem
> To have no power themselves, save in thy will;
> And whether that be good or ill I know not,
> Not being omnipotent, nor fit to judge
> Omnipotence, but merely to endure
> Its mandate; which thus far I have endured.

This powerfully ironic speech acquires, in context, the further
irony of the demonic, for it precedes the sacrifice of Abel to his
brother's inadequately awakened consciousness of man's freedom.
God accepts Abel's lamb, and rejects the fruits of the earth. Cain
overthrows his brother's altar, in the name of the creation. When
Abel interposes himself and cries that he loves God far more than
life, he provokes his brother to murder in the name of life and the
earth. The act done, the terrible irony of having brought death into
the world by his very quest for life destroys Cain's spirit:

> Oh, earth!
> For all the fruits thou hast render'd to me, I
> Give thee back this.

This is the self-imposed culmination of Byron's Prometheanism.
We can leave Blake to make the apt answer, before we pass to the
satiric poems in which Byron found a less arbitrary balance for his
divided universe. Blake replied to *Cain* with the dramatic scene he
called *The Ghost of Abel* (1822), addressed "to Lord Byron in the
wilderness." Byron is in the state that precedes prophecy, an Elijah
or John the Baptist prefiguring a coming of the truth, and his *Cain*
prepares Blake's way before him for *The Ghost of Abel*. Byron's
error, in Blake's judgment, is to have insisted that the Imagination

necessarily participates in the diabolical, so that the poet must be exile, outcast, and finally criminal. This is the pattern of Byron's obsession with incest, an element present in *Cain* in the beautiful relationship between Adah and Cain, who are both sister and brother, and husband and wife. The murder of Abel, in Byron, is a crime of Imagination, not of passion or society. In Blake, as Frye says, "murder cannot be part of genius but is always part of morality," for genius breaks not only with conventional virtue but with conventional vice as well. Byron could not free himself from societal conventions, and so his Promethean poems do not show us the real man, the Imagination, fully at work within him. The digressive, satirical poems and the handful of late lyrics of personal reappraisal come closer to a full expressiveness. The values of the sequence from *Childe Harold* to *Cain* still exist, but Byron's achievement in them is dwarfed by the great Romantic poems of Titanic aspiration, the Ninth Night of *The Four Zoas* and *Prometheus Unbound*.

2   *The Digressive Balance*

Beppo

WRITING to his publisher, John Murray, in October 1817, Byron expressed his admiration for a poem by John Hookham Frere published earlier in the same year. This work, under the pseudonym "Whistlecraft," is an imitation of the Italian "medley-poem," written in *ottava rima,* and inaugurated by the fifteenth-century poet Pulci in his *Morgante Maggiore.* The form is mock-heroic or satirical romance, and the style digressive, colloquial, realistic. Byron, in imitating Frere, had at first no notion that he had stumbled on what was to be his true mode of writing:

> I have written a story in eighty-nine stanzas in imitation of him, called *Beppo* (the short name for Giuseppe, that is, the *Joe* of the Italian Joseph), which I shall throw you into the

balance of the fourth canto to help you round to your money; but you had perhaps better publish it anonymously.

Beppo, thus offered to Murray as a throw-in with the last canto of *Childe Harold,* is a permanent and delightful poem, and hardly one to need anonymous publication, which it received in 1818. Byron's caution and respect for convention were characteristic, but he had embarked nevertheless on the great venture of his career, for out of *Beppo* came the greater poems, *Don Juan* and *The Vision of Judgment,* in which the poet at last found aesthetic balance and an individual ethos.

The story of *Beppo,* based on an anecdote of Venetian life told to Byron by the husband of one of his Venetian mistresses, is so slight as to need only a few stanzas of narration. The final version of the poem contains ninety-nine stanzas, and could as effectively go on for ninety-nine more, for the poem's point is in its charming digressiveness. The Venice of Byron's prose (and life) suddenly flowers in his verse, and the man himself is before us, all but unconcealed.

Venice and the Carnival before Lent set the place and time:

> This feast is named the Carnival, which being
> Interpreted, implies "farewell to flesh."

As the Venetians "bid farewell to carnal dishes," to "guitars and every other sort of strumming," and to "other things which may be had for asking," Byron moves among them with an eye of kindly irony. *Beppo,* like the Carnival, is an escape into freedom. For a little while, as he thinks, Byron puts aside the world of *Childe Harold,* and the Pilgrim becomes a man who can live in the present.

After the introduction, *Beppo* digresses on the happy and parallel themes of Venetian women and gondolas, until Byron introduces his heroine, Laura, whose husband, Beppo, has sailed east on business and failed to return. After a long wait, and a little weeping, she takes a Count as protector:

> He was a lover of the good old school,
> Who still become more constant as they cool.

This leads to a digression on the amiable institution of the "Cavalier Servente," and so to Byron in Italy, who was to play that role for the Countess Teresa Guiccioli, the great love of the poet's life after his half-sister Augusta. Praises of the Italian climate, land-scape, and way of life are followed by Byron's appreciation for Italy's chief adornments, the language and the women:

> I love the language, that soft bastard Latin,
> Which melts like kisses from a female mouth.

This provides a contrast for a backward glance at England, with its "harsh northern whistling, grunting guttural," its "cloudy cli-mate" and "chilly women." Remembering the circumstances of his exile, Byron shrugs himself off as "a broken Dandy lately on my travels" and takes Laura and the Count, after a six-year relation-ship, off to a Carnival ball, where Laura encounters a Turk who is the returned Beppo. A digression on Moselm sexual ways flows into another upon authors, which includes an oblique glance at Byron's central theme of lost innocence. The ball ends; Beppo as Turk follows Laura and the Count to the stairs of their palace, and reveals the inconvenient truth. The three go within, drink coffee, and accept a return to the earlier arrangement, Beppo and the Count becoming friends. Byron's pen reaches the bottom of a page:

> Which being finish'd, here the story ends;
> 'Tis to be wish'd it had been sooner done,
> But stories somehow lengthen when begun.

Don Juan

On the back of his manuscript of Canto I of *Don Juan*, Byron scribbled an exemplary stanza:

> I would to heaven that I were so much clay,
>   As I am blood, bone, marrow, passion, feeling—
> Because at least the past were pass'd away—
>   And for the future—(but I write this reeling,
> Having got drunk exceedingly to-day,
>   So that I seem to stand upon the ceiling)
> I say—the future is a serious matter—
> And so—for God's sake—hock and soda-water!

The empirical world of *Don Juan* is typified in this stanza. The poem is identifiable with Byron's mature life, and excludes nothing vital in that life, and so could not be finished until Byron was. *Don Juan's* extraordinary range of tone is unique in poetry, but Byron's was a unique individuality, pre-eminent even in an age of ferocious selfhood.

Don Juan began (September 1818) as what Byron called simply "a poem in the style and manner of *Beppo,* encouraged by the success of the same." But as it developed, the poem became something more ambitious, a satire of European Man and Society which attempts epic dimensions. In the end the poem became Byron's equivalent to Wordsworth's projected *Recluse,* Blake's *Milton,* Shelley's *Prometheus,* and Keats's *Hyperion.* As each of these attempts to surpass and, in Blake's and Shelley's poems, correct Milton, so Byron also creates his vision of the loss of Paradise and the tribulations of a fallen world of experience. There is no exact precedent for an epic satire of this kind. Byron's poetic idol was Pope, who kept his finest satiric strain for *The Dunciad* and wrote his theodicy, without overt satire, in the *Essay on Man.* Had Pope tried to combine the two works in the form of an Italianate medley or mock-heroic romance, something like *Don Juan* might have resulted. Byron's major work is his *Essay on Man, Dunciad, Rape of the Lock,* and a good deal more besides. Where Byron falls below his Augustan Master in aesthetic genius, he compensates by the range of his worldly knowledge, and the added complexity of bearing the burden of a Romantic Imagination he could neither trust nor eradicate. Much as he wished to emulate Pope, his epic moves in the poetic world of Wordsworth and Shelley, very nearly as much as *Childe Harold* did.

Yet he wills otherwise. The poem's most acute critic, George Ridenour, emphasizes that Byron has chosen "to introduce his longest and most ambitious work with an elaborately traditional satire in the Augustan manner." [37] The seventeen-stanza "Dedication" savages Southey, Wordsworth, and Coleridge, and suggests that Byron is a very different kind of poet and man, whose faults "are at least those of passion and indiscretion, not of calculation, venality, self-conceit, or an impotence which manifests itself in tyranny," to quote Ridenour again. Byron is establishing his *persona* or dramatized self, the satirical mask in which he will present

himself as narrator of *Don Juan*. Southey, Wordsworth, and Coleridge are renegades, revolutionary zealots who have become Tories.
Southey indeed is an "Epic Renegade," both more venal than his
friends (he is poet laureate) and an offender against the epic form,
which he so frequently and poorly attempts. As laureate, he is "representative of all the race" of poets, and his dubious moral status
is therefore an emblem of the low estate to which Byron believes
poetry has fallen:

> And Coleridge, too, has lately taken wing,
>   But like a hawk encumber'd with his hood,—
> Explaining metaphysics to the nation—
> I wish he would explain his Explanation.

Coleridge's flight is genuine but blind. Southey's poetic soarings
end in a "tumble downward like the flying fish gasping on deck."
As for Wordsworth, his "rather long *Excursion*" gives a "new system to perplex the sages." Byron does not make the mistake of
mounting so high, nor will he fall so low:

> For me, who, wandering with pedestrian Muses,
>   Contend not with you on the winged steed,
> I wish your fate may yield ye, when she chooses,
>   The fame you envy, and the skill you need.

He will not attempt the sublime, and thus he need not fall into
the bathetic. From Southey he passes to the Master Tory, "the intellectual eunuch Castlereagh," a pillar of the Age of Reaction that
followed Napoleon, and the master of Southey's hired song:

> Europe has slaves, allies, kings, armies still,
> And Southey lives to sing them very ill.

The mock dedication concluded, the epic begins by announcing
its hero:

> I want a hero: an uncommon want,
>   When every year and month sends forth a new one,
> Till, after cloying the gazettes with cant,
>   The age discovers he is not the true one:
> Of such as these I should not care to vaunt,
>   I'll therefore take our ancient friend Don Juan—

> We all have seen him, in the pantomime,
> Sent to the devil somewhat ere his time.

This last may be a reference to Mozart's *Don Giovanni*. Byron's Don Juan shares only a name with the hero of the legend or of Mozart. At the root of the poem's irony is the extraordinary passivity and innocence of its protagonist. This fits the age, Byron insists, because its overt heroes are all military butchers. The gentle Juan, acted upon and pursued, sets off the aggressiveness of society.

The plot of *Don Juan* is too extensive for summary, and the poem's digressive technique would defeat such an attempt in any case. The poem organizes itself by interlocking themes and cyclic patterns, rather than by clear narrative structure. "A deliberate rambling digressiveness," Northrop Frye observes, "is endemic in the narrative technique of satire, and so is a calculated bathos or art of sinking in its suspense." [38] *Don Juan* parodies epic form and even its own digressiveness. Its organization centers, as Ridenour shows, on two thematic metaphors: the Fall of Man, in terms of art, nature, and the passions; and the narrator's style of presentation, in terms of his rhetoric and his *persona*. Juan's experiences tend toward a cyclic repetition of the Fall, and Byron's style as poet and man undergoes the same pattern of aspiration and descent.

Canto I deals with Juan's initial fall from sexual innocence. The tone of this canto is urbanely resigned to the necessity of such a fall, and the description of young love and of Donna Julia's beauty clearly ascribes positive qualities to them. Yet Julia is rather unpleasantly changed by her illicit love affair, and her parting letter to Juan betrays a dubious sophistication when we contrast it to her behavior earlier in the canto. As Byron says, speaking mockingly of his own digressiveness:

> The regularity of my design
> Forbids all wandering as the worst of sinning.

His quite conventional moral design condemns Julia, without assigning more than a merely technical lapse to the seduced sixteen-year-old, Juan. The self-baffled Prometheanism of *Childe Harold* manifests itself again here in *Don Juan,* but now the emphasis is rather more firmly set against it. "Perfection is insipid in this naughty world of ours," and Byron is not prepared to be even mo-

mentarily insipid, but the price of passion, with its attendant im-
perfections, may be damnation. And so Byron writes of "first and
passionate love":

>   —it stands alone,
>   Like Adam's recollection of his fall;
>   The tree of knowledge has been pluck'd
>   —all's known—
>   And life yields nothing further to recall
>   Worthy of this ambrosial sin, so shown,
>   No doubt in fable, as the unforgiven
>   Fire which Prometheus filch'd for us from heaven.

Imaginatively this is an unfortunate passage, as it reduces both
Man's crime and the Promethean theft from the level of disobedience, which is voluntaristic, to that of sexuality itself, a natural endowment. Byron's paradoxes concerning sexual love are shallow,
and finally irksome. It is not enlightening to be told that "pleasure's
a sin, and sometimes sin's a pleasure."

Byron does better when he finds Prometheanism dubiously at
work in human inventiveness:

>   One makes new noses, one a guillotine,
>   One breaks your bones, one sets them in their sockets.

In an age full of new inventions, "for killing bodies, and for saving souls," both alike made with great good will, the satirist finds a
true function in exploring the ambiguities of human aspiration.
When Byron merely condemns all aspiration as sinful, he repels us.
Fortunately, he does not play Urizen for very long at a time. What
is most moving in Canto I is the final personal focus. After extensive ridicule of Coleridge and Wordsworth, Byron nevertheless
comes closest to his own deep preoccupations in two stanzas that
are no more than a weaker version of the *Intimations* and *Dejection*
odes:

>   No more—no more—Oh! never more on me
>   The freshness of the heart can fall like dew,
>   Which out of all the lovely things we see
>   Extracts emotions beautiful and new;
>   Hived in our bosoms like the bag o' the bee.

> Think'st thou the honey with those objects grew?
> Alas! 'twas not in them, but in thy power
> To double even the sweetness of a flower.

This is a very naïve version of the *Dejection* ode. What we receive is what we ourselves give. Byron's scorn of "metaphysics" and "system" in Coleridge and Wordsworth, which is actually a rather silly scorn of deep thought in poetry, betrays him into a very weak though moving performance in the mode of Romantic nostalgia for the innocent vision both of external and of human nature:

> No more—no more—Oh! never more, my heart,
>   Canst thou be my sole world, my universe!
> Once all in all, but now a thing apart,
>   Thou canst not be my blessing or my curse:
> The illusion's gone for ever, and thou art
>   Insensible, I trust, but none the worse,
> And in thy stead I've got a deal of judgment,
> Though heaven knows how it ever found a lodgment.

The last couplet helps the stanza, as an ironic equivalent to Wordsworth's "sober coloring" of mature vision, but the preceding lines are weak in that they recall *Peele Castle,* and fall far short of it. Not that Byron is thinking of either Coleridge or Wordsworth in these two stanzas; it is more to the point to note that he might have done better to think of them, and so avoid the bathos of unconsciously, and awkwardly, suggesting their major poetic concerns.

In Canto II Juan is sent on his travels, and suffers seasickness, shipwreck, and the second and greatest of his loves. The shipwreck affords Byron a gruesome opportunity to demonstrate fallen nature at its helpless worst, as the survivors turn to a cannibalism that is rather nastily portrayed. From the flood of judgment only Juan is saved, for only he refrains from tasting human flesh. He reaches shore, a new Adam, freshly baptized from the waves, to find before him a new Eve, Haidée, daughter of an absent pirate. She seems innocence personified, but for Byron no person is innocent. Though it is an "enlargement of existence" for Haidée "to partake Nature" with Juan, the enlargement carries with it the burden of man's fall. Byron himself keenly feels the lack of human justice in this association. First love, "nature's oracle," is all "which Eve has left her daughters since her fall." Yet these moments will be paid for "in an endless shower of hell-fire":

> Oh, Love! thou art the very god of evil,
> For, after all, we cannot call thee devil.

Canto III is mostly a celebration of ideal love, but its very first stanza pictures Juan as being

> loved by a young heart, too deeply blest
> To feel the poison through her spirit creeping,
> Or know who rested there, a foe to rest,
> Had soil'd the current of her sinless years,
> And turn'd her pure heart's purest blood to tears!

This seems an equivocal deep blessing for Haidée, "Nature's bride" as she is. Yet, Byron goes on to say, they *were* happy, "happy in the illicit indulgence of their innocent desires." This phrasing takes away with one hand what it gives with the other. When, in the fourth canto, all is over, with Juan wounded and sold into slavery, and Haidée dead of a romantically broken heart, Byron gives us his most deliberate stanza of moral confusion. Haidée has just died, and her unborn child with her:

> She died, but not alone; she held within
> A second principle of life, which might
> Have dawn'd a fair and sinless child of sin;
> But closed its little being without light,
> And went down to the grave unborn, wherein
> Blossom and bough lie wither'd with one blight;
> In vain the dews of Heaven descend above
> The bleeding flower and blasted fruit of love.

This is a pathetic kind of sentimental neo-Calvinism until its concluding couplet, when it becomes a statement of the inefficacy of heavenly grace in the affairs of human passion. At the start of the fourth canto Byron had modulated his tone so as to fit his style to the saddest section of his epic. If a fall is to be portrayed, then the verse too must descend:

> Nothing so difficult as a beginning
> In poesy, unless perhaps the end;

> For oftentimes when Pegasus seems winning
>   The race, he sprains a wing, and down we tend,
> Like Lucifer when hurl'd from heaven for sinning;
>   Our sin the same, and hard as his to mend,
> Being pride, which leads the mind to soar too far,
> Till our own weakness shows us what we are.

Few stanzas in *Don Juan* or elsewhere are as calmly masterful as that. The poet attempting the high style is likely to suffer the fate of Lucifer. Pride goes before the fall of intellect, and the sudden plunge into bathos restores us to the reality we are. The movement from *Childe Harold* into *Don Juan* is caught with fine self-knowledge:

>   Imagination droops her pinion,
> And the sad truth which hovers o'er my desk
> Turns what was once romantic to burlesque.

Self-recognition leads to a gentler statement of mature awareness than Byron usually makes:

> And if I laugh at any mortal thing,
>   'Tis that I may not weep; and if I weep,
> 'Tis that our nature cannot always bring
>   Itself to apathy, for we must steep
> Our hearts first in the depths of Lethe's spring
>   Ere what we least wish to behold will sleep:
> Thetis baptized her mortal son in Styx;
> A mortal mother would on Lethe fix.

This is noble and restrained, and reveals the fundamental desperation that pervades the world of the poem, which is our world. After the death of Haidée most of the tenderness of Byron passes out of the poem, to be replaced by fiercer ironies and a reckless gaiety that can swerve into controlled hysteria. It becomes clearer that Byron's universe is neither Christian nor Romantic, nor yet the eighteenth-century cosmos he would have liked to repossess. Neither grace nor the displaced grace of the Secondary Imagination can move with freedom in this universe, and a standard of reasonableness is merely a nostalgia to be studied. What haunts

Byron is the specter of meaninglessness, of pointless absurdity. He is an unwilling prophet of our sensibility. The apocalyptic desires of Blake and Shelley, the natural sacramentalism of Coleridge and Wordsworth, the humanistic naturalism of Keats, all find some parallels in Byron, but what is central in him stands apart from the other great Romantics. He lacks their confidence, as he lacks also the persuasiveness of their individual rhetorics. Too traditional to be one of them, too restless and driven to be traditional, impatient of personal myth if only because he incarnates his own too fully, he creates a poem without faith in Nature, Art, Society, or the very Imagination he so capably employs. Yet his obsessions betray his uncertainties of rejection. *Don Juan* cannot let Wordsworth alone, and cannot bring itself to mention Shelley, Byon's companion during much of the poem's composition. Until Shelley's death, Byron could not decide what to make of either the man or the poet, both of whom impressed him more than he cared to acknowledge. After Shelley's death, Byron seems to have preferred to forget him, except for one stanza of *Don Juan* where the puzzle of Shelley continues as a troubling presence:

> And that's enough, for love is vanity,
>   Selfish in its beginning as its end,
> *Except where 'tis a mere insanity,*
>   *A maddening spirit which would strive to blend*
> *Itself with beauty's frail inanity,*
>   On which the passion's self seems to depend;
>   And hence some heathenish philosophers
>   Make love the main-spring of the universe.

The italics are mine, and indicate the probable Shelley reference.[39] The stanza's first two lines express the mature judgment of Byron on love, a vanity that begins and ends in selfishness, except in the case of the rare spirits who madden themselves and others by questing as though the world could contain the object of their fierce desire. The tone here is uneasy, as it is in Byron's continuous digressions on Wordsworth's *Excursion. The Excursion* contains just enough of Wordsworth's greatness both to influence and to repel Byron, and its emphasis on the correction of a misanthropic Solitary may have offended him directly. We cannot know, but a surmise is possible. There are moments in *Don Juan* when Byron longs to make nature his altar, and moments when he is drawn toward a desperate religion of love. His rejection of Wordsworth and evasion of Shelley have deep and mysterious roots within *Don Juan*'s underlying assumptions concerning reality.

After the love-death of Haidée, Byron moves Juan into the world of two rapacious empresses, Gulbeyaz of Turkey and the historical Catherine the Great of Russia. Between these tigresses the poem progresses by an account of a battle between Turks and Russians. After Catherine's court, *Don Juan* starts its last, most interesting and unfinished movement, a view of the English society that Byron had known before his exile. A fierce love, a faithless war, another fierce love, and a social satire of what was closest to Byron's heart form a suggestive sequence. Seduced by a young matron, shipwrecked into an idyl of natural and ideal love, wounded and sold into bondage—the passive Juan has encountered all these adventures without developing under their impact. As he falls further into experience, he does not gain in wisdom, but he does maintain a stubborn Spanish aristocratic pride and a basic disinterestedness. Turkish passion and the horror of battle do not seem to affect him directly, but the embraces of Catherine finally convert his disinterestedness into the sickness of uninterestedness. Probably, like Childe Harold and Byron, the Don begins to feel the "fulness of satiety." His diplomatic rest trip to England is a quest for a renewal of interest, and the quest's goal, Lady Adeline, becomes Byron's last vision of a possible and therefore ultimately dangerous woman. In thus patterning the course of the poem, I have moved ahead of my commentary, and return now to Juan in slavery.

The memorable elements in that episode are the digressions. With Juan pausing, involuntarily, between women, Byron is free to meditate upon the impermanence of all worldly vanities, including poetry. He is back in the mood of *Childe Harold*, from which only the therapy of his own epic can rescue him:

> Yet there will still be bards: though fame is smoke,
>   Its fumes are frankincense to human thought;
> And the unquiet feelings, which first woke
>   Song in the world, will seek what then they sought:
> As on the beach the waves at last are broke,
>   Thus to their extreme verge the passions brought

Dash into poetry, which is but passion,
Or at least was so ere it grew a fashion.

Poetry here is expression and catharsis, and nothing more. At
most it can help keep the poet (and his readers) sane. Elsewhere
in *Don Juan* Byron rates poetry as simultaneously higher and
lower, when he sees it as a dangerous mode of evading the consequences of Man's Fall, an evasion that must resolve at last in the
consciousness of delusion. The impermanence of poetry is related
to human mortality and what lies beyond its limits. Before introducing Juan into a Turkish harem, Byron perplexes himself with
the mystery of death, drawing upon "a fact, and no poetic fable."
His acquaintance, the local military commandant, has been slain in
the street "for some reason, surely bad." As Byron stares at the
corpse, he cannot believe that this is death:

> I gazed (as oft I have gazed the same)
> To try if I could wrench aught out of death
> Which should confirm, or shake, or make a faith;
>
> But it was all a mystery. Here we are,
>   And there we go:—but *where?* five bits of lead,
> Or three, or two, or one, send very far!
>   And is this blood, then, form'd but to be shed?
> Can every element our element mar?
>   And air—earth—water—fire live—and we dead?
> *We,* whose minds comprehend all things. No more;
> But let us to the story as before.

What is effective here is the human attitude conveyed, but
Byron's own turbulence weakens the expression. Few great poets
have written quite so badly about death. The Muse of Byron was
too lively to accommodate the grosser of his private apprehensions.
The paradox of an all-comprehensive mind inhabiting a form vulnerable to every element is the basis of Byron's dualism, his own
saddened version of "the ghost in the machine." The inevitable corruption of the body obsesses Byron, and this obsession determines
his dismissal of passionate love as a value. Julia was self-corrupted,
and Haidée the most natural and innocent of sinners, too harshly
judged by her father, himself a great cutthroat but perfectly con-

ventional in questions of his own family's morality. Gulbeyaz is further down in the scale of female culpability. Her features have "all the sweetness of the devil" when he played the cherub. She has the charm of her passion's intensity, but her love is a form of imperial, or imperious, bondage, her embrace a chain thrown about her lover's neck. Her love is a variation of war and preludes Byron's ferocious and very funny satire on the siege, capture, and sack of the Turkish town Ismail by the ostensibly Christian imperial Russian army of Catherine the Great, Juan's next and most consuming mistress. Byron introduces Canto VII and its slaughter by parodying Spenser, whose *Faerie Queene* sang of "fierce warres and faithful loves." For Byron, it is altogether too late in the day to sing so innocently, especially when "the fact's about the same," so his themes are "fierce loves and faithless wars":

> "Let there be light!" said God, "and there was light!"
>   "Let there be blood!" says man, and there's a sea!
> The fiat of this spoil'd child of the Night
>   (For Day ne'er saw his merits) could decree
> More evil in an hour, than thirty bright
>   Summers could renovate, though they should be
> Lovely as those which ripen'd Eden's fruit;
> For war cuts up not only branch, but root.

War completes the Fall of Man, costing us our surviving root in Eden and nullifying the renovating power of nature. This does not prevent Byron from an immense and sadistic joy in recording the butchery and rapine, but his *persona* as Promethean poet, whose every stanza heightens aspiration and deepens guilt, justifies the seeming inconsistency.

Juan has butchered freely, but refrained from ravishing, and next appears as hero at the court of Catherine the Great, where he falls, not into love, but into "that no less imperious passion," self-love. Flattered by Catherine's preference, Juan grows "a little dissipated" and becomes very much a royal favorite. As this is morally something of a further fall, Byron is inspired to reflect again upon his favorite theme:

> Man fell with apples, and with apples rose,
>   If this be true; for we must deem the mode

In which Sir Isaac Newton could disclose
    Through the then unpaved stars the turnpike road,
A thing to counterbalance human woes:
    For ever since immortal man hath glow'd
With all kinds of mechanics, and full soon
Steam-engines will conduct him to the moon.

The triumphs of reason are now also identified as sinfully and gloriously Promethean, and Sir Isaac observing the apple's fall is responsible for the paradox that Man's initial fall with apples was a fortunate one. The glowing of human intellect is "a thing to counterbalance human woes," and soon enough will take us to the moon. Byron quickly goes on to qualify this counterbalance as "a glorious glow," due only to his internal spirit suddenly cutting a caper. Cheerfulness thus keeps breaking in, but does not alter the fundamental vision of our world as "a waste and icy clime." That clime surrounds us, and we are "chill, and chain'd to cold earth," as our hero Prometheus was upon his icy rock. But we look up, and see the meteors of love and glory, lovely lights that flash and then die away, leaving us "on our freezing way." *Don Juan* is not only, its poet tells us, "a nondescript and ever-varying rhyme," but it is also "a versified Aurora Borealis," a northern light flashing over us.

Love and glory have flashed too often for Juan, and he begins to waste into a clime of decay just as his creator laments that Dante's "obscure wood," the mid-point of life, draws close. In "royalty's vast arms," Juan sighs for beauty, and sickens for travel. The now motherly Catherine sends her wasting lover on his last quest, a mission to England, and Byron returns in spirit to the Age of Elegance of his triumphant youth, the London of the Regency.

This, *Don Juan*'s last and unfinished movement, is its most nostalgic and chastened. Byron, once "the grand Napoleon of the realms of rhyme," revisits in vision his lost kingdom, the Babylon that sent him into exile and pilgrimage. "But I will fall at least as fell my hero," Byron cries, completing his lifelong comparison to the other Titan of the age. The poem of Juan, Byron says, is his Moscow, and he seeks in its final cantos his Waterloo. Juan has met his Moscow in Catherine, and evidently would have found a Waterloo in the Lady Adeline Amundeville, cold heroine of the final cantos and "the fair most fatal Juan ever met."

The English cantos are a litany for an eighteenth-century world, forever lost, and by Byron forever lamented. The age of reason and love is over, the poet insists, and the age of Cash has begun. The poem has seen sex displaced into war, and now sees both as displaced into money. Money and coldness dominate England, hypocritically masked as the morality that exiled Byron and now condemns his epic. There are other and deeper wounds to be revenged. The Greek and Italian women of the poet's life have given fully of their passion and spirits, and Byron has returned what he could. But England stands behind him as a sexual battlefield where he conquered all yet won nothing, and where at last he defeated himself and fled. Incest, separation, mutual betrayal of spirit are his English sexual legacy. In his sunset of poetry he returns to brood upon English womankind, products of "the English winter—ending in July, to recommence in August." Beneath the Lady Adeline's snowy surface is the proverbial *et caetera,* as Byron says, but he refuses to hunt down the tired metaphor. He throws out another figure: a bottle of champagne "frozen into a very vinous ice."

> Yet in the very centre, past all price,
> About a liquid glassful will remain;
> And this is stronger than the strongest grape
> Could e'er express in its expanded shape.

Severity and courtliness fuse here into definitive judgment, and bring the spirit of this female archetype to a quintessence:

> And thus the chilliest aspects may concentre
> A hidden nectar under a cold presence.

Adeline is mostly a cold potential in this unfinished poem; her fatality is only barely felt when Byron breaks off, in his preparation for his final and genuinely heroic pilgrimage, to battle for the Greeks. She is Byron's "Dian of the Ephesians," but there is more flesh and activity to "her frolic Grace," the amorous Duchess of Fitz-Fulke. No personage, but an atmosphere, dominates these English cantos, with their diffused autumnal tone and their perfectly bred but desperately bored aristocrats, with whose breeding and boredom alike Byron is more than half in sympathy. *Don Juan,* begun as satiric epic, ends as a remembrance of things past, with Byron's last glance at home, and the poet's last tone one of weary but loving irony. The last word in a discussion of *Don Juan* ought not to be "irony," but "mobility," one of Byron's favorite terms. Oliver Elton called Byron's two central traits his mobility and self-consciousness, and the former is emphasized in *Don Juan*. Adeline is so graceful a social performer that Juan begins to feel some doubt as to how much of her is *real:*

> So well she acted all and every part
> By turns—with that vivacious versatility,
> Which many people take for want of heart.
> They err—'tis merely what is call'd mobility,
> A thing of temperament and not of art,
> Though seeming so, from its supposed facility;
> And false—though true; for surely they're sincerest
> Who are strongly acted on by what is nearest.

This is Byron's own defense against our charge that he postures, our feeling doubts as to how much of *him* is real. An abyss lies beneath mobility, but Adeline and Byron alike are too nimble to fall into it, and their deftness is more than rhetorical. The world of *Don Juan,* Byron's world, demands mobility; there is indeed no other way to meet it. Byron defines mobility in a note that has a wry quality, too sophisticated to acknowledge the tragic dimension being suggested: "It may be defined as an excessive susceptibility of immediate impressions—at the same time without *losing* the past: and is, though sometimes apparently useful to the possessor, a most painful and unhappy attribute."

This is Byron's social version of the Romantic term "Imagination," for mobility also reveals itself "in the balance or reconciliation of opposite or discordant qualities: of sameness, with difference; the individual, with the representative; the sense of novelty and freshness, with old and familiar objects." The great Romantic contraries—emotion and order, judgment and enthusiasm, steady self-possession and profound or vehement feeling—all find their social balance in the quality of mobility. Viewed thus, Byron's achievement in *Don Juan* is to have suggested the pragmatic social realization of Romantic idealism in a mode of reasonableness that no other Romantic aspired to attain.[40]

Byron lived in the world as no other Romantic attempted to live, except Shelley, and Shelley at the last despaired more fully. *Don Juan* is, to my taste, not a poem of the eminence of *Milton* and *Jerusalem,* of *The Prelude* or *Prometheus Unbound* or the two *Hyperions.* But it is not a poem of their kind, nor ought it to be judged against them. Shelley said of *Don Juan* that "every word of it is pregnant with immortality," and again: "Nothing has ever been written like it in English, nor, if I may venture to prophesy, will there be; without carrying upon it the mark of a secondary and borrowed light." Byron despaired of apocalypse, and yet could not be content with Man or nature as given. He wrote therefore with the strategy of meeting this life with awareness, humor, and an intensity of creative aspiration, flawed necessarily at its origins. Mobility is a curious and sophisticated ideal; it attempts to meet experience with experience's own ironies of apprehension. It may be that, as Byron's best critic says, *Don Juan* offers us "a sophistication which (in a highly debased form, to be sure) we have already too much of." [41] We have, however, so little besides that a higher kind of sophistication can only improve us. Whatever its utility, *Don Juan* is exuberant enough to be beautiful in a Blakean sense, little as Blake himself would have cared for Byron's hard-won digressive balance.

3   *The Byronic Ethos*

The Vision of Judgment

THE parody poem *The Vision of Judgment* contains Byron's best work outside of *Don Juan*. It is, as Byron said, "in the Pulci style," like *Beppo* and *Juan,* but its high good nature reveals a firmer balance than Byron maintains elsewhere in his Italian mock-heroic vein. Southey, the battered poet laureate, is the scapegoat again, as he was in the "Dedication" to *Don Juan*. Byron's treatment of his victim is both more humane and more effective in the *Vision,* once the reader gets past the angry prose preface.

George III died in 1820, and poor Southey performed the laureate's task of eulogizing his late monarch in *A Vision of Judgment* (1821), a poem no better than it needed to be, and not much worse than most of Southey. The laureate's misfortune was to write a preface in which he denounced lascivious literature and attacked the "Satanic school" (Byron and Shelley) for producing it: "for though their productions breathe the spirit of Belial in their lascivious parts, and the spirit of Moloch in those loathsome images of atrocities and horrors which they delight to represent, they are more especially characterized by a satanic spirit of pride and audacious impiety, which still betrays the wretched feeling of hopelessness wherewith it is allied."

Byron was not the man to pass this by. His *Vision of Judgment* takes its occasion from Southey's and permanently fixates the laureate as a dunce. But it does something rather more vital besides. *Don Juan* has its Miltonic side, as we have seen, yet the *Vision* as it develops is even closer to *Paradise Lost* in material, though hardly in spirit or tone. Milton's anthropomorphic Heaven is sublime and also sometimes wearisome, too much like an earthly court in its servile aspects. Byron's burlesque Heaven is sublimely funny. St. Peter sits by the celestial gate and can happily drowse, for very little goes in. The Angels are singing out of tune and are by now hoarse, having little else to do. Down below, George III dies, which does not disturb the yawning Peter, who has not heard of him. But the mad old blind king arrives in the angelic caravan, and with him comes a very great being, the patron of the "Satanic school":

> But bringing up the rear of this bright host
>   A Spirit of a different aspect waved
> His wings, like thunder-clouds above some coast
>   Whose barren beach with frequent wrecks is paved;
> His brow was like the deep when tempest-toss'd;
>   Fierce and unfathomable thoughts engraved
> Eternal wrath on his immortal face,
> And *where* he gazed a gloom pervaded space.

Those "fierce and unfathomable thoughts" remind us of Manfred, but this is great Lucifer himself, come to claim George as his own. The gate of heaven opens, and the archangel Michael comes forth to meet his former friend and future foe. There is "a high immortal, proud regret" in the eyes of each immortal being, as if destiny rather than will governs their enmity:

> Yet still between his Darkness and his Brightness
> There pass'd a mutual glance of great politeness.

Michael is a gentleman, but the Prince of Darkness has the superior hauteur of "an old Castilian poor noble." He is not particularly proud of owning our earth, but he does own it, in this quietly Gnostic poem. But, as befits a poor noble with hauteur, he thinks few earthlings worth damnation save their kings, and these he takes merely as a kind of quitrent, to assert his right as lord. Indeed, he shares Byron's theory of the Fall as being perpetually renewed by Man:

> they are grown so bad,
> That hell has nothing better left to do
> Than leave them to themselves: so much more mad
> And evil by their own internal curse,
> Heaven cannot make them better, nor I worse.

Lucifer's charges against George and his calling of witnesses are nimbly handled. Life comes exuberantly into the poem with the intrusion of Southey upon the heavenly scene. The devil Asmodeus stumbles in, under the heavy load of the laureate, and the poor devil is moved to lament that he has sprained his left wing in the carry. Southey has been writing his *Vision of Judgment*, thus daring to anticipate the eternal decision upon George. The laureate, glad to get an audience, begins to recite, throwing everyone into a horror and even rousing the deceased King from his stupor in the horrible thought that his former laureate, the abominable Pye, has come again to plague him. After a general tumult, St. Peter

> upraised his keys,
> And at the fifth line knock'd the poet down;
> Who fell like Phaëton.

Phaëton (or Phaethon) attempted to drive the chariot of the sun across the sky, but could not control the horses, who bolted, and so Phaethon fell to his death. Southey attempts to ride in the chariot of Apollo, god of poetry, and suffers a fall into the depths, a bathetic plunge. The same imagery of falling is associated with

Southey in the "Dedication" to *Don Juan,* but there it is more direct:

> He first sank to the bottom—like his works,
> But soon rose to the surface—like himself.

In the confusion, King George slips into heaven, and as Byron ends his *Vision,* the late monarch is practicing the hundredth psalm, which is only fitting, as it adjures the Lord's people to "enter into his gates with thanksgiving." The ethos of *The Vision of Judgment* is remarkably refreshing. Byron is so delighted by his fable that his good will extends even to Southey, who does not drown like Phaethon but lurks in his own den, still composing. George is in heaven, and the very dignified and high-minded Lucifer back in hell. In this one poem at least, Byron writes as a whole man, whose inner conflicts have been mastered. If the earth is the Devil's, the Devil is yet disinterested, and damnation a subject for urbane bantering. Peculiar as Byron's variety of Prometheanism was, *The Vision of Judgment* makes it clear that we err in calling the poet any genuine sort of a Calvinist:

> for not one am I
> Of those who think damnation better still:
> I hardly know too if not quite alone am I
> In this small hope of bettering future ill
> By circumscribing, with some slight restriction,
> The eternity of hell's hot jurisdiction.

If there is any mockery in the poem which is not altogether good-humored, it is in Byron's conscious "blasphemy":

> I know one may be damn'd
> For hoping no one else may e'er be so;
> I know my catechism; I know we're cramm'd
> With the best doctrines till we quite o'erflow;
> I know that all save England's church have shamm'd,
> And that the other twice two hundred churches
> And synagogues have made a *damn'd* bad purchase.

Religious cant was no more acceptable to Byron than the social or political varieties, however darkly and deeply his own orthodox currents ran. *The Vision of Judgment* is perhaps only a good parody of aspects of *Paradise Lost,* but few of us would prefer Milton's heaven to Byron's as a place in which to live.

Stanzas to the Po

BYRON's lyrics are an index to his poetic development, though only a few of them are altogether adequate in the expression of his complex sensibility. The best of them include the *Stanzas to the Po* (1819), the undated *Ode to a Lady,* which applies the poet's negative Prometheanism to the theme of lost human passion, and the last poems written under the shadow of death at Missolonghi. Byron's personal ethos, the dignity of disillusioned intensity and disinterested heroism, despairing of love and its human limitations but still longing for them, continued to shine out of this handful of lyrics.

The last poems have the poignancy of their occasion, but the *Stanzas to the Po* constitute Byron's finest short poem, and one perfectly revelatory of his mature spirit.

In April 1819 Byron, aged thirty-one, fell in love with the Countess Teresa Guiccioli, aged nineteen, who had been married only a little over a year to the fifty-eight-year-old Count. Byron had already lamented in *Don Juan* the cooling of his heart, now that he was past thirty, but he proved no prophet in this matter. Momentarily separated from Teresa, he wrote the first draft of his *Stanzas to the Po.* The firm diction of this beautiful poem shows an Italian influence, probably that of Dante's *Canzoniere:*

> River, that rollest by the ancient walls,
>   Where dwells the Lady of my love, when she
> Walks by thy brink, and there perchance recalls
>   A faint and fleeting memory of me;
>
> What if thy deep and ample stream should be
>   A mirror of my heart, where she may read
> The thousand thoughts I now betray to thee,
>   Wild as thy wave, and headlong as thy speed!

The movement of this is large and stately, but there is a curious and deliberate reluctance in the rhythm, as if the poet wished to resist the river's swift propulsion of his thoughts toward his absent mistress. As he stares at the river he sees suddenly that it is more than a mirror of his heart. He finds not similitude but identity between the Po and his heart:

> Thou tendest wildly onwards to the main.
> And I—to loving *one* I should not love.

He should not love only because he had said his farewell to love, and is reluctant to welcome it again. But it has come; he longs desperately for his beloved, yet he still resists the longing:

> The wave that bears my tears returns no more:
>   Will she return by whom that wave shall sweep?—
> Both tread thy banks, both wander on thy shore,
>   I by thy source, she by the dark-blue deep.

As the Po is one with the passion of Byron's heart, a love that Teresa reciprocates, the geographical position of the lovers symbolizes the extent to which they have given themselves to their love. Teresa is "by the dark-blue deep," but Byron still lingers by the source, struggling with the past:

> But that which keepeth us apart is not
>   Distance, nor depth of wave, nor space of earth,
> But the distraction of a various lot,
>   As various as the climates of our birth.

> A stranger loves the Lady of the land,
>   Born far beyond the mountains, but his blood
> Is all meridian, as if never fann'd
>   By the black wind that chills the polar flood.

His hesitation keeps them apart, and he traces it to the division within his own nature. But his blood triumphs, though in his own despite:

> My blood is all meridian; were it not,
>   I had not left my clime, nor should I be,
> In spite of tortures, ne'er to be forgot,
>   A slave again of love,—at least of thee.

> 'Tis vain to struggle—let me perish young—
> Live as I lived, and love as I have loved;
> To dust if I return, from dust I sprung,
> And then, at least, my heart can ne'er be moved.

Complex in attitude as these two final stanzas of the poem are, they did not satisfy Byron. As he gives himself again to love, he senses that he also gives himself to self-destruction and welcomes this as a consummation to be wished. By loving again, he is true to both his own past and his own nature, but to a past he had rejected and a nature he had sought to negate. His heart is moved again, and to have its torpor stirred is pain, but this is the pain of life.

Less than two months later, as he made his final decision and moved to join Teresa, he redrafted his poem. Characteristically, the poem is now more indecisive than the man, for he alters the final lines to a lament:

> My heart is all meridian, were it not
> I had not suffered now, nor should I be
> Despite old tortures ne'er to be forgot
> The slave again—Oh! Love! at least of thee!
>
> 'Tis vain to struggle, I have struggled long
> To love again no more as once I loved,
> Oh! Time! why leave this worst of earliest
> Passions strong?
> To tear a heart which pants to be unmoved?

Byron was too courtly to leave the penultimate line as above, and modified it to "why leave this earliest Passion strong?" With either reading, this makes for a weaker and less controlled climax to the poem than the first version, as it denies the strength of the poet's own will. The first set of *Stanzas to the Po* makes a permanent imaginative gesture, and deserves to be read repeatedly as the universal human legacy it comes so close to being. The heart divided against itself has found few more eloquent emblems.

Last Poems

ON the morning of his thirty-sixth birthday, at Missolonghi, where he was to die three months later, Byron finished the poem that is his epitaph:

> 'Tis time this heart should be unmoved,
>> Since others it hath ceased to move:
> Yet, though I cannot be beloved,
>> Still let me love!

He begins with an echo of the final line of the *Stanzas to the Po,* but the emphasis is different. He now fears not that he will love again but that he cannot:

> My days are in the yellow leaf;
>> The flowers and fruits of love are gone;
> The worm, the canker, and the grief
>> Are mine alone!

The Macbeth comparison is perhaps rather too melodramatic, but the next stanza modulates to the more appropriate Promethean image of fire:

> The fire that on my bosom preys
>> Is lone as some volcanic isle;
> No torch is kindled at its blaze—
>> A funeral pile.

The fire is not yet out, the volcano not extinct, but the volcano is isolated and the fire will be consumed with the poet. He wears the chain of love (for the abandoned Teresa?) but he cannot share in its pain and power. In a recovery of great rhetorical power he turns upon his grief and delivers himself up to his destiny:

> Tread those reviving passions down,
>> Unworthy manhood!—unto thee
> Indifferent should the smile or frown
>> Of beauty be.

> If thou regrett'st thy youth, *why live?*
>> The land of honourable death

> Is here:—up to the field, and give
>   Away thy breath!
>
> Seek out—less often sought than found—
>   A soldier's grave, for thee the best;
> Then look around, and choose thy ground,
>   And take thy rest.

Byron seems to have intended this as his last poem, but his Muses had it otherwise, and ended him with an intense love poem for his page-boy Loukas. The suffering conveyed by this poem clearly has its sexual element, so that the complex puzzle of Byron is not exactly simplified for us, but this is a problem for his biographers, who have reached no agreement upon it. Certainly Byron had homosexual as well as incestuous experience; his questing and experimental psyche, and his conviction of necessary damnation, could have led him to no less. In his final lines he liberates himself from his last verbal inhibition and writes a very powerful homosexual love poem:

> I watched thee when the foe was at our side,
>   Ready to strike at him—or thee and me.
> Were safety hopeless—rather than divide
>   Aught with one loved save love and liberty.
>
> I watched thee on the breakers, when the rock
>   Received our prow and all was storm and fear,
> And bade thee cling to me through every shock;
>   This arm would be thy bark, or breast thy bier.

Love and death come dangerously close together in these tense stanzas, so much so that one can understand why Loukas was wary enough to cause Byron to lament:

> And when convulsive throes denied my breath
>   The faintest utterance to my fading thought,
> To thee—to thee—e'en in the gasp of death
>   My spirit turned, oh! oftener than it ought.
>
> Thus much and more; and yet thou lov'st me not,
>   And never wilt! Love dwells not in our will.

Nor can I blame thee, though it be my lot
  To strongly, wrongly, vainly love thee still.

It is very moving that this agonized hymn to hopeless love should
be Byron's last poem. Had he been more of a Promethean he would
still not have achieved a better either sexual or rhetorical balance,
when one remembers the English and European society through
which he had to take his way. But he might have had more faith
in his own imaginings, more confidence in his own inventive power,
and so have given us something larger and more relevant than *Manfred* in the Romantic mode, good as *Manfred* is. We have *Don
Juan,* and the record, still incomplete, of Byron's life. Byron did not
seem to regret his not having given us more, and was himself realistic enough to believe that there was no more to give.

CHAPTER FIVE

PERCY BYSSHE SHELLEY

and where death, if shed,
Presumes no carnage, but this single change,—
Upon the steep floor flung from dawn to dawn
The silken skilled transmemberment of song.

HART CRANE

1 *Urbanity and Apocalypse*

S HELLEY is a prophetic and religious poet whose passionate
convictions are agnostic, and a lyrical poet whose style is a
deliberate gamble with the limits of poetry. He is in consequence likely to remain controversial, but no single generation of
critics will dispose of him. Of all the Romantics, he needs the closest
reading, and a reading whose context ought to be found in traditions of poetry, and not in philosophy or politics. But the critical
fate of his poetry has been obscured by allegorizers who have read it
as Plato versified, or as an apotheosis of Godwin, his father-in-law
and mentor in revolutionary theory.

Shelley drowned at twenty-nine, and made no single poem that shows all his powers working together. His major completed poem, *Prometheus Unbound,* was written a little too early; like Keats, he found his myth before he had matured his style. His unfinished last poem, *The Triumph of Life,* is probably as complete as it could be; like the two *Hyperions* of Keats, it resolves itself by breaking off. The *Triumph* has a more severe and finished style than *Prometheus,* but it is a work that attempts less, for *Prometheus* shares with Blake and Wordsworth an ambition to replace *Paradise Lost.* What distinguishes Shelley from Blake, whom he otherwise resembles, is the urbanity of his apocalypse. Usually intense, Shelley is yet always at ease, though few of his critics want to note this. Shelley's irony is neither the "romantic irony" of pathos, brilliantly manipulated by Byron, nor the "metaphysical" irony so valued in the generation just past. It has more in common with the prophetic and cyclic irony of Blake; like Blake, Shelley is always alert to the combative possibilities of interweaving an antinomian rhetoric with a dialectic that exposes the inadequacies of both the orthodox in morality and religion and any position that seeks merely to negate orthodoxy by an inversion of categories. But Blake's irony is always at the expense of some position, and is usually bitter. Shelley's irony is gentler and relies on incongruities that can suddenly startle us in the midst of the sublime without dropping us into the bathetic. Indeed, Shelley's urbanity is unique in literature in that it can manifest itself on the level of the sublime.[42] We can even say that in *Prometheus,* Acts III and IV, Shelley *civilizes the sublime,* and makes a renovated universe a subject for gentlemanly conversation.

The notions of urbanity and civility rely upon the image of a city, and Blake more than Shelley understands that a redeemed universe must be a city of art and not a garden of happier nature. But it is Shelley who has an instinctive sense of the manners of Blake's City.

When Blake gives us the complete trumpet rhapsody of his Last Judgment ("Night the Ninth," *The Four Zoas*), the aim of his astonishing invention is to compel in us a total response as exuberant as our creative energies can supply. Nothing can exceed the sense of a more human world that Blake gives us, but the solitary reaction within that world is one of exultant wonder:

The roots shoot thick thro' the solid rocks bursting their way
They cry out in joys of existence; the broad stems
Rear on the mountains stem after stem the scaly newt creeps
From the stone and the armed fly springs from the rocky
    crevice
The spider, the bat burst from the harden'd slime crying
To one another: "What are we, and whence is our joy and
    delight?"

In Act III, scene iv, of *Prometheus Unbound* the Spirit of Earth observes the renovation of mankind, as all ugly shapes and images depart upon the winds:

                                and those
From whom they passed seemed mild and lovely forms
After some foul disguise had fallen.

In Blake this would be followed by something strenuous; in Shelley it flows on with an urbane rhythm, as the marvelous is civilized into the ordinary:

                                and all
Were somewhat changed, and after brief surprise
And greetings of delighted wonder, all
Went to their sleep again.

The "somewhat" is masterly; the "brief" not less so, and the concluding turn a triumph of gracious underemphasis.

This spirit of urbanity is so prevalent in Shelley that one learns to distrust the accuracy of any critic who finds Shelley's poetry shrill, without humor, self-centered, or exhibiting only "primary impulses." Ideologically Shelley is of the permanent Left, in politics and religion, and his morality insists on the right of private judgment in every possible human matter. He is nothing short of an extremist, and knew it; he says of himself, "I go on until I am stopped, and I never am stopped." Perhaps it is inevitable that so passionately individual a poet will always make ideological enemies. Nevertheless, it is to be hoped that such enemies will in time cease to misrepresent Shelley's poetry, and not continue to pretend to an aesthetic condemnation that is usually a mask for their own sense of moral and religious outrage.

2 *The Quest*

Alastor

IN the autumn of 1815 Shelley, aged twenty-three, composed a blank-verse rhapsody of 720 lines, a quest-romance called *Alastor* (Greek for "avenging demon") or *The Spirit of Solitude*. This is his first poem of consequence, and is already both characteristic of his genius and premonitory of the development he was to undergo in the less than seven years that remained to him. The burden of *Alastor* is despair of the human condition. A preface sets forth the two possible fates the poem assigns to mankind:

> But that Power which strikes the luminaries of the world with sudden darkness and extinction, by awakening them to too exquisite a perception of its influences, dooms to a slow and poisonous decay those meaner spirits that dare to abjure its dominion.

That Power is the Imagination, in its Wordsworthian formulation, and it brings with it a choice between two kinds of destruction: the Poet's solitude and the unimaginative man's lonely gregariousness. The second, less luminous destruction is ignored in *Alastor,* and receives no adequate treatment in Shelley until his last poem, *The Triumph of Life.* The first becomes a quest for a finite and measured object of desire which shall yet encompass in itself the beauty and truth of the infinite and unmeasured conceptions of the Poet. This quest is necessarily in vain, and leads to the untimely death of the quester.

Such a theme would not have been acceptable to Wordsworth or Coleridge, and yet is the legitimate offspring of their own art and imaginative theory. Indeed *Alastor* is prompted by *The Excursion,* and echoes both the *Intimations* ode and *Kubla Khan.* It seemed to the young Shelley that Wordsworth and Coleridge had inaugurated a mode, liberated an imaginative impulse, but then had repudiated their own creation. With *Alastor*, Shelley published a sonnet addressed to Wordsworth and a powerful lyric ("Oh! there are spirits of the air"), which Mrs. Shelley says was addressed to Coleridge. The sonnet to Wordsworth opens with direct reference to the Great Ode's theme of loss:

> Poet of Nature, thou hast wept to know
> That things depart which never may return.

To this Shelley now adds the loss of Wordsworth himself, who has ceased to be what he was, a maker of "songs consecrate to truth and liberty." The sonnet fails by excessive externalization of Wordsworth's supposed apostasy. Shelley, though more influenced by Wordsworth, felt a closer temperamental affinity with Coleridge, and his lyric to Coleridge is remarkable for its inventive reading of a nature he believed akin to his own:

> With mountain winds, and babbling springs,
>   And moonlight seas, that are the voice
> Of these inexplicable things,
>   Thou didst hold commune, and rejoice
> When they did answer thee; but they
> Cast, like a worthless boon, thy love away.

"These inexplicable things" are the manifestation abroad of the One Life that is also within us. For a while Nature held commune with Coleridge, but finally broke off the dialogue and cast the poet's love away:

> Ah! wherefore didst thou build thine hope
>   On the false earth's inconstancy?
> Did thine own mind afford no scope
>   Of love, or moving thoughts to thee?
> That natural scenes or human smiles
> Could steal the power to wind thee in their wiles?

This is exactly contrary to Coleridge's own reading of his crisis in *Dejection*, where Nature lives only insofar as we give it something of our own life. Nature, Shelley insists, has its own life, but apart from us, and is necessarily false and inconstant to us. Or, to put it as a contrary of Wordsworth's language, Nature always will and must betray the human heart that loves her, for Nature, whether operative in "natural scenes or human smiles," is not adequate to meet the demands made upon her by the human imagination. So, from the beginning, Shelley takes his position with Blake as against Wordsworth.

But how will the poet's soul react when he at last realizes that "the glory of the moon is dead"? Your own soul, Shelley observes to Coleridge, still is true to you, but the misery of loss makes it only a specter of what it was, and this specter of departed power haunts Coleridge like a fiend:

> This fiend, whose ghastly presence ever
>   Beside thee like thy shadow hangs,
> Dream not to chase;—the mad endeavour
>   Would scourge thee to severer pangs.
> Be as thou art. Thy settled fate,
> Dark as it is, all change would aggravate.

That is hardly kind, but Shelley, young and intense, is finally not much kinder to himself in *Alastor,* where the doomed quester is clearly the poem's maker. This last stanza of the lyric to Coleridge is an exact analogue to Blake's theory of Spectre and Emanation. The composite form of all the poet creates or loves, his Emanation, does emanate from him when he is still in possession of the Joy of Imagination. But when it exists as a mere external form, independent of him, it is likely to seem mocking and tantalizing. In response to this mockery, his sense of self may seek refuge in abstractions, as Coleridge's does in *Dejection,* until the self and the abstraction merge into the menacing and self-accusing figure of the Spectre. You are in your Spectre's power, Shelley's poem warns Coleridge, and a continued struggling will only intensify that power, and aggravate an already darkly settled fate.

Shelley ends the preface to *Alastor* by ironically quoting the Wanderer's introduction to the tragic tale of Margaret in Book I of *The Excursion:*

> The good die first,
> And those whose hearts are dry as summer dust,
> Burn to the socket!

In the light of the poems printed with *Alastor,* Wordsworth and Coleridge are held among those who burn to the socket. The poem *Alastor* is itself a prophetic celebration of Shelley's own career, moving rapidly toward a more dramatic "sudden darkness and extinction." Only the image is inappropriate, for Shelley's heart did not find its hoped-for death by the fire of his own desires, but by the watery waste of the world of experience.

Alastor opens with a Wordsworthian invocation of Nature as "Great Parent." Speaking as the element of fire, the poet addresses earth, ocean, and air as his brothers, and claims a "natural piety" that enables him to feel their love and to offer his own in recompense. Yet, like Wordsworth's Child in the Great Ode, he has felt "obstinate questionings of thee and thine," of Nature and her phenomenal manifestations. But Nature has not yet unveiled her inmost sanctuary, and he is puzzled as to the mystery "of what we are." Like Coleridge and Wordsworth, he calls upon nature for a greater measure of inspiration, and offers himself up to the wind as an aeolian lyre

> that serenely now
> And moveless, as a long-forgotten lyre
> Suspended in the solitary dome
> Of some mysterious and deserted fane,
> I wait thy breath, Great Parent, that my strain
> May modulate with murmurs of the air,
> And motions of the forests and the sea,
> And voice of living beings, and woven hymns
> Of night and day, and the deep heart of man.

To modulate with is to adjust to a certain measure or proportion, yet the strain need not be lost in the music of nature. The poem's music is toned down by the melody of earth and air, but still strives for distinctness.

Shelley begins his story of a Poet with a vision of an untimely tomb built by moldering leaves in the waste wilderness. Not hands, but "the charmed eddies of autumnal winds" have built this sad monument to one who lived, died, and sang in solitude. He began as a Wordsworthian poet must, with every natural sight and sound sending to his heart its choicest influences. Leaving an alienated home behind him, he sets forth to seek strange truths, and to pursue "Nature's most secret steps" to their *Kubla Khan*–like sources:

> where the secret caves
> Rugged and dark, winding among the springs
> Of fire and poison, inaccessible
> To avarice or pride, their starry domes
> Of diamond and of gold expand. . . .

In this quest for the secret spring of things the Poet is oblivious of the love felt for him by an Arab maiden. Instead he has a vision of a veiled maid whose voice is like that of his own soul and the themes of whose converse are his own. They meet in love; sleep returns, and the Poet awakens to find her gone:

> His wan eyes
> Gaze on the empty scene as vacantly
> As ocean's moon looks on the moon in heaven.

He is as empty as the scene, and his eyes are now only a reflection of the ideal he has loved. As in *Endymion,* which is influenced by *Alastor,* the Poet now pursues his quest with renewed intensity and hopelessness. The sexual element changes the nature of the poem, as Shelley intended it to do. Wordsworth, in his disciple's view, was sexually timid in not directly associating the poet's love of nature with his love of woman. If sight and sound send to the heart its choicest impulses, then surely the other senses are also natural modes of imaginative discernment. The quest for the hiding places of natural power is now also a quest for complete sensual fulfillment.

The Poet wanders on driven by the bright shadow of his dream, and enters into a premature autumn of the body. He rejects the gentle advances of youthful maidens, for he is pursued now by his own Spectre, the *alastor* or avenging demon of his self-chosen solitude.

He moves on to the foothills of the Caucasus, retracing in reverse the march of civilization. Though most of the poem until the climax is scenery, it is scenery charged with a furious energy of perception, for all of it shudders at the edge of the destructive ideal toward which the Poet surges. When he dies, his ideal still unattainable, his life ebbs and flows as the great horned moon goes down. What is left behind is not "the passionate tumult of a clinging hope" but

> cold tranquillity,
> Nature's vast frame, the web of human things.

Beautiful and extreme as it is, *Alastor* remains a dead end, as any poem of a ruined quest must be, for it closes in a wasteland from which no salvation is possible. Half a year later, in the summer of 1816, in the Swiss Alps and lakes, and frequently in the company of Byron, Shelley found his way out of this premature vision of despair. He found, in one startling revelation, both myth and poetic technique, and did not abandon them until the end.

3   *The Hidden Power*

Hymn to Intellectual Beauty

VOYAGING round the Lake of Geneva with Byron, Shelley occupied himself by reading Rousseau's *Nouvelle Héloïse* for the first time. Rousseau's influence is added to Wordsworth's in the *Hymn to Intellectual Beauty*, conceived at this time. "Intellectual" in the title simply means "spiritual," or "beyond the senses." The poem's subject is very nearly that of the *Intimations* ode, but Shelley takes a very different attitude to the problem of the glory's departure:

> The awful shadow of some unseen Power
> Floats though unseen among us,—visiting
> This various world with as inconstant wing
> As summer winds that creep from flower to flower.

The splendor in nature is due to this shadow but is not identical with it, as the shadow of an unseen Power is itself unseen even when it moves among us, fitful as the creeping summer wind. Wordsworthian natural glory is thus three degrees removed from

an unknown reality. Yet it does intimate reality to us, and such
reality is fleetingly manifested in any phenomenon that moves us
by its grace and mystery.

The next stanza relates the evanescence of this spirit of Beauty
to man's scope for negations, to his contradictory capacity "for love
and hate, despondency and hope." These dualities remain inexplicable, and the attempts of superstition and religion to deal with
them are vain endeavors, frail spells that cannot dismiss "doubt,
chance, and mutability." Only the momentary visitations of beauty's light give grace and truth to appearances, and redeem man from
his natural despair:

> Love, Hope, and Self-esteem, like clouds depart
>   And come, for some uncertain moments lent.
>   Man were immortal, and omnipotent,
> Didst thou, unknown and awful as thou art,
> Keep with thy glorious train firm state within his heart.
>   Thou messenger of sympathies,
>   That wax and wane in lovers' eyes—
>   Thou—that to human thought art nourishment,
>   Like darkness to a dying flame!
>   Depart not as thy shadow came,
>   Depart not—lest the grave should be,
>   Like life and fear, a dark reality.

This stanza is the heart of Shelley's hymn. The Christian triad
of virtues—love, hope, and faith—are replaced here by the Shelleyan triad of love, hope, and self-esteem, this last meaning esteem
for the Imagination as the great agency of moral good within each
of us. These virtues come and go like cloud movements, and are
only lent us by the visitations of Imagination or the Intellectual
Beauty. If they remained with us, we would be as gods. Human
love and thought wax and wane in cycle insofar as they are alternately nourished and abandoned by the unseen Spirit, just as if first
the Spirit fed the flame and then left it to die in darkness. The
stanza closes in the desperation of a hopeless prayer. Doctrinal center of the poem as it is, the fourth stanza is a little strident in tone.

Until now the hymn has dealt with a general phenomenon, the
arrival and departure of the spirit of Beauty. The poem's second
half particularizes both the gain and the loss, and more directly

recalls Wordsworth. Shelley abandons sensuous observation for memory, in the manner of the Great Ode. As a boy he actively sought ghostly revelations, and "called on poisonous names with which our youth is fed," the names presumably being those of Christian doctrine. But nothing came of this seeking. In the wise passivity of "musing deeply on the lot of life," in the spring of the year, suddenly the shadow of Beauty fell upon him with the force of a religious awakening. In response, he vowed that he would dedicate his powers to this spirit. The final stanza renews this vow, and echoes the Wordsworthian "sober coloring" of mature Imagination:

> The day becomes more solemn and serene
>   When noon is past—there is a harmony
>   In autumn, and a lustre in its sky,
> Which through the summer is not heard or seen,
> As if it could not be, as if it had not been!
>   Thus let thy power, which like the truth
>   Of nature on my passive youth
> Descended, to my onward life supply
>   Its calm—to one who worships thee,
>   And every form containing thee,
>   Whom, SPIRIT fair, thy spells did bind
> To fear himself, and love all human kind.

The first five lines here are thoroughly Wordsworthian; they would fit into the last stanza of the *Intimations* ode. In what follows, Shelley breaks with Wordsworth, as he has several times previously in the poem. The hidden Power descends on the poet's passive youth like the truth of nature, but in his onward life he must learn to worship the Power only, and not its ebbing natural manifestations. When the imagination becomes more active, nature loses its power as truth. We have seen this dialectic operative in Blake and Wordsworth, involuntarily in the latter case. To worship every form containing the Power is to worship Blake's human form divine, or the imagination incarnate. So drastic a humanism Wordsworth could not bring himself to accept, though he comes close to it in his visions of shepherds against the sky in *The Prelude*. Shelley bluntly declares for such a humanism here in his hymn. The final effect of the Spirit of Beauty on the young poet is to strengthen his imaginative virtues of "Love, Hope, and Self-esteem." "To fear himself" is to hold his imagination in reverence and awe as a mark of divinity; to "love all human kind" is to see them as potential imagination; and the calm he requests finds its foundation in his visionary hope. Shelley has thrown off his *alastor* or Spectre, his selfhood of despair, and has found in its place a quasi-religious impulse, the desire to make a myth out of the heart's responses to the hidden godhead whose light moves so precariously through the natural world.

Mont Blanc

THE reasons of the heart find their expression in Shelley's hymn of Beauty. The report of the head, searching out the nature of the hidden power that governs thought and the universe, is involved in the other nature ode of 1816, the irregularly rhymed *Mont Blanc*.[43] Here the dominant influence is *Tintern Abbey*, and the dissent from Wordsworth becomes more explicit.

Wordsworth had a sense of "a motion and a spirit" that rolled through all external phenomena and that simultaneously moved both the thinker and the object of his thought. This motion and spirit was benevolent, and moral in its human effects. Shelley is not so sure as he contemplates Mont Blanc, Europe's highest peak, and seeks to commune with the spirit hidden behind the glaciers and icy torrents. The mountain and its ravine testify to Shelley of the difficulties inherent in natural theology, in our seeking to find the wisdom of God in the creation. Job abnegated himself before the Behemoth and Leviathan, God's fearful handiwork. Shelley belongs to a different tradition, as do Blake when he ironically questions *The Tyger*'s idiot questioner, and Melville's Ahab when he assaults that snowy Leviathan and king over all the children of pride, Moby Dick.

Mont Blanc opens with a majestic evocation of the power of nature:

> The everlasting universe of things
> Flows through the mind, and rolls its rapid waves,
> Now dark—now glittering—now reflecting gloom—
> Now lending splendour, where from secret springs

The source of human thought its tribute brings
Of waters,—with a sound but half its own,
Such as a feeble brook will oft assume
In the wild woods, among the mountains lone,
Where waterfalls around it leap for ever,
Where woods and winds contend, and a vast river
Over its rocks ceaselessly bursts and raves.

The poem's subject is the relation between individual mind and the universe, and also the problem of what rules the universe, and to what moral end. Unifying this double subject is the imaginative postulate of a universal mind, or hidden Power in nature. The ravine masks and metaphorically represents universal mind; the Arve River, the "everlasting Universe of things," and the "feeble brook," the human mind that borrows inspiration from the external world, even as the brook's force depends upon the river's. The Arve gives splendor to the ravine and reflects the ravine's colors, just as impressions reach the individual mind through the senses but the mind gives its personal coloring to these impressions. The Arve seems to take on something of the meaning of "Alph, the sacred river" when the passage's final lines echo *Kubla Khan*.

The next section of the poem directly addresses the ravine and its lurking Power. As Shelley gazes upon the ravine, he muses upon his reaction to its vivid force:

One legion of wild thoughts, whose wandering wings
Now float above thy darkness, and now rest
Where that or thou are no unbidden guest,
In the still cave of the witch Poesy,
Seeking among the shadows that pass by
Ghosts of all things that are, some shade of thee,
Some phantom, some faint image; till the breast
From which they fled recalls them, thou art there!

Here the legion of thoughts is the state of the poet's mind, distracted as he composes the poem, but still at rest in the refuge of poetry's cave. In the cave, the poet's mind gazes out at phenomena and seeks a shade of the ravine's reality in the ghostly world of imagination. These phantoms and images have emanated from the poet's own breast; when he recalls them he admits defeat in his metaphoric quest. But, suddenly, when he ceases to search, the natural scene gives him his symbol: "thou art there"; the ravine itself is an emblem of a mind more comprehensive than the poet's, a power akin to the light that sweeps through the world in the *Hymn to Intellectual Beauty*. But the powers, though close, are not one. The Intellectual Beauty compels the heart's response, but "the secret Strength of things" in *Mont Blanc* addresses itself to the mind, and terrifies the heart. Shelley is verging on a strange revelation of a divided Godhead, half of it totally withdrawn and indifferent to us, but nevertheless governing thought; the other half free-floating, sometimes among us, benevolent, and governing the emotions.

Mont Blanc's third section establishes the moral indifference of the secret power enshrined in the mountain, yet suggests how the power can be tapped for revolutionary moral ends:

> The wilderness has a mysterious tongue
> Which teaches awful doubt, or faith so mild,
> So solemn, so serene, that man may be,
> But for such faith, with nature reconciled;
> Thou hast a voice, great Mountain, to repeal
> Large codes of fraud and woe; not understood
> By all, but which the wise, and great, and good
> Interpret, or make felt, or deeply feel.

The "awful doubt" is of any orthodox view of nature that sees it as the direct handiwork of a benevolent God. The "faith so mild" is the solemn and serene natural piety of Wordsworth which is too timid to apprehend that nature is not concerned with man's specific good. To reconcile oneself with nature, one needs to recognize its potential malevolence. The mountain's voice, if understood, tells us that the power of good or evil is in our own wills, for we can choose how to utilize natural power. Indeed, even without full understanding, the voice can be interpreted properly (as it was by Shelley's father-in-law, Godwin) or can be deeply felt (as it was by Wordsworth, who also knew how to make it felt by others).

The fourth section of the poem develops the vision of the natural scene, emphasizing the remote serenity of the Power that dwells apart behind the mountain. As the section deals with the dual capacity of the Power for creation and destruction, it is not surprising that memories of *Kubla Khan* are again evoked:

> Below, vast caves
> Shine in the rushing torrents' restless gleam,
> Which from those secret chasms in tumult welling
> Meet in the vale, and one majestic River,
> The breath and blood of distant lands, for ever
> Rolls its loud waters to the ocean-waves,
> Breathes its swift vapours to the circling air.

As in *Kubla Khan,* natural creation and destruction are paralleled to the Imagination's capacity for creation, with a dark hint that the human negation of imaginative making will lead to destruction.

In its fifth and final section, *Mont Blanc* reinforces its Blake-like point that there is no natural religion. We are told again that the ultimate power of things finds its emblem in the mountain, and we are now given the understanding of this emblem's importance to us, which is in the "human mind imaginings." Our imaginings can draw upon "the secret Strength of things," and but for our imaginings the phenomena of nature would be meaningless to us:

> And what were thou, and earth, and stars, and sea,
> If to the human mind's imaginings
> Silence and solitude were vacancy?

"Thou" here is Mont Blanc only, and not the Power behind natural forms. The phenomena of mountain, and earth, and stars, and sea would continue to exist even if our imaginings could do nothing with them, but they would lose their human significance. Their vacancy would be our poverty. But if we purged our poverty, then we could see these phenomena as outer forms of the inner Strength of things, and our imaginings would be a means of grace for us. This pattern of natural inspiration as a reciprocal process or dialogue between phenomena and the poet's imaginings becomes clearer in Shelley's most powerful shorter poem, the fierce and apocalyptic *Ode to the West Wind.*

Ode to the West Wind

WITH this ode we move ahead three years in Shelley's life, to the autumn of 1819, when the poet had finished the first three acts of

Prometheus Unbound but before he had added the astonishing afterthought of the fourth (October 1819). The tentative myth-making apprehensions of the poems of 1816 have now been confirmed, and Shelley sees himself as the prophet of a rising wind which heralds destruction of an old world and creation of a new. He raises his psalm to the glory of what is coming, and as a celebration of much that departs.

Shelley's note to his ode places the circumstances of its composition. In a wood that skirts the Arno, near Florence, on a day when the wind is rising and collecting the vapors that pour down the autumnal rains, the poet at sunset observes the turning of the year, the passage into fall. As the night comes on, a violent tempest of hail and rain descends. In this autumnal advent the poet reads the signs of a creative destruction that will affect the whole condition of man. Even as the destroying westerly wind now sweeps toward the winter of the world, so another wind from the same quarter will bring in the spring the following year. But though the poem salutes the second wind ("thine azure sister of the Spring"), it concerns itself not with cycle but with the possibility of breaking out of cycle into a spring that shall not pass away:

> O wild West Wind, thou breath of Autumn's being,
> Thou from whose unseen presence the leaves dead
> Are driven, like ghosts from an enchanter fleeing,
>
> Yellow, and black, and pale, and hectic red,
> Pestilence-stricken multitudes! O thou
> Who chariotest to their dark wintry bed
>
> The wingèd seeds, where they lie cold and low,
> Each like a corpse within its grave, until
> Thine azure sister of the Spring shall blow
>
> Her clarion o'er the dreaming earth, and fill
> (Driving sweet buds like flocks to feed in air)
> With living hues and odours plain and hill;
>
> Wild Spirit, which art moving everywhere;
> Destroyer and preserver; hear, oh, hear!

The wind, like the Beauty of the *Hymn,* is an "unseen presence." Before this presence's exorcising enchantment the dead leaves flee to their necessary destruction, but the live seeds are "charioted" to the salvation of a winter's sleep, akin to that of the sleepers who will awake into resurrection. The spring wind is a shepherdess of a renewed pastoral innocence, whose clarion of judgment will awaken earth to renewal. The stanza ends with a confronting call to the wind to hear its prophet. This pattern is repeated in the second and third stanzas, which also end in summoning the wind to heed the poet's prayer. In the first stanza, observing the wind's effect upon the forest, Shelley sees the dead leaves driven along beneath tangled boughs still covered with leaves. In the second he transfers his gaze to the sky:

> Thou on whose stream, mid the steep sky's commotion,
> Loose clouds like earth's decaying leaves are shed,
> Shook from the tangled boughs of Heaven and Ocean,
>
> Angels of rain and lightning! there are spread
> On the blue surface of thine aëry surge,
> Like the bright hair uplifted from the head
>
> Of some fierce Maenad, even from the dim verge
> Of the horizon to the zenith's height,
> The locks of the approaching storm. Thou dirge
>
> Of the dying year, to which this closing night
> Will be the dome of a vast sepulchre,
> Vaulted with all thy congregated might
>
> Of vapours, from whose solid atmosphere
> Black rain, and fire, and hail will burst: oh, hear!

The tangled boughs of Heaven and Ocean are the higher, more stationary clouds; the loose clouds beneath them are driven by the wind, just as the dead leaves are driven below. The heavens, like the forest, are dying, and yielding their substance up to the destroying wind. As the wind sweeps on, the woods act as a vast aeolian lyre and give forth a dirgelike sound. The year and its dependent life are imprisoned in the sepulcher dominated by the blackening dome of the stormy evening sky, from which the black rain, fire, and hail of destruction will burst. The figure of black rain has in it a hint of revolution, and reminds us that Shelley is heralding also an overthrow of the age of Metternich and Castlereagh. What is destroyed in the third stanza is a natural peace and beauty, which scarcely needs the fierce destructive grace of the abolishing wind. The sweep of apocalypse carries away the best of the old order as well as what needs burial:

> Thou who didst waken from his summer dreams
> The blue Mediterranean, where he lay,
> Lulled by the coil of his crystàlline streams,
>
> Beside a pumice isle in Baiae's bay,
> And saw in sleep old palaces and towers
> Quivering within the wave's intenser day,
>
> All overgrown with azure moss, and flowers
> So sweet, the sense faints picturing them! Thou
> For whose path the Atlantic's level powers
>
> Cleave themselves into chasms, while far below
> The sea-blooms and the oozy woods which wear
> The sapless foliage of the ocean, know
>
> Thy voice, and suddenly grow gray with fear,
> And tremble and despoil themselves: oh, hear!

Azure is Shelley's color for the triumphant joy of imagination made manifest in nature. He uses it to mean what is delicate, gracious, clear, pleasant, sometimes even without reference to color. The Mediterranean is only lulled, but the illusion of peace is itself an Elysian value, and Shelley laments its sacrifice to the wind. The "old palaces and towers," once tokens of tyranny, have been mellowed by time and receive their ultimate imaginative form by being reflected on the calm waters of the sea. This is the best that nature's own art can do with reality, and it is beautiful, but it cannot abide the intensity of the wind.

So far the poet himself has not entered his poem, but in the last two stanzas he replaces leaf, cloud, and wave as the object of the

wind's force. The poem's meaning turns upon the deliberate contrast between the fourth and fifth stanzas. In the fourth the poet
pleads for a negation of his human status; he wishes to be only
an object for the wind, like leaf, cloud, wave. His despair here is like
the despair of Job, who calls upon the wind to dissolve his substance. The final stanza recoils from this surrender, and cries out
for a mutual relation with the wind. Yet even the Jobean fourth
stanza is far removed from self-pity, modern critical opinion to the
contrary:

> If I were a dead leaf thou mightest bear;
> If I were a swift cloud to fly with thee;
> A wave to pant beneath thy power, and share
>
> The impulse of thy strength, only less free
> Than thou, O uncontrollable! If even
> I were as in my boyhood, and could be
>
> The comrade of thy wanderings over Heaven,
> As then, when to outstrip thy skiey speed
> Scarce seemed a vision; I would ne'er have striven
>
> As thus with thee in prayer in my sore need.
> Oh, lift me as a wave, a leaf, a cloud!
> I fall upon the thorns of life! I bleed!
>
> A heavy weight of hours has chained and bowed
> One too like thee: tameless, and swift, and proud.

If I were merely part of nature, or if I still possessed the imaginative strength of my boyhood, then I would not be striving with
you now in prayer in my sore need. These lines mix a Wordsworthian plangency for the hiding places of imaginative power with
the accents of wrestling Jacob, who would not let the angel go until
a divine blessing was bestowed. Yet this Jacob momentarily lets go
in despair of his struggle and, as a mere natural object, falls back,
out of the Spirit, and onto the thorns of life. Job, feeling his abandonment, cried out, "He hath cast me into the mire, and I am become like dust and ashes." A rhetorical critic could as justifiably,
and as inaptly, accuse Job of self-pity, as he does Shelley. The *Ode*

to the West Wind, like the Book of Job, is a religious poem, and the conventions of religious rhetoric apply equally to each work. Shelley's song falters in the fourth stanza with the deliberation of religious despair and the pathos of the rejected and wasted prophet.

The last stanza of the *Hymn to Intellectual Beauty* echoed the "sober coloring" of the last stanza of Wordsworth's *Intimations* ode by speaking of "a harmony in autumn, and a lustre in its sky." Similarly, the final stanza of Shelley's greatest ode modulates to "a deep, autumnal tone":

> Make me thy lyre, even as the forest is:
> What if my leaves are falling like its own!
> The tumult of thy mighty harmonies
>
> Will take from both a deep, autumnal tone,
> Sweet though in sadness. Be thou, Spirit fierce,
> My spirit! Be thou me, impetuous one!
>
> Drive my dead thoughts over the universe
> Like withered leaves to quicken a new birth!
> And, by the incantation of this verse,
>
> Scatter, as from an unextinguished hearth
> Ashes and sparks, my words among mankind!
> Be through my lips to unawakened earth
>
> The trumpet of a prophecy! O Wind,
> If Winter comes, can Spring be far behind?

The twentieth-century equivalent to this marvelous stanza is in Hart Crane's powerful elegy for his own poetic career, *The Broken Tower:*

> The bells, I say, the bells break down their tower;
> And swing I know not where. Their tongues engrave
> Membrane through marrow, my long-scattered score
> Of broken intervals . . . And I, their sexton slave!

The bells break down their tower, even as the leaves of the humanized aeolian lyre fall like the autumn leaves of the forest. The leaves are the poet's thoughts, falling dead to earth. But these dead leaves fall, to be lifted again by the wind and to be driven by it over the universe to quicken a new birth. Quite humbly, Shelley is suggesting that his thoughts may be useful to fertilize the age he wishes to stir into life. For his poem, he claims more. The prayer to the wind stresses mutual need; if the prophet needs the divine, the divine as assuredly needs the prophet if the message is to be heard by men. Shelley is praying for energy and life, and offers in recompense a human voice, to be the trumpet of a prophecy.

In his passionate prose essay *A Defence of Poetry* (1821), Shelley was to return to the figure of "an unextinguished hearth" as an emblem of his poetic mind: "The mind in creation is as a fading coal, which some invisible influence, like an inconstant wind, awakens to transitory brightness; this power arises from within, like the colour of a flower which fades and changes as it is developed."

The mind of Shelley, in creating his *Ode,* is such a coal or hearth, never quite faded, never altogether extinguished. The west wind awakens it to a transitory brightness, but the poem's color still comes from a power within the mind. The prophecy is Shelley's own, for it must pass through his lips if it is to reawaken man as well as earth, and his lips modify even as they sound forth the wind's song. With Isaiah the prophet, the agnostic poet of the *Ode to the West Wind* could have said that a live coal from the divine altar had touched his lips.

To a Skylark

THE beautiful ode *To a Skylark,* composed a year later, can be taken as Shelley's lyrical farewell to the theme of the power hidden behind nature and the poet's relation to that power. As the poem begins, the bird is already out of sight; it is flying too high for visibility. The poet hears the lark's song coming out of the clear, still, blue sky; the impression is astonishingly disembodied. Delighted surprise is the tone of this ecstatic first stanza:

> Hail to thee, blithe Spirit!
> Bird thou never wert,
> That from Heaven, or near it,
> Pourest thy full heart
> In profuse strains of unpremeditated art.

The unseen bird is all swiftness and fire in the second stanza; he goes on soaring and singing, higher and higher, into the blue of his happiness. He goes on until he is stopped, and he never is stopped. He moves in an upper paradise, in which infinite desire is gratified, and this is possible because, appearance aiding fancy here, he is "unbodied," he is only song.

In Stanzas iv and v, the lark is compared to the morning star, Shelley's prime emblem of desire, poetry, relationship. The lark is unseen as the star is unseen in daylight, but the clear, piercing song of the lark can be heard, as *keen* to hear as the lines of light are *keen* (that is, clear and bright) to be viewed, when the star's lamp narrows. Neither the lark's song nor the star's light fades out in dimness; rather, they vanish by intensification, until only one clear note or one clear arrow of light is left. They intensify until one hardly hears or sees them anymore, but, rather, feels that they are there.

Stanzas vi and vii continue the simile between song and light, quite straightforwardly, and the same simile flows over into Stanza viii, where the poet's song emanates from the light of his thought, so that this similitude has been brought over to an identity that is at the heart of the poem's meaning. The poem's central image is of an abundance of joy and song so great that it must *overflow* and graciously give itself in this effusiveness. But its nature remains hidden; Shelley's poem holds to the myth of confrontation, contenting itself with inverse analogies:

> What thou art we know not;
> What is most like thee?

Those two lines are central as we proceed to that famous series of "likes": A poet, a high-born maiden, a glow-worm golden, a rose embowered. Impatient readers may protest that they cannot see in what way a lark is like any of that series; the answer is that Shelley is not comparing the lark to them or even them to the lark, but, rather, he is comparing a series of visionary tableaux to the showering forth, the flowing over, of the lark's song. The unbidden poet singing away, obscured by the light of his own conceptions, is able to temper the world with his song. The high-born maiden, lovelorn in her tower, soothes her soul with music, and the music "overflows her bower," imparts something to others as well. The glow-worm golden (and this is an urbane jest) is screened from the view

by flowers and grass, but its own appearance, "its aëreal hue," overflows, as it were, and is scattered as light among flowers and grass
(the song-light simile is implied here again; the glow-worm scatters
light as lark, poet, maiden scatter song). The rose, robbed by the
winds, flows its musk over into those winds. In each tableau the
giver of song, light, perfume is *hidden,* just as the lark is hidden;
in each case also there is a giving to excess, and without the necessity of the receivers having deserved the gift.

But even these inverse analogues are rejected as being inadequate; the lark's music "doth surpass" them. With the thirteenth
stanza, the poem begins a new movement. No analogue of free,
overflowing relationship will serve; the uniqueness of the lark's song
remains. Only a direct appeal to the reality incarnate in the song
will serve to bring the poet into relationship with the ecstasy of the
unheard singer; from seeking to appropriate part of the reality of
the lark-song for himself, the poet enters into a prayer to know the
reality only through sharing it. As in the *Ode to the West Wind* and
the *Hymn to Intellectual Beauty,* the prayer is for the confrontation
of relationship although too often it has been read as a prayer for
escape:

> Teach us, Sprite or Bird,
>   What sweet thoughts are thine: . . .
>
> What objects are the fountains
>   Of thy happy strain?
> What fields, or waves, or mountains?
>   What shapes of sky or plain?
> What love of thine own kind? what ignorance of pain?

The lark loves, without "love's sad satiety." The burden of
mortality (Stanza XVII) is therefore not existent; "things more true
and deep" about death than anything we can visualize are in the
lark's possession. The inference is not that the lark knows the
truth of immortality (hence its happy song) but simply that one
way or the other the bird's knowledge is definite, and that, again
either way, it accepts that knowledge as final.

The poem climaxes in humility:

We look before and after,
      And pine for what is not:
Our sincerest laughter
      With some pain is fraught;
Our sweetest songs are those that tell of saddest thought.

Yet if we could scorn
      Hate, and pride, and fear;
If we were things born
      Not to shed a tear,
I know not how thy joy we ever should come near.

Better than all measures
      Of delightful sound,
Better than all treasures
      That in books are found,
Thy skill to poet were, thou scorner of the ground!

Teach me half the gladness
      That thy brain must know,
Such harmonious madness
      From my lips would flow,
The world should listen then, as I am listening now.

In his prayer to be the west wind's lyre, Shelley had promised
that the tumult of the wind's harmonies would take from him a
deep autumnal tone, "sweet though in sadness," the paradox expressed here again in "our sweetest songs are those that tell of
saddest thought." This poem ends in sadness because it has not
accounted for the joy that gives life to the skylark's song. Nor has
it been able to suggest what determines the bounteousness of that
effluence of melody. Enough that it affirms the limitless possibility
of relationship; content to be a lyric, it does not attempt finalities.

4 *Titan on the Rock*

Prometheus Unbound

THE Titans were, by Orphic tradition, our sinful and perpetually defeated ancestors. The most cunning of them, Prometheus, whose name means "prophetic," separated mankind from the gods and then atoned for this dark gift by stealing fire from heaven and so ensuring man's survival. Empedocles identified the stolen fire with the burden of human consciousness, so that Prometheus brings in one act of graciousness the dual capacity for joy and despair.

The Promethean fire, in Blake and Shelley, comes naturally to represent the creating fire of the poet's shaping imagination. The ambiguities of Milton's Promethean Satan are explored in *The Marriage of Heaven and Hell, A Defence of Poetry,* and in the "Preface" to *Prometheus Unbound,* in which Shelley says that Satan resembles Prometheus but is a less poetical character: "The character of Satan engenders in the mind a pernicious casuistry which leads us to weigh his faults with his wrongs, and to excuse the former because the latter exceed all measure."

This casuistry is pernicious because it militates against imaginative apprehension of Satan, and for such casuistry Shelley holds Milton responsible. The Satan of Books I and II is, in Shelley's reading, better poetry than the Satan of the remainder of *Paradise Lost.* The Prometheus of Shelley's lyrical drama has the "courage, and majesty, and firm and patient opposition to omnipotent force" of Milton's Satan, but he is "exempt from the taints of ambition, envy, revenge, and a desire for personal aggrendisement" which disfigure the great and imperfect hero-villain of *Paradise Lost.*

Act I of *Prometheus* opens with the Titan bound to a precipice in the Caucasus, chained to the rock like the babe of *The Mental Traveller* or Orc in *The Book of Urizen.* The rock is the stony world of Urizen, "the gray particular of man's life," as Wallace Stevens called it. Thus far the Poet of *Alastor* came in his death agony, and from these icy summits Shelley's Man must rise, if he is to rise at all.

The first speech of the bound Prometheus is an epitome of the entire poem. Directed to Jupiter, the speech nevertheless makes clear that the Titan's bondage has been largely internal, self-caused, for he has been "eyeless in hate." Blake states the essence of the situation with clarity: "The bounded is loathed by its possessor." Jupiter is only the boundary or outward circumference of the Titan's energies and desires. Prometheus is nailed down, not by an external principle of evil, but by his own separated faculties, gone wrong in their isolation from each other. Jupiter resembles Urizen or any other of Blake's Zoas cut off from the unity of Albion, who finds his parallel in Prometheus, the archetypal Divine Man or primal reality. The awakening of Albion is the unbinding of Prometheus; Urizen and Jupiter than vanish because they have no existence once Man has reintegrated himself.

The Nature upon which the bound Titan gazes is, like himself, fallen and fragmented. Mankind, his creation, worships its own Jupiter aspect, the principle of barren restraint, and their god requites them "with fear and self-contempt and barren hope." "Love, Hope, and Self-esteem," the imaginative virtues of the earlier *Hymn to Intellectual Beauty,* have departed. The function of Prometheus, in his powerful speech of self-recognition, is to call them back, and so bring earth and the human again into the reality of a shared freedom.

The process of renewal begins with the Titan's desire to recall his self-stultifying curse against Jupiter. He appeals to the fragmented phenomena of the universe to render back the curse that it may be cast forth. Until the curse is externalized, it cannot be recalled. But the mountains, springs, air, whirlwinds refuse to deliver up their burden; they are too afflicted by fear, self-hatred, hopelessness. Even the Earth, the Titan's mother, has not the requisite courage. Wordsworthian Nature cannot herself be an agency of liberation. Yet she can and does suggest that she will speak the curse in the language of mortality, which proves inadequate. Bound Man, though encumbered, is still too divine to gain full understanding from the language of mutability. Nature is not enough. Prometheus breaks through this paradox by calling upon a world of forms that are not our own, a *Doppelgänger* world of correspondences, of other Selves with whom we reunite in death. If nothing living will repeat the curse, then the phantasm of the curse's object, of Jupiter, will have to externalize it. Evidently this phantasm world is like the world of Blake's Spectres, our shadowy self-accusing halves formed by the ghosts of our unfulfilled desires and self-abandoned aspirations.

The repeated curse has an elaborate and largely oblique meaning. The power of Jupiter comes from Prometheus' acknowledging Jupiter as an existent negation, and then wishing pain and destruction upon that negation. To hate and reject so intensely is to become that which one hates. By deciding that Jupiter is a contrary force to be transcended, Prometheus achieves a dialectic of release. He recants his curse:

> It doth repent me: words are quick and vain;
> Grief for awhile is blind, and so was mine.
> I wish no living thing to suffer pain.

But Jupiter himself achieves no such wish and still is enslaved by the repetitious morality of revenge. The release of Prometheus has begun, yet Jupiter sees only a negation of his own will: a rebellion, not a strife of contraries. His response is to inflict subtler tortures upon his chained victim. Furies are sent upon Prometheus, but only to remind him of the futility of his own sacrifice:

> Behold an emblem: those who do endure
> Deep wrongs for man, and scorn, and chains, but heap
> Thousandfold torment on themselves and him.

This is the irony of the Orc cycle; even Christ at last becomes a tyrant of the upper sky. Good and the human means of good are irreconcilable. The best lack all conviction, while the worst are full of passionate intensity:

> In each human heart terror survives
> The ravin it has gorged: the loftiest fear
> All that they would disdain to think were true:
> Hypocrisy and custom make their minds
> The fanes of many a worship, now outworn.
> They dare not devise good for man's estate,
> And yet they know not that they do not dare.

The good want power, but to weep barren tears.
The powerful goodness want: worse need for them.
The wise want love; and those who love want wisdom;
And all best things are thus confused to ill.

Love, wisdom, power, goodness; to find that fourfold excellence
in the human form divine is the quest of Shelley as of Blake before him. The contradictions of existence, the recalcitrance of the
unwilling dross in the self, the evasions of natural reality defeat
the quest in Shelley. After the Furies have left, the tortured
Prometheus is comforted by the song of "subtle and fair spirits"
called up by his mother, the Earth. But even their visionary and
Wordsworthian consolation resolves itself in the paradox of desolation and ruin:

> Desolation is a delicate thing:
>   It walks not on the earth, it floats not on the air,
> But treads with lulling footstep, and fans with silent wing
>   The tender hopes which in their hearts the best and gentlest
>   bear;
> Who, soothed to false repose by the fanning plumes above
>   And the music-stirring motion of its soft and busy feet,
> Dream visions of aëreal joy, and call the monster, Love,
>   And wake, and find the shadow Pain, as he whom now we
>   greet.

The next song speaks of ruin as "love's shadow," and reinforces
the warning of the "desolation" lyric, a warning implicit in the
whole of *Prometheus Unbound*. The shadow of each aspiration
moves behind it; there is a dialectical counterpoise to every thrust
toward a more human mode of relationship. The shadow falls
lightly over the closing lines of Act I, as night gives way to dawn.
The greater shadow of Demogorgon, that tremendous gloom, dominates the mysterious second act.

Prometheus, separated from his unitary nature, is also divided
from his emanation (as Blake would have called her), Asia. He has
her emblems with him as comforters in the first act, in the form
of her sisters, Panthea and Ione, but they are intermediaries only.
The morning of the Titan's dawn into release finds Asia alone but

saluting the advent of spring and confidently awaiting reunion with Prometheus.

The mythic action of Act II is descent. The female principle goes down into the depths of being, seeking an answer to the questions that ultimately torment mankind, but finding instead a transfiguration into radical innocence, a rebirth into the form of highest human excellence and sexual beauty. Asia goes down to find truth, but finds only her own beauty, the objective exemplification of Promethean desire, a means of good reconcilable with the gratification of good, the realization of human sexual completion. Truth does indeed dwell in the depths, but it is the deep truth of Demogorgon and as such is imageless. The agnostic Shelley finds his most appropriate mythic figure in Demogorgon, who cannot be visualized because he is a dialectical *process,* not a god. The Demogorgon of tradition is the god of the abyss, the genius of chaos, dreadful in himself and the father of all the pagan gods, according to Boccaccio. The Demogorgon of Shelley is shapeless, without form or outline, and is called "a mighty darkness," but he has more to do with time than with space. The poem speaks of "Demogorgon's mighty law," and Demogorgon is its agent of apocalypse, who overthrows Jupiter and so emancipates mankind. Prometheus inaugurates the process, turning again to Asia. To come again to him she must be born again, and so begins her dark descent, ostensibly to discover the time of rebirth. The secret desired by Jupiter is the identity of his displacer, a secret known to Prometheus alone. In the dialectic of displacement Jupiter is thesis, Prometheus antithesis, and Demogorgon the transcending agent of synthesis, the dark force turning the cycle over. He calls himself "Eternity," but hints that he has "a direr name." "Eternity" in this sense is the *now* of Prometheus, when he repents. The "direr name" is whatever an individual poet wants to call the process of making and defeating myths, of forming a new story and ending an old one. Demogorgon sees to it that no one custom, good or bad, corrupts the world, for he rises at the turning, and he sinks down again bearing with him all that was in the ascendent. W. B. Yeats thought Demogorgon a product of nightmare, balancing Shelley's fierce images of infinite desire, negating the superhuman by the terrible. But the law of Demogorgon is double-edged and finds its emblem in the *amphisbaena,* the snakelike doom that has a head at either

end and so can go two ways, down and out to Fall, or up and in
to Redemption. Demogorgon's is that place that Yeats, following
Blake, spoke of: at the bottom of the graves, where all contraries
are equally true. To be subjected to him is either to fall from innocence into experience, or to rise again into a second and higher
innocence.

When Asia reaches the cave of Demogorgon, she discovers that
he can tell her no more about the ultimate than she herself already
knows. As process, he knows only his own nature, which is as imageless as the deep truth, but is only part of that truth. Mutability
rules the cyclic world; "Eternal Love" is free of such domination.
So much both he and Asia know. But "of such truths," Asia says,
"each to itself must be the oracle." Having learned that, she asks
only one thing more: "When shall the destined Hour arrive?" The
answer is simply "Behold!" and the vision of an Hour in which
time turns on itself is granted to her.

Time has already been suspended in this drama of renovation,
for the dawn that closes Act I and begins Act II has been suspended: "The sun will not rise until noon." Suddenly a light
radiates from Asia as she ascends again to the upper world. A voice
in the air, saluting her, sings a remarkable song celebrating her
transfiguration:

> Life of Life! thy lips enkindle
>   With their love the breath between them;
> And thy smiles before they dwindle
>   Make the cold air fire; then screen them
>   In those looks, where whoso gazes
>   Faints, entangled in their mazes.

The fire she gives forth is more constant than the beholder's eye
can bear. What exists to be confronted is beyond our powers of
confrontation, and its very brightness shrouds it from us:

> Child of Light! thy limbs are burning
>   Through the vest which seems to hide them;
> As the radiant lines of morning
>   Through the clouds ere they divide them;
>   And this atmosphere divinest
>   Shrouds thee wheresoe'er thou shinest.

As a child of light Asia is pure revelation, without concealment, burning through what only seems to hide her. The limbs are themselves the unconcealing vest, just as the clouds reveal the dawn behind them. The burning-through quality is a *shrouding* atmosphere that is also a *shining* forth; the paradox is complete. Shelley has deliberately put together a stanza whose imagery resists explication. Asia's revelation is to be confronted, but not analyzed.

> Fair are others; none beholds thee,
>   But thy voice sounds low and tender
> Like the fairest, for it folds thee
>   From the sight, that liquid splendour,
> And all feel, yet see thee never,
> As I feel now, lost for ever!

None beholds her because she cannot be visualized; she offers no analogues to the world experienced by sight. The fire of love which is her voice kindles the air (first stanza) and folds her from sight. She is a felt presence, but her unseen radiance leaves a sense of deprivation that first exalts and then abandons her admirer:

> Lamp of Earth! where'er thou movest
>   Its dim shapes are clad with brightness,
> And the souls of whom thou lovest
>   Walk upon the winds with lightness,
> Till they fail, as I am failing,
> Dizzy, lost, yet unbewailing!

As she leaves, her brightness abandons shapes to their previous dimness, and her imparted lightness goes with her as well, causing the souls she loves to fail in a sudden heaviness, and experience a vertigo of vision, yet without lament. The glory she has become can be met only in moments of confronting grace, and these cannot be sustained.

She sings, in reply to the Voice in the Air, one of the finest of Shelley's lyrics. She is going back to the roots of life, and her song moves through varying states of existence:

> My soul is an enchanted boat,
>   Which, like a sleeping swan, doth float
> Upon the silver waves of thy sweet singing;

> And thine doth like an angel sit
> Beside a helm conducting it,
> Whilst all the winds with melody are ringing.
> It seems to float ever, for ever,
> Upon that many-winding river,
> Between mountains, woods, abysses,
> A paradise of wildernesses!
> Till, like one in slumber bound,
> Borne to the ocean, I float down, around,
> Into a sea profound, of ever-spreading sound.

The "Life of Life" song is the ocean upon which her solitary soul voyages, under no power external to itself, for it is an enchanted boat. The boat of the soul floats out of time and space down to the primal sea of birth and being, with a dreamlike movement.

Free of spatial and temporal limitations, the poem moves into the sphere of that which relates itself to love in harmony and system, and becomes its own subject matter, a theme for its own music:

> Meanwhile thy spirit lifts its pinions
> In music's most serene dominions;
> Catching the winds that fan that happy heaven.
> And we sail on, away, afar,
> Without a course, without a star,
> But, by the instinct of sweet music driven;
> Till through Elysian garden islets
> By thee, most beautiful of pilots,
> Where never mortal pinnace glided,
> The boat of my desire is guided:
> Realms where the air we breathe is love,
> Which in the winds and on the waves doth move,
> Harmonizing this earth with what we feel above.

The Voice in the Air incarnates poetry, and moves the boat of Asia's desire against nature, utilizing the winds that are the breath of creative inspiration. The transfigured Asia becomes a harmony of will and desire, and moves through the watery Beulah world of an earthly paradise, back toward the realm of the unborn:

> We have passed Age's icy caves,
> And Manhood's dark and tossing waves,

And Youth's smooth ocean, smiling to betray:
Beyond the glassy gulfs we flee
Of shadow-peopled Infancy,
Through Death and Birth, to a diviner day;
A paradise of vaulted bowers,
Lit by downward-gazing flowers,
And watery paths that wind between
Wildernesses calm and green,
Peopled by shapes too bright to see,
And rest, having beheld; somewhat like thee;
Which walk upon the sea, and chant melodiously!

To descend, backward and out of cycle, to this "diviner day" is to court the doom of Blake's pathetic Thel, when she flees back into her prison-paradise. But Asia is no Thel, dreading the sexual rhythms of the generative world. She is the bride of the Great Marriage of apocalypse, revisiting the paradise of innocence only to prepare herself for a more exuberant sexuality, a vitality of release appropriate to a reintegrated universe.

The urbanity of Shelley in this last stanza is strikingly evident, in its ironic perception and complex presentation of a purely Byzantine reality, in Yeats's sense. What Asia voyages into is both more and less real than our state of existence. The stanza smooths its imagery down to a precarious glassiness, as it moves from the icy caves of Age and rough ocean of Manhood to the deceptively smooth ocean of Youth and on to the treacherous surface of the glassy gulfs of Infancy. The pattern of retreat from the realm of experience necessarily involves a fragile imagery like *The Book of Thel*'s, a world of appearances so illusory as to suggest an absence of *the given*, the hard phenomenal universe of most adult experience and literature. The discursive antithesis between what is and what is not wavers; we flee back beyond the "shadow-peopled" realm of Infancy, not through Birth alone, but "through Death and Birth." The two words have very nearly the same meaning in this sophisticated context, as Birth into experience is a Death compared to the paradise existence, as it is a movement into a lower reality, but the lower reality is more alive in imaginative potential. The paradox is the same that Blake explored in his dialectical interplay of Innocence and Experience. Asia is at once dying into life and livng into death, depending upon the perspective of one's view.

In this paradise of vaulted bowers, pulsating with life, Asia moves again among the Shining Ones of Bunyan, "too bright to see," whom yet she beholds. She comes to rest, in creative repose, surrounded by beings who can defy natural law, and walk upon ocean. This image of her latent strength closes Act II, and is juxtaposed by Shelley against the fierce but illusory speech of triumph delivered by Jupiter on his heavenly throne, which opens Act III. Here chance and choice become one, and Jupiter goes down to the rich, dark nothingness of Demogorgon's abyss.

Jupiter has summoned all heaven to hear the boast that henceforth he is to be omnipotent, for the lingering Promethean resistance in mankind is now to be repressed:

> The soul of man, like unextinguished fire,
> Yet burns towards heaven with fierce reproach, and doubt,
> And lamentation, and reluctant prayer,
> Hurling up insurrection, which might make
> Our antique empire insecure, though built
> On eldest faith, and hell's coeval, fear;
> And though my curses through the pendulous air,
> Like snow on herbless peaks, fall flake by flake,
> And cling to it; though under my wrath's night
> It climbs the crags of life, step after step,
> Which wound it, as ice wounds unsandalled feet,
> It yet remains supreme o'er misery,
> Aspiring, unrepressed, yet soon to fall.

The agent of repression is to be Jupiter's "fatal child," supposedly begotten upon Thetis by the sky tyrant. At "the destined hour" this child will rise from Demogorgon's throne, having usurped the might of that dread power, and ascend unto his father, Jupiter. But the dialectical irony of the destined hour has trapped Jupiter; he has engendered no child at all, this being the secret known only to Prometheus as the ultimate representative of the human Imagination. The sky god is sterile; the Car of the Hour arrives bearing no fatal child but Demogorgon himself. Act IV of the drama presents two apocalyptic infants born at this hour, but they belong to a world that replaces Jupiter.

When Demogorgon moves toward the throne, he utters the final irony of his instrumentality. Jupiter cries out: "Awful shape, what art thou? Speak!" The reply is massive and sublime:

> Eternity. Demand no direr name.
> Descend, and follow me down the abyss.
> I am thy child, as thou wert Saturn's child;
> Mightier than thee: and we must dwell together
> Henceforth in darkness. Lift thy lightnings not.
> The tyranny of heaven none may retain,
> Or reassume, or hold, succeeding thee.

Demogorgon is Jupiter's son only in that he displaces him, as Jupiter had dethroned Saturn. The shapeless spirit is the child of Jupiter's dark aspirations in that he transcends and so obliterates them. Father of all the gods, he has come now to end forever the tyranny of heaven, to cancel the cycles of futurity.

The three remaining scenes of this great act describe a renovated universe, gradually awakening to the delighted consciousness of its liberation. The sound of waves is now "the unpastured sea hungering for calm." "The warmth of an immortal youth" revives the marble nerves of the Earth. The painted veil of illusion is torn aside:

> The loathsome mask has fallen, the man remains
> Sceptreless, free, uncircumscribed, but man
> Equal, unclassed, tribeless, and nationless,
> Exempt from awe, worship, degree, the king
> Over himself; just, gentle, wise: but man
> Passionless?—no, yet free from guilt or pain,
> Which were, for his will made or suffered them,
> Nor yet exempt, though ruling them like slaves,
> From chance, and death, and mutability,
> The clogs of that which else might oversoar
> The loftiest star of unascended heaven,
> Pinnacled dim in the intense inane.

Man is now the Prolific, in Blake's sense, but still needs the contrary of the Devourer to receive the excess of his energies. The

Devourer appears as chance, death, mutability—realities unlike guilt and pain, which are willed entities and so vanish. Yet even chance, death, and mutability are to be ruled as man's slaves, mere clogs that ballast his existence. They serve self-liberated man by assuring the continuity of his progress, the humanness of his existence. Like Blake, Shelley refuses to visualize a static heaven, an upper paradise without change, choice, danger, and the naturalistic completion of death. There is no mysterious invisible in Shelley's vision of the last things; death survives, but so do we, by mastering death without ending it and replacing the religion of the remote sky with a renewed earth. The death that is Promethean man's slave is itself a part of life, another dimension or starting point of the human, not the start of a state other than life's. Shelley's Promethean man, mastering death for life, finds his modern analogue in the "major man" or "central man" of Wallace Stevens, "formed out of our lives to keep us in our death," a character "beyond reality" but "composed thereof." Shelley's Prometheus in Act III is very like this fictive man "created out of men." The world of Act III is free of the categories of space and time. As in Blake's Eden, space is replaced by the more significant form of art, and time by the pulsations of artistic creation. Death has no form and is unmeasurable by creation, and so becomes, with chance and mutability, only the outward boundary or circumference, the definite outline, of eternity, always to be moved outward so long as imaginative energy is able to prevail.

The difficulties of Act III are consumed in the fiery last act, a rhapsody equal in force and invention to the astonishing Ninth Night of Blake's *Four Zoas*. From the piercing voice that cries, "The pale stars are gone!" to the organ voice of Demogorgon proclaiming what alone is "Life, Joy, Empire, and Victory," Shelley sustains a varied and triumphant song for 578 lines, a remarkable technical achievement that can be pardoned its sporadic flaws. To apprehend this long chant is difficult and requires patience; even sympathetic readers of Shelley can stumble here, as I did in the past.[44] The first third of the act is the weakest, but is still very far from being "an aesthetic disaster." Prometheus and Asia are absent from this act, as it is a nuptial song celebrating their passionate reunion. Nothing is more difficult than the technical task Shelley set himself here: to convince us of a rejoicing beyond the measure of fallen human de-

light. Even a partial success is a victory for the imagination equal to
the *kind* of achievement in Dante and Blake.

The act begins with a deliberately confused flight of Spectres,
dark shadows of the dead Hours bearing their ruler, Time, "to his
tomb in eternity." Hours and Spirits of earth and air sing a series
of antiphons of joy, until they depart for the two swift visions that
dominate the act, both of which are derived from Ezekiel's fiery
chariot and Enthroned Man, who is a manifestation of God. The
first vision, which is the milder, is granted to Ione, the gentler of
Asia's sisters:

> I see a chariot like that thinnest boat,
> In which the Mother of the Months is borne
> By ebbing light into her western cave,
> When she upsprings from interlunar dreams;
> O'er which is curved an orblike canopy
> Of gentle darkness, and the hills and woods,
> Distinctly seen through that dusk aery veil,
> Regard like shapes in an enchanter's glass;
> Its wheels are solid clouds, azure and gold,
> Such as the genii of the thunderstorm
> Pile on the floor of the illumined sea
> When the sun rushes under it; they roll
> And move and grow as with an inward wind;
> Within it sits a wingèd infant, white
> Its countenance, like the whiteness of bright snow,
> Its plumes are as feathers of sunny frost,
> Its limbs gleam white, through the wind-flowing folds
> Of its white robe, woof of ethereal pearl.
> Its hair is white, the brightness of white light
> Scattered in strings; yet its two eyes are heavens
> Of liquid darkness, which the Deity
> Within seems pouring, as a storm is poured
> From jaggèd clouds, out of their arrowy lashes,
> Tempering the cold and radiant air around,
> With fire that is not brightness; in its hand
> It sways a quivering moonbeam, from whose point
> A guiding power directs the chariot's prow
> Over its wheelèd clouds, which as they roll

> Over the grass, and flowers, and waves, wake sounds,
> Sweet as a singing rain of silver dew.

The chariot resembles the old moon in the new moon's arms, and bears an apocalyptic infant heralding a storm of change. The chariot is instinct with spirit and is moved by no force external to itself. Visualization is deliberately made difficult for us; the wheels are "solid clouds," the child's plumes are as "sunny frost," and its eyes shine "with fire that is not brightness." White beyond whiteness is suggested by the total vision; white fire comes from the child's eyes and its moonbeam wand. The Son of Man in Revelation, also derived from Ezekiel, appears with head and hair "white like wool, as white as snow; and his eyes were as a flame of fire."

The myth of renewal in Prometheus is human and agnostic in its emphasis, but this winged infant of a new innocence transcends that emphasis and is a divine emblem. The hope of Act IV is that the new birth will bring about finality and the infant of the new moon, as an augury of innocence, portends the permanence of uncovered reality.

The infant spirit of Earth makes an even swifter entrance:

> And from the other opening in the wood
> Rushes, with loud and whirlwind harmony,
> A sphere, which is as many thousand spheres,
> Solid as crystal, yet through all its mass
> Flow, as through empty space, music and light:
> Ten thousand orbs involving and involved,
> Purple and azure, white, and green, and golden,
> Sphere within sphere; and every space between
> Peopled with unimaginable shapes,
> Such as ghosts dream dwell in the lampless deep,
> Yet each inter-transpicuous, and they whirl
> Over each other with a thousand motions,
> Upon a thousand sightless axles spinning,
> And with the force of self-destroying swiftness,
> Intensely, slowly, solemnly roll on,
> Kindling with mingled sounds, and many tones,
> Intelligible words and music wild.
> With mighty whirl the multitudinous orb
> Grinds the bright brook into an azure mist

Of elemental subtlety, like light;
And the wild odour of the forest flowers,
The music of the living grass and air,
The emerald light of leaf-entangled beams
Round its intense yet self-conflicting speed,
Seem kneaded into one aëreal mass
Which drowns the sense.

This vision is analogous to Ezekiel's of "the wheels and their work," the cherubim who form the Divine chariot. The "orbs" in Shelley's myth are both spheres and eyes, just as "their rings were full of eyes round about them" in Ezekiel. Shelley's spheres within spheres form a paradoxical single sphere, as solid as "the terrible crystal" of Ezekiel. This movement of rings is most regular where it seems most irregular, for it delights eyes more enlarged in perception than our own. Music, light, song mingle in this divine dance of the spheres as the earth whirls on to a revelation of its true form. Self-destroying swiftness, a menace to the poet from the early lyrics on to *Adonais*, here becomes a movement toward imaginative finality. The sphere is peopled by *unimaginable* shapes that shall be revealed, while the previously evident phenomena of nature undergo a transmemberment of song into "an azure mist of elemental subtlety," like the luminous substance of Imagination in Coleridge's *Dejection*. Yet Shelley, like Blake, is too much a humanist to treat these whirling gyres without irony:

Panthea.   Within the orb itself,
Pillowed upon its alabaster arms,
Like to a child o'erwearied with sweet toil,
On its own folded wings, and wavy hair,
The Spirit of the Earth is laid asleep,
And you can see its little lips are moving,
Amid the changing light of their own smiles,
Like one who talks of what he loves in dream.
Ione.   'Tis only mocking the orb's harmony.

The sleeping infant Spirit smilingly mocks the harmony of his own orb, the non-human outline of its intricate mazes. Urbanity of this kind is almost uniquely Shelleyan; the finality that comes mocks our state, but is urbanely scorned by the human dimension within it. The ironies of Yeats's *Byzantium* are akin to Shelley here, but lack his gentle persuasiveness.

The whirling sphere is an instrument for the increase of natural self-knowledge, a more fully revealed earth, and an indication that time has stopped, for the flashing of its beams reveals the "ruins of cancelled cycles."

Earth and moon, their freedom established by these fiery infants, sing forth the hymns of their awakening. One of the Earth's songs ("It interpenetrates my granite mass") stands among the handful of Shelley's unrivaled lyrics:

> Man, one harmonious soul of many a soul,
>   Whose nature is its own divine control,
> Where all things flow to all, as rivers to the sea;
>   Familiar acts are beautiful through love;
>   Labour, and pain, and grief, in life's green grove
> Sport like tame beasts, none knew how gentle they could be!
>
> His will, with all mean passions, bad delights,
>   And selfish cares, its trembling satellites,
> A spirit ill to guide, but mighty to obey,
>   Is as a tempest-wingèd ship, whose helm
>   Love rules, through waves which dare not overwhelm,
> Forcing life's wildest shores to own its sovereign sway.
>
> All things confess his strength. Through the cold mass
>   Of marble and of colour his dreams pass;
> Bright threads whence mothers weave the robes their children
>   wear;
>   Language is a perpetual Orphic song,
>   Which rules with Daedal harmony a throng
> Of thoughts and forms, which else senseless and shapeless were.

The human will here is exalted in its dual capacity for divine control of self and of the materials of art. Here, as in the *Defence of Poetry*, the Imagination achieves again its Blakean eminence as the great agency of moral good in the universe.

The close of the lyrical drama demonstrates Shelley's power over his difficult theme. The scattered elements of a disintegrated universe, to whom Prometheus appealed in vain at the poem's start, are now gathered together by the "universal sound like words" which is the voice of the freshly risen Demogorgon. The dread agent of process now comes as the greatest of shepherds, herding reality together in a pastoral unity. His final lines end the poem with majestic firmness and assurance:

> This is the day, which down the void abysm
> At the Earth-born's spell yawns for Heaven's despotism,
>   And Conquest is dragged captive through the deep:
> Love, from its awful throne of patient power
> In the wise heart, from the last giddy hour
>   Of dread endurance, from the slippery, steep,
> And narrow verge of crag-like agony, springs
> And folds over the world its healing wings.
>
> Gentleness, Virtue, Wisdom, and Endurance,
> These are the seals of that most firm assurance
>   Which bars the pit over Destruction's strength;
> And if, with infirm hand, Eternity,
> Mother of many acts and hours, should free
>   The serpent that would clasp her with his length;
> These are the spells by which to reassume
> An empire o'er the disentangled doom.
>
> To suffer woes which Hope thinks infinite;
> To forgive wrongs darker than death or night;
>   To defy Power, which seems omnipotent;
> To love, and bear; to hope till Hope creates
> From its own wreck the thing it contemplates;
>   Neither to change, nor falter, nor repent;
> This, like thy glory, Titan, is to be
> Good, great and joyous, beautiful and free;
> This is alone Life, Joy, Empire, and Victory.

We have come so dark a way since these lines of triumphant Romanticism that we are likely too quickly to reject them as the song of a soul singing to cheer itself in the darkness of a past age. The self-deception may have been in Shelley's heart, but it is not present in his poem. The "verge of crag-like agony" has receded here, but the cliff of fall still hovers. The pit over Destruction's strength is barred, but only the firmness of a hand that is finally our own keeps imprisoned the serpent Time. Like Blake, Shelley has offered a vision of a last judgment that each man passes upon himself, by his own assertion and in the cultivation of his own understanding. The Life and Joy available here are created by Hope from its own wreck, and in the image of the thing it contemplates. This is not the apocalypse of any time-bound sect, political or religious or philosophical, but the humanizing dream of the autonomous Imagination, holding to a faith in the truth and effectuality of its own disinterestedness.

5 *Dialectics of Vision*

The Two Spirits: An Allegory

SHELLEY wrote nothing so hopeful again. The ruin and desolation that shadow the heart's affections in *Prometheus* haunt all of his later poetry.

The unwilling dross that cannot be tortured into spirit, the hardened element that will not wish its own redemption, becomes increasingly the feared antagonist in Shelley's poetry, until at last it wins over Imagination the triumph of life and closes Shelley's poetic career in the welter of a watery chaos. The episodes of that strife, with momentary escapes into visionary possibility, find their record in the series of marvelous poems that distingush Shelley's last and most productve years, 1820–1822. The great but imperfect structure of *Prometheus* is made out of hopes and desires that still seek their object, but the more perfectly structured later poems seek no resolution beyond their own form.

The most beautiful of Shelley's shorter poems, to me, is the neglected lyric of 1820, *The Two Spirits: An Allegory,* published posthumously in 1824. Here Blake's theme of Spectre and Emanation, independently worked out by Shelley in his earlier poetry through *Prometheus,* finds its definitive statement as a dialectic of

infinite desire and the finite limits that attempt to defeat desire.
The First Spirit begins:

> O thou, who plumed with strong desire
> Wouldst float above the earth, beware!
> A Shadow tracks thy flight of fire—
> Night is coming!
> Bright are the regions of the air,
> And among the winds and beams
> It were delight to wander there—
> Night is coming!

The Shadow is the ruin haunting love, the Spectre that will displace the strongly desired Emanation after the desire is frustrated by the menace of coming night. But the Second and more Shelleyan Spirit is undaunted:

> The deathless stars are bright above;
> If I would cross the shade of night,
> Within my heart is the lamp of love,
> And that is day!
> And the moon will smile with gentle light
> On my golden plumes where'er they move;
> The meteors will linger round my flight,
> And make night day.

The shade of night is the shadow thrown into the heavens by our earth, and it ends at the sphere of Venus, the lamp of love which is the evening star and which the Second Spirit carries within him as an eternal and unfailing day. The First Spirit warns him again of the coming storm, but he utters a finer defiance:

> I see the light, and I hear the sound;
> I'll sail on the flood of the tempest dark,
> With the calm within and the light around
> Which makes night day:
> And thou, when the gloom is deep and stark,
> Look from thy dull earth, slumber-bound,
> My moon-like flight thou then mayst mark
> On high, far away.

This has the accent of Ariel scorning Caliban and marks the poem as containing the theme of Icarus' courage, the vision that makes night day. The dialogue between Spirits is over, and the poem resolves itself in two stanzas of myth-making:

> Some say there is a precipice
> Where one vast pine is frozen to ruin
> O'er piles of snow and chasms of ice
> Mid Alpine mountains;
> And that the languid storm pursuing
> That wingèd shape, for ever flies
> Round those hoar branches, aye renewing
> Its aëry fountains.

This would be the First Spirit's spectral interpretation of the Second Spirit's ruinous fate. In a Promethean setting of cyclic and frozen pursuit the winged shape expiates its daring by perpetual flight from the languid but ever renewed storm. But the poem's last stanza, the most exquisite in all of Shelley, tells a different story of the Second Spirit's destiny:

> Some say when nights are dry and clear,
> And the death-dews sleep on the morass,
> Sweet whispers are heard by the traveller,
> Which make night day:
> And a silver shape like his early love doth pass
> Upborne by her wild and glittering hair,
> And when he awakes on the fragrant grass,
> He finds night day.

The subtle music of De la Mare is anticipated in this perfect stanza. The traveler hears sweet whispers that make night day in a visionary sense, like the Second Spirit's earlier transfiguration of night into day. The shape of early desire, of lost youth and abandoned vision, comes to the traveler in the form of the inviolable Second Spirit, now revealed in its allegorical meaning of early love. When the traveler awakes from vision, it is literally to find night day, as Arthur awakes in *The Faerie Queene,* to find himself alone on the fragrant grass. Desire suffers both fates, the Spectre's prophecy of cyclic desolation, and the Emanation's fulfillment of a vision that cannot die, for it has the potency of renewable though wavering life. The mood of this enigmatic final stanza, the fantasy of realized wish, is extended at least once by Shelley in his most beautiful longer poem, *The Witch of Atlas*, composed in three days of inspired creativity in August 1820. The dream of love and beauty does not seek reality in *The Witch of Atlas*, but for once contents itself to move in a world entirely of Shelley's making.

The Witch of Atlas

EXCEPT for *The Faerie Queene* and Blake's epics, no poem in English contains as much exuberant invention as *The Witch of Atlas*. The tone and versification of the *Witch* owe something to the first canto of *Don Juan*, though Shelley's use of *ottava rima* is more slowly paced than Byron's. Urbane digressiveness characterizes both poems, but Shelley digresses from one vision only to depict another.

The courtly tone of Shelley's fantasy is already marked in its initial stanza:

> Before those cruel Twins, whom at one birth
> Incestuous Change bore to her father Time,
> Error and Truth, had hunted from the Earth
> All those bright natures which adorned its prime,
> And left us nothing to believe in, worth
> The pains of putting into learnèd rhyme,
> A lady-witch there lived on Atlas' mountain
> Within a cavern, by a secret fountain.

Shelley, in *Mont Blanc*, had spoken of "the still cave of the witch Poesy," calling poetry a witch because of its magical associations in contradistinction to philosophy or religion. The lady-witch here is to be approached through poetry, though she embodies the awakened imagination, which comprehends poetry without being limited by it.

She lived on Atlas' mountain before the end of the golden age of Saturn. Mutability, Saturn's incestuous daughter, bears to her father, Kronos, two cruel twins, Error and Truth, Blake's "cloven fiction." These antithetical gods hunt all the "bright natures" of myth from the earth and leave nothing to be believed in, to be "worth the pains" of the "learnèd rhyme" that *The Witch of Atlas* is. The cruel twins find their kingdom in philosophy and religion, realms of negations. But Shelley's verses, as his dedication to his wife insists, "tell no story, false or true." The Witch and her world are and are not; they invalidate the discursive antitheses of our prose existence.

The Witch lived alone within her cavern, with a secret fountain of creative energy. Her own creation was by an *aura seminalis,* like that of Belphoebe and Amoret in Spenser's Gardens of Adonis:

> Her mother was one of the Atlantides:
> > The all-beholding Sun had ne'er beholden
> In his wide voyage o'er continents and seas
> > So fair a creature, as she lay enfolden
> In the warm shadow of her loveliness;—
> > He kissed her with his beams, and made all golden
> The chamber of gray rock in which she lay—
> She, in that dream of joy, dissolved away.

The Spenser allusion tells us that the Witch's pastoral scene, in the ensuing poem, is identical with the Gardens of Adonis. When the Witch is born she is already full-grown, for the sun's force was too great for her mother, dissolved that lady away, and made the cavern the womb for so powerful and prodigal a birth:

> A lovely lady garmented in light
> > From her own beauty—deep her eyes, as are
> Two openings of unfathomable night
> > Seen through a Temple's cloven roof—her hair
> Dark—the dim brain whirls dizzy with delight,
> > Picturing her form; her soft smiles shone afar,
> And her low voice was heard like love, and drew
> All living things towards this wonder new.

A "chamber of gray rock" may refer obliquely to the poet's brain, inspired by Apollo to bring forth the Witch. Yet this poem is not an allegory but a mythopoeic fantasy; the more general interpretation seems truer to it. The Witch as the Sun's child shares in a more than human energy; her form will survive any other in her Spenserian world, for mutability governs even the earthly paradise of the Gardens of Adonis. Like the transfigured Asia, she suggests no image that can be visualized, being garmented only by the light from her own beauty, a light that darkens the poet's eyes. Her voice goes out into her pastoral universe as love, and draws her subjects to her. Before they can behold her unshadowed beauty, she weaves a veil to protect them from the ill consequences of too direct a confrontation:

> For she was beautiful—her beauty made
>   The bright world dim, and everything beside
> Seemed like the fleeting image of a shade:
>   No thought of living spirit could abide,
> Which to her looks had ever been betrayed,
>   On any object in the world so wide,
> On any hope within the circling skies,
> But on her form, and in her inmost eyes.
>
> Which when the lady knew, she took her spindle
>   And twined three threads of fleecy mist, and three
> Long lines of light, such as the dawn may kindle
>   The clouds and waves and mountains with; and she
> As many star-beams, ere their lamps could dwindle
>   In the belated moon, wound skilfully;
> And with these threads a subtle veil she wove—
> A shadow for the splendour of her love.

Her beauty would condemn its beholder to the fate of the wandering poet in *Alastor*, by withdrawing all hope and beauty from attainable objects of experience. Out of her compassion she weaves her veil of white magic, of mist, dawnlight, and beams of the evening star. In the *Hymn to Intellectual Beauty* the spirit's shadow floated among us "like hues and harmonies of evening," "like clouds in starlight," "like mist o'er mountains driven." The Witch deliberately makes her presence as apparently transient and willful, though in actuality she does not waver like the Intellectual Beauty.

In spite of her care, the Witch's beauty enchants the most vital forms in her world, the nymphs, into the illusion that they can abide forever in her presence. In four stanzas that are at once the poem's thematic center and its greatest achievement, the Witch firmly, gently, and finally in grief, dissolves the illusion:

> The Ocean-nymphs and Hamadryades,
>   Oreads and Naiads, with long weedy locks,

Offered to do her bidding through the seas,
   Under the earth, and in the hollow rocks,
And far beneath the matted roots of trees,
   And in the gnarlèd heart of stubborn oaks,
So they might live for ever in the light
Of her sweet presence—each a satellite.

"This may not be," the wizard maid replied;
   "The fountains where the Naiades bedew
Their shining hair, at length are drained and dried;
   The solid oaks forget their strength, and strew
Their latest leaf upon the mountains wide;
   The boundless ocean like a drop of dew
Will be consumed—the subborn centre must
Be scattered, like a cloud of summer dust.

"And ye with them will perish, one by one;—
   If I must sigh to think that this shall be,
If I must weep when the surviving Sun
   Shall smile on your decay—oh, ask not me
To love you till your little race is run;
   I cannot die as ye must—over me
Your leaves shall glance—the streams in which ye dwell
Shall be my paths henceforth, and so—farewell!"—

She spoke and wept:—the dark and azure well
   Sparkled beneath the shower of her bright tears,
And every little circlet where they fell
   Flung to the cavern-roof inconstant spheres
And intertangled lines of light:—a knell
   Of sobbing voices came upon her ears
From those departing Forms, o'er the serene
Of the white streams and of the forest green.

Nymphs live a very long time, much longer than humans, but they die at last. Love and mutability meet in conflict here, and mutability must triumph. Though the nymphs offer their perpetual worship to the Witch, this may not be, as she sadly replies, for the world to which the nymphs are so inseparably linked is itself mutable. When the fountains are drained and dried, the naiads will vanish with them. The solid oaks will forget their strength, and die, and their dryads with them. As the time when there will be no more change finally approaches, the boundless ocean will be consumed, and when there is no more sea there will be no ocean nymphs. When, at the very end, the center cannot hold, things will fall apart, the earth will be scattered like summer dust, and the oreads who had offered their homage "under the earth, and in the hollow rocks" will cease to exist.

Few poets have been accused of sentimentality more frequently than Shelley has, and few have so little deserved the charge. Here he handles an immense pathos with urbane tact that does not forget the necessity of sympathy, yet refuses to surrender aesthetic control. The Witch's determination persists, as it must, yet it gives way to grief in lines that catch the tensions of self-struggle. She begins by insisting that she will not sigh or weep at what must be, and therefore cannot allow herself to love the nymphs. As she goes from thought to thought in her struggle to maintain composure, the verse moves with her. "I cannot die as ye must"; she is not a figure of atonement; only life is possible for her. Then, "over me your leaves shall glance," which is an attempt to be cruel, but a cruelty turned only toward herself. She makes her greatest attempt at stoic control with the still more deliberate dismissal of streams into paths, but then her control gives way—"She spoke and wept." Shelley dissolves the scene with a tableau of departure akin to the leave-taking of Adam and Eve from their garden. We watch the dark and azure fountain that can never cease to flow. It sparkles beneath the shower of the Witch's tears, themselves mutable. They cast circles of light which are "inconstant spheres." The distress of the Witch is reflected by the "intertangled lines of light" on the walls of her cavern. The "departing Forms" leave behind the knell of their sobbing voices to join for a final time with the Witch's tears.

All day the solitary Witch now sits alone, forgetting her grief by weaving poetry "upon her growing woof." It becomes clear that the Witch incarnates the myth-making faculty, of which poetry is only one manifestation. She weaves a fire that outshines natural flame:

> While on her hearth lay blazing many a piece
> Of sandal wood, rare gums, and cinnamon;

> Men scarcely know how beautiful fire is—
>   Each flame of it is as a precious stone
> Dissolved in ever-moving light, and this
>   Belongs to each and all who gaze upon.
> The Witch beheld it not, for in her hand
> She held a woof that dimmed the burning brand.

This is a fire like that of Blake's Eden or Yeats's Byzantium, a fire that cannot be quenched, and yet less "real" than mortal fire. Within it the Witch lies in trance all winter, awaiting the serious play she is henceforth to enjoy.

When she voyages forth she utilizes a curious boat and a more curious companion. The boat has its origins in the sphere of the morning star, which Yeats properly called Shelley's "star of infinite desire." The morning star, surviving the night longer than the other stars but fading at last with dawn into the sunlight, is an apt emblem for Shelley's desire to convert objects of experience into subjects of innocence, capable of the mutuality and dialogue of relationship. This imaginative personalism of Shelley is misinterpreted as animism or a deliberate refusal to acknowledge an inanimate world. In his myth-making poems Shelley does not know an inanimate world.

The Witch's boat is, then, like Asia's pinnace, the boat of her desire. To accompany her on the voyage, she creates an ambiguous being:

> Then by strange art she kneaded fire and snow
>   Together, tempering the repugnant mass
> With liquid love—all things together grow
>   Through which the harmony of love can pass;
> And a fair Shape out of her hands did flow—
>   A living Image, which did far surpass
> In beauty that bright shape of vital stone
> Which drew the heart out of Pygmalion.
>
> A sexless thing it was, and in its growth
>   It seemed to have developed no defect
> Of either sex, yet all the grace of both,—
>   In gentleness and strength its limbs were decked;
> The bosom swelled lightly with its full youth,

The countenance was such as might select
Some artist that his skill should never die,
Imaging forth such perfect purity.

From its smooth shoulders hung two rapid wings,
    Fit to have borne it to the seventh sphere,
Tipped with the speed of liquid lightenings,
    Dyed in the ardours of the atmosphere:
She led her creature to the boiling springs
    Where the light boat was moored, and said: "Sit here!"
And pointed to the prow, and took her seat
Beside the rudder, with opposing feet.

This Hermaphrodite finds its literary source in Book III of Spenser's *Faerie Queene,* where a False Florimell is made by a witch out of a "repugnant mass" of purest snow. As a false emblem of natural beauty, this monster is also a Hermaphrodite and resembles Belial, patron of sodomy.

The Witch of Atlas is later described by the poem as "a sexless bee," so that her creation of the Hermaphrodite for company's sake is free of sexual purpose. Beautiful as the Hermaphrodite is, it is merely "a living Image," like Yeats's visions of an image of "the superhuman" in *Byzantium,* "Shade more than man, more image than a shade," and of a golden cock that scorns the common bird as a complexity of mire and blood, for it has the glory of changeless metal and is an artifice of eternity.

Yet the Hermaphrodite, for all its "perfect purity," is only an object, like Yeats's golden bird, and as much a deceitful image of real flesh as Spenser's False Florimell is. Like Yeats's artifice, it is a robot; it needs to be led to the boat, ordered to sit in the prow, while the Witch takes the rudder, and then falls asleep, to be awakened only for use when the Witch desires the boat to go against nature, against a stream, or through the air.

The point of the Hermaphrodite is that it is the best permanent being the sexless Witch can create. The nymphs are capable of relationship, but they are mutable and must die. The Hermaphrodite is more beautiful than the nymphs, but its beauty is too perfect and unchanging. The nymphs must die, but they can love. The Hermaphrodite is sexually self-sufficient because it is a cold but unful-

fillable perfection. A mere artifice remains the best product of the
myth-making faculty, and so the Hermaphrodite is an involuntary
criticism of *The Witch of Atlas*. Fictions intimate relationships to
us, but cannot substitute for them.

The remainder of the poem is occupied by the Witch's voyages
and antinomian tricks. As she goes about the earth she delights in
upsetting orthodox moralities, religions, and political orders, by en-
couraging human desire to subvert them. Her final service for
mortals is against the last orthodoxy, death:

> To those she saw most beautiful, she gave
>   Strange panacea in a crystal bowl:—
> They drank in their deep sleep of that sweet wave,
>   And lived thenceforward as if some control,
> Mightier than life, were in them; and the grave
>   Of such, when death oppressed the weary soul,
> Was as a green and overarching bower
> Lit by the gems of many a starry flower.
>
> For on the night when they were buried, she
>   Restored the embalmers' ruining, and shook
> The light out of the funeral lamps, to be
>   A mimic day within that deathy nook;
> And she unwound the woven imagery
>   Of second childhood's swaddling bands, and took
> The coffin, its last cradle, from its niche,
> And threw it with contempt into a ditch.

The gesture here is of death annexed to life, as in the apocalypse
of *Prometheus Unbound*. Yeats, in his death poem, *Under Ben
Bulben*, begins with a reference to Shelley's poem:

> Swear by what the sages spoke
> Round the Mareotic Lake
> That the Witch of Atlas knew,
> Spoke and set the cocks a-crow.

Yeats is remembering the Witch's voyage:

> By Moeris and the Mareotid lakes,
>   Strewn with faint blooms like bridal chamber floors,

> Where naked boys bridling tame water-snakes,
> Or charioteering ghastly alligators,
> Had left on the sweet waters mighty wakes
> Of those huge forms—within the brazen doors
> Of the great Labyrinth slept both boy and beast,
> Tired with the pomp of their Osirian feast.

These boys resemble the spirits who ride into Yeats's *Byzantium*, "astraddle on the dolphin's mire and blood," and so provide fresh substance to be broken up by the Emperor's smithies, and made into "those images that yet / Fresh images beget," auguries of eternity. Yeats's Emperor and his smithies probably have their origin in the seventy-fourth and seventy-fifth stanzas of *The Witch of Atlas,* where "a gaudy mock-bird" scorns earthly power, and the Emperor's soldiers sleep-walk, dream that they are blacksmiths, and stand around the red anvils beating their swords to plowshares. *The Witch of Atlas* seems to have haunted the imagination of the old Yeats. When, on September 4, 1938, he anticipated his death in *Under Ben Bulben* he called upon his memories of Shelley's poem to give him an image of triumphant contempt for dying. Nothing could be more Yeatsian than the Witch's action in unwinding the mummy cloth of the gyres of man's life, "the woven imagery of second childhood's swaddling bands," or her further action when she took

> The coffin, its last cradle, from its niche,
> And threw it with contempt into a ditch.

Yeats, in *Under Ben Bulben,* follows Blake and Shelley by insisting that man has invented death:

> Though grave-diggers' toil is long,
> Sharp their spades, their muscles strong,
> They but thrust their buried men
> Back in the human mind again.

The Witch's power is that of a muse of mythopoeia, but she cannot invent life, which is the other human prerogative. What she heard round the Mareotic Lake, Shelley does not tell us, but the sages of that region wrote *The Book of the Dead* and thus, Yeats says, set the cocks of Hades a-crow, presumably as the cocks of *Byzantium* are also set a-crow, in scorn of the still-living, still-dying world. *The Witch of Atlas* shows Shelley playing with the dialectics of his vision, balancing the ironies of experience against the subtler ironies of innocence. Benevolent as the Witch is, she is also a little remote from the tortured intensities of man's condition. *Prometheus Unbound* exhausted Shelley's drive toward the realization of his humanist quest; *The Witch of Atlas* makes light of finalities. This lightness, which finds its tonal expression as an urbane graciousness, is barbed with the thorns of life. Shelley wrote no more poems like *The Witch of Atlas;* the remainder of his work follows a downward path to the wisdom of disillusion.

6   *Darkening of the Quest*

Epipsychidion

EPIPSYCHIDION was composed in January–February 1821, half a year after *The Witch of Atlas*. The rhapsodic, invocatory strain in Shelley here reaches its climax, in his most original poem. *Epipsychidion* is an impassioned six-hundred-line direct address, in a high lyrical style, on the theme of free love, and is therefore Shelley's equivalent to Blake's *Visions of the Daughters of Albion*. The occasion for *Epipsychidion* was Shelley's love for Emilia Viviani, the ideal "Emily" of the poem, but the biographical situation is almost totally absorbed into the poem's mythopoeic speculations.

Keats's hymn to heterosexual love, *The Eve of St. Agnes,* juxtaposes Eros against an environment that seeks to nullify it. Shelley's hymn is characteristically different. The final barrier to the completion of love is the separateness that shadows the human, and causes every relationship to collapse into experience. The title of *Epipsychidion* probably means "a work about the soul out of my soul," the epipsyche, or emanation, as Blake calls it. The name does not matter; Dante's Beatrice is Shelley's probable model, and her name will do as well as any other. Emily is a woman who incarnates all that a woman can, and the poet desires to confront her in the full and free relationship of love. The poem records both this aspiration and the problem of finding apt language for voicing it. Finally, it records the defeat of both aspiration and wording.

The poem opens with twenty lines that suggest frustrated intensity, and give the impression of a work starting in its own middle. Emily is addressed in a heightening sequence from "Sweet Spirit!" to "Poor captive bird!" to "High, spirit-wingèd Heart!" This series then is kindled into a profusion of alternate images, each rejected as soon as it is invoked:

> Seraph of Heaven! too gentle to be human,
> Veiling beneath that radiant form of Woman
> All that is insupportable in thee
> Of light, and love, and immortality!
> Sweet Benediction in the eternal Curse!
> Veiled Glory of this lampless Universe!
> Thou Moon beyond the clouds! Thou living Form
> Among the Dead! Thou Star above the Storm!
> Thou Wonder and thou Beauty, and thou Terror!
> Thou Harmony of Nature's art! Thou Mirror
> In whom, as in the splendour of the Sun,
> All shapes look glorious which thou gazest on!

The poem affirms images of Emily, but no single image, and proceeds to recount the struggle of image-making, for this is a poem about poetry:

> Ay, even the dim words which obscure thee now
> Flash, lightning-like, with unaccustomed glow;
> I pray thee that thou blot from this sad song
> All of its much mortality and wrong,
> With those clear drops, which start like sacred dew
> From the twin lights thy sweet soul darkens through,
> Weeping, till sorrow becomes ecstasy:
> Then smile on it, so that it may not die.

There is genuine urbanity here: the consciousness of a convention of love-making, and of its way of speaking. Unique again in Shelley is the attempt to heighten this kind of graciousness so that it can be manifest on the level of the sublime.

Emily is "Youth's vision thus made perfect," a humanized form of the shadowy light for which the poet quests. He declares his love

for this vision, and suddenly directs his poem as polemic against
what threatens his love. The poem's opening couplet has an oblique
reference to the institution of marriage. The theme is mentioned
again here lines (46–51) and emerges again later in the poem in its
most famous lines (147–159), which will be considered below. Coun-
terpointed against the theme of marriage's iniquities is the poem's
most fervent element, an overwhelming desire for a more than sexual union with Emily which will transcend human limitations. The
key line is a sudden exclamation: "Would we two had been twins
of the same mother!" For Shelley, as for his fellow luminary of the
"Satanic school," Byron, incest was a very poetical circumstance.
Laon and Cythna, the hero and heroine of an early allegorical epic
by Shelley, are both brother and sister and lovers. Incest is dimly
hinted at in *Prometheus;* becomes the principal subject of *The
Cenci,* Shelley's attempt at theatrical drama; and is the metaphysical
spring of desire here in *Epipsychidion.* Relationship with another
cannot be sustained; the other becomes only an object of desire, and
dwindles into the experiential. Why not then find a closer and surer
way, through another allied initially to the self? The myth of *Epipsychidion* drives toward relationship and life, but is countered by
an incestuous antimyth of despair, moving toward death. The poem
alternates between the two quests: for an emanation and for a female counterpart of the spectral self. Line 52 is a momentary victory
for the second: "I am not thine: I am a part of thee." This love-
death mystical annihilation struggles through the poem as its dark
undersong, and then wins out in the closing lines.

Recovering from the eclipse of line 52, the poem again affirms
images, but now with an overt consciousness of poetic limits:

> Sweet Lamp! my moth-like Muse has burned its wings
> Or, like a dying swan who soars and sings,
> Young Love should teach Time, in his own gray style,
> All that thou art. Art thou not void of guile,
> A lovely soul formed to be blessed and bless?
> A well of sealed and secret happiness,
> Whose waters like blithe light and music are,
> Vanquishing dissonance and gloom? A Star
> Which moves not in the moving heavens, alone?
> A Smile amid dark frowns? a gentle tone

> Amid rude voices? a belovèd light?
> A Solitude, a Refuge, a Delight?
> A Lute, which those whom Love has taught to play
> Make music on, to soothe the roughest day
> And lull fond Grief asleep? a buried treasure?
> A cradle of young thoughts of wingless pleasure?
> A violet-shrouded grave of Woe?—I measure
> The world of fancies, seeking one like thee,
> And find—alas! mine own infirmity.

Here the reality of the epipsyche, "all that thou art," is likened to a series of delights encased by the world of experience. The Muse's infirmity is manifested by its singed wings and swan song of creative self-destruction. Shelley measures the resources of his imagination against the immediacy of confrontation and is compelled to admit the inadequacy of his image-making. The confronted reality belongs to form and creation, not to space and time, and no mimetic image can be similarly unconditioned. To set his desire in the context of space and time, he turns to detailing its history:

> She met me, Stranger, upon life's rough way,
> And lured me towards sweet Death; as Night by Day,
> Winter by Spring, or Sorrow by swift Hope,
> Led into light, life, peace. An antelope,
> In the suspended impulse of its lightness,
> Were less aethereally light: the brightness
> Of her divinest presence trembles through
> Her limbs, as underneath a cloud of dew
> Embodied in the windless heaven of June
> Amid the splendour-wingèd stars, the Moon
> Burns, inextinguishably beautiful.

This is again very like the paradoxes of Asia's transfiguration in the "Life of Life" lyric. We are met by a divine brightness trembling through limbs, but only the limbs give evidence for the brightness, and themselves tremble through it. Shelley has found a verbal figure in which the outer covering and the inner essence are interchangeable. Such figured brightness cannot be contained:

> The glory of her being, issuing thence,
> Stains the dead, blank, cold air with a warm shade

Of unentangled intermixture, made
By Love, of light and motion: one intense
Diffusion, one serene Omnipresence,
Whose flowing outlines mingle in their flowing,
Around her cheeks and utmost fingers glowing
With the unintermitted blood, which there
Quivers, (as in a fleece of snow-like air
The crimson pulse of living morning quiver,)
Continuously prolonged, and ending never,
Till they are lost, and in that Beauty furled
Which penetrates and clasps and fills the world.

This is one of the most extraordinary passages in Shelley, and no description can hope to be adequate to it. As *The Witch of Atlas* had it, "all things together grow / Through which the harmony of love can pass." "Glory" in line 91 sets the tone for this passage. The epipsyche's reality here has diffused into a serene Omnipresence, the very air that Shelley breathes. The form of that reality has become one with the fleeting presence of Intellectual Beauty "which penetrates and clasps and fills the world." The "unintermitted blood" glows through this vision to remind us of its human grounding. This is the poem's positive climax, its finest realization of relationship.

Knowing now that no images can convey this reality, the poet nevertheless renews his figurative quest. Before he abandons this self-defeating process to give a history of his love, he delivers three sermons on the nature of true love. The passionate assurance of rhetoric in these addresses carries them through their fierce polemic as they justify the will's rejection of everything that impedes its quest. The best of these passages is the first, with its chilling denunciation of the institution of marriage:

Thy wisdom speaks in me, and bids me dare
Beacon the rocks on which high hearts are wrecked.
I never was attached to that great sect,
Whose doctrine is, that each one should select
Out of the crowd a mistress or a friend,
And all the rest, though fair and wise, commend
To cold oblivion, though it is in the code
Of modern morals, and the beaten road
Which those poor slaves with weary footsteps tread,

Who travel to their home among the dead
By the broad highway of the world, and so
With one chained friend, perhaps a jealous foe,
The dreariest and the longest journey go.

Aside from their rhetorical power, these lines contribute a crucial reminder to the poem's story. The poem celebrates love more than it does a particular love for Emily, as a single epipsyche. Shelley is not affirming his immediate passion over his marriage so much as he affirms the continual and open possibility of love over either.

After two subsidiary sermons, the poem turns to the history of the poet's quest (lines 190–344). As is traditional, it proceeds through misadventures and anticipations until at last he again encounters "youth's vision thus made perfect." Having found her, he desires to hold not only her (pictured as "an Incarnation of the Sun") but two earlier ladies as well (a Moon figure and a Comet form, probably to be interpreted on the biographical level as Mrs. Shelley and her stepsister, Claire Clairmont, one of Byron's former mistresses). This is undoubtedly to be taken as a pragmatic program for polygamy, but then *Epipsychidion* is an idealizing poem and contemplates a world rather different from ours (or Shelley's). If relationship is always to be as wavering as the appearances of Intellectual Beauty, then a sun-moon-comet alternation provides an incessant substitute for the single relationship that, of itself, necessarily must fail.

Shelley is too tactful to argue the feasibility of his fairly desperate solution. The poem's myth seeks defeat, and finds it, for the understanding of human limitations has now conflicted openly with the theme of transcendent desire. Two antithetical movements end the poem. The first envisions an earthly paradise to be shared with Emilia:

Meanwhile
We two will rise, and sit, and walk together,
Under the roof of blue Ionian weather,
And wander in the meadows, or ascend
The mossy mountains, where the blue heavens bend
With lightest winds, to touch their paramour;
Or linger, where the pebble-paven shore,

Under the quick, faint kisses of the sea
Trembles and sparkles as with ecstasy,—
Possessing and possessed by all that is
Within that calm circumference of bliss,
And by each other, till to love and live
Be one.

Beautiful as this is, it cannot be sustained. Shelley passes from
this vision of attempted union to its necessary failure:

We shall become the same, we shall be one
Spirit within two frames, oh! wherefore two?
One passion in twin-hearts, which grows and grew.
Till like two meteors of expanding flame,
Those spheres instinct with it become the same,
Touch, mingle, are transfigured; ever still
Burning, yet ever inconsumable:
In one another's substance finding food,
Like flames too pure and light and unimbued
To nourish their bright lives with baser prey,
Which point to Heaven and cannot pass away:
One hope within two wills, one will beneath
Two overshadowing minds, one life, one death,
One Heaven, one Hell, one immortality,
And one annihilation. Woe is me!
The wingèd words on which my soul would pierce
Into the height of Love's rare Universe,
Are chains of lead around its flight of fire—
I pant, I sink, I tremble, I expire!

Love unites in act, not in essence. The countermyth demands
union in essence, and so destroys the poem, in the movement to
"one annihilation." The attempt both to extend and to realize the
limits of relationship and expression fails, yet the poem remains.
Four months later, in *Adonais* (June 1821), Shelley extended his
chronicle of a quest's darkening. *Adonais* is an elegy on the death
of John Keats, but also on the waning of Shelley's own quest.

Adonais

SHELLEY and Keats, brought together by Leigh Hunt, failed to become friends. Hunt puts it briefly: "Keats did not take to Shelley as kindly as Shelley did to him." Still, they saw enough of one another in the spring of 1817 for Keats to fear the other poet's personal and literary influence upon *Endymion,* and they continued to see one another until Shelley left England for a last time in March 1818.

In July 1820 Shelley, knowing of Keats's illness, asked him to come to Italy, to avoid the English winter. The invitation was for Keats to take up his residence with the Shelleys. Yet the same generous letter contains criticism of Keats's poetry which he was not likely to accept. After praising *Endymion* for "the treasures of poetry it contains," Shelley adds, "though treasures poured forth with indistinct profusion." This becomes a more general censure: "In poetry I have sought to avoid system and mannerism. I wish those who excel me in genius would pursue the same plan."

Keats's reply was equally apt. "You, I am sure, will forgive me for sincerely remarking that you might curb your magnanimity, and be more of an artist, and load every rift of your subject with ore." Each poet had hold of a limited critical truth about the other, but Keats, ill and irritated, understandably showed less graciousness in the exchange.

The poets did not meet again, for Keats came to Italy only to die, at Rome, on February 23, 1821. Shelley had, in the meantime, read the *Hyperion* fragment in Keats's volume of 1820 and thereby changed his estimate of Keats's poetry. "If the *Hyperion* be not grand poetry, none has been produced by our contemporaries." Shelley went to his own death with the rereading of Keats, evidently his last act. Trelawny, identifying his friend's body, catches this final and affecting detail: "The tall slight figure, the jacket, the volume of Sophocles in one pocket, and Keats's poems in the other, doubled back, as if the reader, in the act of reading, had hastily thrust it away."

Keats was only three months dead when Shelley composed his elegy. He said of the poem that it was "perhaps the least imperfect" of his compositions, and certainly it is a highly finished work. Responding to his friends' praise of it, he very truly observed: "The poet and the man are two different natures: though they exist together, they may be unconscious of each other, and incapable of deciding on each other's powers and efforts by any reflex act." We may apply this to the subject of *Adonais;* it is the formalized lament of Shelley the poet for Keats the poet. It has rather less to do with the very real but remote grief that Shelley felt for Keats as a man. As in Milton's *Lycidas,* the poet's concern is with the fate of poets in a world that resists their prophecies and a nature that seems indifferent to their destruction.

Shelley's form is the pastoral elegy, modeled on Bion's *Lament for Adonis* and Moschus' *Lament for Bion,* Hellenic poems of the second century B.C. Shelley had translated fragments of both poems and turned to them as archetypes of the kind of elegy he wished to write. Bion laments the death of the vegetation god, Adonis, the doomed lover of Venus. Moschus adopts the form of his friend's poem as appropriate for lamenting Bion's death and so initiates the tradition of one poet associating the death of another poet with the fabled death of Adonis. Spenser's lament for Sir Philip Sidney, *Astrophel,* and Milton's for Edward King continue this tradition, which culminates in *Adonais.*

Shelley chooses to believe, for his poetic purposes, that Keats was slain by the attacks upon *Endymion,* particularly the one made in the *Quarterly Review.* What counts here is imaginative, rather than literal, correctness. Shelley means, as Northrop Frye observes, that the hatred of genius by mediocrity is a death principle in society.[45]

The epigraph to *Adonais* is a little poem attributed to Plato, which Shelley himself translated:

> Thou wert the morning star among the living,
>   Ere thy fair light had fled;—
> Now, having died, thou art as Hesperus, giving
>   New splendour to the dead.

Keats has passed from the sphere of Lucifer, star of the morning, to that of Hesperus or Venus, first light of evening. This is a prefiguration of his fate within the poem.

Adonais consists of fifty-five Spenserian stanzas, and falls into two principal movements, with the thirty-eighth stanza marking the point of transition. The last seventeen stanzas are much finer than what precede them. Shelley casts off his poem's machinery in its final third and chants an astonishing hymn that recapitulates his darkened quest and seeks at last the quest's realization in a transvaluation of death. The movement of the first two thirds of the poem is much clearer than that of the final third, but is considerably less inspired.

Adonais, or Keats, is dead as the poem opens, and the Hour of death mourns him, and is to call the other hours to similar mourning. The dead poet was the youngest and dearest son of the Muse Urania, patroness of his poems *Endymion* and *Hyperion,* who was slumbering in her paradise when the murder occurred. She is called upon to weep, and yet her lament will be in vain. The poet's creations lament with her. The poem's first crisis comes in the counterpoint between the rebirth of nature and the soul's failure to revive:

> Ah, woe is me! Winter is come and gone,
> But grief returns with the revolving year;
> The airs and streams renew their joyous tone;
> The ants, the bees, the swallows reappear;
> Fresh leaves and flowers deck the dead Seasons' bier;
> The amorous birds now pair in every brake,
> And build their mossy homes in field and brere;
> And the green lizard, and the golden snake,
> Like unimprisoned flames, out of their trance awake.

> Through wood and stream and field and hill and Ocean
> A quickening life from the Earth's heart has burst
> As it has ever done, with change and motion,
> From the great morning of the world when first
> God dawned on Chaos; in its stream immersed,
> The lamps of Heaven flash wtih a softer light;
> All baser things pant with life's sacred thirst;
> Diffuse themselves; and spend in love's delight,
> The beauty and the joy of their renewèd might.

> The leprous corpse, touched by this spirit tender,
> Exhales itself in flowers of gentle breath;

> Like incarnations of the stars, when splendour
> Is changed to fragrance, they illumine death
> And mock the merry worm that wakes beneath;
> Nought we know, dies. Shall that alone which knows
> Be as a sword consumed before the sheath
> By sightless lightning?—the intense atom glows
> A moment, then is quenched in a most cold repose.

This is a first and relatively crude formulation of the poem's greatest concern; the shaping spirit alone vanishes, while everything grosser turns over and reappears in cycle. This grief becomes that of Urania when she seeks her son's death chamber. She desires to join him in death, but she is "chained to Time, and cannot thence depart." After her lament, she is joined by the Mountain Shepherds, the surviving poets, including Byron, Thomas Moore, and Leigh Hunt, only the last of whom, in fact, cared for Keats. Once again, Shelley deliberately ignores the poets as men, and emphasizes only their symbolic aspect. Amid the others, comes Shelley himself:

> A pardlike Spirit beautiful and swift—
> A love in desolation masked;—a Power
> Girt round with weakness;—it can scarce uplift
> The weight of the superincumbent hour;
> It is a dying lamp, a falling shower,
> A breaking billow;—even whilst we speak
> Is it not broken? On the withering flower
> The killing sun smiles brightly: on a cheek
> The life can burn in blood, even while the heart may break.

In his other stanzas of self-description here, Shelley compares himself to Actaeon, Cain, and Christ. Like Actaeon, he has "gazed on Nature's naked loveliness," and Nature strikes back by turning his own thoughts upon him, as Actaeon was pursued by his own hounds. Like Cain, he has perhaps failed to be his brother's keeper, though he had tried to preserve and shelter Keats. Again, like Cain, he is in fact an outcast from his family's and nation's society, for he is more reviled in orthodox English circles than Keats or Byron or any other contemporary writer. The Christ comparison is frankly impious; Shelley means to parallel his sufferings for mankind with those of Christ, for he desires to make his own sufferings vicarious, though not an atonement. In the stanza just quoted he compares his own power to the mutable strength of natural process, caught at the moment of its downward passage, "a falling shower, a breaking billow." Like the confronted reality of Asia or Emilia, his power can scarcely be apprehended before it wavers and vanishes. He has caught for us, imperishably, the basis of his style, its deliberate evanescence, and has given us its thematic justification: to be true to what *he* observes as most vital in nature.

Renewed lament for Adonais is followed by the poorest stanza in the poem (xxxvii), in which the Quarterly Reviewer is castigated as a "noteless blot on a remembered name." From this bathos the next stanza recoils, and the poem soars into greatness:

> Nor let us weep that our delight is fled
> Far from these carrion kites that scream below;
> He wakes or sleeps with the enduring dead;
> Thou canst not soar where he is sitting now.—
> Dust to the dust! but the pure spirit shall flow
> Back to the burning fountain whence it came,
> A portion of the Eternal, which must glow
> Through time and change, unquenchably the same,
> Whilst thy cold embers choke the sordid hearth of shame.

Shelley remains agnostic as to literal immortality; Keats "wakes *or* sleeps with the enduring dead," and survives only as they survive. But though he agrees with Ecclesiastes on "dust to the dust," he affirms the return of creative spirit back to a source neither temporal nor mutable, "the burning fountain" where life-giving water is aflame with the energy of imagination. In the light of that fountain, the dead poet is neither dead nor asleep, but "awakened from the dream of life" by having "outsoared the shadow of our night." Urania is represented in the heavens by Venus, the star of evening, to whose sphere Keats has soared. As the shadow of earth stops at the sphere of Venus, the poet is now free "from the contagion of the world's slow stain," and becomes a presence of transcendent Nature:

> He is made one with Nature: there is heard
> His voice in all her music, from the moan

> Of thunder, to the song of night's sweet bird;
> He is a presence to be felt and known
> In darkness and in light, from herb and stone,
> Spreading itself where'er that Power may move
> Which has withdrawn his being to its own;
> Which wields the world with never-wearied love,
> Sustains it from beneath, and kindles it above.

There is a touch of Keats's *Ode to a Nightingale* here. More vital, Shelley moves in this stanza to his most overt affirmation of the benevolence of the unknown Power he has pursued since *Alastor*. The Power is withdrawn, and has taken Keats into that remote tranquillity, but it still dominates and directs the world with love, by both giving reality a firm existence at a phenomenal level and kindling the spirit rising out of phenomena:

> He is a portion of the loveliness
> Which once he made more lovely; he doth bear
> His part, while the one Spirit's plastic stress
> Sweeps through the dull dense world, compelling there,
> All new successions to the forms they wear;
> Torturing th' unwilling dross that checks its flight
> To its own likeness, as each mass may bear;
> And bursting in its beauty and its might
> From trees and beasts and men into the Heaven's light.

This majestic stanza completes one aspect of Shelley's imaginative apprehension of reality. The Spirit itself now directs the successions of mutable appearances, as part of its ultimate desire to mold the world into its own likeness. The unwilling dross of things resists, but finally in vain, as the Spirit bursts triumphantly through the forms of nature and man up into the light of Heaven. Until the Spirit kindles itself for a last time in the final four stanzas, this is all that Shelley is willing to put in terms of a faith.

Keats, like Chatterton or Sidney, is one of "the splendours of the firmament of time," and he goes now to join them, the Vesper of their throng. But Shelley's thought returns to groundling earth, where he himself still abides. As he ponders the problem of earthly consolation, his mind turns to Rome, scene of Keats's death and burial, and to the Protestant cemetery where lie the remains of

Keats, and where he himself was to lie not so long after. Though the Spirit's breath moves, the world's wind remains bitter:

> From the world's bitter wind
> Seek shelter in the shadow of the tomb.
> What Adonais is, why fear we to become?

This is the poem's great moment of transition, its dialectical resolution as Shelley chooses the fate of Keats for himself. In a stanza justly celebrated two opposing realities are brought together, with neither negating the other:

> The One remains, the many change and pass;
> Heaven's light forever shines, Earth's shadows fly;
> Life, like a dome of many-coloured glass,
> Stains the white radiance of Eternity,
> Until Death tramples it to fragments.—Die,
> If thou wouldst be with that which thou dost seek!
> Follow where all is fled!—Rome's azure sky,
> Flowers, ruins, statues, music, words, are weak
> The glory they transfuse with fitting truth to speak.

Though life *stains* the white radiance of Eternity, the staining is not all loss, for the dome produces the colors that Eternity merely subsumes. Death smashes the dome and tramples it into fragments, but the fragments are at least brightly colored, for they are identical with the azure sky, with flowers, ruins, statues, music, and the words of Shelley's own poem. Yet he turns from them and seeks the deathly glory they transfuse:

> Why linger, why turn back, why shrink, my Heart?
> Thy hopes are gone before: from all things here
> They have departed; thou shouldst now depart!
> A light is passed from the revolving year,
> And man, and woman; and what still is dear
> Attracts to crush, repels to make thee wither.
> The soft sky smiles,—the low wind whispers near:
> 'Tis Adonais calls! oh, hasten thither,
> No more let Life divide what Death can join together.

The low wind that rises here is like the west wind of Shelley's *Ode*, the creative and destructive agent, which begins my destroying. The year revolves again, yet a light has passed away from it forever, and everything left behind is caught in the strife of contraries, "attracts to crush." For a last time Shelley states his now pragmatically hopeless faith:

> That Light whose smile kindles the Universe,
> That Beauty in which all things work and move,
> That Benediction which the eclipsing Curse
> Of birth can quench not, that sustaining Love
> Which through the web of being blindly wove
> By man and beast and earth and air and sea,
> Burns bright or dim, as each are mirrors of
> The fire for which all thirst; now beams on me,
> Consuming the last clouds of cold mortality.

In this straining upward, the natural world that is given to us becomes only a darkness, into which we are born by an eclipsing Curse, and within which we weave our sustaining web of Love quite blindly. This is the undersong of the Spirit's immense declaration, for the overt emphasis here is on the salvation that brings us finally back to the burning fountain. The poem now refers us back to the *Ode to the West Wind*, as the force invoked there now descends on its prophet:

> The breath whose might I have invoked in song
> Descends on me; my spirit's bark is driven
> Far from the shore, far from the trembling throng
> Whose sails were never to the tempest given;
> The massy earth and spherèd skies are riven!
> I am borne darkly, fearfully, afar;
> Whilst, burning through the inmost veil of Heaven,
> The soul of Adonais, like a star,
> Beacons from the abode where the Eternal are.

We mistake this triumph of rhetoric if we read it as other than a triumph of human despair. The imagination holding life open to death is not the burden of this great but suicidal stanza. Shelley is surrendering to Heaven, though it is the Heaven not of any orthodoxy but of his own agnostic will. A known is yielding to an unknown, and a vision collapses into mystery. *Adonais* is an imperishable poem, but it is also the sepulcher of a humanist and heroic quest.

7   *Transmemberment of Song*

Final Lyrics

SHELLEY died at sea, off Leghorn, on July 8, 1822, a month before what would have been his thirtieth birthday. The lyrics of his final half-year of life have both perfection of form and a melancholy serenity of tone. *The Zucca* is a darker recasting of the *Hymn to Intellectual Beauty,* as it concerns the departure of that Spirit:

> By Heaven and Earth, from all whose shapes thou flowest,
>   Neither to be contained, delayed, nor hidden;
> Making divine the loftiest and the lowest,
>   When for a moment thou art not forbidden
> To live within the life which thou bestowest;
>   And leaving noblest things vacant and chidden,
> Cold as a corpse after the spirit's flight,
> Blank as the sun after the birth of night.
>
> In winds, and trees, and streams, and all things common,
>   In music and the sweet unconscious tone
> Of animals, and voices which are human,
>   Meant to express some feelings of their own;
> In the soft motions and rare smile of woman,
>   In flowers and leaves, and in the grass fresh-shown,
> Or dying in the autumn, I the most
> Adore thee present or lament thee lost.

The tragic love song "When the lamp is shattered" also records the death of relationship.[46] The Spirit's light departs, but "the light in the dust" abides in the dead heart. Love ends, and its weaker victim despairingly cradles its dead form:

When hearts have once mingled
Love first leaves the well-built nest;
   The weak one is singled
To endure what it once possessed.
   O Love! who bewailest
The frailty of all things here,
   Why choose you the frailest
For your cradle, your home, and your bier?

In the love poems to Jane Williams, Shelley's last compositions
before the unfinished *Triumph of Life,* this bitterness of tone disappears, and a gracious resignation usurps its place. The finest of
these poems, *Lines Written in the Bay of Lerici,* depicts a state of
immediacy intense enough to remind the poet, momentarily, of the
possibility of living again in the present:

She left me, and I stayed alone
Thinking over every tone
Which, though silent to the ear,
The enchanted heart could hear,
Like notes which die when born, but still
Haunt the echoes of the hill;
And feeling ever—oh, too much!—
The soft vibration of her touch,
As if her gentle hand, even now,
Lightly trembled on my brow;
And thus, although she absent were,
Memory gave me all of her
That even Fancy dares to claim:—
Her presence had made weak and tame
All passions, and I lived alone
In the time which is our own;
The past and future were forgot,
As they had been, and would be, not.

But the daemon reassumes his throne in the poet's heart; he remembers the hopelessness of a lifetime's quest. He looks out to sea
and indulges in Elysian intimations, until he is recalled to himself
by an image of reality:

And the scent of wingèd flowers,
And the coolness of the hours

Of dew, and sweet warmth left by day,
Were scattered o'er the twinkling bay.
And the fisher with his lamp
And spear about the low rocks damp
Crept, and struck the fish which came
To worship the delusive flame.
Too happy they, whose pleasure sought
Extinguishes all sense and thought
Of the regret that pleasure leaves,
Destroying life alone, not peace!

Love's pleasure drives his love away, and he realizes again that whatever flames upon the night is fed by his own heart alone. The theme of life's triumph over everything imaginative that seeks to redeem life had been a long time in coming to Shelley's poetry, but when it did come it came as devastation. That Shelley had the power to submit the theme to the transmemberment of his last and most finely wrought poem is the crown of his tragic life and poetic career.

The Triumph of Life

WILLIAM HAZLITT reviewed Shelley's *Posthumous Poems* in 1824, and complained of the paradoxical title of Shelley's last poem: "The poem entitled the *Triumph of Life,* is in fact a new and terrific *Dance of Death;* but it is thus Mr. Shelley transposes the appellations of the commonest things, and subsists only in the violence of contrast."

The *Triumph* is in *terza rima* and shows the influence of Dante throughout, particularly of the *Purgatorio.* Keats was dead when Shelley composed the *Triumph,* and Keats's *Fall of Hyperion* was not published until 1856, so there is no question of mutual influencing or example in the extraordinary fact that both poets left as their last considerable fragments work dominated by the *Purgatorio.* Both were attempting visions of judgment, and Dante seemed the inevitable model.

The *Triumph*'s vision is of a public way:

Thick strewn with summer dust, and a great stream
Of people there was hurrying to and fro,
Numerous as gnats upon the evening gleam,

All hastening onward, yet none seemed to know
Whither he went, or whence he came, or why
He made one of the multitude, and so

Was borne amid the crowd, as through the sky
One of the million leaves of summer's bier.

This recalls the opening stanza of the *Ode to the West Wind*. The people are as dust, as gnats, as dead leaves, crowding along to their own destruction. They lack individuality and will, and all the objectives of their trek are equally unreasonable. As Hazlitt said, this is a dance of death, compulsive and busy, replete with meaningless activity and serious folly:

Old age and youth, manhood and infancy,

Mixed in one mighty torrent did appear,
Some flying from the thing they feared, and some
Seeking the object of another's fear.

Down the sterile, flowerless path they run the way of competition. As the poet gazes in wonder, the passing crowd's dance becomes wilder:

And as I gazed, methought that in the way
The throng grew wilder, as the woods of June
When the south wind shakes the extinguished day,

And a cold glare, intenser than the noon,
But icy cold, obscured with blinding light
The sun, as he the stars. Like the young moon.

The glare comes from an advancing chariot, which rolls over the fierce dancers in its path, and whose blinding cold glare, light without heat, obscures the warm light of the sun, even as the sun's light obscures the light of the stars. We have touched this optical theme

before in Shelley, but in the *Triumph* it assumes a new importance. The chariot's glare is the light of life; the sun's, of nature;
the stars', the visionary light of imagination and poetry. Nature's
light obliterates that of the poet, only to be destroyed in turn by
the light of life, the moonlike cold car of Life. The chariot of Life
is introduced by the sinister image of the new moon with the old
moon in its arms, prophetic of an oncoming storm:

> So came a chariot on the silent storm
> Of its own rushing splendour, and a Shape
> So sate within, as one whom years deform,
>
> Beneath a dusky hood and double cape,
> Crouching within the shadow of a tomb.

Like Ezekiel's visionary chariot, Shelley's comes in a storm.
Ezekiel's cherubim each have four faces and four wings; we see no
beasts drawing the chariot because so divine a vehicle can be moved
by no force external to itself. Shelley's charioteer has four faces,
and we are not allowed to see the shapes drawing it, for they are
lost "in thick lightenings." The vision in Shelley is a deliberate "diabolic" parody of the chariot of Ezekiel, as well as its derivatives in
the *Purgatorio* and *Paradise Lost*. Shelley's Shape, within the chariot, is called simply "Life," is deformed, dusky, and also shrouded
and indefinite:

> And o'er what seemed the head a cloud-like crape
> Was bent, a dun and faint aethereal gloom
> Tempering the light.

The Enthroned Man in Ezekiel's chariot, or the Christ in Revelation's chariot modeled after Ezekiel, nakedly blazed with light, and
had the hard, definite form of agate. The Shape of Life is hooded,
and rather less human, being merely natural, to be identified with
all the life lived by the natural man. With the Shape we see her
charioteer:

> All the four faces of that Charioteer
> Had their eyes banded; little profit brings
>
> Speed in the van and blindness in the rear,
> Nor then avail the beams that quench the sun,—
> Or that with banded eyes could pierce the sphere

Of all that is, has been or will be done;
So ill was the car guided—but it passed
With solemn speed majestically on.

The four-faced Charioteer is derived from the Ezekiel-Revelation-Dante-Milton tradition of a divine chariot made up of four-faced cherubim. Every text in that tradition emphasizes the innumerable eyes of the cherubim. Blake, in his illustration of the *Purgatorio*'s Triumphal Chariot of the Church, carries this emphasis to an extreme, for his painting is dominated by a plethora of eyes over everything else in the scene. The eyes are open; like Keats's "intlligences," which were "atoms of perceptions," these eyes also "know and they see and they are pure, in short they are God." But all four faces of Shelley's Charioteer "had their eyes banded." The Charioteer cannot guide, and so the light given off by the chariot is of no help to him in his blindness. This chariot's progress is therefore meaningless, for all its majestic appearance and solemn speed.

The chariot passes on, and the poet sees a horde following it, captives in its triumphal procession:

—all those who had grown old in power
Or misery,—all who had their age subdued

By action or by suffering, and whose hour
Was drained to its last sand in weal or woe,
So that the trunk survived both fruit and flower;—

All those whose fame or infamy must grow
Till the great winter lay the form and name
Of this green earth with them for ever low.

Counting up all these "alls," one counts up to everybody as having been conquered by Life, except for "the sacred few" who are considered next in the poem. "The sacred few" escaped this defeat only by choosing to die to this life, like the poet at the end of *Adonais:*

All but the sacred few who could not tame
Their spirits to the conqueror's—but as soon
As they had touched the world with living flame,

Fled back like eagles to their native noon.
For those who put aside the diadem
Of earthly thrones or gems till the last . . .

Whether of Athens or Jerusalem,
Were neither mid the mighty captives seen,
Nor mid the ribald crowd that followed them

Nor those who went before fierce and obscene.

These sacred few certainly include Socrates and Jesus, though many of their followers are later seen among the captives, whom Shelley divides into three groups. These are: the mighty ones chained to the chariot (Rousseau will describe them later, after he makes his striking entrance into the poem); the ribald old following the chariot; the young dancing to destruction before it. The young at least are destroyed by the failure of love, like the poet in *Alastor,* but the old sink to corruption "with impotence of will." The given condition of natural man is depicted in its dual modes of hopelessness, after which the poem mounts to its first climax:

Struck to the heart by this sad pageantry,
Half to myself I said—"And what is this?
Whose shape is that within the car? And why—"

I would have added—"Is all here amiss?—"
But a voice answered—"Life!"—I turned, and knew
(O Heaven, have mercy on such wretchedness!)

That what I thought was an old root which grew
To strange distortion out of the hill side,
Was indeed one of those deluded crew,

And that the grass, which methought hung so wide
And white, was but his thin discoloured hair,
And that the holes he vainly sought to hide,

Were or had been eyes.

This is what remains of Rousseau, who has attained completely to the state of nature, Blake's Vegetative universe of Generation.

Rousseau enters the poem as the chastened prophet of the state of nature, the disillusioned poet of natural religion and natural passion. As Virgil guided Dante, so the relic of Rousseau is to guide Shelley, to purify his vision. Rousseau himself can no longer see; Life's chariot has blinded him. He hears Shelley's words and replies to them. Out of his grim knowledge he gives the younger poet a warning not to join the dance, "which I had well forborne." He passes judgment upon himself in the poem's finest lines:

> Before thy memory,
>
> I feared, loved, hated, suffered, did and died,
> And if the spark with which Heaven lit my spirit
> Had been with purer nutriment supplied,
>
> Corruption would not now thus much inherit
> Of what was once Rousseau,—nor this disguise
> Stain that which ought to have disdained to wear it.

Rousseau began with flame in his spirit, a spark that had both heat and light. He needed only to supply proper nutriment for this spark, but he failed, and he recognizes his own responsibility for the failure. Corruption veils the aged victims of the chariot (line 174) but not Rousseau, merely "what was once Rousseau," is thus disguised by the contagion of the world's slow stain. The disguise stains "that which ought to have disdained to wear it," imagination. Rousseau is now as corrupt as any of Life's victims, but the way of his corruption was nobler than that of other "sages":

> —The wise,
>
> The great, the unforgotten,—they who wore
> Mitres and helms and crowns, or wreaths of light,
> Signs of thought's empire over thought—their lore
>
> Taught them not this, to know themselves; their might
> Could not repress the mutiny within
> And for the morn of truth they feigned, deep night
>
> Caught them ere evening.

These leaders include bishops, warriors, rulers, and canonized saints and mystics; their headgear indicates "thought's empire over thought," tyrannies of the spirit. No system of belief has brought them knowledge of the selfhood of mutiny within, and so their truth is only "feigned" and they too are conquered by Life.

Among them is Napoleon, the fallen Titan, whose appearance now inspires the central statement of Shelley's poetry:

> —I felt my cheek
> Alter, to see the shadow pass away,
> Whose grasp had left the giant world so weak
>
> That every pigmy kicked it as it lay;
> And much I grieved to think how power and will
> In opposition rule our mortal day,
>
> And why God made irreconcilable
> Good and the means of good.

The last and subtlest Fury had reminded Prometheus that goodness and power, wisdom and love, were antithetical, "and all best things are thus confused to ill." The contraries are now sharper; power and will are in opposition, and thus good and the means of good are irreconcilable by the very nature of things. Life, our life, can be met only by quietism or by willful self-destruction.

What remains in this poem of total despair is the story closest to Shelley's individual fate, the overcoming by Life of the poet's unextinguished imaginative spark. While Shelley broods on the irreconcilable contraries, Rousseau completes his naming of the mighty captives by listing the "spoilers spoiled," Voltaire and his disciples, the "benevolent despots":

> For in the battle Life and they did wage,
> She remained conqueror. I was overcome
> By my own heart alone, which neither age,
>
> Nor tears, nor infamy, nor now the tomb
> Could temper to its object.

None of Life's weapons succeed in limiting Rousseau's desire by reducing his heart's infinite capacity to desire. If his heart had been so tempered to its object, then it would have been content with Life's gratifications, and so would have been conquered by Life. He has been overcome nevertheless, but by his own heart alone, not by Life. He is self-defeated, and his account of how this came to be forms the closing movement of the poem as we have it.

Rousseau's story resembles that of Wordsworth in the *Intimations* ode, for both describe a process of rebirth, of the transition from Innocence to Experience, from boyhood to manhood, from absolute dependence upon nature for imaginative vision to the realization that nature's vision fails its seer.

In the April prime of the year the young Rousseau falls asleep in a cavern with an opening to the west, actually a deep ravine that cuts through a mountain, probably to be related to Dante's mountain of Purgatory. The mountain is north-south, the ravine through it east-west. On the east of the mountain Rousseau passed his infancy and early childhood. He progresses through the mountain as he grows older, until as a young man he reaches a center point within the cavern where a fountain or well takes its rise. The fountain issues in a west-flowing gentle rivulet, the sound of which lulls Rousseau to sleep. The rivulet broadens into a stream and then a river as it flows westward out of the mountain.

As Rousseau sleeps under the rivulet's influence his childhood vanishes into oblivion. When he awakens, he faces the Wordsworthian situation of the fading of an earlier phenomenal glory:

> I arose, and for a space
> The scene of woods and waters seemed to keep,
>
> Though it was now broad day, a gentle trace
> Of light diviner than the common sun
> Sheds on the common earth, and all the place
>
> Was filled with magic sounds woven into one
> Oblivious melody, confusing sense
> Amid the sliding waves and shadows dun.

For a while he can still see the diviner light, and still experience the fused or organic sense that haunted Coleridge and Wordsworth. But then the light of nature has its way with him. The vision of a Shape, representing Wordsworthian nature, now appears to him:

there stood

Amid the sun, as he amid the blaze
Of his own glory, on the vibrating
Floor of the fountain, paved with flashing rays,

A Shape all light, which with one hand did fling
Dew on the earth, as if she were the dawn,
And the invisible rain did ever sing

A silver music on the mossy lawn;
And still before me on the dusky grass,
Iris her many-coloured scarf had drawn.

The rays of the sun flow in from the eastern side of the cavern. The "sun's image" burns on the fountain, and a rainbow appears within that image. The rainbow is the emblem of salvation, of a continuity in nature, in Wordsworth's *Ode,* but here it is employed ironically, against Wordsworth's vision. The Shape moves upon the surface of the water, a movement that parodies Dante's *Purgatorio,* XXVIII–XXIX, where the poet meets Matilda in her earthly paradise, on top of the mount of Purgatory. Dante sees Matilda across the water of the river of Lethe, a draught of which will wash away all memory of sin. Rousseau sees the Shape all light upon the waters of a Lethe-like river, but she carries a crystal glass the contents of which will wash away all memory whatsoever, including the divine youth of Rousseau, the spark with which his earlier spirit was illuminated. As the Shape approaches Rousseau, her pragmatic malevolence becomes unmistakable:

And still her feet, no less than the sweet tune
To which they moved, seemed as they moved to blot
The thoughts of him who gazed on them; and soon

All that was, seemed as if it had been not;
And all the gazer's mind was strewn beneath
Her feet like embers; and she, thought by thought,

Trampled its sparks into the dust of death;
As day upon the threshold of the east
Treads out the lamps of night, until the breath

Of darkness re-illumine even the least
Of heaven's living eyes.

The Shape tramples the sparks of Rousseau's mind, thought by thought, "into the dust of death." Day treads out the stars, "the lamps of night," which are equivalent to the poets who are the lamps of earth and who are extinguished by the light of common day.

The Shape is like Keats's Belle Dame, and from her tempting him to a strange drink, Rousseau will awaken to Shelley's version of Keats's cold hill's side. She offers her nepenthe, Rousseau drinks of it, and suddenly his brain becomes as sand where tracks are more than half erased. And the cold vision of Life bursts upon him:

> —so on my sight
> Burst a new vision, never seen before,
>
> And the fair Shape waned in the coming light,
> As veil by veil the silent splendour drops
> From Lucifer, amid the chrysolite
>
> Of sunrise, ere it tinge the mountain-tops.

Even as the sun dims Lucifer, the morning star, now the glare of Life's chariot dims the rainbow, emblem of the sun. Rousseau has surrendered to nature, but nature either cannot or will not keep faith with him. The mature Wordsworth would have said the first, Blake the second, for Shelley's Shape is very like Blake's Vala in her effect. Either way, the rainbow fades, and the memory of it replaces the now extinct memory of an earlier and more divine light. Rousseau is swept into the chariot's procession until at last he falls by the wayside. The poem breaks off in the despairing cry of Shelley or Rousseau:

> "Then, what is life?" I cried.

The poem has already provided the answer. Life is what triumphs over nature, even as nature triumphs over imagination. Life is death-in-life, Ulro, a cold, common hell in which we wake to weep. The quest of Shelley comes full circle from *Alastor* to *The Triumph of Life*, and the total structure of his poetic canon is seen to resemble the ironic cycle of Blake's *Mental Traveller*. Shelley was too honest an agnostic and too good a poet merely to repeat the cycle again. He went forth to suffer a sea change, abandoning behind him the rich strangeness of his poetry.

CHAPTER SIX

JOHN KEATS

The imagination spans beyond despair,
Outpacing bargain, vocable and prayer.
HART CRANE

1 *Gardens of the Moon*

Sleep and Poetry

SLEEP AND POETRY, Keats's first considerable poem, is
his version of Wordsworth's *Tintern Abbey*. It is a hymn of
poetic dedication that charts the stages of imaginative development, and begins the statement of the personal word or individual myth of the new poet.

The universe of *Sleep and Poetry* is that of pastoral innocence. A
bowery nook, Keats says, will be Elysium for him. He looks forward
to being a glorious denizen of poetry's wide heaven, and prays
ardently for a breath of inspiration:

> That I may die a death
> Of luxury, and my young spirit follow
> The morning sun-beams to the great Apollo
> Like a fresh sacrifice.

It is sadly prophetic, more so than Keats could have intended. He asks for ten years that he may overwhelm himself in poetry, but he got scarcely four of life, and only three of poetry after writing these lines.

To do the deed that his own soul to itself decrees, he needs to pass through the countries of the mind, and taste continually from the pure fountains existent in each state of being:

> First the realm I'll pass
> Of Flora, and old Pan: sleep in the grass,
> Feed upon apples red, and strawberries,
> And choose each pleasure that my fancy sees;
> Catch the white-handed nymphs in shady places,
> To woo sweet kisses from averted faces,—
> Play with their fingers, touch their shoulders white
> Into a pretty shrinking with a bite
> As hard as lips can make it.

Keats's state of innocence is directly erotic, and he does not evade the naturalistic honesty that parallels the biting of apples and of shoulders. His first realm retains but inverts the orthodox popular imagination's identification of the Fall with sexuality. He completes his view of Elysium by identifying repose within nature and sexual union:

> Another will entice me on, and on
> Through almond blossoms and rich cinnamon;
> Till in the bosom of a leafy world
> We rest in silence.

Here there is no clash of contraries or strife of hearts, and yet to this innocence and these joys he must bid farewell. He seeks experience, with "the agonies, the strife of human hearts." A vision of the ideal within experience comes to him in the shape of the charioteer with his car and steeds, a vision of the figure of the youth as virile poet. Ultimately this youth is both the Romantic Apollo (as in Blake's Orc, Collins' rich-haired youth of morn, Coleridge's youth with flashing eyes and floating hair) and the Romantic successor to the Son of God figure who rides the Flaming chariot of Deity in Ezekiel, Revelation, and *Paradise Lost*. When Keats's charioteer descends and addresses natural objects, they come alive with a vitality more intense than the animate personifications of Collins:

> The charioteer with wond'rous gesture talks
> To the trees and mountains; and there soon appear
> Shapes of delight, of mystery, and fear,
> Passing along before a dusky space.

The "wond'rous gesture" is the gesture a poem makes, and by the poem's confrontation the trees and mountains become persons, to whom the charioteer-poet can talk. They appear as abstract human emotions, but their behavior is concrete and particular:

> Lo! how they murmur, laugh, and smile, and weep:
> Some with upholden hand and mouth severe;
> Some with their faces muffled to the ear
> Between their arms; some, clear in youthful bloom,
> Go glad and smilingly athwart the gloom;
> Some looking back, and some with upward gaze;
> Yes, thousands in a thousand different ways
> Flit onward

The variety and multitude of shapes is Keats's first image for what he will later (in the *Ode to Psyche*) refer to as the complex feigning of the gardener Fancy, "who breeding flowers, will never breed the same." The uniqueness of each shape is part of its value, but testifies also to its aspect of feigning. The ideal departs, and the high flight of the imagination returns to earth:

> The visions all are fled—the car is fled
> Into the light of heaven, and in their stead
> A sense of real things comes doubly strong,
> And, like a muddy stream, would bear along
> My soul to nothingness

The effect of the poetic ideal is both to double the sense of real things and to expose such reality as being like a muddy stream. Caught in the mire of the actual, Keats vows that he will strive against all doubtings to keep alive the thought of the chariot of poetry and its journey. Such strife leads him into Romantic polemic. Why cannot the high imagination freely fly as she did of old, when she prepared her steeds and performed the rich activities

that constitute the poems of Spenser, Shakespeare, Milton? What
caused the native Muses to be forgotten?

> a schism
> Nurtured by foppery and barbarism,
> Made great Apollo blush for this his land.
> Men were thought wise who could not understand
> His glories: with a puling infant's force
> They sway'd about upon a rocking horse,
> And thought it Pegasus.

Not a very good thrust at the school of Pope, as Keats is weak at
this kind of wit. Blake puts it better in one Proverb of Hell: "bring
out number, weight and measure in a year of dearth." Keats is a
more persuasive critic, both in praise and blame, when he goes on
to speak of his older contemporaries:

> fine sounds are floating wild
> About the earth: happy are ye and glad.

> These things are doubtless: yet in truth we've had
> Strange thunders from the potency of song;
> Mingled indeed with what is sweet and strong;
> From majesty: but in clear truth the themes
> Are ugly clubs, the Poets Polyphemes
> Disturbing the grand sea.

The reference is probably to Wordsworth and Byron together.
"We hate poetry that has a palpable design upon us," Keats was to
write, and here he repudiates what he takes to be tendentiousness,
the use of poetry to teach a moral doctrine or aggrandize a personality. The *themes* are ugly clubs; they are so many blind Cyclopses
enragedly throwing stones at an elusive Odysseus out on the im-
mensity of water, and merely disturbing it. But poems do not exist
to flesh themes:

> A drainless shower
> Of light is poesy; 'tis the supreme of power;
> 'Tis might half slumb'ring on its own right arm.
> The very archings of her eye-lids charm
> A thousand willing agents to obey,
> And still she governs with the mildest sway.

Poetry is the supreme of power because it need not put forth its strength in order to rule; it governs by suggestion, and defines itself by its own potential, or sense of possibility. It is a Titan under self-restraint:

> But strength alone though of the Muses born
> Is like a fallen angel: trees uptorn,
> Darkness, and worms, and shrouds, and sepulchres
> Delight it; for it feeds upon the burrs,
> And thorns of life; forgetting the great end
> Of poesy, that it should be a friend
> To sooth the cares, and lift the thoughts of man.

The reference here is to Byron, but is prophetic of the other Titan of the "Satanic school," Shelley, whom Keats had already met and whose *Alastor* finds its echo and reply in *Endymion*. Keats is predicting poems like *The Sensitive Plant* and the *Ode to the West Wind,* with their fierce emphasis on a despair of mutable nature, and their hints at an apocalyptic hope arising from the ruin of nature. More directly, Keats may be thinking of *Childe Harold,* and protesting its ironic quest and Promethean expressionism. Either way, Keats's complaint is Wordsworthian. The nature of poetry is to be disinterested, but its function is consolatory and enlightening.

Keats is more himself when, in the remainder of his poem, he considers his own destiny as poet. He is aware that he will be called presumptuous, and that he may fail, but if he does, it will be the fate of an Icarus who has dared to attempt his own freedom and powers. His ambition is founded upon a vision of poetry as a higher mode than any other. He acknowledges that others surpass him in strength of reason:

> yet there ever rolls
> A vast idea before me, and I glean
> Therefrom my liberty; thence too I've seen
> The end and aim of Poesy.

He does not identify the idea in what remains of the poem, but the reader can surmise it from its context. A poem is neither thought nor personality; it does not affirm anything, not even the poet himself. A poem grows out of consciousness as naturally as leaves come to a tree. The poem transcends nature, and yet is a natural outgrowth from nature. Keats's vast idea is of the apocalyptic use of poetry, which is to apprehend a full truth of nature and man which less disinterested and more artificial modes cannot arrive at, and to express this apprehension by unobtrusively being itself, a wording that cannot be reduced. Keats's idea of poetry is best expressed outside of his own work by the latest embodiment of the figure of the youth as virile poet, the rider, "no chevalere and poorly dressed," who gallops past Wallace Stevens' *Mrs. Alfred Uruguay* as she slowly approaches her reductive real, upon her mountain, with lofty darkness. The youth as reborn Apollo lives again in the "figure of capable imagination" who creates in his mind "the ultimate elegance: the imagined land":

> Was it a rider intent on the sun,
> A youth, a lover with phosphorescent hair,
> Dressed poorly, arrogant of his streaming forces.

Here again is might half-slumbering on its own right arm, a youth who is arrogant of his streaming forces, for he knows them to be a drainless shower of light.

Endymion

THE poetic romance *Endymion* begins by establishing the state of existence, intense and mutable, inhabited by its protagonist. An enclosed world, frequently likened to a bower and covert, it is a natural temple, dominated by the moon, which is scarcely differentiated from the poetry made by its celebrants:

> so does the moon,
> The passion poesy, glories infinite,
> Haunt us till they become a cheering light
> Unto our souls.

The shepherd prince, Endymion, is introduced as presiding over a Dionysiac procession. Adonis-like, he carries a boar spear. This intimation of self-destruction is reinforced by a comparison to Ganymede and by "a lurking trouble" in his countenance. The procession climaxes in a hymn to Pan, which is an extraordinary prayer and rather more than Wordsworth's condescension ("a very pretty piece of paganism") would grant it to be. The hymn salutes Pan as "a new birth," the refuge of imaginings that "dodge conception," and implores him to

> Be still a symbol of immensity;
> A firmament reflected in a sea;
> An element filling the space between;
> An unknown.

Be what cannot be categorized discursively is the prayer. The poem *Endymion,* though flawed in structure and diction, is as successful as *The Book of Thel* and *The Witch of Atlas* in consciously resisting kinds of analysis alien to it. The pattern of *Endymion* follows the Spenserian tradition of Romantic Pastoral as we have observed it in Blake and Shelley. The young shepherd poet wanders in his garden of the moon, a land of eternal spring, given over to a delicious indolence, a state relaxed, passive, even a little drowsy. Endymion is the hero of romance denied his quest, or a youthful Orc in Blake's symbolism. He is tormented and comforted, in recurrent cycle, by the contrary goddess who has visited him. She is both virginal and wanton, and as elusive in sleep as in waking, triumphant in her silver moon of love as its reflection moves slowly across the mysterious water in whose crystal depths Circe builds her cabinet to ensnare shepherd princes wandering on their quests. Rhythms here are triple, as befits a watery world of eternal recurrence, of cycles never to be canceled.

In such a world, action carries always its confused reflections, and in the poem *Endymion* the reader needs to struggle if he is to grasp even the sequence of events or what must pass as events. But a little patience yields large rewards. *Endymion* is Keats's only completed poem of real length. The fragmentary *Hyperions* are greater, but they end before Keats does more than indicate the pattern of his myth-making. *Endymion* is a work even more premature than *Prometheus Unbound;* Keats attempted large structures too quickly. But the poem, like *Prometheus,* exposes the complete anatomy of a great mythical structure, and is our fullest revelation of the reach and power of Keats's poetic mind.

In the hymn sung to Pan, he has been saluted as the

> Dread opener of the mysterious doors
> Leading to universal knowledge.

Presumably it is universal knowledge toward which Endymion is
to quest. He has had his first encounter with an unknown goddess.
He does not identify her with Cynthia, Diana, or Hecate, the triple
goddess of moon, woods, and the underworld, commonly called the
Great or White Goddess, but he has intimations that this first
amatory visitation will lead toward fulfillment of his dreams and his
desires. And these resemble the stages toward insight already
marked out in *Sleep and Poetry:*

> Wherein lies happiness? In that which becks
> Our ready minds to fellowship divine,
> A fellowship with essence; till we shine,
> Full alchemiz'd, and free of space. Behold
> The clear religion of heaven!

This is not yet very clear. A sort of oneness, a state like a floating spirit's, awaits us if our minds can be brought into that freedom
from spatial limitations which constitutes a fellowship with essence.
Whatever that is, it is not yet the desirable chief intensity, which
depends upon

> Richer entanglements, enthralments far
> More self-destroying.

These are friendship and love, and only love destroys the selfhood. This cannot be done without pain and pleasure both, and
these Endymion has begun to taste in the encounter he believes to
have been more than visionary.

Book I has opened with a declaration that the phenomena of
beauty will endure. Book II starts with a passionate rejection of the
reality of human history except insofar as it is the history of human
love. The next invocation, heading Book III, is to the regality of
the four elements, combined with a fierce denunciation of all political regalities. The fourth and last book starts with the long-delayed
invocation to the Muse, which is in effect the muse of Thomas
Chatterton, of British native genius, of deep prophetic solitude and
Druidic rhapsodizings. This invocation is basic in the poem, and

needs close consideration later in its context. Here it matters for patterning and the total structure of *Endymion.*

From beauty, to love, to the kingship of the elements, to poetry: that is the movement of Endymion's quest, in Keats's overt plan. These stages of existence parallel the general structures of the Romantic quest in Blake and Wordsworth. The beauty is that of first innocence; the love, of generative experience. To rise to the height of the elements is to reach the point of survey which is the upper or organized limit of the innocent natural world. Beyond this, only the imagination can go, after surmounting the crisis of vision and triumphing over what Blake calls Ulro, Wordsworth visionary dreariness or desolation, and Keats, in *Endymion,* the Cave of Quietude.

Keats's special emphasis in Endymion's baffled quest is on the value of instinctive impulses, which bind us to the earth and will eventually, if obeyed, lead us to that essential truth that the imagination can seize on as beauty. But this naturalistic quest, carried out in a largely supernatural context, does not seem to bear out Keats's overt emphasis, for Endymion's fate is mostly a series of frustrations, and he ultimately achieves his quest only by abandoning it. The most intense experience available to Endymion within nature is sexual, but his malaise, though it has sexual origins, expresses a more complex longing, a sickness unto action. The hero needs an antagonist; ultimately, in romance, this is likely to be mortality itself. The immense strength and variety of Spenser's invention in *The Faerie Queene* is owing to that great poet's abundant projections of the quest's adversaries. Endymion's only opponents are his own confusions and frequent despairings, and we weary of these, as they are all too much alike. And yet Keats is true to himself and to the temper and needs of his age by refusing to externalize the quest's adversary. Shelley's wandering poet, in *Alastor,* falls victim to the spirit of his own solitude. The influence of Wordsworth's *Excursion* is basic in *Alastor,* as we have seen. The determining influences on the internalized theme of *Endymion* are the combined ones of *Alastor* and the *Excursion,* as both emphasize the destructiveness of an inward-turning and stagnant solitude. The man cut off from others and from his own true imagination is in hell, for the Romantic hell is neither other people nor oneself but the absence of relationship between the two. The world through which Endymion must move appears to be only a barrier to his quest, and the tribulations of others seem to be irrelevant to his high desires, but Keats, following Wordsworth, wants Endymion to learn otherwise. Shelley's young poet, for all his fragility, had too much intensity to cease his drive toward a glorious extinction. Keats, even in as ideal a romance as *Endymion,* does not surrender his sense of existential contraries. The reality of the earth and the strength of natural impulse toward adhering to it will both save Keats's hero and give him his ideal in a form that flesh can touch.

Book II commences Endymion's active search for the vision that has abandoned him. History is denied by Keats in the book's opening passage because it cannot affect poetic consciousness, which depends altogether upon love. Endymion's quest for love now leads him down in search of the evasive truth, as in Book IV it will lead him up, pursuing an equally evasive beauty.

But the deep truth is too dark for this seeker, and he becomes lost in a labyrinthine underworld, away from the light of heaven and the pastoral beauty of his earth. He is in danger of "the deadly feel of solitude" and so prays to Diana, at once the queen of his woodland and the crescent glimmering of air's freedom. It is an ironic prayer in its context, for he does not know that it is Diana herself who has visited him and provoked the quest that has brought him into the darkness from which he now begs her for liberation. He asks to see his native bowers again, in contrast to the rapacious deep around him. His prayer is answered, and he stumbles out into the Garden of Adonis, his underground adventures thus ensuing in a sexually instructive interlude.

Adonis awakens from his recurrent six months' slumber, and Venus takes him off to a six months' embrace in the upper regions. Endymion is strongly affected, and wanders on to his own bower of delight, where his unknown goddess awaits him. The amatory scene between them unfortunately moves Keats to some astonishing diction (Endymion refers to his beloved's lips as "slippery blisses"), but it serves its structural purpose well enough. The physical meeting causes even the goddess both bliss and pain, for she confesses that she cannot yet uplift the youth to her starry eminence, and so must leave him.

When Endymion awakens from sleeping in her arms, he is alone.
And his sexual adventure has transvalued his vision of essences:

> Now I have tasted her sweet soul to the core
> All other depths are shallow: essences,
> Once spiritual, are like muddy lees,
> Meant but to fertilize my earthly root,
> And make my branches lift a golden fruit
> Into the bloom of heaven.

He is mistaken, and needs to plunge still deeper if he is to know
it. The quest moves from underground to undersea, as in an act of
instinctive sympathy with the forbidden love of Alpheus and
Arethusa, Endymion plunges down after those metamorphosized
lovers. They have been turned to water by Diana herself, and
Endymion, before descending, names her as goddess of his pilgrimage and prays to her to yet grant them fulfillment in one another.

Book I climaxed in the sexual invitation of the quest. Book II has
brought sexual completion, but renewed alienation. In the watery
world of Book III, which exposes the ambiguities of natural forms,
Endymion seeks a release from natural cycle and an escape from a
self that is alternately favored and victimized by that cycle. He finds
the materials for imaginative vision, but not the vision itself. But
he does begin to understand some of the limitations of the moon
world he inhabits, dim as the understanding is. The imaginative
reader, puzzling over the pattern revealed in the depths, can grasp
better the cyclic dilemma of the poem's hero.

Before his sea adventure properly begins, Endymion addresses
the moon. It was moonlight that was what Shelley would have
called the "intellectual beauty" of Endymion's youth, blending art,
nature, friendship into a higher unity. With the advent of his
"strange love," the moonlight faded, but survived as "an under-pas-
sion." Endymion begins to apprehend that he may be caught in a
conflict between two diverse but allied loves:

> Now I begin to feel thine orby power
> Is coming fresh upon me: O be kind,
> Keep back thine influence, and do not blind
> My sovereign vision.—Dearest love, forgive

That I can think away from thee and live!—
Pardon me, airy planet, that I prize
One thought beyond thine argent luxuries!
How far beyond!

He now encounters Glaucus, an old man of the sea who has been thrall to the temptress Circe. Keats borrowed the incident from Sandys' commentary on Ovid, but transformed it into an analogue of Blake's symbol of the crystal cabinet.

The story of Glaucus is rather like that of Endymion himself. Glaucus is a kind of shepherd of the ocean, a follower of Neptune as Endymion was of Pan. But he is not contented, and feels "distemper'd longings." He plunges into the sea, "for life or death," and learns to live beneath the waves, where he falls in love with a timid sea nymph, Scylla, who flees from him. After he vows to seek help from Circe, he is seduced in a deceptive bower by an "arbitrary queen of sense." One day he discovers his seductress presiding over a witch's sabbath and calls on Circe to break his bondage, but Circe is revealed to be his mistress, and he is cursed by her to a watery death-in-life.

Glaucus now becomes a kind of subterranean Wordsworthian solitary, haunting the waters, until he finds a magical scroll from a shipwreck. The scroll predicts his liberation

If he explores all forms and substances
Straight homeward to their symbol-essences

To this complex achievement of mind he needs to add one of action, which is preparatory of apocalypse. He must preserve the bodies of all drowned lovers until a youth shall come to him and be instructed "how to consummate all." Endymion is clearly this messianic figure, and Glaucus leads him to a curious structure, "a fabric crystalline, rubb'd and inlaid with coral, pebble and pearl." This is a place "vast and desolate and icy cold," which Circe apparently has appointed as a grisly storehouse for drowned lovers. Glaucus has installed Scylla, drowned by Circe, in it, and to "that crystal place" where no decay and no life has come, Endymion is brought to perform a magical ritual of deliverance. This humanistic service is followed by a communion in which "the two deliverers tasted a pure wine of happiness." A celebration in which all the

revived lovers take part climaxes the book, which ends characteristically with Endymion swooning away as he hears his beloved
Diana's voice. He is revived by her assurance that he has won immortal bliss for her, and finds himself back in the forest.

This summary is sufficiently absurd as action to compel us to try
the pattern on our imaginations, in the hope that what is literal
nonsense makes sense on another level of meaning. Endymion's
quest for the object of his love liberates Glaucus from a state of
death-in-life, though Endymion does not descend with any such in-
tention. Glaucus is betrayed initially by a thirst for a more imaginative existence. His Circe experience puts him into a state of involuntary solipsistic isolation, and his efforts to work out of it are doomed
to be ghoulish without Endymion's intervention. The crystal cabinet in which he stores drowned lovers is merely an illusion of mercy
until its unreal structure is startled into life by the engendering of a
relationship of sympathy between Endymion and himself. Our best
imaginative clue as to the nature of the apocalyptic consummation
in which the dead lovers come alive is the admonition given to
Glaucus by the scroll. All forms *and* substances, the outer and the
inner of phenomena, need to be explored straight homeward to
their essences, and these essences are themselves symbols—symbols
of fellowship, we may surmise, remembering Endymion's account
of wherein lies happiness in Book I. Happiness is a state achieved
by a humanistic alchemy that results in our being made free of the
limitations of materialistic conceptualizations of reality. And the
way to this is through what beckons our ready minds to the fellowship divine that Keats terms a fellowship with essence. Keats seems
to be edging on a Neoplatonic statement, but he is too naturalistic
to cross over into it. What he does give is a version of myth-making
very close to Wordsworth, Blake, and Shelley. The subject-object
experience, in which we are not free of space, can be surmounted
by a relationship in which life confronts life, an alchemized sharing
of essence between two equal partners. Friendship as such a mode
has been illustrated by Book III of the poem. Book IV is devoted
to richer entanglements, enthrallments far more self-destroying,
leading, by degrees, to the chief intensity of love.

The last book of *Endymion* is, thankfully, much clearer than the
first three, and has less disproportion in structure. The invocation
to the British Muse salutes that subdeity for its patience, with un-

intentional irony. Underlying this glad hailing is an intimation of mortality, with an implied reminder that this poem is dedicated to Chatterton and a hint of Keats's lack of time.

Endymion's story begins again with the fine complication of his falling in love with an Indian maid who has been swept from her native land by a Bacchic procession. The shepherd prince reveals "a triple soul," as he now loves simultaneously Diana, the unknown visitant not yet identified with her, and the immediately available earthly maiden. Shelley, confronted by a similar galaxy in *Epipsychidion*, finds no problem in loving all, but Keats was more nearly conventional in these matters, and Endymion groans in vexation. Nevertheless, he surrenders to his love of the human, and so humanizes himself.

Although he has made a choice, Endymion is claimed by the power above, and so must ascend into the heavens with his new love. As he had gone down to discover truth, he now goes up to encounter the ultimate in beauty. They sleep as they climb, and when Diana's crescent rises in his dream, Endymion recognizes her as his very goddess. When he awakens, he finds his sleeping earthly mistress next to him, and is torn again by his double love. He begins to doubt his own soul, and fears he has "no self-passion or identity." He thus has attained a stage further toward the negative capability that Keats saw as the mark of the true poet, the loss of self in the conflict between imaginative contraries. Before he attains this laurel, he experiences his supreme despair, and his purgation. First, the moonlight dissolves his earthly bride:

> He saw her body fading gaunt and spare
> In the cold moonshine. Straight he seiz'd her wrist;
> It melted from his grasp: her hand he kiss'd,
> And, horror! kiss'd his own—he was alone.

Diana seems to be another Circe, and the fate of the Indian maid at this point approximates Scylla's. As Glaucus fell into a death-in-life beneath the surface, so Endymion falls into the Cave of Quietude, a den of Ulro, a deathly isolation, yet with an unsuspected Eden in the heart of it.

No other passage in Keats features a rhetoric more replete with oxymorons, verbal figures by which the effect of self-contradiction is produced. For the Cave pictures the calm ecstasy that despair can ultimately bring, and we cannot know whether to term its last sensation a joyful sorrow or a sorrowful joy. The Cave is a prophecy of the lesson that Keats will read in the silent countenance of Moneta in the climactic passage of *The Fall of Hyperion*. Within this quietude anguish does not sting, nor pleasure pall. In this "happy gloom" and "dark Paradise" health and sickness become interchangeable, and dreariest silence is most articulate. Hopes infest, and despairs lose all force. The verbal evidence suggests that Keats's notion of this state is aesthetic, and only secondarily psychological. A poet needs a stance beyond the reach of primary human emotions before he can attain an art relevant to them. Endymion comes out of the Cave sufficiently disinterested to disqualify him for more questing. He has passed from innocence to experience, touched the hell within experience, and is ready for a more organized innocence that may precede the vision of art.

In a very great line, he returns to ordinary reality:

> His first touch of the earth went nigh to kill.

It is the earth that he chooses, but he comes to it from a world beyond, and pain attends his rebirth into common things. Keats is imaginatively right in equating Endymion's first touch of earth, pain, and the pleasure of finding the Indian maid lying by his side again. The returned shepherd salutes Pan as his deity, and renounces his quest as "a great dream." He has been presumptuous against love, the sky, the tie of mortals each to each, and against the whole earth of flowers and rivers. There comes to him the realization that he has barely escaped the fate that Keats will later visualize as that of the knight of arms in *La Belle Dame Sans Merci*, for

> There never liv'd a mortal man, who bent
> His appetite beyond his natural sphere,
> But starv'd and died.

Farewell then to caverns lone, and air of visions, and the monstrous swell of visionary seas. He still loves his dream, but not unto the death. Shelley's poet in *Alastor* ignored the love of the Arab maiden, and died into his vision, but Endymion will be content with "one human kiss, one sigh of real breath" from his mistress.

Probably Keats ought to have ended the poem there, but instead he strives for a premature union of contraries, a rather desperate attempt to unite overtly the real with the ideal, and truth with beauty. The Indian maid rejects Endymion, claiming that to love him is now forbidden. He wanders off, vowing to be a hermit, but the maid is transfigured into the Moon goddess, and Endymion vanishes with her. It is a mechanical end to the luxuriant, natural overgrowth of the poem, and probably the least satisfactory episode in the entire structure. Keats had resolved none of his inner conflicts, and one wonders at the appropriateness of the derived mythical material to the very personal synthesis that Keats hoped to achieve. *Alastor* attempts less than *Endymion,* although it is an equally confessional poem, but *Alastor* is an articulated whole, where the poet is entirely at one with both his subject and the form his story takes. The matter of *Alastor* has at times rather little to do with flesh and blood, so that *Endymion* can better afford its confusions in its attempt to give the natural man some just treatment, even in the form of the pastoral romance. *Endymion* is primarily an erotic poem, and its Wordsworthian doctrines sometimes seem oddly uttered in that context. Keats's exquisite sense of the luxurious foreshadows the Wallace Stevens of *Harmonium,* and does not always suit his abstract theme of the identity of ideal beauty, love, and truth. The implicit burden of *Endymion* is a humanistic hedonism, and the poem's only realized apocalypses are the naturalistic consummations of sexual love. In *The Eve of St. Agnes,* Keats was to write an overt hymn to Eros which is a glowing unity of all his poetic impulses. *Endymion,* beautiful as it so frequently is, abandons too often the sensuous world it exists to celebrate.

2 *Hymns of Eros*

The Eve of St. Agnes

IT seems fairly certain that *The Eve of St. Agnes* had some impulse from Keats's falling in love, and possibly from his anticipation

of marriage. The poem was created January–February 1819, and
Keats seems to have declared his love to Fanny Brawne on December 25, 1818, a few months after meeting her.

Keats's subject may be taken from Boccaccio, or else from the
Anatomy of Melancholy, which suggested the material of *Lamia,*
although Burton is not exactly in the Keatsian vein on women:

> 'Tis their only desire if it may be done by Art, to see their
> husbands' picture in a glass, they'll give anything to know when
> they shall be married, how many husbands they shall have, by
> Crommyomantia, a kind of divination with Onions laid on the
> Altar on Christmas Eve, or by fasting on St. Agnes' Eve or
> Night, to know who shall be their first husband.

The power of Keats as poet and humanist is in an apotheosis of
the human senses. Until Wallace Stevens, no other poet was to
attain so immense a celebration of the risen body in the here and
now, with the senses given their delighted primacy and playing the
measures destined for the soul:

> The adventurer
> In humanity has not conceived of a race
> Completely physical in a physical world.

In *The Eve of St. Agnes,* Keats comes close to so prodigious a
conception. His lovers are completely physical in a physical world,
and their sensuous concreteness is emphasized by an ironic interplay with worlds that fail to be completely physical, whether by an
extreme resort to spirituality or by a grossness that abolishes the
individuality of the atoms of perception which make up Keats's
human reality. The "spiritual" that seeks to establish itself by denying life and "life's high meed," death, is the more important of these
juxtaposing realms in the poem. Indeed Keats begins with it:

> St. Agnes' Eve—Ah, bitter chill it was!
> The owl, for all his feathers, was a-cold;
> The hare limp'd trembling through the frozen grass,
> And silent was the flock in woolly fold:
> Numb were the Beadsman's fingers, while he told
> His rosary, and while his frosted breath,
> Like pious incense from a censer old,

> Seem'd taking flight for heaven, without a death,
> Past the sweet Virgin's picture, while his prayer he saith.

The Beadsman is cold with nature's cold, but he converts his privation into a prayer for immediate entry into heaven, without any intermediate natural death. His own vision of purgatory (next stanza) sees it as an extension of winter. He goes off to his harsh St. Agnes' Eve penance, to sit all night amid rough ashes and wait for death. His icy faith frames the passionate center of the poem, where warmth and sexual passion glow more brightly against the Beadsman's death-in-life.

Between the icy bordering and the glowing center is "the argent revelry" of the ball that whirls on while the lovers meet for their first union. The other connecting link between frost and fire is Angela, the pious servant who reluctantly agrees to conceal Porphyro in his lady's chamber. Even the names have their roughly symbolic function; Angela with her fumbling pieties is obvious enough. Porphyro is chosen for the purple-red color implied by the name:

> Sudden a thought came like a full-blown rose,
> Flushing his brow, and in his pained heart
> Made purple riot.

It is the thought of appearing to Madeline, and of the likely consummation. The name Madeline, in its root form of Magdalen, appears in the canceled stanza that comes between Stanzas VI and VII in one manuscript:

> 'Twas said her future Lord would there appear
> Offering as sacrifice—all in the dream—
> Delicious food even to her lips brought near:
> Viands and wine and fruit and sugar'd cream,
> To touch her palate with the fine extreme
> Of relish: then soft music heard; and then
> More pleasures followed in a dizzy stream
> Palpable almost: then to wake again
> Warm in the virgin morn, no weeping Magdalen.

The morn remains virgin, and the Madeline who goes out into renewal at the poem's close is no weeping Magdalen but a transfigured epitome of love. For *The Eve of St. Agnes* is a hymn in honor of the senses but particularly the sense of touch, and it celebrates at its climax the "solution sweet" when

> Into her dream he melted, as the rose
> Blendeth its odour with the violet.

At the heart of the poem (Stanzas xxix–xxxvi) Keats strives to suggest a supreme intensity by particularizing a wealth of concrete sensuous details, which not only deliberately confuse and mix senses, but tend to carry the other senses over into the tactile. Salvation, according to *The Eve of St. Agnes,* is only through the intense manifestation of all phenomena as being truly themselves. The lovers are saved by surrendering themselves to a world of objects, and to one another.

The extraordinary profusion of sensuous apprehensions is certainly the characteristic that distinguishes *The Eve of St. Agnes* from Keats's other poems in which minute particulars give themselves to the poet's delighted receptiveness. Porphyro conceals himself as Angela hurries away, tormented by her remorse. What he sees and does becomes subordinated to the strenuous exercise of the reader's sensory imagination as Keats allows his own imagination to be indulged by a luxurious object world.

A prevalent procedure of Romantic poetry, as we have seen, is the displacement of religious vocabulary into secular and literary, sometimes erotic contexts:

> Full on this casement shone the wintry moon,
> And threw warm gules on Madeline's fair breast,
> As down she knelt for heaven's grace and boon;
> Rose-bloom fell on her hands, together prest,
> And on her silver cross soft amethyst,
> And on her hair a glory, like a saint:
> She seem'd a splendid angel, newly drest,
> Save wings, for heaven:—Porphyro grew faint:
> She knelt, so pure a thing, so free from mortal taint.

The moon of winter shines on the flowry casement (described in the previous stanza) and on Madeline's white breast, even as she kneels to pray. A rose color falls on her hands, and a paler red on the silver cross she wears. The light makes an aureole about her head, and Porphyro grows faint, for complex reasons. He is reacting both to her beauty and to her apparent sacredness, "so free from mortal taint."

But "his heart revives," and her body is revealed to him. When she falls asleep, she goes to an abode beyond the world of the oxymoron, to where she is "blissfully haven'd both from joy and pain." As she sleeps, her lover begins his ritual of supplication:

> Then by the bed-side, where the faded moon
> Made a dim, silver twilight, soft he set
> A table, and, half anguish'd, threw thereon
> A cloth of woven crimson, gold, and jet:—
> O for some drowsy Morphean amulet!
> The boisterous, midnight, festive clarion,
> The kettle-drum, and far-heard clarinet,
> Affray his ears, though but in dying tone:—
> The hall door shuts again, and all the noise is gone.

The stanza is a triumph. Porphyro is "half anguish'd" because his desire is to involve her in joy and pain, in the oxymoronic world of "mortal taint." He begins to set the reality of rich objects against the world of dream, for his is a sure lover's instinct, underlying the psychology of the lover's gift. Physical love *is* the wealth of the world, and the "cloth of woven crimson, gold, and jet" is the proper cloth for a lover's communion table. Bordering the altar of passion is the now "dim, silver twilight" of the faded winter moon of body-denying spirituality and, on the other side of the stanza, the mere grossness of the revel that goes on below in the castle. When the hall door shuts again, and all the noise is gone, we are in the enchantment of the sexual world of the next seven stanzas until the marvelous re-entry of an outer world in Stanza xxxvi:

> Into her dream he melted, as the rose
> Blendeth its odour with the violet,—
> Solution sweet: meantime the frost-wind blows
> Like Love's alarum pattering the sharp sleet
> Against the window-panes; St. Agnes' moon hath set.

The cold of nature and of spirituality has re-entered the poem. Indeed, as the sleet comes down, Keats calls it "flaw-blown," and the flaw is in nature and in the spirituality that merely repudiates that flaw. But before we describe the orders of reality striving again in the poem, we can enjoy the seven stanzas of tender luxury that ensue in the "Solution sweet" of sexual love.

As Madeline sleeps, Porphyro heaps high the table with a profusion of spiced foods thrown upon sumptuous vessels. His impulse is of course not merely that which contributes to the art of the seducer. It is the same that drives the lover of the Song of Solomon into the imagery of gold and silver, myrrh and frankincense, into saying that "thy temples are like a piece of a pomegranate within thy locks" and "thy lips drop as the honey-comb: honey and milk are under thy tongue." *The Eve of St. Agnes* is Keats's Song of Solomon, and to allegorize either poem prematurely is to abandon a value.

From *Sleep and Poetry* onward, Keats had played with the reality of dream and the illusions of reality. In the beautiful alternation of Madeline's dreaming and waking he now experiments further with this visionary device. Donne, in *A Dreame,* had explored the same paradoxes, but in a spirit alien to the naturalistic rapture of Keats's lovers.

Porphyro summons Madeline to an awakening, vowing that she is his heaven and he her hermit, in contrast to the heaven sought by and the suppliance represented in the Beadsman. But she does not awake until he sings to her the song most appropriate to the occasion, the "La belle dame sans mercy" that Keats is meditating and is soon to compose. In that poem, the knight at arms awakens to disenchantment on the cold hill's side. To forestall such a fate for Porphyro, Madeline awakens out of a dream centered upon her lover. For a moment she is caught, painfully and finely, between contending realities:

> Her eyes were open, but she still beheld,
> Now wide awake, the vision of her sleep:
> There was a painful change, that nigh expell'd
> The blisses of her dream so pure and deep
> At which fair Madeline began to weep,
> And moan forth witless words with many a sigh;
> While still her gaze on Porphyro would keep;
> Who knelt, with joined hands and piteous eye,
> Fearing to move or speak, she look'd so dreamingly.

The real lover before her, with his sad eyes, his "pallid, chill, and drear" countenance, compares unfavorably with the dream lover whose eyes were spiritual and clear and whose looks were immortal. This is the crisis of their love, and she triumphs in it. Rather than reject physical reality for a dream of heaven, she invites reality to become that dream.

The remainder of the poem is a movement of exodus. Love flees the castle with the lovers, and nightmare descends upon the revelers, death upon the pious. The lovers leave behind an inferno, and carry their heaven with them. The wakeful bloodhound they elude is a kind of Cerberus, and the besieging wind that conceals the sound of their departure blows up an "elfin-storm from faery land" for them, but a storm of woe and death for the other inmates of the castle:

> And they are gone: aye, ages long ago
> These lovers fled away into the storm.
> That night the Baron dreamt of many a woe,
> And all his warrior-guests, with shade and form
> Of witch, and demon, and large coffin-worm,
> Were long be-nightmar'd. Angela the old
> Died palsy-twitch'd, with meagre face deform;
> The Beadsman, after thousand aves told,
> For aye unsought for slept among his ashes cold.

Nothing comes to seek the heaven-aspiring Beadsman among his now cold, rough ashes, and Angela dies the death her pious and sinful fears make inevitable. The lovers are gone away into their storm, out of the castle's purgatorial and finally infernal reality to the naturalistic fruition of their love and the ultimate high meed of their death.

La Belle Dame Sans Merci

THE poet who writes incessantly of the Gardens of Adonis owes his vision a rendering also of a Bower of Bliss. The song of Beulah land requires its contrary in a song of Ulro. Heaven's lower counterpart is Earth, the hell we are never out of, but the lower paradise finds its diabolic double in the false garden of desire simulated, provoked, but never gratified—the bower of Acrasia, the world of Blake's Vala. Against his perpetual epipsyche visions of Beulah, Shelley set at last the deceiving "Shape all light" of the cold hell of *The Triumph of Life*. Keats's vision of Ulro is more ambiguous and more modest: the terse and haunting ballad of *La Belle Dame Sans Merci*.

For Robert Graves, himself a great poet of the Orc cycle, a Worshiper of Vala under her name of the White Goddess, Keats's poem is a *celebration* of the poet's destruction by his muse. But Keats had a muse of his own making, Moneta, and she did not destroy her poets, nor is she involved in this ballad. For Graves, La Belle Dame is consumption, poetry, Fanny Brawne, love, death, and finally the Triple Goddess herself, the blue-white hag who mothers, marries, and buries poets. This is an undeniable and terrible vision, akin to Blake's Shadowy Female, though it takes toward her an attitude opposed to Blake's.

The answer to the question that opens the ballad *is* the meaning of the poem:

> O what can ail thee, knight-at-arms,
>   Alone and palely loitering?

What is his illness? He loiters by the lake, where all is withered and bird song is over. Against the background of a completed and full harvest, he is "haggard and so woe begone." The withering flowers of his countenance reinforce the impression that he is *starved,* though the landscape has yielded enough for all granaries. But the stigma of his thralldom is his starvation, his putting aside earthly food for the "roots of relish sweet / And honey wild and manna dew" that he can no longer obtain. His vision on the cold hill's side had warned him of just such a fate:

> I saw their starv'd lips in the gloom,
>   With horrid warning gaped wide,
> And I awoke, and found me here
>   On the cold hill's side.

He has had no other vision except this warning that he has become addicted to what he can never again taste. The question next becomes, what has he eaten, and who gave him to eat that he might become accursed?

Our clues are wonderfully, deliberately infinite, and defeat our antipoetic reductiveness. But let us try a few. To a scholarly critic of Romanticism, it would seem unnecessary to seek for literary sources for Keats's ballad too widely afield. Spenser's Acrasia and Phaedria we can feel here directly; Malory, Alan Chartier, the Ballad of Thomas the Rhymer seem more remote. But Wordsworth and Coleridge are very close; this poem is written in their diction and echoes their phrasing. It would have found a place in the *Lyrical Ballads,* though it might have been moralized a bit in the process.

> I met a Lady in the Meads,
> Full beautiful—a faery's child,
> Her hair was long, her foot was light,
> And her eyes were wild.

The movement of that is Wordsworth's, and the last line is of course palpably his. The third and fourth lines have their quite obvious parallel in Coleridge's "the Night-mare LIFE-IN-DEATH":

> *Her* lips were red, *her* looks were free,
> Her locks were yellow as gold.

Kubla Khan ends with the vision of a youthful Promethean poet, an Orc with flashing eyes and floating hair, who is best kept inside a magic circle away from us, and whom holy dread forbids us to gaze upon,

> For he on honey-dew hath fed,
> And drunk the milk of Paradise.

"Honey wild, and manna dew" comes close enough. The outcast, driven like the Baptist into the Wilderness, lives on wild honey. The faithful, in the Wilderness, live upon the miracle of manna. Keats, at the least, is both glossing Coleridge and naturalizing the Bible for us. Like Nebuchadnezzar in the last plate of Blake's *Marriage of Heaven and Hell,* the knight at arms has been reduced to feeding like a beast upon the grass, though earlier "she found me roots of relish sweet." A close analogue is in the most famous of Dante's "stony rimes," "Al poco giorno e al gran cerchio d'ombra" ("To the dim light and the large circle of shade"), where the poet is at last reduced to crying:

che mi torrei dormire in petra
tutto il mio tempo e gir pascendo l'erba,
sol per veder do'suoi panni fann' ombra.

Who would sleep away in stone my life
Or feed like beasts upon the grass
Only to see her garments cast a shade.

In these shattering visions of the sudden descent of a too literal
return to nature we have one part of Keats's meaning; in the deification of the youthful poet at the close of *Kubla Khan* we have another. The knight at arms has devoured, apparently under the in-
structions of the Belle Dame, "a faery's child," a natural food that
has made him both less than and more than human. Either way, he
has little use for human food again. He is in thrall forever. To
whom?

We cannot tell, for we have only the knight's evidence, and he
may be self-deceived. He does not know her language, nor do we.
Whatever her purpose, the knight falls asleep, with the fated food
within him, to dream of the truth and awaken to find himself in a
withered natural world, forever cut off from it. The clearest of all
Romantic analogues is Blake's *The Crystal Cabinet,* which follows
the same pattern: the protagonist coming out of his momentary
earthly paradise (Beulah) to find himself, not in the ordinary world
of Generation from which he entered it, but in a solitary hell (Ulro)
infinitely worse than his state of being at the poem's onset.

Lamia

KEATS had a special fondness for *Lamia,* but this beautiful poem
is a puzzle to the imagination. The poet's tragic love for Fanny
Brawne is probably the crucial element in the poem's genesis. *Lamia*
tells us something about that love relationship, but does not allow
our knowledge of Keats's life to help much in sorting out the poem's
complex feignings.

Keats took his story from Burton's *Anatomy of Melancholy,* but
Burton only hints at the sympathetic aspects of the lamia, or serpent woman. When Apollonius the sophist found her out, says

Burton, "she wept, and desired Apollonius to be silent, but he would not be moved." Keats is very moved, and his Lamia is simultaneously a deceptive sorceress and a beautiful innocent, a destroyer and a sensual ideal. When she dies, Lycius, her victim and lover, dies also, and so his teacher Apollonius is pragmatically wrong though theoretically right in exposing reality. She is a serpent, but Lycius is surely better off "made a serpent's prey" and yet in the bliss of sexual possession than he is at the poem's close when his friends find him alone on the bridal couch:

> —no pulse, or breath they found,
> And, in its marriage robe, the heavy body wound.

There is a serpent suggestion here, and the irony is that the reasoning eye of Apollonius has given his pupil to the serpent death, precisely by attempting to save him from a sexual serpent of life. The basic theme of *Lamia* is not so much that of illusion against reality as it is of two illusions or two realities in conflict. Like Geraldine in Coleridge's *Christabel*, Lamia is to be both feared and pitied, shunned and loved. Her deceptiveness imparts the most intense of sexual fulfillments, and completes even as it threatens to destroy. Keats sums up what he took to be his poem's moral by distributing poetic crowns:

> What wreath for Lamia? What for Lycius?
> What for the sage, old Apollonius?
> Upon her aching forehead be there hung
> The leaves of willow and of adder's tongue;
> And for the youth, quick, let us strip for him
> The thyrsus, that his watching eyes may swim
> Into forgetfulness; and, for the sage,
> Let spear-grass and the spiteful thistle wage
> War on his temples.

Lamia is thus an unlikely composite of Ophelia and Circe. Lycius is a representative of Dionysus, for the thyrsus is a Bacchic staff, tipped by the pine cone and twined with ivy and vine branches. The Dionysiac fate is to be torn apart in the joy of one's own revelation, in a violent increase of sensual fulfillment, followed by the forgetfulness of Hades. This is the fate of bright destruction that

Apollonius has cost Lycius. The "spear-grass and the spiteful this-
tle" for the aged sophist tell their own story, for

> Do not all charms fly
> At the mere touch of cold philosophy?
> There was an awful rainbow once in heaven:
> We know her woof, her texture; she is given
> In the dull catalogue of common things.
> Philosophy will clip an Angel's wings,
> Conquer all mysteries by rule and line,
> Empty the haunted air, and gnomed mine—
> Unweave a rainbow, as it erewhile made
> The tender-person'd Lamia melt into a shade.

Keats does not accede to the reductive fallacy here, as even acute
critics have insisted, any more than Wallace Stevens subscribes to
it in his wonderfully funny masterpiece *Mrs. Alfred Uruguay,*
which also turns upon the dark trick of the mind by which we first
explain a phenomenon in terms more elementary than its own, and
then replace the discredited phenomenon by our own explanation.
This is the spirit of Mrs. Alfred Uruguay, who says, "I have wiped
away moonlight like mud," and of Apollonius, who would "unweave
a rainbow." The opposing spirit, urged by Keats, is to take appearance as reality, to accept natural phenomena as presences, and
beauty as truth. The beauty of Lamia is not the beauty of art and
is perhaps not true, if one analyzes it. But Keats has so built his
poem that we cannot know which is the true Lamia, serpent or
woman. When we see her first she is serpent, but astonishingly
beautiful:

> She was a gordian shape of dazzling hue,
> Vermilion-spotted, golden, green, and blue;
> Striped like a zebra, freckled like a pard,
> Eyed like a peacock, and all crimson barr'd;
> And full of silver moons, that, as she breathed,
> Dissolv'd, or brighter shone, or interwreathed
> Their lustres with the gloomier tapestries—
> So rainbow-sided, touch'd with miseries,
> She seem'd, at once, some penanced lady elf,
> Some demon's mistress, or the demon's self.

The detail here is an exuberance of natural color, and the moral identity offered ranges a wide choice. Hermes, the divine messenger who transforms her into a woman by the magic of his rod of twined serpents, believes her story that her original shape was human. Yet her transformation creates doubts in us:

> So that, in moments few, she was undrest
> Of all her sapphires, greens, and amethyst,
> And rubious-argent: of all these bereft,
> Nothing but pain and ugliness were left.
> Still shone her crown; that vanish'd, also she
> Melted and disappear'd as suddenly.

There are three stages here. First she has a serpent appearance and is beautiful. Next, we do not know whether she is serpent or woman, but in this most reductive stage, the "truth" of her (if you would call it so) is pain and ugliness. Finally she is "now a lady bright" and is termed, accurately, "a full-born beauty new and exquisite." Keats has defeated moral analysis; we cannot ascertain which of the three Lamias is least illusory.

Lamia is Keats's equivalent of Shelley's play poem *The Witch of Atlas,* which sets itself still more deliberately against a reductive reading. Too honest to deny a kind of truth to Apollonius, Keats makes a double point for the magic of his own poetry against the world's reasoners. The deep truth is known neither to the poet nor to the sophist, and the poet's and the sophist's truths both kill, but the poet's more gloriously. If death awaited Lycius in Lamia's folds, it would have been a death better worth the dying, and better worth the poet's imaginings.

3   *Temples of the Sun*

Hyperion

KEATS published his first attempt at mature epic, *Hyperion,* as a fragment in his 1820 volume. He had composed it between the autumn of 1818 and early spring 1819. Between August and December 1819 Keats tried again with *The Fall of Hyperion,* subtitled *A Dream.* This second fragment (about 525 lines of *Hyperion*'s 880 or so) Keats simply abandoned in manuscript. He wrote only a few lines of verse after December 1819, and so the putting aside of *The Fall of Hyperion* is parallel to Shelley's failure to finish *The Triumph of Life;* it was probably involuntary. The *Fall,* like the *Triumph,* is a poem of desperate crisis, and both works derive their structure and temper from Dante's *Purgatorio,* an inevitable influence for poems so self-chastening, and so bitterly determined to seek a new knowledge of internal realities.

The first *Hyperion* is very unlike the second, as its massive strength and coolness represent the triumph of Keats's early idea of poetry as a disinterested mode, free from didactic emphasis or personalistic self-dramatization. *Hyperion* is Miltonic, whereas *The Fall of Hyperion* is Dantesque. Keats is outside *Hyperion,* but, like Dante or the Shelley of the *Triumph,* he is altogether the protagonist of the *Fall. Hyperion* is the poem of Apollo, but in the *Fall* the god is from the onset incarnated in a Romantic poet caught in suffering the crisis of his own vision.

The Romantic fortunes of the theme of warfare between Titans and Olympians we have followed already in Blake, Byron, and Shelley. Keats in his quiet way was as antinomian as any of these, but he cared too little for Christianity to bother quarreling with orthodoxy. Byron's inverted Calvinism, Blake's persuasive redefinitions of the doctrine of forgiveness, and Shelley's longings for apocalypse were all equally alien to Keats's firm naturalism. The others (including Wordsworth and even Coleridge) are Bible-haunted, but there are only a handful of Biblical allusions in Keats's entire body of work, and they are never central. Keats's Bible was made up of Spenser, Shakespeare, Milton, and, to some extent, Wordsworth. It is this that helps to give Keats his peculiar modernity for many contemporary readers of poetry. What Matthew Arnold preached, Keats had anticipated him by practicing: to make a faith out of the tradition of high and serious poetry. The swiftness of Blake and Shelley is the swiftness of the spirit answering the prophetic call to put off the burden of deathly nature; the paced slowness of Keats is the deliberate leisure of a more-than-Wordsworthian naturalist, moving at the body's own sensuous pace toward a thoroughly hedonistic and aesthetic humanism. Kierkegaard would not have rated Keats as ever attaining the ethical, let alone the religious stage, but Keats is too healthy a human phenomenon to be subsumed by any categories made by a poet who thought less of the earth than he did. As his sage Moneta remarks in *The Fall of Hyperion,* he strove toward being one of those humanists who "seek no wonder but the human face." The night world of Romantic demonism and religiosity, which the Age of Kierkegaard moves in, has nothing to do with the natural sun of Keats.

It is a crisis of the sun that the first *Hyperion* takes as its theme, for the poem accepts as given that moment in myth at which the old gods depart and the new have not fully manifested themselves. The glorious but rough Titan Hyperion still keeps his uneasy place in heaven; the young Apollo, below on the earth, is dying into life, being twice born into his poetic powers.

The background in theogony of Keats's poem is to be found in Chapman's versions of Hesiod and Homer, Sandys' version of Ovid, and various mythologists of Keats's own day. But Keats's Saturn is so entirely different from any before him that source study is of little aid in comprehension. Keats's fall of the Titans is as much an individual myth-making as Blake's fall of the Zoas or Shelley's unbinding of Prometheus.

Few poems open so beautifully as *Hyperion.* Keats creates the fallen Saturn for us as a nobler Lear, massive even in his decayed godhood. With Thea, Hyperion's wife, mourning at his feet, the scene is presented as what Keats aptly calls "natural sculpture":

> the while in tears
> She touch'd her fair large forehead to the ground,
> Just where her falling hair might be outspread
> A soft and silken mat for Saturn's feet.
> One moon, with alteration slow, had shed
> Her silver seasons four upon the night,
> And still these two were postured motionless,
> Like natural sculpture in cathedral cavern;
> The frozen God still couchant on the earth,
> And the sad Goddess weeping at his feet.

The Titans are children of heaven and earth, but except for Hyperion they have all been forced to return to their mother.

"Smother'd up" on the earth, Saturn cannot understand his fate, and doubts his own identity:

> —I am gone
> Away from my own bosom: I have left
> My strong identity, my real self,
> Somewhere between the throne, and where I sit
> Here on this spot of earth.

The desperate god, in a sublime attempt at recovery, summons his imaginative powers, and his resolution, though hopeless in itself, is enough to frighten the Olympians and to put some last hope into Thea:

> "But cannot I create?
> Cannot I form? Cannot I fashion forth
> Another world, another universe,
> To overbear and crumble this to naught?
> Where is another chaos? Where?"

Thea leads the stricken god to the covert where his fallen race is hidden, locked in grief. Keats shifts perspective for the rest of Book I, while Saturn and Thea make their journey. We move into the heavens, to the blazing palace of the tormented but still powerful and unfallen Titan, Hyperion.

Though still worshiped by mortals as the sun's god, Hyperion is insecure, troubled by omens. In a titanic failure of nerve, he attempts to hasten sunrise by six hours, but cannot master the universe he must serve:

> No, though a primeval God:
> The sacred seasons might not be disturb'd.
> Therefore the operations of the dawn
> Stay'd in their birth, even as here 'tis told.
> Those silver wings expanded sisterly,
> Eager to sail their orb; the porches wide
> Open'd upon the dusk demesnes of night;
> And the bright Titan, phrenzied with new woes,
> Unus'd to bend, by hard compulsion bent
> His spirit to the sorrow of the time.

The sky, Hyperion's father, seeks to comfort him, but the comfort becomes itself ominous:

> vague fear there is:
> For I have seen my sons most unlike Gods.
> Divine ye were created, and divine
> In sad demeanour, solemn, undisturb'd,
> Unruffled, like high Gods, ye liv'd and ruled:
> Now I behold in you fear, hope, and wrath;
> Actions of rage and passion; even as
> I see them, on the mortal world beneath,
> In men who die.

At the sky's prompting, Hyperion plunges down to the earth, to find and assist Saturn. This ends the first book, and begins the second, for at the same moment that Hyperion starts his slide, Saturn and Thea reach the den that conceals the Titans from the "insulting light." Their impulse to hide is the overwhelming mark of the inwardness of their defeat, for the light they avoid is still their own, that of Hyperion. At the close of the second book, Keats emphasizes the irony of their condition by showing their reaction to the sudden influx of radiance which announces Hyperion's arrival:

> Despondence seiz'd again the fallen Gods
> At sight of the dejected King of Day,
> And many hid their faces from the light.

The structure of the Titan's situation is clearly based on that of the fallen angels at the opening of *Paradise Lost,* and the powerful but turbulent and despairing Hyperion is closely related to the Promethean Satan who dominates the first two books of Milton's epic. Keats parallels the poems still more closely by presenting a debate of the Titans, as they attempt to estimate their condition and prospects. The structural analogues take their point as a kind of parody. The contrast is between Milton's overt moralizings against the beings who yet represent his own creative energies, insofar as those talents are necessarily fallen, and Keats's refusal to take sides for or against the Titans, who yet have his deep and pained sympathy, but who have existed merely to be transcended by what is more excellent, more true and beautiful, than themselves.

The technical achievement of Keats, throughout these first two (and only completed) books of his poem, is subtly to advance the

Titans toward the condition of mortality. With this progressive humanization, they gain in our sympathetic self-identification and yet
become less in truth and beauty, for they move toward the organic
paradox of human existence. They can mature only by dying into
merely human life, and its limits will become their limits. Apollo,
the young Olympian counterpart of Hyperion, shows a contrary pattern in the fragmentary third book, for his dying into life is a dying
into godhead, a movement toward truth, beauty, and the power of
poetry.

The debate commences with Saturn's poignant confession of his
bafflement. He can find no reason for the terrible change, and
though he desires to go back to war, he does not know the means
by which the battle can be carried back to the Olympians. He appeals first to Oceanus, displaced god of the sea, whom he is astonished to find full of a "severe content."

What Oceanus proclaims is the imaginative center of the fragment, but for all its glowing power, Keats himself was not to find
it finally satisfactory. Oceanus refuses to make his voice "a bellows
unto ire," and offers only truth for comfort. The Titans fall "by
course of Nature's law," and the only sovereignty left for them is "to
bear all naked truths" and to be calm as they envisage the necessity of their own decline. For reality moves toward perfection, and
no stage in this dialectical process is refuted merely because it is
over:

> So on our heels a fresh perfection treads,
> A power more strong in beauty, born of us
> And fated to excel us, as we pass
> In glory that old Darkness: nor are we
> Thereby more conquer'd, than by us the rule
> Of shapeless Chaos.

This dispassionate observation is thrilled into a sudden beauty by
Oceanus' acceptance of his own displacement:

> Have ye beheld the young God of the Seas,
> My dispossessor? Have ye seen his face?
> Have ye beheld his chariot, foam'd along
> By noble winged creatures he hath made?
> I saw him on the calmed waters scud,

With such a glow of beauty in his eyes,
That it enforc'd me to bid sad farewell
To all my empire.

This is the truth offered to the Titans as balm. Before he has Enceladus, the volcanic Moloch of these defeated, fiercely reject such comfort, Keats inserts a more surprising instance of the effect of the new age upon the old. Oceanus' has been a voice of experience, but innocence is more apt to sense the unique element in what has come. The timid Clymene, whose tragic fate in mythology was to bear the doomed Phaethon to Apollo, has had a prophetic encounter with the new melody that has brought into the world "a living death."

Her only knowledge is that joy is gone, yet the sorrow that she tells is mixed with a new delight. A melody has come to her which is the birth music of the last of the new gods, Apollo, the leader of the Muses. This music makes her "sick of joy and grief at once." The entry of the oxymoron, here as elsewhere in Keats, is the emblem of an awakening into reality. The song that heralds "the morning-bright Apollo" is a living death for Clymene and all her race because it marks the precise moment at which she and they have joined the natural and human realm of the mortal.

Book II ends with the defiant war cry of Enceladus and the hollow roar of Saturn's name by the just arrived Hyperion and the Titans still defiant enough to greet him. The fragmented Book III opens with Keats bidding his Muse to leave the Titans to their woes, which surpass the possibility of expression, and to turn instead to the initiatory period of the young god who is "the Father of all verse."

Even as Hyperion stands bright, "amid the sorrow of his peers," the boy Apollo wanders forth in the morning twilight on the island sanctuary of Delos, leaving his mother, Leto, and his twin sister, Artemis, sleeping in their bower. He weeps, in a baffled expression of his still inchoate creativity, as he listens to the murmurous noise of waves. Mnemosyne, who is to be mother of the Muses by Zeus, comes to him, in betrayal of her fellow Titans, and asks the cause of his grief:

Show thy heart's secret to an ancient Power
Who hath forsaken old and sacred thrones

> For prophecies of thee, and for the sake
> Of loveliness new born.

Mnemosyne's function in the poem has little to do with memory in the narrow sense. Nor is she an admonitory figure, like the Moneta who replaces her in *The Fall of Hyperion*. She figures as a preceptress without needing to say anything; her lesson is in her face, as the final truth taught by Moneta will become clear in an unveiling of her countenance.

Apollo's pangs are those of death and birth, of dying into godhood, as he half seems to know. He spurns the green turf as hateful to his feet, for he is immediately destined for higher regions. He seeks his own power and suddenly finds it by reading a wondrous lesson in the silent face of Mnemosyne:

> Knowledge enormous makes a God of me.
> Names, deeds, grey legends, dire events, rebellions,
> Majesties, sovran voices, agonies,
> Creations and destroyings, all at once
> Pour into the wide hollows of my brain,
> And deify me, as if some blithe wine
> Or bright elixir peerless I had drunk,
> And so become immortal.

It is history, or, as we would say, mythology, which pours in to widen his consciousness. The contraries of existence, whether of gods or of men, come upon him at once, majesties and agonies, creations and destroyings together. The struggle within him carries the oxymoronic stage to its limits of intensity, heat and cold, life and death:

> Most like the struggle at the gate of death;
> Or liker still to one who should take leave
> Of pale immortal death, and with a pang
> As hot as death's is chill, with fierce convulse
> Die into life.

The fragment breaks off with the moment in which godhood is achieved. Mnemosyne upholds her arms in a prophetic gesture; Apollo shrieks a cry of death and birth, and his limbs are suddenly described as "celestial." He has risen to his heavenly power. But why does Keats break off so abruptly?

In a sense, *Hyperion* is already a complete poem once Apollo has realized himself, and the poet in Keats seems to have recognized this by refusing to go on. Whatever the planned length, nothing could be added to the fragment as it is without some redundancy. Keats's invention has been absolute. Human tragedy has claimed the Titans, who are doomed to mortality by no fault of their own. Indeed, their only flaws are those inherent in the human condition that they so rapidly and unwillingly must assume. The birth of an artist and art beyond tragedy has been enacted in the transformation of Apollo, whose growing pains are his only human element, and whose completion is an apotheosis of poetry itself. *Hyperion,* thus viewed, becomes a large image of the theme of the ode *To Autumn,* a naturalistic acceptance of the human necessity of tragedy. But, like *To Autumn, Hyperion* is written without overt personal reference. We feel that Apollo's painful struggle into consciousness is very like Keats's own, that to become a god of poetry within a poem or a poet within life are very much the same thing. Yet Keats has struggled for a disinterested stance all through *Hyperion,* and the relative unsteadiness of what exists as Book III shows him struggling still, but with the myth of self breaking in to capture the poem. One's guess is that Keats began to find himself writing the kind of poem that *Endymion* had been, a work in the *Alastor* tradition of Romantic self-recognition. This is precisely what the first two books of *Hyperion* had tried to get away from, but Keats discovered, with rare emotional honesty, that this was necessarily the proper mode for his age. Keats gave up *Hyperion* to recast it as *The Fall of Hyperion,* and the *Fall* is very nearly the archetypal Romantic poem. However Christian or classical some of his commentators might want him to be, Keats himself in the *Fall* chose to be a poet very much of the Shelleyan or Blakean kind, a vitalist of the imagination. Keats began the theme of the Titans as an attempt at epic, but found himself on the edge of composing his equivalent of the *Intimations* or *Dejection* odes, in concealed form. Having discovered this, he abandoned epic and turned to romance again, to a dream vision that could accommodate the great Romantic theme of the poet relating himself to the content of his own vision. The myth of the Titans and Olympians had to be made honestly representative of the poet's own state of mind. *The Fall of Hyperion* is a subjective version of the romance, just as *Childe*

Harold, Endymion, and most of Shelley's major poems are psychologized versions of the ancient patterns of quest and alienation which typify the romance as a form. Keats's quest in the *Fall* is remarkably like the final desperate quest of Shelley in *The Triumph of Life,* for both poets seek an end to alienation, a release from subjectivity through a bold embrace of the subjective. They enter for a last time into the abyss of their own selves that they may liberate their imaginations from their selfhoods. There the parallel ends. Shelley in the *Triumph* identifies what is anti-imaginative within the self as nature, while Keats reaffirms his naturalism and his faith that death is the mother of beauty, that mortality is the necessary condition for human greatness or the power of human art.

Ode to Psyche

THE *Ode to Psyche* has little to do with the accepted myth of Eros and Psyche. That myth is itself scarcely classical; it comes very late, and as an obvious and deliberate allegory. Aphrodite, jealous of the beautiful Psyche who is drawing her admirers away, commands Eros to afflict her with love for a base creature. But he falls in love with her, and comes to her regularly, always in the darkness. When, against his wishes, she lights a candle to see him, he flees from her. She quests for Eros by performing tasks set by Aphrodite, the last of which is a descent into the underworld. Psyche's inquiring spirit, which has previously caused her the loss of her lover, now all but destroys her. Warned by Persephone not to open a box sent by that goddess to Aphrodite, Psyche forsakes control again, and is about to be pulled down forever into the darkness when Eros intervenes, persuades Zeus to make Psyche immortal and to reconcile Aphrodite to her. Restored to each other, the lovers dwell together in Olympus.

Keats begins by bringing the reunited Eros and Psyche down to earth. We do not know whether Keats has seen the lovers in a dream or "with awaken'd eyes" in a vision of reality, but either way he has seen them. He finds them at that moment of Keatsian intensity when they are neither apart nor joined together, but rather in an embrace scarcely ended and another about to commence.

Eros he recognizes immediately, but Psyche is revealed to him in a moment of astonished apprehension.

The next two stanzas are parallel in structure, and are deliberately contrary to each other in emphasis and meaning. In the first the machinery of worship—altar, choir, voice, lute, pipe, incense, shrine, grove, oracle, and "heat of pale-mouth'd prophet dreaming" —is subtly deprecated. In the second, though the wording is almost identical, the same apparatus is humanized and eulogized. Keats said ironically that he was "more orthodox" in the old Olympian religion than the ancients, too orthodox "to let a heathen Goddess be so neglected." This heathen Goddess is the human-soul-in-love, which can well dispense with the outward worship ironically regretted in the second stanza, but which deserves and needs the inner worship of the imagination that is offered to it in the third stanza.

The changes of wording between the stanzas are so slight that a careless reading may overlook them. In the first, the Olympian hierarchy is "faded," and Psyche is the loveliest of the gods still evident. The other surviving Olympians are Phoebe and Aphrodite, and they live only in the light of the moon and the evening star. They were worshiped by the ancients; Psyche was not, but she is now fairer than either of them:

> though temple thou hast none,
> Nor altar heap'd with flowers;
> Nor virgin-choir to make delicious moan
> Upon the midnight hours;
> No voice, no lute, no pipe, no incense sweet
> From chain-swung censer teeming;
> No shrine, no grove, no oracle, no heat
> Of pale-mouth'd prophet dreaming.

As the catalog piles up, it is deliberately made to seem a little ludicrous, and the thrust (in context) is against the outer ceremonial of organized religion itself, not just against the Olympian worship. The choir is of virgins, and they make "delicious moan" at midnight: a sly hint of the sexual sublimation in aspects of worship. Then comes the long list of negative properties, whose absence makes them seem faintly ridiculous, until at the incantatory climax the celebrant prophet is evoked, with his heat of possession, his "pale-mouth'd" dreaming, as he longs for Phoebe or Aphrodite. The element of sexual suppression is again subtly conveyed.

When Keats turns to the positive, he employs similar phrases with a different emphasis. First comes a very forceful transition in which the sanctified elements are replaced by the poet finding his inspiration in his own perception of the elements:

> O brightest! though too late for antique vows,
>   Too, too late for the fond believing lyre,
> When holy were the haunted forest boughs,
>   Holy the air, the water, and the fire;
> Yet even in these days so far retir'd
>   From happy pieties, thy lucent fans,
>   Fluttering among the faint Olympians,
> I see, and sing, by my own eyes inspir'd.

Too late for antique vows, but in good time for the imaginative vow that Keats is about to give. On one level Keats is still voicing an ostensible regret for the days not "so far retir'd / From happy pieties" (happy in contrast to later pieties), when earth and its forest growths and the other elements were all accounted holy. Now they are not, for other pieties and the analytical mind combine to take away their sanctification. Yet even in these days Keats can *see* one movement, one light, fluttering among the faint Olympians, and because he can see her he can sing, inspired by his own eyes. Atoms of perception become intelligences, as Keats once remarked, because they *see*, they know, and therefore they are God. Seeing Psyche, he knows her, and moves to a union with her in which he becomes a god, a movement of incarnation. The poet is born in his own mind as he moves to become a priest of Psyche, and as a priest he participates in a humanistic and naturalistic communion, an act of the imagination which is a kind of natural supernaturalism. In the passage ending the third stanza the change from "no voice" and "no lute" to "thy voice" and "thy lute" utterly transforms the same phrasing employed earlier:

> So let me be thy choir, and make a moan
>   Upon the midnight hours;
> Thy voice, thy lute, thy pipe, thy incense sweet

> From swinged censer teeming;
> Thy shrine, thy grove, thy oracle, thy heat
> Of pale-mouth'd prophet dreaming.

The entire paraphernalia of worship is transformed in this internalization. Not only is Keats himself substituted for the deliciously moaning virgin choir, but Keats's poem, the *Ode to Psyche,* which he is in the act of composing, becomes the "moan upon the midnight hours." The voice, the lute, and the pipe become emblems of the poem that features them. The sweet incense rises from the poem itself, now identified as a "swinged censer teeming," and identified also with Keats himself. The particular change in wording here is revelatory—from "chain-swung censer" to "swinged censer," with the mechanical element omitted. The shrine becomes the fane that Keats will build in his own mind; the grove, the visionary foliage that will rise there as "branched thoughts." The oracle or prophet will be Keats in his role of the figure of the youth as virile poet, the youth of the poet's paradise in Collins and Coleridge, the questing poet shepherd in a state of innocence. The final transformation comes in a triumph of contextualization, as no word needs to be changed in "thy heat / Of pale-mouth'd prophet dreaming." This is not the frustration felt by the aspirant for Phoebe or Aphrodite, because it is *thy* heat, Psyche's, and so Keats and Psyche share it. If it is a reciprocal heat, then the "pale-mouth'd prophet" is at least dreaming of reality.

So far Keats has reached a point parallel to Collins' most imaginative moment in the *Ode on the Poetical Character,* for Keats has identified himself as a prophet of the loving human soul, and is poised before declaring that the paradise for the soul is to be built by the poet's imagination within the poet's own consciousness. In the final stanza Keats goes beyond Collins, with the general influence of Wordsworth determining the extent of that advance:

> Yes, I will be thy priest, and build a fane
> In some untrodden region of my mind,
> Where branched thoughts, new grown with pleasant pain,
> Instead of pines shall murmur in the wind.

Collins wrote in the light of Milton; Keats in the more inward-shining light of Wordsworth. In the lines from *The Recluse,* prefac-

ing *The Excursion,* Keats had read Wordsworth's invocation of a
greater Muse than Milton's:

> if such
> Descend to earth or dwell in highest heaven!
> For I must tread on shadowy ground.

That "shadowy ground" is the haunt of Keats's "shadowy
thought," and its place is "the Mind of Man," which Wordsworth
calls "the main region of my song." Wordsworth seeks his "groves
Elysian" in a wedding between "the discerning intellect of Man"
and "this goodly universe" of nature. Keats, in the last stanza of
To Psyche, finds the goodly universe to be produced within the
discerning intellect by the agency of poetry.

The opening lines of this stanza state that Psyche's temple will
be built "in some untrodden region" of Keats's mind. The implication is that the process is one of soul-making in an undiscovered
country; to build Psyche's temple is to widen consciousness. But
an increase in consciousness carries with it the dual capacity for
pleasure or for pain. The thoughts that will grow like branches in
that heretofore untrodden region will be grown "with pleasant
pain"; the oxymoron, Keats's most characteristic rhetorical device,
is peculiarly appropriate to any rendition of an earthly or poet's
paradise, a Beulah land where, as Blake said, all contrary statements
are equally true.

The branched thoughts, in this inner nature, replace pines, and
murmur in the wind of inspiration.

> Far, far around shall those dark-cluster'd trees
> Fledge the wild-ridged mountains steep by steep;
> And there by zephyrs, streams, and birds, and bees,
> The moss-lain Dryads shall be lull'd to sleep.

It takes an effort to recollect that these mountains and other
phenomena are all within the mind. The pastoral landscape is completed by the Dryads, who can no longer be lulled to sleep in the
external woods now "retir'd from happy pieties" but who find their
repose in this mental paradise. Having created a more ideal nature,
Keats proceeds to embower within it a sanctuary for Psyche:

> And in the midst of this wide quietness
> A rosy sanctuary will I dress

With the wreath'd trellis of a working brain,
With buds, and bells, and stars without a name,
With all the gardener Fancy e'er could feign,
Who breeding flowers, will never breed the same.

The "wide quietness" framed by the "wild-ridged mountains,"
themselves plumed by the "dark-cluster'd trees," reminds us of the
Wordsworthian landscape near Tintern Abbey, where the steep and
lofty cliffs impressed thoughts of deeper seclusion on an already se-
cluded scene, and connected the landscape with the quiet of the
sky. But whereas Wordsworth's scene is a given outward phenomenon, Keats's is built up within. And so he refers to the function of
his working brain within his general consciousness as being that of
a "wreath'd trellis," a gardener's support for clinging vines. In
Keats's most definitive vision of a poet's paradise, at the opening of
The Fall of Hyperion, this natural emblem appears again:

. . . and by the touch
Of scent, not far from roses. Turning round
I saw an arbour with a drooping roof
Of trellis vines, and bells, and larger blooms,
Like floral censers, swinging light in air.

It is Psyche's rosy sanctuary, but also the arbor where "our
Mother Eve" had her last meal in Paradise, a feast of summer fruits.
In the *Ode* the sanctuary is dressed not only with buds and bells
but with "stars without a name," for here the unrestricted invention
of the Fancy is at work. But Paradise was lost, and the Paradise
of the poet's fancy has an ambiguous and fragile nature. What follows is the triumph of Keats's *Ode,* and the most complex effect
in it: the somber but defiant acknowledgment of invention's limits,
and the closing declaration of the human love that surmounts even
imaginative limitations. Where Collins' *Ode* ends in a grim acknowledgment that the time cannot be imaginatively redeemed, at
least not by himself, Keats chooses to end with an image of an open
casement, through which the warm Love, Psyche's Eros, shall yet
enter.

Keats prepares his poem's rhapsodical climax by coming to a full but open stop after a couplet that rivals any as an epitome of the myth-making faculty:

> With all the gardener Fancy e'er could feign,
> Who breeding flowers, will never breed the same.

Keats, in his use of "feign" in this context, may be recalling the critic Touchstone in *As You Like It*. Audrey says: "I do not know what poetical is. Is it honest in deed and word? Is it a true thing?" Touchstone replies: "No, truly; for the truest poetry is the most feigning." Keats's rich word "feign," with its mingled dignity and ruin, is parallel to the word "artifice" in Yeats's myth of poetic self-recognition in *Sailing to Byzantium*. Yeats appeals to the beings who stand in the holy fire of the state Blake called Eden, where the creator and the creation are one. It is a fire that can be walked through; it will not singe a sleeve. Yet it can consume the natural heart away. This is Yeats's prayer to his masters in the fire, who would include Blake and Shelley and Keats: consume away what is sick with desire and yet cannot know itself, for it is fastened to dying, to the contrary to desire. And, having done this, gather me into the *artifice* of eternity. The gardener Fancy only feigns, and when he makes his artifice, breeds his flower, he cannot make or breed the same again, as a natural gardener could. But the orders of reality contend here; the natural gardener breeds only in finite variety, but the abundance of the imagination is endless, and each imaginative breeding is unique.

The poem *Ode to Psyche* is unique, and also central, for its art is a natural growth out of nature, based as it is upon a very particular act of consciousness, which Keats arrests in all its concreteness. Keats's real parallel among the myth-makers is Wallace Stevens, as Collins' is Coleridge, and Blake's is, more or less, Yeats. Keats's Psyche is a sexual goddess who renews consciousness and thus renews the earth, and for Stevens as for Keats the earth is enough. The ode *To Autumn* finds its companion in Wallace Stevens' *Sunday Morning*, and *To Psyche* is closely related to some of the *Credences of Summer*. Stevens writes of seeing nature as "the very thing and nothing else," and "without evasion by a single metaphor." Keats grows a foliage within his mind so as to have a natural shrine for Psyche which shall be eternal. Stevens says, take the phenomenon of nature and

> Look at it in its essential barrenness
> And say this, this is the centre that I seek.
> Fix it in an eternal foliage
>
> And fill the foliage with arrested peace,
> Joy of such permanence, right ignorance
> Of change still possible. Exile desire
> For what is not. This is the barrenness
> Of the fertile thing that can attain no more.

The gardener Fancy, breeding flowers, will never breed the same, for his feigning gives us that same barrenness, the barrenness of the fertile thing that can attain no more, a fixed perfection that lacks both the flaw and the virtue of green life. This paradox is more overt in the *Ode on a Grecian Urn* and in *Byzantium,* where the glory of changeless metal can scorn common bird or petal, and yet must be embittered by the changing and sexually governing moon. What unites Keats and Stevens is a temper of naturalistic acceptance, without bitterness or protest, of the paradox of the Romantic Imagination. Keats carries the honesty of acceptance to the point where it is impossible to judge whether the flaw or virtue of the gardener Fancy is offered to Psyche as the poet's best gift. *"With all the gardener Fancy e'er could feign,"* he says. The final offer is Keats's human absolute; he does not offer Psyche the truth of the Imagination, for he is uncertain of the kind of truth involved, but gives her instead the holiness of the heart's affections:

> And there shall be for thee all soft delight
>   That shadowy thought can win,
> A bright torch, and a casement ope at night,
>   To let the warm Love in!

There is a play, in these final lines, upon the familiar myth of Eros and Psyche which Keats has put aside in the main body of his ode. The mythical love of Eros and Psyche was an act in darkness; the bright torch burns in the natural tower of consciousness which Keats has built for the lovers' shrine. The open casement may remind us of the magic casements that open on the faery vision of the *Nightingale* ode, in the fading of the song of that more ambitious poem. Here, in *To Psyche*, it emphasizes the openness of the imagination toward the heart's affections. The subtle genius of Keats shades his ode even at its exultant surrender; there shall be for the soul "all soft delight / That *shadowy* thought can win." Thought is foliage here, and the green shade will shelter the soul, but the green thought itself is shadowy, which again suggests its limitations. Like the other great Romantics, Keats distrusted the Beulah of earthly repose, the natural garden of a world that he longed for. And, like his major contemporaries, he went on from it to a myth that promised a humanism that could transcend nature's illusions.

4   *Naturalistic Humanism*

Ode to a Nightingale

THE *Ode to a Nightingale* opens with the hammer beats of three heavily accented syllables—"My heart aches"—signaling the sudden advent of a state of consciousness unlike the Beulah state of "indolence," soft, relaxed, and feminine, which marks Keats's usual mode of heightened awareness and creativity. Like Shelley in the *Skylark*, Keats is listening to an unseen bird whose location he cannot specify—it is "In *some* melodious plot / Of beechen green, and shadows numberless." But the sharp immediacy of its song is nevertheless emphasized, for it sings "of summer in full-throated ease." The effect of the song on Keats is dual and strongly physical, indeed almost deathly. His heart aches, and his sense is pained with a drowsy numbness that suggests, first, having been poisoned; next, having taken a narcotic. Not the sound alone of the song, but Keats's empathizing with the bird, has done this. He is not envious of the bird, but is "too happy" in its happiness. He cannot sustain his own "negative capability" in this case; he has yielded his being too readily to that of the bird.

And yet, he welcomes this dangerous vertigo, for the next stanza of the poem seeks to prolong his condition by its wish for drunkenness, for "a beaker full of the warm South." The slackening intensity from poison to narcotic to wine is itself a return to an ordinary wakeful consciousness, a sense of the usual reality from which Keats here would "fade away into the forest dim," to join the nightingale in its invisibility and enclosed joy; to leave behind the world of mutability, where every increase in consciousness is an increase in sorrow. But the leave-taking is the contrary of Keats's expectation; the flight is not an evasion, but an elaboration of waking reality:

> Away! away! for I will fly to thee,
>   Not charioted by Bacchus and his pards,
> But on the viewless wings of Poesy,
>   Though the dull brain perplexes and retards:
> Already with thee!

Suddenly, having put aside the last aid to invocation, but by the act of writing his poem, he is where he wills to be, with the nightingale. The wings of Poesy are "viewless," not just because they are invisible, but because the flight is too high for a vision of the earth to be possible. And the state that now commences is a puzzle to the retarding "dull brain." The sweep of the imagination here is more than rational in its energy. Between the ecstatic cry of "Already with thee!" and the bell-like tolling of the word "forlorn" at the poem's climax, Keats enters the inner world of his poem, that highest state of the imagination which Blake called Eden. The mystery of Keats's unresolved contraries is in his quite anti-Blakean association of this state of more abundant life with what seems to be the death impulse. What for Blake is a state of greater *vision* is for Keats the realm of the *viewless:*

> Already with thee! tender is the night,
>   And haply the Queen-Moon is on her throne,
>   Cluster'd around by all her starry Fays;
>   But here there is no light,
>   Save what from heaven is with the breezes blown
>   Through verdurous glooms and winding mossy ways.

It is the night that is tender, the paradoxical darkness of the Keatsian vision constituting the mark of that tenderness. Nature is not blacked out; moon and stars may be present, but their light must first submit to the diminishing maze through which the night winds are blown.

Sight goes; the other senses abide in this trance, which at once equals nature and poetry. He cannot see, but odor, taste, and sound, in an instructive ordering, are called upon to describe the phenomena of the world he has at once entered and created. First, odor and taste, in the form of "soft incense" and "dewy wine":

> I cannot see what flowers are at my feet,
>   Nor what soft incense hangs upon the boughs,
> But, in embalmed darkness, guess each sweet
>   Wherewith the seasonable month endows
> The grass, the thicket, and the fruit-tree wild;
>   White hawthorn, and the pastoral eglantine:
>   Fast fading violets cover'd up in leaves;
>   And mid-May's eldest child,
>   The coming musk-rose, full of dewy wine,
>   The murmurous haunt of flies on summer eves.

The sensuous imagery here is the luxury of the lower paradise, of the Gardens of Adonis or of Beulah, but set in a context more severe. The odors and tastes are almost those of a more abandoned Milton, a blind poet intensifying the glory he cannot apprehend. But this is closer to the blindness of faith, the evidence of things not seen. Keats cannot see the flowers, but they do him homage at his feet. The "soft incense hangs upon the boughs" for him; and the darkness is "embalmed," a hint of the death wish in the next stanza. The month has kept faith; it is seasonable, and so aids Keats in guessing the identity of each odor. The significance of the "musk-rose" is that it is "coming," still a potential, for it is "mid-May's eldest child" and Keats is writing his ode early in May. Even as he anticipates the taste of the "musk-rose, full of dewy wine," Keats empathizes in advance with the insects, tasting of that wine on still-to-come summer eves. The rose as *"murmurous* haunt of flies" summons in the sense of hearing:

> Darkling I listen; and, for many a time
>   I have been half in love with easeful Death,
> Call'd him soft names in many a mused rhyme,
>   To take into the air my quiet breath.

THE VISIONARY COMPANY *410*

He listens, in the nightingale's own darkness, to the ecstasy of the bird's song. A clue to the poet's deliberate blinding of himself is heard here in a slight but haunting echo of a plangent passage of Milton. In the great invocation to light which opens Book III of *Paradise Lost,* the blind poet prepares himself to describe the glory of God the Father, "bright effluence of bright essence increate," a light so intense as to put out our earthly sight. As he reflects on his own sightless eyes, Milton's thoughts turn to the nightingale singing in darkness:

> Then feed on thoughts, that voluntary move
> Harmonious numbers; as the wakeful Bird
> Sings darkling, and in shadiest Covert hid
> Tunes her nocturnal note.

How consciously Keats remembered this passage one cannot say, but it contains the whole kernel of the *Ode to a Nightingale,* including the identification of poet and bird in their situations; involuntary in Milton, voluntary in Keats.

As he listens in the bird's own darkness, Keats approaches that supreme act of the Romantic Imagination so prevalent in his master, Wordsworth, the fluid dissolve or fade-out in which the limitations of time and space flee away, and the border between being and non-being, life and death, seems to crumble:

> Now more than ever seems it rich to die,
> To cease upon the midnight with no pain,
> While thou art pouring forth thy soul abroad
> In such an ecstasy!
> Still wouldst thou sing, and I have ears in vain—
> To thy high requiem become a sod.

Two attitudes toward death, the first shading into the second, are involved in this beautiful but disturbed stanza. Previous to the occasion this ode celebrates, the poet says, he has frequently invoked Death, under his "soft names" of ease, calling on Death to take his breathing spirit "into the air," that is, to die by the very act of exhaling. As he has called upon Death in "many a mused rhyme," this exhaling is equivalent to the act of uttering and composing his poem, and we are reminded that spirit means both soul and breath, and that the poet invoking his muse calls upon a breath greater than his own to inspirit him. Death, then, is here a muse, but this was previously only partly the case:

> I have been *half* in love with easeful Death.

But

> Now more than ever seems it rich to die,
> To cease upon the midnight with no pain.

"Rich" and "cease" are marvelously precise words. Now, in the shared communion of the darkness out of which the nightingale's song emerges, it seems rich to die, and he is *more than half* in love with easeful Death. For he has reached the height of living experience, and any descent out of this state into the poverty of ordinary consciousness seems a death-in-life, a pain to be avoided, in contrast to the life-in-death "with no pain" to be maintained were he "to cease upon the midnight." "To cease," suddenly not to be, and thus to cross over into non-being attended by the "requiem," the high mass of the nightingale's song. For the nightingale itself is pouring forth its soul abroad in an ecstasy that transcends the division between life and death; the bird lives, but its breath-soul is taken into the air as it gives itself freely in the extension of its ecstasy.

Two notes deliberately jar within this passion: "and I have ears in vain—" and "become a sod." At the very moment of Keats's most exultant self-surrender to the bird's song, he yet intimates his own mortality, his separateness from the immortality of the song:

> Thou wast not born for death, immortal Bird!
> No hungry generations tread thee down;
> The voice I hear this passing night was heard
> In ancient days by emperor and clown:
> Perhaps the self-same song that found a path
> Through the sad heart of Ruth, when, sick for home,
> She stood in tears amid the alien corn;
> The same that oft-times hath
> Charm'd magic casements, opening on the foam
> Of perilous seas, in faery lands forlorn.

The sadness of this stanza is double, for there is the explicit burden of Keats as he explores his separateness from the bird's song, and the implicit lament in the stanza's coming to rest upon the fateful word "forlorn," the repetition of which serves to shatter the inner world of the nightingale's song. The pathos of the reference to Ruth becomes tragic in its implied transference to the poet, through whose heart the self-same song now finds its path to indicate *his* coming alienation, not from home, but from the song itself. The closing lines of the stanza, with their hint of the Spenserian world, to Keats the universe of poetry itself, are a final presage of the loss that is to come. The "faery lands" are forlorn, not that the poet has forsaken them, but that, like the bird's song, they have abandoned him:

> Forlorn! the very word is like a bell
>   To toll me back from thee to my sole self!
> Adieu! the fancy cannot cheat so well
>   As she is fam'd to do, deceiving elf.
> Adieu! adieu! thy plaintive anthem fades
>   Past the near meadows, over the still stream,
>   Up the hill-side; and now 'tis buried deep
>   In the next valley-glades:
>   Was it a vision, or a waking dream?
>   Fled is that music:—Do I wake or sleep?

The double tolling of "forlorn" converts the nightingale's song into a "plaintive anthem," a requiem for the shattered communion between poet and song, as it rings the poet back to the isolation of his sole self. The movement of imagination becomes the deception of an elf, like the Belle Dame, Keats's triple mistress, Poetry, Consumption, and Death. The song fades with the unseen flight of the bird, until it is "buried deep." There remains only the resolution of the nature of the poetic trance—fully manifest, as in a vision, or merely the latent content of a waking dream? The answer is uncertain, for "fled is that music." At the close, Keats is left pondering the contraries: are the act and state of creation a heightening or merely an evasion of the state of experience? Once back in experience, the honest answer is only in the continued question, both as to fact and to will: "Do I wake or sleep?"

Ode on Melancholy

THE difficulties of the *Ode on Melancholy* are infrequently realized because the poem is not often closely read. Yet even a superficial reading involves us in Keats's deliberately unresolved contraries. The admonition of the first stanza is against false melancholy, courted for the sake of the supposed oblivion it brings. But oblivion is not to be hired; for Keats true melancholy involves a sudden increase in consciousness, not a gradual evasion of its claims.

Keats canceled the initial opening stanza of this ode presumably because he saw that the poem's harmony was threatened if fully half of it was concerned with the useless quest after "the Melancholy." His sense of proportion did not fail him in this, and yet something went out of the poem with the exclusion of that stanza:

> Though you should build a bark of dead men's bones,
>   And rear a phantom gibbet for a mast,
> Stitch shrouds together for a sail, with groans
>   To fill it out, blood-stained and aghast;
> Although your rudder be a dragon's tail
>   Long sever'd, yet still hard with agony,
>   Your cordage large uprootings from the skull
> Of bald Medusa, certes you would fail
>   To find the Melancholy—whether she
>   Dreameth in any isle of Lethe dull.

The "whether" in the ninth line may be read as "even if." This remarkable and grisly stanza is more than the reverse of an invitation to the voyage. Its irony is palpable; its humor is in the enormous labor of Gothicizing despair which is necessarily in vain, for the mythic beast, Melancholy, cannot thus be confronted. The tone of the stanza changes with the dash in line 9; with it the voice speaking the poem ceases to be ironical. With the next stanza, the first of the received text, the voice is passionate, though its message is the same. By excluding the original first stanza, Keats lost a grim humor that finds only a thin echo at the poem's close. That humor, in juxtaposition to the poem's intensities, would have been parallel to successful clowning in a tragedy.

As the poem stands, the idle quest after the Melancholy is yet inviting:

> No, no, go not to Lethe, neither twist
>   Wolf's-bane, tight-rooted, for its poisonous wine;
> Nor suffer thy pale forehead to be kiss'd
>   By nightshade, ruby grape of Proserpine;
> Make not your rosary of yew-berries,
>   Nor let the beetle, nor the death-moth be
>   Your mournful Psyche, nor the downy owl
> A partner in your sorrow's mysteries;
>   For shade to shade will come too drowsily,
>   And drown the wakeful anguish of the soul.

What is most important here is *"too* drowsily" and *"wakeful* anguish." The truest parallel is in the first stanza of the *Ode to a Nightingale.* There the drowsiness is not excessive; it numbs, but the soul's anguish remains wakeful. The properties of questing after the Melancholy are there also: hemlock, a dull opiate, Lethe, but only in the form of "as though." The melancholy is genuine there, as it is here. It is as though Keats had quested after the epiphanies of these poems, but he has not. The negative grace of the state of being these odes embody falls suddenly, comes with the sharp immediacy of a blow. "My heart aches"; the three heavily accented syllables begin the poem by battering three times at the poet's and our consciousness. "But when the melancholy fit shall fall / Sudden from heaven . . ." is the equivalent in this ode. But when it falls without one's having provoked it, "Then glut thy sorrow"; one need show no restraint in feeding it further. On what? The melancholy fit has fallen as the rains of April fall, to "foster the droop-headed flowers," to cover the hills with green. The shock is that this green fostering, for all its beauty, *is* like the fall of melancholy, for April's green is here called "an April shroud." The enduring color of fresh life is only a grave color, and so your sorrow can also be glutted on the loveliness of such supposedly nonsorrowful emblems as a morning rose, a shore rainbow, or the wealth of globed peonies. To complete the complexity, Keats offers as food for sorrow the *wealth* of ones' beloved's "rich anger."

The force of this second stanza is that it is inexplicable, unre-

solved, until it is suddenly clarified by the first line of the final
stanza:

> She dwells with Beauty—Beauty that must die.

The line relies on its immediate expository force after the puzzle
of the preceding stanza; it requires a long pause after reading. The
emphasis needs to be put upon *"must* die"; the anger of the mistress, which so delights the sadism-hunting scholar, is significant
only in its richness, not in any sexual implication. It is rich because it offers a possibility of feeding deeply upon an animated
beauty that is doomed to lose all motion, all force. Animation, as
in its root meaning, here reveals the living soul in full activity, with
the special poignance that in this poem is definitive of true melancholy, consciousness of mutability and death. Like Wallace Stevens in *Sunday Morning, Esthétique du Mal* (especially Section
XV, the poem's conclusion), and *The Rock,* Keats is insisting on
the mingled heroic ethic and humanistic aesthetic that the natural
is beautiful and apocalyptic precisely because it is physical and
ephemeral. Keats's contrast is in his tense insistence that *something*
in nature *must* prevail, and his final despair that nothing can, even
as the parallel and contrast to Stevens is Yeats, in his insistence
(however ironic) that Byzantine realities are superior to mere natural beauties. Spenser in the *Mutabilitie* Cantos and Milton
throughout his work resolve these conflicts by a cosmic dialectic.
It remained for Blake and Wordsworth, in their very different ways,
to humanize these resolutions. With younger and modern Romantics it has been too late in the day to offer full measure in these
conflicts; bitterness, however visionary, necessarily keeps breaking
in.

The magnificence of the *Ode on Melancholy*'s final stanza is in
its exactness of diction as it defines the harmony of continued apprehension of its unresolved contraries. Only Beauty that *must* die
is beauty; Joy cannot be present without simultaneously bidding
adieu; and *aching* Pleasure (the adjective triumphantly embodies a
pair of contraries) is immanent only by turning to poison for us,
even as we sip its real (not supposed) honey. For, like the rest of
Keats's odes, this poem is tragic; it reaches beyond the disillusion-
ments of a state of experience into the farther innocence of a poet's

paradise, as in the shrine of Moneta in the *Fall of Hyperion,* to which this is surely a reference (the "has" helps establish it):

> Ay, in the very temple of delight
> Veil'd Melancholy has her sovran shrine.

And, as in the *Fall of Hyperion,* this truth is seen by none except those who earn the poet's melancholy, which is not to be usurped. The *strenuous* tongue does not simply sip the grape's juice; it *bursts* the grape of Joy, with the inevitable double consequence of tasting might and the sadness of might, Moneta's or the Melancholy's double aspect, the Goddess as Muse and as Destroyer:

> And be among her cloudy trophies hung.

Ode on a Grecian Urn

THE still urn is a bride of quietness, but the marriage is unconsummated; the urn speaks. By speaking, it reveals itself as only a "foster-child of silence and slow time"; its true parents are its creator and marble, but its creator communicates through silence, and the unchanging marble has arrested time, and slowed it toward the eternity of art.

The urn as sylvan historian expresses a tale more sweetly than our rhyme because it presents a tale in space and without the duration of time. Liberated from the sourness of temporal presentation, the tale lacks the either/or referential clarity of language:

> What leaf-fring'd legend haunts about thy shape
>   Of deities or mortals, or of both,
>   In Tempe or the dales of Arcady?
>   What men or gods are these? What maidens loth?
> What mad pursuit? What struggle to escape?
>   What pipes and timbrels? What wild ecstasy?

The scene cannot quite be identified, except in its deliberately typical elements. Reluctant maidens flee the mad pursuit of men or gods, but the struggle and reluctance are only part of a myth of pursuit, a ritual of delayed rape spurred on to wild ecstasy by pipes and timbrels. The sexual power of the depicted scene is one with the aesthetic; it depends on potential, on something ever more about to be, and suggests the sense of possible sublimity that art can communicate. In the second stanza, Keats intensifies the expectation:

> Heard melodies are sweet, but those unheard
>   Are sweeter; therefore, ye soft pipes, play on;
> Not to the sensual ear, but, more endear'd,
>   Pipe to the spirit ditties of no tone.

The taking famishes the receiver; it is the greatest of the Romantic paradoxes. The darkness of this situation is presented in *La Belle Dame Sans Merci,* but here Keats explores the twilight. Shelley thought good and the means of good irreconcilable, and made love and poetry the good. In Keats the means can serve the end of good, but tend to serve it too well. The accomplished good requires the rhetoric of the oxymoron, where every qualifier negates what is qualified. And so fulfillment for Keats is a betrayal of potential. The ideal for Keats is to be poised before experience. The ideal for Shelley is to find an experience in which the means and the end, the subject and the object, become indistinguishable one from the other.

As he gazes at the urn's musicians, Keats asks them to play on tonelessly, piping only to his spirit. A train of association carries from the soundless song through the trees that will never know winter to the sexual stasis of the kiss that cannot take place. The gardener Fancy of the *Ode to Psyche* feigned, but breeding flowers he never bred the same. The happy melodist, unwearied, forever pipes songs that are forever new. The urn's youth is forever panting, but also forever young. All these, the urn's foliage, song and singer, beloved and lover, are

> All breathing human passion far above,
>   That leaves a heart high-sorrowful and cloy'd,
>   A burning forehead, and a parching tongue.

They can scorn the complexities of blood and mire, the common bird and the human singer, and the lover who moves in flesh. The art of Keats triumphs in the line "All breathing human passion far above," for to Keats nothing is more to be desired than "breathing human passion," the sexual experience, which heightens nature to its own limits. For Keats, as for Wordsworth before him, to call something "human" is to eulogize it. Keats does not deprecate the human in this line or anywhere else, and we miss the line's meaning if we do not read it as including its own contrary. The "more happy, happy love" depicted on the urn is as far below breathing human passion as it is far above. A mouth that has no moisture and no breath may be able to summon breathless mouths, but it can as easily be called death-in-life as life-in-death. Confronted by an impassable paradox, Keats resolves his poem by a dialectic dependent on the simultaneous existence and non-existence of what is presented by art. In a perfect Shakespearean stanza, he shifts perspective and looks at another picture on the urn:

> Who are these coming to the sacrifice?
>   To what green altar, O mysterious priest,
> Lead'st thou that heifer lowing at the skies,
>   And all her silken flanks with garlands drest?
> What little town by river or sea shore,
>   Or mountain-built with peaceful citadel,
>   Is emptied of this folk, this pious morn?
> And, little town, thy streets for evermore
>   Will silent be; and not a soul to tell
>   Why thou art desolate, can e'er return.

What Keats sees is a procession; the rest is conjecture. The green altar and the little town exist not on the urn but in the past and future that are phenomenological implications of the poem's existence. They belong to the world that critics of poetry have no reason to inquire into: the world of the childhood of Shakespeare's heroines, and of the married life of Jane Austen's Mr. and Mrs. Collins. This is precisely the world that is not given by a work of art. Keats speculates on it for just that reason, to establish what are the limits of poetry. The nature of poetic time, Keats finds, is such that it teases us out of thought, just as eternity defies our conceptualizations. The procession has emptied some little town, but that town is far in what Shelley called the Unapparent. The procession, because it is portrayed, both is and is not, as Hamlet is and is not. The discursive antithesis between being and non-being is revealed by art as a conceptual fiction, a convenience for the tired imagination. The little town is not, even by the canons of art, and the imagination can tell us nothing of it. There is not a soul to tell us why it is desolate, and so the reality of art is only in its eternal present. So also the urn is an eternal present, and its freedom from the restrictions of time eludes our categorization:

> O Attic shape! Fair attitude! with brede
>   Of marble men and maidens overwrought,
> With forest branches and the trodden weed;
>   Thou, silent form, dost tease us out of thought
> As doth eternity: Cold Pastoral!

Keats begins his final stanza by reminding himself that it is only an artifice of eternity before him. The men and maidens are merely wrought over the urn's surface; they are but marble. Yet the weed is trodden beneath their feet, evidence which teases thought's antitheses. We cannot think of eternity because duration is inextricable with our thinking; time passes as we try to apprehend timelessness. The urn is a silent form, and speaks to us. Its subject is a passionate idyl, and yet it is a cold pastoral, for marble sensuality is at an extreme from "a burning forehead, and a parching tongue." Cold though it be, it is a friend to man, for its temporal freedom intimates to us another dimension of man's freedom:

> When old age shall this generation waste,
>   Thou shalt remain, in midst of other woe
> Than ours, a friend to man, to whom thou say'st,
>   "Beauty is truth, truth beauty,"—that is all
>   Ye know on earth, and all ye need to know.

Keats wrote, in one of his letters, that what the imagination seizes as beauty *must* be truth. The imagination he compared to Adam's dream, during which Eve was created. Adam woke to find it true, presumably because she *was* beautiful. The urn's beauty is truth because age cannot waste it; our woes cannot consume it. The urn's truth, its existence out of time, is beauty because such freedom is beautiful to us. The condition of man, for Keats, is such that all we shall ever know we know on earth, and the sum of our knowledge is the identity of beauty and truth, when beauty is defined as what gives joy forever, and truth as what joy seizes upon as beauty. The image of an eddying joy, making its own definitions by circularity, closed Coleridge's *Dejection: An Ode* and reappears in abstract form at the close of Keats's *Ode on a Grecian Urn.* To know the truth of the imagination is to live again, and living, the soul will know the beauty of its own truth. The defiant naturalist in Keats takes him a liberating step beyond Coleridge; the soul that knows the identity of beauty and truth knows also its own freedom, which is all it needs to know.

Ode on Indolence

In the *Ode on Indolence* Keats loafs and invites his soul to consider the lilies of the field. The poem is in the mood of the *Grecian Urn,* but the mood is turned inward toward Keats himself. The subject is not poetry, but the poet.

Both odes begin with a confrontation of a classical scene, but in the *Indolence* Keats starts with an allegory, and then compares the personified figures to those on an urn. The strength of his obsessions—Love, Ambition, Poesy—and his rueful disregard for them in favor of what is seen as a more imaginative fourth abstraction, Indolence, determine the shape of a poem remarkable in itself and illustrative of the conflicts within the poet.

The three figures move like three graces, serene and disinterested, but they are Keats's three fates, and their triple passing has an ominous potential for him. They restore him to that state of consciousness he seeks to evade:

> Ripe was the drowsy hour;
> The blissful cloud of summer-indolence
>   Benumb'd my eyes; my pulse grew less and less;
> Pain had no sting, and pleasure's wreath no flower:
>   O, why did ye not melt, and leave my sense
>   Unhaunted quite of all but—nothingness?

The poem dismisses Love as that which can neither be defined nor located, and Ambition as mutable, but it makes a more involved farewell to Poesy. She is a "maiden most unmeek," even "my demon," and yet Keats loves her more, the more of blame is heaped upon her. Even she, whose faults are thus translated to virtues, has no joys to give Keats which are

> so sweet as drowsy noons,
> And evenings steep'd in honied indolence.

The sensuous concreteness of indolence makes the three figures
ghosts by contrast. Keats's mood is a *penseroso* one; he is sinking
back deliberately into the bower celebrated as the poet's first phase
in *Sleep and Poetry*. Yet he makes it clear that he wants a creative
repose, to gather force for his final attempts at poetry:

> Farewell! I yet have visions for the night,
> And for the day faint visions there is store.

He parallels Shelley's lyric *To Night*, in which imaginative consciousness is equated with natural darkness, and ordinary consciousness with the heavy burden of noon. The farewell to Poesy in the
Indolence is a farewell to the conventional idea of poetry, the
pseudo-pastoral namby-pamby land of Leigh Hunt:

> For I would not be dieted with praise,
> A pet-lamb in a sentimental farce!

This is Keats's break with any sentimentalities about nature, and
its "places of nestling green for poets made." From his defiant indolence, a true poet's trance, there arises the vision of tragic humanism that ends his career as poet, *The Fall of Hyperion*.

5 *Tragic Humanism*

The Fall of Hyperion

KEATS begins *The Fall of Hyperion* by distinguishing poetic from
religious and primitive dreams. The religious (here unkindly called
"fanatics") have their dreams, and use them as evidence for the
existence of a paradise beyond sensuous apprehension, and reserved
for members of a particular sect. Primitive man has his dreams,
from which he less confidently attempts to guess at Heaven. The

content of both the fanatic's and the savage's dream remains largely
latent, for both believe themselves to possess a reality beyond the
reach of language, and so both lapse into mystery:

> For Poesy alone can tell her dreams,—
> With the fine spell of words alone can save
> Imagination from the sable chain
> And dumb enchantment.

Imagination is involved in the dreamings of religion and primal
mythology, but imagination is ill-served by them, and is bewitched
into silence and darkness. Keats implies that the fanatic and the
savage are imperfect poets, with a further suggestion that religious
speculation and mythology are poetry not fully written. Keats is
about to give his own dream of paradise, and knows that only pos-
terity will decide if it is a realized poem or not:

> Whether the dream now purpos'd to rehearse
> Be poet's or fanatic's will be known
> When this warm scribe, my hand, is in the grave.

The visionary paradise Keats finds himself standing in is the paradise lost by our Mother Eve. He sees an arbor, and before it, spread
upon a mound of moss, a feast of summer fruits. As he comes
closer, he sees the feast as what it is, the refuse of an apparently
interrupted meal. The reference may be to the repast given by Eve
to the Angel Raphael in *Paradise Lost*, or, more likely, I think, to a
meal Milton does not mention, the last eaten in paradise by Adam
and Eve before their expulsion into the fallen world. In vision Keats
has re-entered Eden, and he now eats deliciously of the remnants
of the fruit forever barred to us. This feast of naturalistic communion with archetypal man is climaxed by a toast to mortal life existent and remembered:

> And, after not long, thirsted; for thereby
> Stood a cool vessel of transparent juice,
> Sipp'd by the wander'd bee, the which I took,
> And, pledging all the mortals of the world,
> And all the dead whose names are in our lips,
> Drank. That full draught is parent of my theme.

He sinks down into a slumber within a dream, and wakens to find
himself within a ruined and gigantic ancient sanctuary, with a dome

over his head and marble at his feet. As he looks down he finds
not the remnants of a feast of summer fruits but the abandoned
paraphernalia of religious worship—robes, golden tongs, censer,
holy jewelries. He raises his eyes to fathom the space around him:

> The embossed roof, the silent massy range
> Of columns north and south, ending in mist
> Of nothing; then to eastward, where black gates
> Were shut against the sunrise evermore.
> Then to the west I look'd, and saw far off
> An image, huge of feature as a cloud,
> At level of whose feet an altar slept,
> To be approach'd on either side by steps
> And marble balustrade, and patient travail
> To count with toil the innumerable degrees.

For this faith, the way east is barred; there are to be no more
dawns. To turn aside, north or south, is to seek to evade reality,
only to end in the mist of nothing. Keats faces to the west, to the
stairs of purgation and the unknown altar, to natural completion,
sunset, man's death.

The structure that Keats slowly moves toward is derived primarily from Dante, probably by way of the Cary translation, but also
from the description of the sanctuary of Jehovah in Exodus, and
from reminiscences of Keats's readings about ancient Egyptian,
Greek, and Celtic temples. The steps and marble pavement are like
those leading up the graded and steep sides of Mount Purgatory.
The temple horns are those grasped by the suppliant in Jehovah's
sanctuary and symbolized His power and glory, and man's salvation
by them. The details of the dome, pillars, and hall mix Pericles'
temple, Egyptian monuments, and Fingal's cave. Keats blends five
religious traditions—Christian, Jewish, Egyptian, Olympian, Druidic—because he wants the abandoned temple of Saturn to represent the shrine of religious consciousness itself. The death of one
god is for Keats the death of all, and Saturn in this second version
of *Hyperion* is not less than ancient and displaced piety, in all its
historical forms. Moneta, who serves the ruined altar, is a priestess
of intense consciousness doing homage to the dead faiths which
have become merely materials for poetry. Keats, in approaching the
altar and its purgatorial steps, is assuming the position of the young

Apollo of *Hyperion* as the god approached Mnemosyne. But the differences are profound: Apollo met sympathy and love; Keats encounters scorn and a challenge of his right to exist.

As he draws closer to the shrine, he sees a sacrificial flame rising from it:

> and there arose a flame.
> When in mid-May the sickening east-wind
> Shifts sudden to the south, the small warm rain
> Melts out the frozen incense from all flowers,
> And fills the air with so much pleasant health
> That even the dying man forgets his shroud;—
> Even so that lofty sacrificial fire,
> Sending forth Maian incense, spread around
> Forgetfulness of everything but bliss,
> And clouded all the altar with soft smoke.

This passage is derived from the *Purgatorio*, where it precedes a blessing on those whose hunger is measured by righteousness, and follows the appearance of a tree that is a shoot from the one whereof Eve tasted the fruit. Keats's use of it is ironic, for, like Eve, he has just tasted fruit of paradise, but, unlike Dante, the breeze's fragrance upon him presages not a blessing but a sharp and painful test. Out of the white fragrant curtains of smoke the voice of Moneta comes, to begin a series of dialectical exchanges akin to those between Rousseau and Shelley in *The Triumph of Life*. As in Shelley, the tense and lucid dialogue moves on a poetic level of sublimity more chastened and austere than either poet had achieved before. Menace and energy, and an ultimate inevitability of diction are combined in Moneta's challenge:

> "If thou canst not ascend
> These steps, die on that marble where thou art.
> Thy flesh, near cousin to the common dust,
> Will parch for lack of nutriment,—thy bones
> Will wither in few years, and vanish so
> That not the quickest eye could find a grain
> Of what thou now art on that pavement cold.
> The sands of thy short life are spent this hour,
> And no hand in the universe can turn

> Thy hourglass, if these gummed leaves be burnt
> Ere thou canst mount up these immortal steps."

The thrust and power of this passage are unmistakable, and so is the reference to Keats's own approaching death, imported into the poem because the poet's mortality is at the center of its theme. The poet requires nutriment that can be gained only by ascending these purgatorial steps, and warmth which lies beyond these icy stairs. And there is only a limited time; the leaves are burning. Keats hears the warning, sees the burning leaves, and pauses to reflect on the fineness and subtlety of the two senses that feel the tyranny of that fierce threat. The pause and reflection are characteristic of this most sensuous of all poets, and they nearly undo him:

> —when suddenly a palsied chill
> Struck from the paved level up my limbs,
> And was ascending quick to put cold grasp
> Upon those streams that pulse beside the throat!
> I shriek'd, and the sharp anguish of my shriek
> Stung my own ears.

The shriek is parallel to Apollo's shriek of death and birth as he dies into life. It arouses Keats to a supreme effort:

> I strove hard to escape
> The numbness, strove to gain the lowest step.
> Slow, heavy, deadly was my pace: the cold
> Grew stifling, suffocating, at the heart;
> And when I clasp'd my hands I felt them not.
> One minute before death, my iced foot touch'd
> The lowest stair; and, as it touch'd, life seem'd
> To pour in at the toes.

He has died into life, and is naturalistically twice-born. But he does not know why he has been saved, and is confused, like Apollo, as to his very identity. He questions Moneta, and the still-veiled Shade replies:

> "Thou hast felt
> What 'tis to die and live again before
> Thy fated hour; that thou hadst power to do so

> Is thy own safety; thou hast dated on
> Thy doom."

But why had he the power? What is he, to stand on a height that ought to have slain him?

> "High Prophetess," said I, "purge off,
> Benign, if so it please thee, my mind's film."
> "None can usurp this height," returned that shade,
> "But those to whom the miseries of the world
> Are misery, and will not let them rest.
> All else who find a haven in the world,
> Where they may thoughtless sleep away their days,
> If by a chance into this fane they come,
> Rot on the pavement where thou rotted'st half."

This magnificent reply, with its significant allusions to Wordsworth's *Excursion* and Shelley's *Alastor,* is the beginning of the poem's attempt to awaken the imagination by distinguishing among the classes of men. Keats half rotted on the pavement before his painful salvation. Those who enter this temple of poetry and are not humanists rot altogether on the icy marble. And yet, why is Keats in the shrine alone? He knows of greater humanists than himself:

> "Are there not thousands in the world," said I,
> Encourag'd by the sooth voice of the shade,
> "Who love their fellows even to the death;
> Who feel the giant agony of the world;
> And more, like slaves to poor humanity,
> Labour for mortal good? I sure should see
> Other men here, but I am here alone."

There is great pride in these lines, but a great desolation, and a Wordsworthian weight of solitude as well. Moneta's reply is both a rebuke to pride and an affirmation, and seems to me the finest moment in Keats's poetry:

> "Those whom thou spak'st of are no visionaries,"
> Rejoin'd that voice,—"they are no dreamers weak;
> They seek no wonder but the human face,
> No music but a happy-noted voice—

They come not here, they have no thought to come—
And thou art here, for thou art less than they.
What benefit canst thou do, or all thy tribe,
To the great world? Thou art a dreaming thing,
A fever of thy self—think of the earth;
What bliss, even in hope, is there for thee?
What haven? every creature hath its home;
Every sole man hath days of joy and pain,
Whether his labours be sublime or low—
The pain alone, the joy alone, distinct:
Only the dreamer venoms all his days,
Bearing more woe than all his sins deserve.
Therefore, that happiness be somewhat shar'd,
Such things as thou art are admitted oft
Into like gardens thou didst pass erewhile,
And suffer'd in these temples: for that cause
Thou standest safe beneath this statue's knees."

These lines are the culmination of Keats's work, and need the closest kind of reading, while they demand an energy of response which vitalizes the reader's imagination. Humanists, Moneta replies, are of two kinds, and Keats is alone in his generation in being the lesser kind, both a humanist and a visionary. The pragmatic humanists do not need the invented wonders of weak dreaming. The object of their quest is directly before them. They write no poems, for their music is in human happiness, and their truth and beauty in the human face. The poet is a fever of himself, caught in the anguish of his own selfhood. But the earth is enough, if he would but think of it, and the earth need surrender to no heaven. Those for whom the earth is not enough can have no home, and no happiness even in their own hopes. Having moved so close to Keats's own malady, his involvement in the pain of the unresolved contraries of nature and imagination, Moneta strikes at what is most central in Keats, his inability to unperplex joy from pain. Men, humanists or not, except the dreamer, can experience joy and pain unmixed. No line in Keats is more intense with baffled aspiration than the one that separates him from the generality of men:

The pain alone, the joy alone, distinct.

The indictment seems crushing, and the rhetorical irony turned on Keats by Moneta is cruel. Such things as Keats is, Moneta tells him, are admitted into a state of innocence, that happiness may be *somewhat* shared, and are suffered within the temple of poetry. Moneta's tone has the ironic and mocking pity that Blake extends to the "gentle souls," the quietists like St. Teresa and Fénelon, who are given minor gates of Jerusalem to guard. But Keats is more than a gentle wanderer in Beulah, and his sense of the dignity of poetry provokes a dialectical response that compels Moneta to modify her severe categories:

> "That I am favour'd for unworthiness,
> By such propitious parley medicin'd
> In sickness not ignoble, I rejoice,
> Aye, and could weep for love of such award."
> So answer'd I, continuing, "If it please,
> Majestic shadow, tell me: sure not all
> Those melodies sung into the world's ear
> Are useless: sure a poet is a sage;
> A humanist, physician to all men.
> That I am none I feel, as vultures feel
> They are no birds when eagles are abroad.
> What am I then: thou spakest of my tribe:
> What tribe?"

It is an astonishing and very great recovery, expressed with tact and firmness. Keats accepts the admonitions, but deftly refers to the poet's oxymoronic sickness as being "not ignoble." Poetry has its humanist use, as Moneta in her dialectical zeal seems to have forgotten. The poet is a great therapist, in the Wordsworthian sense of consolation and spiritual renewal. Yet, Keats modestly admits, he himself is not quite a poet in so high a sense. His questioning moves the dialectic onto a more earnest level, and Moneta now corrects herself by distinguishing between two kinds of poets, another cross-category to add to the distinctions between poets and other humanists, and between humanists and men who merely rot if they attempt greatness:

> "Art thou not of the dreamer tribe?
> The poet and the dreamer are distinct,

> Diverse, sheer opposite, antipodes.
> The one pours out a balm upon the world,
> The other vexes it."

Keats's dialectical victory is that for the first time she must reply with a question. He has asked again for his identity, but this time in such a way that the question compels her to a more generous answer. She is now in doubt. Is Keats one of those who heal or vex the world by their writing? His own response to her last distinction settles the issue. With a vehement outcry, he separates himself from those who merely seek relief and aggrandizement for the ego by their poetry:

> Then shouted I
> Spite of myself, and with a Pythia's spleen,
> "Apollo! faded! O far-flown Apollo!
> Where is thy misty pestilence to creep
> Into the dwellings, through the door crannies
> Of all mock lyrists, large self-worshippers
> And careless Hectorers in proud bad verse?
> Though I breathe death with them it will be life
> To see them sprawl before me into graves."

In *Sleep and Poetry,* Keats had begun to separate himself from his chief contemporary rivals, Wordsworth, Byron, and Shelley. *Endymion* had attempted to refute *Alastor,* and the great odes practice an art of Mammon, loading every rift with ore, which is what Keats had none too kindly advised Shelley to do. I am one of the few readers now extant, so far as I can see, who think Keats a very great poet but Shelley an even greater one, so I am not altogether happy with this passage, though its principal reference is probably to Byron rather than to Wordsworth or Shelley. Keats himself half-apologizes for these lines, but they are necessary to his poem. He shouts with the spleen of Apollo's Pythian oracle, directly inspired by the god of poetry, and in spite of himself. It is not a pretty sentiment to say that it will be life for him to see his rival poets sprawl before him into graves, even on the undoubted symbolic level that is intended, where the reference is clearly to their poetry and not their persons. In any case, this outburst of spleen is what convinces Moneta to give her ultimate gift of enlightenment to

Keats. This is, after all, a very harsh and purgatorial poem, written with the heart's blood of a poet who senses that death is all but upon him. If he is harsh toward others, he is also terribly harsh toward himself.

This Pythian spleen reminds us that Apollo, father of all verse and of medicine, is father also of pestilence. And pestilence haunts the remainder of *The Fall of Hyperion,* though it is the pestilence of tragedy, "an immortal sickness that kills not."

Keats has won for himself a fuller sense of identity, but he still needs to know where he is, at whose altar he stands, and who Moneta is. She replies with altered tone to his fresh questionings. But what she tells, which is essentially the story of the first Hyperion, is less important to Keats or to us than is her own silent countenance, when she finally unveils it to the poet. Just as the *Purgatorio* climaxes at the end of the thirty-first canto, when Beatrice unveils herself to Dante, so *The Fall of Hyperion* attains its vision of truth when Keats gazes upon the revealed face of the surviving Titaness:

> Then saw I a wan face,
> Not pined by human sorrows, but bright-blanch'd
> By an immortal sickness which kills not;
> It works a constant change, which happy death
> Can put no end to; deathwards progressing
> To no death was that visage; it had pass'd
> The lily and the snow; and beyond these
> I must not think now, though I saw that face.
> But for her eyes I should have fled away.
> They held me back with a benignant light,
> Soft mitigated by divinest lids
> Half closed, and visionless entire they seem'd
> Of all external things.

The face of Moneta is a symbolic eternity, for it has passed beyond the strife of contraries, passed the lily and the snow, passed even the discursive antithesis between being and non-being. It is a wan face, but it has assumed the authentic expression of tragedy, and is no longer pined by human sorrows. A series of oxymorons follows, playing upon the meanings of sickness, change, and death,

and so modifying those barren meanings that they become a thousand things, and so their barrenness exists no more.

Keats's problem from this passage on is precisely the reverse of
the problem that caused him to abandon *Hyperion,* and one may
wonder whether a solution was possible in either poem. In *Hyperion,* Keats began with the myth of the fall of Saturn, and had
to manage a transition to his personal myth of poetic incarnation.
In the *Fall,* he began with his own dying into the life of tragic
poetry, and next had to externalize this theme into its affinities with
the story of the Titans. But the affinities are strained, and the
Titanic myth is irrelevant to Keats's more intense concerns. Apollo
is really all Keats needs for his own myth, and so *The Fall of
Hyperion* tends to break into two poems, the one I have been dis-
cussing and the remainder, which is mostly a revision of the first
Hyperion. Only two passages more add anything to the theme of
Keats's relation to the content of his own vision, his status in his
own poetry. In the first, as soon as he sees Saturn, and hears Moneta
identify the god, he applies to himself Apollo's words of self-
deification:

> whereon there grew
> A power within me of enormous ken,
> To see as a god sees, and take the depth
> Of things as nimbly as the outward eye
> Can size and shape pervade.

To see as a god sees, in depth, is now to see as a poet sees,
directly into the phenomenology of inner realities. In a second passage, Keats lauds the strength of what is mortal as being enough to
sustain the final intensities of tragic vision:

> Without stay or prop,
> But my own weak mortality, I bore
> The load of this eternal quietude,
> The unchanging gloom and the three fixed shapes
> Ponderous upon my senses, a whole moon.

This is not the kind of expressiveness one expects to find in epic
or even in romance; Keats is moving toward the tragic drama he
was not to survive to compose. *The Fall of Hyperion* has neither

the high finish or style nor the radical unity of *The Triumph of Life*, but like the *Triumph* it leaves us with the impression of a perfection grasped, and of a personal art brought to its moral limits.

To Autumn

To AUTUMN is the subtlest and most beautiful of all Keats's odes, and as close to perfection as any shorter poem in the English language. That is of course cliché, but it cannot be *demonstrated* too often (it is more frequently asserted than evidenced). The incredible richness of this ode is such that it will sustain many readings, and indeed will demand them. To paraphrase G. Wilson Knight, *To Autumn* is a round solidity casting shadows on the flat surfaces of our criticism; we need as many planes at as many angles as we can get.

I am studying Romantic argument in these pages, and the argument of *To Autumn* is largely implicit. The problem here is to externalize it without removing it from the poem's own context.

The Autumn of the first stanza is a process and a beneficent agricultural conspirer, plotting secretly with the sun to bring ripeness to a state of all. The stanza is aureate, Spenserian in the globed fullness of its style, replete with heavily accented, single-syllabled parts of speech. As process Autumn loads, blesses, bends, fills, swells, plumps, and sets budding. The only receptive consciousness of all this activity is that of the bees, who sip their aching pleasure nigh to such a glut that "they think warm days will never cease," for the honey of harvest pleasure has "o'er-brimm'd" their natural storehouses. The fullness of nature's own grace, her free and overwhelming gift of herself, unfallen, is the burden of this ripe stanza. There is only a slight, but vital premonitory shading: the *later* flowers have deceived the bees.

The first stanza is natural process; the remaining two stanzas are sensuous observation of the consequences of that process: first, sights of the harvest in its final stages; then, post-harvest sounds, heralding the coming-on of winter. The sequence of the three stanzas then is pre-harvest ripeness, late-harvest repletion, and post-harvest natural music. The allocation of the senses is crucial: the late-harvest art is plastic and graphic—the art of millennium. The art past ripeness and harvest is the art of the ear, apocalyptic, the final harmonies of music and poetry. Here Keats, like Shelley, is Wordsworth's pupil. In the *Intimations* ode the visible glory departed with the summer of the body; the ear, far inland, could yet hear the immortal sea, and so brought the eye back to the autumnal coloring of a sobered but deepened imagination. The same process of heightened autumnal vision is celebrated by Shelley in the final stanzas of his *Hymn to Intellectual Beauty* and *Ode to the West Wind*. A more serene triumph awaits the modification of Wordsworth's myth in the final stanza of *To Autumn*. The very same movement from sight to sound to final sight may be traced also in the Night the Ninth of Blake's *The Four Zoas*, where the beauty of the harvest of Millennium yields to the clamor of Apocalypse, to be succeeded by a final beauty beyond harvest. The ultimate literary archetype for all this Romantic tradition is of course Biblical.

As the second stanza of *To Autumn* opens, we see Autumn already "amid" her store. The promised overabundance of the first stanza has been fulfilled; the harvest plot has been successful, the blessing so overflowing that nature's grace abounds. Autumn is no longer active process, but a female overcome by the fragrance and soft exhaustion of her own labor. She is passive, an embodiment of the earthly paradise, the place of repose, after the sexual and productive activity hinted at by her having been "close bosom-friend of the maturing sun." But she is also the peasant girl drunk with the odors and efforts of gathering, winnowing, reaping, and gleaning. She sits *"careless"* on the granary floor; the word is very rich. She is careless because there is more to be stored, though she sits, and yet amid all the fresh abundance she can indeed be without care. But the wind, softly lifting her hair, which *is* the unreaped grain, reminds us of the winnowing yet to be done. Again, she lies on her "half-reap'd furrow sound asleep, drows'd with the fume of poppies," late bee-deceiving flowers, which in a sense deceive her also. But the poem celebrates her drowsiness even as it gently chides her, for her hook, in *sparing* the next swath, spares also its twined flowers.

The final four lines of the stanza take us to the very end of harvest, the gleaner bearing her laden head so steadily as to suggest motionlessness even as she moves, which further suggests the running-down to stasis of a process. Finally we are shown the girl patiently watching, hours by hours, the meaningful sameness of the "cyder-press" with its final oozings, the last wealth of complete process itself. With those "hours by hours" we are ready for the music of time in the final stanza. We begin with only the "stubble-plains," but even as they are seen to have their own peculiar visual beauty, so we are able to say that the songs of Spring have been replaced by a different but not a lesser music.

> Where are the songs of Spring? Ay, where are they?
>   Think not of them, thou hast thy music too,—
> While barred clouds bloom the soft-dying day,
>   And touch the stubble-plains with rosy hue;
> Then in a wailful choir the small gnats mourn
>   Among the river sallows, borne aloft
>   Or sinking as the light wind lives or dies;
> And full-grown lambs loud bleat from hilly bourn;
>   Hedge-crickets sing; and now with treble soft
> The red-breast whistles from a garden croft;
>   And gathering swallows twitter in the skies.

This stanza looks back to the concluding lines of Coleridge's *Frost at Midnight,* where we hear

>   the redbreast sit and sing
> Betwixt the tufts of snow on the bare branch
> Of mossy apple-tree, while the nigh thatch
> Smokes in the sun-thaw

and also forward to the final stanza of Stevens' *Sunday Morning,* where

>   at evening,
> In the isolation of the sky,
> Casual flocks of pigeons make
> Ambiguous undulations as they sink
> Downwards to darkness, on extended wings.

Coleridge is extolling the sweetness even of winter as it will present itself to the country-reared, still-infant Hartley. Stevens, possibly remembering Keats even as Keats may be remembering Coleridge, is offering an image of natural death as an imaginative finality, a human consummation to be wished, though not devoutly. Keats is doing both: praising the red-breast and winter's other singers, and finding in the predeparture twitterings of the gathering swallows an emblem of natural completion. Winter descends here as a man might hope to die, with a natural sweetness, a natural movement akin to the extended wings of Stevens' pigeons or the organizing songs of Keats's swallows as they gather together for flight beyond winter. The day dies soft in this great stanza; the late flowers and poppies of Stanzas I and II are replaced by the barred clouds that bloom the twilight and touch the stubble-plains with rosy hue. And though the *small* gnats mourn in a wailful choir, the sound of their mourning is musically varied by the caprice of the *light* wind, as it lives or dies; the poet's touch itself is light here. A final music replaces the lightness of the mourning. The "full-grown lambs" are now ready for their harvest, having completed their cycle. The "hedge-crickets" are heard across the exhausted landscape; the winter singer, the "red-breast," adds his soft treble, and the departing birds, seeking another warmth, close the poem, which has climaxed in an acceptance of process beyond the possibility of grief. The last seven lines are all sound: natural music so varied and intense as to preclude even natural lament. We feel that we might be at the end of tragedy or epic, having read only a short ode. Where the *Nightingale, Urn,* and *Melancholy* odes left us with the contraries, *To Autumn* fulfills the promise of the *Ode to Psyche: t*o let the warm love in, to resolve contraries, because there is no further need for progression.

Bright Star

BRIGHT STAR, the best of Keats's sonnets, left by him unpublished, written on a blank page in Shakespeare's Poems, facing *A Lover's Complaint,* is a direct analogue to the ode *To Autumn,* for it also is a poem beyond argument, though not also calm in mind, for passion informs it throughout. The octet is one of the major expressions of Keats's humanism; the sestet one of the most piercing of his longings after the world of Beulah land, the breathing garden of repose beyond bounds. The unity of the poem is constituted by its total freedom from Keats's characteristic conflicts. The octet shares in the resolution to *To Autumn,* giving us an anagoge of poetic eternity, without contraries. The sestet, as a Beulah poem, is set in that state of being where, according to Blake, "all contraries are equally true."

The initial line is a prayer. The next seven lines *describe* the steadfastness of the star, after making it clear that Keats wants to be as steadfast as the star, but not in the star's way of steadfastness. The sestet describes Keats's mode of desired being, and finally declares for an eternity of this being, or an immediate swoon to death. This tight structure confines a remarkable contrast, between the state of Eden and the state of Beulah, Blake would have said, but Keats, by his own choice, clearly opts for the lower paradise as his own.

The Miltonic bright star is not God's hermit but nature's patient, sleepless eremite. Never sleeping, its "eternal lids apart," like Milton's Eyelids of the Morning, it watches

> The moving waters at their priestlike task
> Of pure ablution round earth's human shores.

"Human shores" is powerfully Blakean; the contrast here is between the star as motionless, solitary hermit, and the waters as moving, companionable priest, the one watching, the other cleansing man. We miss the force of this if we do not see it as humanistic, not Christian, in its religious emphasis. The oceans themselves, as a part of unfallen nature, perform their task of *pure* ablution, and the shores of earth are themselves *human.* That last is more than similitude, i.e., metaphor; it is identity, anagogical typology. As Blake saw the physical universe as having itself an ultimately human form, so here also Keats sees the shores of earth as being "men seen afar." As in *To Autumn,* nature alone is sufficient for purifying herself and ourselves, insofar as we can still be hers. Nature's own grace, akin to Keats's poetry, reveals the human countenance of earth:

> Or gazing on the new soft fallen mask
> Of snow upon the mountains and the moors.

The snow is a mask because it covers the human features of earth—that is, mountains and moors. Keats does not ask for himself the priestlike work of the moving waters, though he had asked for

the equivalent in *The Fall of Hyperion*. Here, at the furthest reach
of his poetry, he prays instead for the hermit star's eminence and
function, to watch, benevolently, nature's work of humanizing herself. But in his own place; "not in lone splendour hung aloft the
night," but in his own Gardens of Adonis, where, still steadfast,
still unchangeable (though how, there, can he expect that?) he
will be able

> Pillow'd upon my fair love's ripening breast,
> To feel for ever its soft fall and swell,
> Awake for ever in a sweet unrest,
> Still, still to hear her tender-taken breath
> And so live ever.

Her breast would be forever ripening, never ripe; keeping its
sleeping rhythm forever while Keats, awake forever in his sweet
unrest, could hear always that recurrence of her breath. This poem
can help explain Keats's life; his life cannot explain the poem.
Alternatively, the poem can help explain certainly contemporary
psychological reductions of human desire, but *they* cannot explain
it. Bunyan or Blake can explain the poem better than Freud or
Keats's biography. Keats had come a long road before coming to
the desired bower of *Sleep and Poetry* and *Endymion* again, but
to that paradisal bower he returned. Had Keats lived longer, his
poetry might have gone on from the broken arch of *The Fall of
Hyperion;* the octet of this sonnet can be taken as demonstration.
But the sestet is the ballast, as the poet, being one with the body of
the man, must accept its limits.

The poet and man alike, at the end, longed for "the Country of
Beulah, where the Air was very sweet and pleasant, the way lying
directly through it." *Through* it, Bunyan insists, as Blake did after
him, for "it was upon the borders of Heaven." But Keats's is a
vision more natural and less strenuously human, more merely human, than that of Blake, or the theocentric Bunyan. Keats, and his
poetry, at the last, would have been well content to rest permanently
"within the sight of the City they were going to."

CHAPTER SEVEN

BEDDOES, CLARE, DARLEY, AND OTHERS

My word I poured. But was it cognate, scored
Of that tribunal monarch of the air
Whose thigh embronzes earth, strikes crystal Word
In wounds pledged once to hope—cleft to despair?

HART CRANE

THE two decades between the deaths of Keats, Shelley, and Byron and the full emergence of the representative Victorian poets are the twilight time of English Romanticism. A remarkable group of poets sustained imaginative defeat in this period, two of them men whose imaginative power promised at least as much as the Victorians performed. Beddoes and Clare, ruins of given circumstance, survive as poets of extraordinary individuality. Darley, Hood, Hartley Coleridge, and Wade are lesser figures, but all of them wrote poems that are genuine and firm successes in what was only beginning to be a period style. Each in his way came close to incarnating again the poetical character whose rebirth Collins had celebrated, and Blake, Wordsworth, Coleridge, and their younger successors had exemplified.

1   *Thomas Lovell Beddoes: Dance of Death*

BEDDOES should have been a great poet, but failed for want of a subject. As a poet of death he is equal to the Shelley he imitated, the poet of *The Cenci* and *The Sensitive Plant*. Only death met the desire of his imagination, but a poet cannot demonstrate his creative exuberance in a celebration of death alone. Beddoes' "death" is as lively as it can be, and yet does not afford him much opportunity to redress the poverty of life.

Beddoes, born in 1803, was a physician by profession, but more of a wanderer than anything else. He spent most of his mature life in Germany and Switzerland, as a student of medicine, a revolutionary agitator, an infrequently practicing doctor, and a companion of actors and journalists. Homosexuality seems to have been the cause of Beddoes' self-exile, but his Shelleyan Romanticism would probably have led him out of the England of 1825 even if his rebellion had been without a sexual aspect.

Beddoes poisoned himself in 1849, after an earlier attempt at suicide had resulted in self-mutilation. He left in manuscript his enormous and unfinished major work, *Death's Jest-Book,* a poem of Romantic apocalypticism barely disguised by its form of Jacobean revenge-drama. Scattered through the blank-verse scenes of this endless play are dozens of songs, many of them very beautiful. Beddoes' imagination is a grotesque version of his master Shelley's, and lacks Shelley's range and sanity, though it possesses an intensity hardly short of Shelley's own. The plot of *Death's Jest-Book* is not worth paraphrase, but the obsessive themes of the drama and Beddoes' other works are interesting for their own power and as evidences of the dying phase of the movement of imagination that Blake and Wordsworth had so greatly begun.

As an Oxford student in 1822, Beddoes wrote a little elegy for Shelley in a blank leaf of the *Prometheus Unbound,* saluting the drowned poet as an angelic Spirit "sphered in mortal earth." The homage thus declared persists through Beddoes' poetry, but even the poet of *Adonais* and *The Triumph of Life* would have been uncomfortable with the work of his deathly disciple. For Beddoes seeks no triumph over death, chance, and time, but surrenders his being to them. He embraces the grave for what is very nearly its own sake:

> The earth is full of chambers for the dead,
> And every soul is quiet in his bed;
> Some who have seen their bodies moulder away,
> Antediluvian minds,—most happy they,
> Who have no body but the beauteous air,
> No body but their minds. Some wretches are
> Now lying with the last and only bone
> Of their old selves, and that one worm alone
> That ate their heart: some, buried just, behold
> Their weary flesh, like an used mansion, sold
> Unto a stranger, and see enter it
> The earthquake winds and waters of the pit,
> Or children's spirits in its holes to play.

The inventiveness of this passage (written at Geneva, 1824) makes it almost playful. In a verse letter sent to his friend Procter, from Göttingen, in March 1826, Beddoes states his purpose in working at *Death's Jest-Book:*

> But he who fills the cups and makes the jest
> Pipes to the dancers, is the fool o' the feast.
> Who's he? I've dug him up and decked him trim
> And made a mock, a fool, a slave of him
> Who was the planet's tyrant: dotard Death:
> Man's hate and dread: not with a stoical breath
> To meet him like Augustus standing up,
> Nor with grave saws to season the cold cup
> Like the philosopher, nor yet to hail
> His coming with a verse or jesting tale
> As Adrian did and More: but of his night,
> His moony ghostliness and silent might
> To rob him, to uncypress him i' the light,
> To unmask all his secrets; make him play
> Momus o'er wine by torchlight is the way

To conquer him and kill; and from the day
Spurned, hissed and hooted send him back again
An unmask'd braggart to his bankrupt den.
For death is more "a jest" than Life, you see
Contempt grows quick from familiarity.
I owe this wisdom to Anatomy.

Beddoes was a skilled anatomist, but he scarcely fools himself here in his boast that he will rob death of its mystery. He is truer to the nature of *Death's Jest-Book* in the very fine *Dedicatory Stanzas* intended for it. The poet who, like Shelley, finds comfort in the stars appareling the evening sky, thus solacing himself for the world's harm, will receive no response from them:

Yet they, since to be beautiful and bless
Is but their way of life, will still remain
Cupbearers to the bee in humbleness,
Or look, untouched down through the moony rain,
Living and being worlds in bright content,
Ignorant, not in scorn, of his affection's bent.

Beddoes goes on, in the next stanza, to repeat Shelley's quest in the accents of the *Hymn to Intellectual Beauty:*

So thou, whom I have gazed on, seldom seen,
Perchance forgotten to the very name,
Hast in my thoughts the living glory been,
In beauty various, but in grace the same.
At eventide, if planets were above,
Crowning anew the sea of day bereft,
Swayed by the dewy heaviness of love,
My heart felt pleasure in the track thou'dst left:
And so all sights, all musings, pure and fair,
Touching me, raised thy memory to sight,
As the sea-suns awakes the sun in air,—
If they were not reflections, thou the light.
Therefore bend hitherwards, and let thy mildness
Be glassed in fragments through this storm and wildness.

This central and Shelleyan desire cannot prevail in Beddoes. The next and last stanza gives itself to death, for Beddoes, in the words of his esoteric drama, hungers "after wisdom, as the red sea after ghosts," and wisdom for him is itself ghostly. The world of *Death's Jest-Book* is strained and distracted, replete with creators and destroyers, and with the portents of death about to break into life. The ship that brings some of the drama's protagonists back to shore is called the *Baris*, the Orphic name for Charon's boat. Death is as close, human, and immediate as he was in Chaucer's *Pardoner's Tale*. Isbrand, the revenger turned court jester who is the poem's hero, resigns his emblem to death in these terms: "I will yield Death the crown of folly. He hath no hair, and in this weather might catch cold and die." The despairing Duke who is Isbrand's antagonist tries to summon back his dead beloved:

> She died. But Death is old and half worn out;
> Are there no chinks in 't? Could she not come to me?

There are many chinks, but through them come the unwanted, not the desired, dead. Beddoes' myth of resurrection has the grotesque power of its cabbalistic source, when it answers the question, "What tree is man the seed of?":

> Of a ghost;
> Of his night-coming, tempest-waved phantom:
> And even as there is a round dry grain
> In a plant's skeleton, which being buried
> Can raise the herb's green body up again;
> So is there such in man, a seed-shaped bone,
> Aldabaron, called by the Hebrews Luz,
> Which, being laid into the ground, will bear
> After three thousand years the grass of flesh,
> The bloody, soul-possessed weed called man.

The resurrection of the body has lost all its spiritual force here and is only another oddity of an obscure natural world. In such a world, death itself "is a hypocrite, a white dissembler," against whose authority rebellion is possible. The Duke, having evoked his dead enemy in the attempt to summon a loved one, takes the ghost home with him as a gesture of Romantic irony:

> Then there is rebellion
> Against all kings, even Death. Murder's worn out

And full of holes; I'll never make 't the prison,
Of what I hate, again. Come with me, spectre;
If thou wilt live against the body's laws,
Thou murderer of Nature, it shall be
A question, which haunts which, while thou dost last.
So come with me.

Out of this grisly companionship the Duke draws one of the
play's overt morals:

If man could see
The perils and diseases that he elbows,
Each day he walks a mile; which catch at him,
Which fall behind and graze him as he passes;
Then would he know that Life's a single pilgrim,
Fighting unarmed amongst a thousand soldiers.

This fine image is lessened by its context, which sets a low value
on life's unarmed courage. The attractions of death become more
overtly sexual as the play's horrors multiply. A phantom wooer
tempts his earthly love by assuring her that the dead are full of
"grace and patient love and spotless beauty," and she yields to him.
A prince, self-poisoned, awaits death with a rhetoric finer than any
he has turned toward life:

I begin to hear
Strange but sweet sounds, and the loud rocky dashing
Of waves, where time into Eternity
Falls over ruined worlds.

The emptiness of the drama is redeemed only in the self-parody
of its songs, the best of which are triumphs of Romantic irony. A
ghost sings the song he learned "one May-morning in Hell," an
inventive lyric in which Adam and Eve are reborn as two carrion
crows, the new lords of creation, nesting in the skull of human
beauty. Another ghost wins a mortal maiden with an exquisite love
lyric with a sinister refrain:

Sweet and sweet is their poisoned note,
The little snakes of silver throat,
In mossy skulls that nest and lie,
Ever singing "die, oh! die."

The finest of these lyrics, the *Song of the Stygian Naiades,* retells the story of Proserpine, involuntary queen of Hell, who wanders "red with anger, pale with fears" as her amorous king, Pluto, nightly comes home with yet another earthly maiden. The poem's content and its delicate, complex metrical form are deliberately inconsonant, which is typical of Beddoes' work. Beddoes, in despair of his time and of himself, chose to waste his genius on a theme that baffled his own imagination. The postulate of Beddoes' poetry is a world in which every metaphor resolves itself as another figure of death. For Beddoes the separation between subject and object is bridged not by any imaginative act, as in Blake, Wordsworth, and Shelley, but by dying. Memory conquers death for life in Wordsworth, while Blake and the Shelley of *Prometheus* tried to see death as only another dimension of life, as Stevens did after them. But Beddoes abandoned hope in earth's renewal. In him the apocalyptic impulse of Romanticism degenerated into the most ironic of its identifications, and death and the imagination became one.

2 *John Clare: The Wordsworthian Shadow*

Clare is a poet who became homeless at home, naturally and tragically conscious of exclusion from nature.

GEOFFREY GRIGSON

> *And Memory mocked me, like a haunting ghost,*
> *With light and life and pleasures that were lost.*
> *As dreams turn night to day, and day to night,*
> *So Memory flashed her shadows of that light*
> *That once bade morning suns in glory rise,*
> *To bless green fields and trees and purple skies,*
> *And wakened life its pleasures to behold;—*
> *That light flashed on me, like a story told*
>
> CLARE, *The Dream* (1821)

CLARE is the most genuine of poets, and yet it does not lessen him to say that much of his poetry is a postscript to Wordsworth's, even as Beddoes, Darley, and Thomas Hood are epigoni in their poetry to Shelley and Keats. It is not that Clare is just a Hartley Coleridge, writing, however well, out of greater men's visions. Clare's vision is as unique as Grigson has insisted it is.[47] But the mode of that vision, the kind of that poetry, is Wordsworth's and Coleridge's. Clare's relation to Wordsworth is closer even than Shelley's in *Alastor* or Keats's in *Sleep and Poetry*. Clare does not imitate Wordsworth and Coleridge. He either borrows directly, or else works on exactly parallel lines, intersected by the huge Wordsworthian shadow.

Clare's dialectic begins like Wordsworth's, passes into a creative opposition resembling that in Coleridge's *Dejection: An Ode,* and climaxes, in a handful of great poems, remarkably close to Blake's. Here is a Song of Experience Blake would have joyed to read, written perhaps twenty years after Blake's death, and in probable ignorance of the greater visionary:

> I hid my love when young till I
> Couldn't bear the buzzing of a fly;
> I hid my love to my despite
> Till I could not bear to look at light:
> I dare not gaze upon her face
> But left her memory in each place;
> Where'er I saw a wild flower lie
> I kissed and bade my love goodbye.

It is terrifying, altogether beautiful, and thoroughly Blakean. The language itself is almost Blake's: it lacks only the terminology. He had put his emanation away from him, in Blake's terms, and he suffered the intolerable consequences. With the total form of all he created and loved put aside, he could not bear the minutest of natural particulars, for he had concealed his vision behind nature. Averted from light, like the protagonist in Blake's *Mad Song,* he peopled nature with "her memory," substituting that treacherous faculty for the direct imaginative apprehensive of a human face. And so, necessarily, his bondage to nature is completed.

> I met her in the greenest dells,
> Where dewdrops pearl the wood bluebells;

> The lost breeze kissed her bright blue eye,
> The bee kissed and went singing by,
> A sunbeam found a passage there,
> A gold chain round her neck so fair;
> As secret as the wild bee's song
> She lay there all the summer long.

Amid so much magnificence, it is the word "secret" that takes the stanza's burden of meaning. The fly's buzzing of the first stanza is reinforced here by the bee's song; the entire second stanza is an intensification of the last couplet of the first. His imaginings are reduced to illusions, the deceptions of fancy: the sunbeam as gold chain, the dewdrops on bluebells as her eyes. What remains is the madness of destroyed vision:

> I hid my love in field and town
> Till e'en the breeze would knock me down;
> The bees seemed singing ballads o'er,
> The fly's bass turned a lion's roar;
> And even silence found a tongue,
> To haunt me all the summer long;
> The riddle nature could not prove
> Was nothing else but secret love.

Part of the sudden increase in rhetorical power here is due to skillful repetition, augmenting the increased weakness of the protagonist and the growth in power of the hostile Spectre he has created in nature. The breeze, the fly's roar, the bee's cyclic repetitiveness in song are the lengthening external shadow of the Selfhood within, which comes entirely to dominate the speaker, confining him in solipsistic isolation from his beloved nature itself. Like all solipsists, he must subside in tautology, which is almost a definition of Blake's state of Ulro. So even silence finds a tongue to haunt him. The final couplet is difficult. Nature could not "prove" the riddle of secret love in any sense, test or demonstrate or solve. Nature, either before or after the hiding of his love, was inadequate to conceal or retain or even identify her. He has lost both, nature and love.

In this poem, and in *I Am!*, *A Vision*, and *An Invite to Eternity*, Clare wrote as Blake wrote, against the natural man (Grigson notes

this for *A Vision*). These poems are palinodes; they need to be
set against some of Clare's best Wordsworthian poems: *Pastoral
Poesy, To the Rural Muse, To the Snipe, The Eternity of Nature,*
and the late poems, *The Sleep of Spring* and *Poets Love Nature,*
which belong to the so-called asylum poems written during Clare's
confinement in an insane asylum. Taking these together, we will
still not have considered all of Clare, even in modest representation.
Nothing in either group of poems resembles the grim and meticu-
lous power of *Badger,* a poem prophesying Edward Thomas and
Frost, or the Shakespearean purity of a song like *Clock-a-clay.* But
these two groups of poems, which contain some of his most characteristic (and best) work do show the Romantic Clare, as a Wordsworthian and as a final independent visionary, equal at his most
intense to Smart and Blake. And a consideration of them should
further illuminate the varieties of Romantic dialectic, in its endless
interplay between nature and imagination.

In *Joys of Childhood* (no certain date) Clare is closest to Wordsworth. Here, in eight Spenserian stanzas, the *Intimations* ode is
recalled in two of its aspects, the child's glory and the sense of loss,
but not in its dialectic of saving memory. As in Wordsworth, the
child, knowing no mortality, *is* immortal:

> Their home is bliss, and should they dream of heaven
> 'Tis but to be as they before have been;
> The dark grave's gulf is naught, nor thrusts its shade between.

But, unlike Wordsworth, this initial consciousness of immortality
has no apocalyptic overtones:

> Oh, I do love the simple theme that tries
> To lead us back to happiness agen
> And make our cares awhile forget that we are men.

In his madness, Clare came again to overt celebration of his love
for that "simple theme":

> Wordsworth I love, his books are like the fields,
> Not filled with flowers, but works of human kind.

This sonnet, *To Wordsworth,* is perceptive both in analyzing the
master and in implying the disciple's affinity:

> A finer flower than gardens e'er gave birth,
> The aged huntsman grubbing up the root—
> I love them all as tenants of the earth:
> Where genius is, there often die the seeds.

Partially, this is the tribute of the man who could say:

> I found the poems in the fields
> And only wrote them down.

But it is more than that, for it records also the death of the *seeds* of genius, not the flowers. Clare's desire was the desire of Wordsworth, to find the unfallen Eden in nature, to read in her a more human face. But Clare ended with a tragic awareness of apocalyptic defeat, akin to Coleridge's, and hinting, in the very last poems, at Blake's and Shelley's rejection of nature. Clare's sensibility was more acute than Wordsworth's, and Clare, as a poet and as a man, died old.

Grigson has remarked that Clare's involvement in the visionary complex of the *Intimations* and *Dejection* odes is most clearly indicated in the radiance of *Pastoral Poesy:*

> But poesy is a language meet,
> And fields are every one's employ
> The wild flower 'neath the shepherd's feet
> Looks up and gives him joy.

So far Wordsworth, but the burden is darker:

> An image to the mind is brought,
> Where happiness enjoys
> An easy thoughtlessness of thought
> And meets excess of joys.

> And such is poesy; its power
> May varied lights employ,
> Yet to all minds it gives the dower
> Of self-creating joy.

"Self-creating joy": without arguing, but by a mysterious synthesis, Clare has passed to Coleridge. As in Wordsworth, the resolution is in a particular silence, from which the varied autumnal music emerges:

And whether it be hill or moor,
   I feel where'er I go
A silence that discourses more
   Than any tongue can do.

Unruffled quietness hath made
   A peace in every place
And woods are resting in their shade
   Of social loneliness.

The storm, from which the shepherd turns
   To pull his beaver down,
While he upon the heath sojourns,
   Which autumn pleaches brown,

Is music, ay, and more indeed
   To those of musing mind
Who through the yellow woods proceed
   And listen to the wind.

Listening to the wind is an honored mode of summoning the Muse, and the wind is the music of reality to those of musing mind when they yield themselves to the "social loneliness" of nature. Without the strife of contraries, Clare passes from this *Tintern Abbey* vision to the *Dejection* climax:

The poet in his fitful glee
   And fancy's many moods
Meets it as some strange melody,
   A poem of the woods,

And now a harp that flings around
   The music of the wind;
The poet often hears the sound
   When beauty fills the mind.

So would I my own mind employ
   And my own heart impress,
That poesy's self's a dwelling joy
   Of humble quietness.

Whether the simplicity here is deliberate or not, we cannot say; in either case it is only *apparent* simplicity. When Blake employs an apparent simplicity in the *Songs of Innocence*, he takes care to hint, however subtly, that he is deliberate. Clare sets no traps; his "organized innocence" is straightforward, but not naïve. Clare's resolution in *Pastoral Poesy* of the Wordsworth-Coleridge visionary conflict is as "modern" as Rimbaud or Hart Crane; the *poem itself* is more than the therapy, as it was for Wordsworth and Coleridge, if less than the apocalyptic act it was for Blake. For Clare his poem is not a second nature but a kindly nurse or foster mother, and yet not a nurse who would have us forget the primal joy:

> That poesy's self's a dwelling joy
> Of humble quietness.

This goes beyond "a timely utterance gave that thought relief." Clare's desperation is still clearer in *The Progress of Rhyme:*

> O soul-enchanting poesy,
> Thou'st long been all the world with me;
> When poor, thy presence grows my wealth,
> When sick, thy visions give me health,
> When sad, thy sunny smile is joy
> And was from e'en a tiny boy.
> When trouble came, and toiling care
> Seemed almost more than I could bear,
> While threshing in the dusty barn
> Or squashing in the ditch to earn
> A pittance that would scarce allow
> One joy to smooth my sweating brow
> Where drop by drop would chase and fall,
> Thy presence triumphed over all.

The point of *The Progress of Rhyme* is to develop this early dependence until the chant's conclusion is inevitable for all of its breadth of identification:

> And hope, love, joy, are poesy.

In some of the asylum poems, this Wordsworthian vision attains a final authority. The perfect sonnet of Romanticism may be the *Bright Star* of Keats, or Wordsworth on Westminster bridge or the Calais sands, or it may be this:

> Poets love nature and themselves are love,
> The scorn of fools, and mock of idle pride.
> The vile in nature worthless deeds approve,
> They court the vile and spurn all good beside.
> Poets love nature; like the calm of heaven,
> Her gifts like heaven's love spread far and wide:
> In all her works there are no signs of leaven,
> Sorrow abashes from her simple pride.
> Her flowers, like pleasures, have their season's birth,
> And bloom through regions here below;
> They are her very scriptures upon earth,
> And teach us simple mirth where'er we go.
> Even in prison they can solace me,
> For where they bloom God is, and I am free.

The concern for liberty here is not just the obsessional desire of an asylum-pent countryman; the liberty is freedom from Self, the mocking of the Spectre. The flowers are nature's scriptures *because* they teach mirth, and mirth endows Clare with the greater joy of liberty.

The most poignant of the asylum poems that look backward to Clare's early vision is *The Sleep of Spring,* a hymn of home yearnings, remarkable alike for its clear identification of Nature as a loving mother and its chilled recognition that there is no way back to her love:

> I loved the winds when I was young,
>   When life was dear to me;
> I loved the song which Nature sung,
>   Endearing liberty;
> I loved the wood, the vale, the stream,
> For there my boyhood used to dream.

In a few of the asylum poems, the sense of loss is transformed into a rejection of nature for a humanistic eternity, an apocalypse akin, as has been remarked, to Blake's. *Secret Love* is such a poem. But if one had to present only the best of Clare, the poems that are indisputably an absolute poetry, I would suggest a trilogy of *An Invite to Eternity, I Am,* and, most perfectly, *A Vision.* These are "Songs of Experience," as the aged Blake might have written, had he not by then gone on to a stage that he alone, finally, can demonstrate to be perhaps beyond the reach of a lyrical art.

Clare's invitation to eternity presents a problem in tone: how are these lines to be read?

> Wilt thou go with me, sweet maid
> Say, maiden, wilt thou go with me
> Through the valley depths of shade,
> Of night and dark obscurity,
> Where the path has lost its way,
> Where the sun forgets the day,—
> Where there's nor light nor life to see,
> Sweet maiden, wilt thou go with me?

Is it merely a Hades, nature projected in its worst aspects? Rather, a displacement of nature is involved, when the path "loses its way" and the sun "forgets," in a land

> Where stones will turn to flooding streams,
> Where plains will rise like ocean waves,
> Where life will fade like visioned dreams
> And mountains darken into caves,
> Say, maiden, wilt thou go with me
> Through this sad non-identity,
> Where parents live and are forgot,
> And sisters live and know us not.

More terrify than Hades and the eternities of Dante, this vision is of a state of changed natural identities and human non-identity. What is the moral and spiritual meaning, the trope and the anagoge, of a vision so hopeless, especially when it is presented as an invitation to a maiden?

> Say, maiden, wilt thou go with me
> In this strange death of life to be,
> To live in death and be the same
> Without this life, or home, or name,
> At once to be and not to be—
> That was and is not—yet to see
> Things pass like shadows, and the sky
> Above, below, around us lie?

This is, at its close, something like a vertigo of vision, necessary to sustain the paradox of simultaneously affirming both of Hamlet's contraries. Clare is attacking, as Blake did, the most rugged of the "cloven fictions," the dichotomy of being and non-being, a discursive antithesis alien to the imagination. But is *this* enough for a symbolic eternity?

> The land of shadows wilt thou trace,
> And look—nor know each other's face;
> The present mixed with reason gone,
> And past and present all as one?
> Say, maiden, can thy life be led
> To join the living with the dead?
> Then trace thy footsteps on with me;
> We're wed to one eternity.

This is more than enigmatic and yet less than obscure. Perhaps dark with excessive light, again like so much of Blake. What meaning can the poem's last line have if eternity is a state merely of non-identity? Why "wed" rather than "bound"? The poem seems to be an appeal for love and courage, and the close has a tone of something like triumph. Why, then, the striking "the present mixed with *reason gone*"? Last, and most crucial, if this *is* an invitation, where is the voluntary element in the vision? What lies in the will of the maiden?

The same questions, in kind, are evoked by the more powerful *I Am*, a poem on the nature of Coleridge's "great I Am," the Primary Imagination:

> I am: yet what I am none cares, or knows,
>   My friends forsake me like a memory lost,
> I am the self-consumer of my woes—
>   They rise and vanish in oblivious host,
> Like shadows in love's frenzied, stifled throes:—
> And yet I am, and live—like vapours tost
>
> Into the nothingness of scorn and noise,
>   Into the living sea of waking dreams,
> Where there is neither sense of life or joys,
>   But the vast shipwreck of my life's esteems;

Even the dearest, that I love the best,
Are strange—nay, rather stranger than the rest.

I long for scenes, where man hath never trod,
    A place where woman never smiled or wept—
There to abide with my Creator, God,
    And sleep as I in childhood sweetly slept,
Untroubling, and untroubled where I lie,
The grass below—above the vaulted sky.

"I am," God's *ehyeh asher ehyeh* reply to the questioning of His Name, is Coleridge's universal creative word, the primal imaginative act. The force of Clare's *I Am* is negative—I am, but what I am is uncared for and unknown, consumes its own woes, is as a vapor tossed into a sea of chaos, an infinity of nothingness. Memory is only a forsaking; it is necessarily lost. The yearning is apocalyptic —not for childhood but for scenes "where man hath never trod"; the break with Wordsworth is complete. For Clare the Fortunate Fields *are* "a history only of departed things." There is no goodly universe to be wedded to man in a saving marriage. The dower of a new heaven and a new earth, given by joy when we take nature as bride, is not to be paid. And Clare is looking for a place beyond the possibility of any marriage—"where woman never smiled or wept." This final yearning, to be free of nature and woman alike, is the informing principle of Clare's most perfect poem, the absolutely Blakean *A Vision:*

I lost the love of heaven above,
    I spurned the lust of earth below,
I felt the sweets of fancied love,
    And hell itself my only foe.

I lost earth's joys, but felt the glow
    Of heaven's flame abound in me.
Till loveliness and I did grow
    The bard of immortality.

I loved but woman fell away,
    I hid me from her faded fame,

> I snatch'd the sun's eternal ray
> And wrote till earth was but a name.
>
> In every language upon earth,
>   On every shore, o'er every sea,
> I gave my name immortal birth
>   And kept my spirit with the free.

Grigson applies to *A Vision* Blake's version of the Pauline distinction between the natural and the spiritual man, that is, the natural and the imaginative, seeing it as "repentance, an immortal moment reached after and attained." The best analogue in Blake is *To Tirzah*, where Blake's rejection of nature as the mother of his imagination is fitted into Jesus' denial of Mary as mother of more than his mortal part:

> Whate'er is Born of Mortal Birth
> Must be consumed with the Earth
> To rise from Generation free:
> Then what have I to do with thee?

Free from Generation and rejecting the changing earthly paradise of Beulah (Wordsworthian nature), Clare and Blake elect the creative paradise of Eden, in which the poet's pen is an eternal ray of the sun and the poem reduces earth to but a name. Clare's rejection of the earth is not merely orthodox, for, like Blake, he has lost the love of the heaven that is above. The crucial process of imaginative incarnation is in

> Till loveliness and I did grow
> The bard of immortality.

This is not Platonic loveliness, in simple contrast to "earth's joys," but a loveliness of vision. Clare himself, by this mutual interpenetration of growth with loveliness, grows into a world he helps create, the world of the Blakean visionary, where the earth as "hindrance, not action" is kicked away and the poet sees through the eye, not with it. *A Vision* is a lucid moment of immortality attained on August 2, 1844. Clare lived another twenty years without expressing such a moment so lucidly again. But the poems of those years are more serene; another Wordsworthian rose in Clare, remote without coldness. The very last poem, written in 1863, can be taken as an emblem of these last decades. The beauty of the verse here is more than its pathos; it stems from a perfect equilibrium between nature and a poet who has learned its limitations for the imagination, but yearns after it still. *Birds' Nests* is a simple pastoral description, but the arrangement, in its alternation of descriptive detail, is meaningful. Spring, the chaffinch nesting, the poet charmed by the bird's song, are succeeded by the bleakness of the wind over the open fen, hinting at the essential inadvertence of nature. But the picture is quietly resolved in warmth and leisure:

> 'Tis spring, warm glows the south,
> Chaffinch carries the moss in his mouth
> To filbert hedges all day long,
> And charms the poet with his beautiful song;
> The wind blows bleak o'er the sedgy fen,
> But warm the sun shines by the little wood,
> Where the old cow at her leisure chews her cud.

3   George Darley and Others: The Strangling Tide

DARLEY, a minor Keats, was born in Dublin in 1795. A stammerer from childhood, he sought refuge in poetry and mathematics, finding in their ultimate apprehensions consolation for his neuroses. He is very nearly the popular archetype of a Romantic poet in his deliberate rejection of a harsh actuality and his desperate adherence to more ideal realms than experience. But his art shows a continual awareness of the consequences of withdrawal. His favorite image is drowning, and most of his poems are siren songs that dissolve themselves in despair. Like Beddoes, he attempted pseudo-Elizabethan drama, but his more characteristic work is in rhapsody and lyric. In 1822, the year of Shelley's death, he published the rhapsodic *The Errors of Ecstasie,* which shows the influence of *Endymion* but not much coherence. His important effort is the still more

rhapsodic *Nepenthe* (privately circulated in 1839), a dream-poem
richer in latent than in manifest content, in the quest-romance
tradition of *Alastor* and *Endymion*. *Nepenthe* is in octosyllabics,
except for the interspersed lyrics, and has excellent movement if
murky significance. Overtly, it hymns what would have to be called
a manic-depressive cycle, with the first canto dedicated to over-joy
and the second to excessive melancholy. The poem's pattern is
purgatorial, and its explicit references to Dante's *Purgatorio* link it
to *The Fall of Hyperion* and *The Triumph of Life*. Sun and earth
dominate the joyous, moon and water the melancholy, canto.[48]

At the poem's opening the poet is alone and content in an earthly
paradise, pastoral and sunny. Dante, during his first night in Purgatory (Canto IX), dreams of an eagle that swoops down and snatches
him up to the fiery sphere, where he and the eagle burn together.
The visionary flame so scorches Dante that he awakes, to find that
he must climb higher in Purgatory. The eagle is a symbol of moral
purification and of baptismal regeneration, as by tradition an eagle,
in his old age, flies up into a circle of fire, is all but consumed there,
and then falls into a fountain of water, from which he rises renewed
and young. As Darley dreams, an eagle carries him off to the burning desert, where he beholds the death by fire and rebirth of the
Phoenix:

> O blest unfabled Incense Tree
> That burns in glorious Araby,
> With red scent chalicing the air
> Till earth-life grow Elysian there!

The rebirth of the Phoenix transforms the desert to Elysian oasis,
and inspires the poet to a Titanic quest for the Nepenthe or elixir
of life and poetry. Content until now with the sensuous world, he
seeks, like Endymion, for a more transcendental good. The Phoenix
is an image of life destroying itself in a manic intensity of gladness.
Darley drinks a drop of Phoenix blood and is carried along in a
Bacchic procession (derived from *Endymion*) of frustrating over-
joy, a sensual passion that finds no object. He receives an Icarian
warning of death by water, ignores it, and is pursued by maenads
until he plunges into deep ocean, again like Endymion, though
Endymion's descent for truth is voluntary.

The second canto is dark with images of sexual repression and self-induced melancholy, in contrast to the hysterical intensities of the first canto. The masculine aggressiveness of the poet-protagonist is expiated in a moon-governed watery world. The Nepenthe reappears, and under its influence Darley rises from his sea grave. He performs a purgative journey to the Nile's source, where he frees Memnon, the son of the Dawn Goddess, an act of liberation Heath-Stubbs accurately compares to Endymion's release of Glaucus. But he himself is no more freed than Endymion is. He continues his quest until he encounters the Unicorn, symbol of ultimate melancholy as the Phoenix was of a final gladness. His purgation fulfilled, he comes out of the desert again to ocean:

> Till I found me once again
> By the ever-murmuring main,
> Listening across the distant foam
> My native church bells ring me home.
> Alas! why leave I not this toil
> Thro' stranger lands, for mine own soil?
> Far from ambition's worthless coil,
> From all this wide world's wearying moil,—
> Why leave I not this busy broil,
> For mine own clime, for mine own soil,
> My calm, dear, humble, native soil!
> There to lay me down at peace
> In my own first nothingness?

In these deliberately helter-skelter verses, with their recurrent rhyme, the rhapsody comes to exhausted rest. *Nepenthe* is less an allegory than it is a direct projection of unresolved psychic torment, surrealistic in its abandonment and redundant sexual imagery. It is *Alastor* or *Endymion* with the informing control gone, and as a purgatorial poem of confession it lacks a bounding outline that could give it more than autobiographical significance. Like *Death's Jest-Book*, it represents a waste of imagination, and is more a tormented dream than a shaped vision.

Outside of the astonishing *Nepenthe*, Darley's best poem is the carefully paced *It Is Not Beauty I Demand*. Here, as in Beddoes and in the weaker aspect of Shelley, is an epitome of the Romantic resolution by suicide of the irreconcilable good and the means of good, beauty and the mode of its apprehension, love and its ex-

periential containment and reversal. The glory of Darley's lyric is
the completeness of its expression of contraries beyond hope, and
the coolness of tone that expression attains throughout:

> It is not Beauty I demand,
> A crystal brow, the moon's despair,
> Nor the snow's daughter, a white hand,
> Nor mermaid's yellow pride of hair.

This first stanza is the poem in little; the poem's procedure is
only to expand from these properties. The mermaid's attractions
are like

> Coral beneath the ocean-stream,
> Whose brink when your adventurer sips
> Full oft he perisheth on them.

The white hand holds an urn not to be praised, for its contents
are the dust of consumed hearts. The climax is one of the major
imaginative gestures of Romanticism, where the Syren's hair becomes at once the overwhelming ocean and the snaky locks of a
muse revealed as a succuba:

> For crystal brows—there's naught within,
> They are but empty cells for pride;
> He who the Syren's hair would win
> Is mostly strangled in the tide.

It is Darley's vision of his own imaginative fate, and the fate of
the poets of his transitional generation—"mostly strangled in the
tide." Thomas Hood, who spent his life struggling with the demons
of sickness and poverty, also knew the strangling favors of the Syren.
Hood's world is an exhausted version of Keats's sensuous domain,
with natural process run down into the stasis of death-in-life. In
Hood's poems light is torpid and Time sleeps, but only as does "a
dark dial in a sunless place." Hood's subjects are death, silence,
and nostalgia for childhood's lightness of spirit. Hartley Coleridge,
at his best in sonnets founded upon Wordsworth's, is most moving
in them when, like Clare or Hood, he laments the lost joys of childhood.

The last of the Romantics of the third generation is the now
forgotten poet Thomas Wade—like Beddoes, a disciple of Shelley.

Wade, born in 1805, continued a long and unsuccessful literary career until 1875, but his best and characteristic work was over by 1839, and the man survived the poet. The dark and majestic hymns *The Coming of Night* and *The Winter Shore* are like fragments of *Alastor* or *Mont Blanc,* relics of an energetic questing defeated by the inconsequence of natural reality. The note of Shelleyan rapture at confronting a sudden human radiance is struck for a last time in the experimental sonnets called *The Face:*

> So interflex'd, that, star by star, its graces
> Were noted not; but still in constellation:
> A harmony of grace, such as embraces
> The innermost spirit with its concord fine,
> But which sense cannot note by note define.

That, until our own day, is the dying fall of Romanticism, expiring in a graceful but tenuous indefinable. A dead Romantic, as Stevens remarked, is a falsification, and the Word of the autonomous human imagination had hardly been spoken for a last time. The last word here can fittingly be from Hart Crane's *The Broken Tower,* one of the greater Romantic odes of self-recognition, of the seer passing a last human judgment upon himself. The Romantic imagination ends, if at all, in an open question, and in the humanist conviction that mortality itself stirs the sense of possible sublimity, and so renews the latent power of something evermore about to be:

> The steep encroachments of my blood left me
> No answer (could blood hold such a lofty tower
> As flings the question true?)—or is it she
> Whose sweet mortality stirs latent power?

EPILOGUE:
THE PERSISTENCE
OF ROMANTICISM

1

I N T H E beginning, modern poetry abandoned most of what had served as the subject matter of European literary tradition from Homer to Pope. Wordsworth was the inventor of modern poetry, and he found no subject but himself. Even if we still held to the Arnoldian simplification of Wordsworth as poet of nature, we would recognize that Wordsworthian landscapes are all the products of an inward estrangement, that Wordsworth sees nothing but things-in-their-farewell. His consciousness of external nature is consciousness of separation, and if the nature with which he seeks a reciprocal relationship is frighteningly other than himself, the guilt for widening that separation is remarkably his own. Self-awareness of the intensity found in Rousseau and Wordsworth either did not exist before them, or for good reason was defined as a mode of madness. In Blake, paradoxically a less revolutionary, less modern poet than Wordsworth, intense self-awareness is still regarded as wholly a horror, and Blake's struggle in *Jerusalem* is to cast out the crippling self-consciousness embodied in that sublimely horrible creation, the Spectre of Urthona, a poor fiend in each of us, who is aware of every injury, and capable of no forgetfulness.

Much of Wordsworth's poetry is involved with Wordsworth's own struggle to cast out his spectral self-concern, and we tend in our time to think of Wordsworth as the poet of *The Prelude* and of such major lyrics as *Resolution and Independence* and the Great Ode, crisis poems concerned with the dangers of the poetic vocation. But the Wordsworth who dominated nineteenth-century poetry from his own time onward was the author of *The Excursion,* a poem we mostly do not read, and rightly dislike when we do compel ourselves to its experience. This Wordsworth, though he overtly preaches against the Solitary's errors, nevertheless fathered the poetry of his century though the figure of the Solitary. The line from the Solitary of *The Excursion* to the Shelley of *Alastor,* the Byron of *Childe Harold's Pilgrimage,* the Keats of *Endymion* is quite clear, as are the lines that lead from those poems to the early and decisive work of Browning, Tennyson, Arnold, and Yeats. At the end of this tradition of the Wordsworthian Solitary and his quest stand the great parody-poem, *The Comedian as the Letter C,* and the tormented questers of *The Waste Land* and *The Bridge.* If modern poetry has found its way out of Wordsworthianism, that way is not yet evident, though many critics have taken the opposite for granted.

Wordsworthian poetry moves us by its absolute relevance, and repels us by its as absolute repetitiveness. Our disease is not so much alienation as it is solipsism, and the subject of modern poetry is endlessly solipsism, or more simply the hopeless question: why is there no subject? There is a recent fashion for confessional verse, stemming from the conversion of Lowell's style that took place in *Life Studies.* The fallacy of the fashion, and even of its distinguished inventor, is that confessional verse is indeed too easy, vulgar, and disgusting when all verse is necessarily afflicted by self-consciousness anyway. The obliqueness of *The Auroras of Autumn* is self-revelatory, while the directness of Lowell's recent volumes is not. The old man walking the twilight beach, oppressed by creative loss and pondering the lesson of the northern lights, is as genuinely open to our understanding as the perplexed poet confronting the leech-gatherer was, but the middle-aged man shown in all the personal, even clinical detail that a wry nobility turns against itself remains as opaque to our apprehension as he is to his own. To embrace personality is as irrelevant for modern poetry as to flee it (in the pronouncements of Eliot and his school). Our poets were and are Romantic as poets used to be Christian, that is, whether they want to be or not.

2

POETRY, as the crown of articulate speech, was defended by Shelley against the ironic strictures of his friend Peacock, who prophesied the degradation of the art, "not from any decrease either of intellectual power, or intellectual acquisition, but because intellectual power and intellectual acquisition have turned themselves into other and better channels." Shelley's profound insight subverted Peacock's prophecy by returning to a sense of necessary priority: "Every original language near to its source is in itself the chaos of a cyclic poem: the copiousness of lexicography and the distinctions of grammar are the works of a later age, and are merely the catalogue and the form of the creations of poetry."

Our contemporary Peacock (though he lacks a saving irony) is Claude Lévi-Strauss, whose respect for mythical thought extends to music, but not to poetry: "Music and myth are languages which, each in its own way, transcend the level of articulate speech." Poetry, he tells us, is a descent from words to phonemes, a fall into language, a failure to transcend daily limitation. The meaning of a myth, he finds, is only to be conveyed by another myth, as the meaning of music is in other music, but Lévi-Strauss does not want to know what all the Romantics knew, that the meaning of any poem can only be another poem. Octavio Paz has attempted to be Shelley to Lévi-Strauss's Peacock, defending poetry as a greater transcendence than myth or music, but the anthropological reductiveness is likelier to be influential in a post-Romantic age. Romantic poetry has survived several varieties of reduction, and so will survive the structuralists, against whom it offers a fierce countercritique. In the structuralist view, myths have no authors and come into existence only when incarnated in a tradition, but the myths of Romanticism have authors, and then are embodied by tradition. Milton's Penseroso becomes Wordsworth's Solitary, and the Solitary in turn becomes Byron's pilgrim, Shelley's wandering poet, Keats's shepherd-prince, Browning's Paracelsus and Childe Roland, and later the wandering Oisin and Forgael of Yeats and the sublimely defeated Crispin of Stevens. This mythic quester, who is defeated every day yet to victory is born, has become more than a literary tradition, if we must yield to the anthropologists the notion that merely literary traditions are insufficiently authentic. So many nonliterary lives —British and American—in the nineteenth and twentieth centuries have wasted themselves in this erotic quest-pattern of the Romantic Solitary, that we can call this myth as grimly authentic as most we encounter.

Paz and others have investigated the odd blend of Buddhism and Marxism to which the structuralist vision itself reduces; as Paz says, "not the knowledge of the void: an *empty knowledge.*" Beyond the oddness is the tragic impulse to dehumanize, and no mode of criticism has dehumanized poetry more than structuralism. Freud, who recognized how little we understood of the poetic imagination, remains a greater dialectical critic of Romanticism than any analyst who has emerged from structuralism, including Lacan. Blake found in the word the true Minute Particular of his vision, an ascent out of language into a larger intelligibility. He may have been self-deceived; on structuralist premises he had to be, but then on those premises neither he nor Wordsworth nor any Romantic master can be regarded as more than a would-be mythmaker, a fanatic hoping to be a god.

3

FROM our current perspective, the Romantics are closer to the prophets of the Enlightenment than they can be to ourselves, despite their insurgence against mere rationalisms, and the persistence of their mythologies in all the major poets of our time (all of whom, after all, were born in the nineteenth century). Whatever our interpretation of Romantic poetry may be, however much we agree with or dissent from one another in our readings, we cannot read that poetry as it was meant to be read. Between the Romantics and ourselves too many shadows have fallen, and by the sad paradox of cultural history we know much less than Blake and Wordsworth knew, even as they knew less than Milton did. Not the knowledge of particulars is involved in this judgment, nor even the knowledge of knowledge, but a freedom to know appears to have been lost. The sorrows of poetic influence blight readers and critics even as they afflict poets, and the man who comes too late in the story is uncertain of his part in its design. Our readings are swervings or falls into language, and not the completions these poets rightfully expected. Blake was no gnostic, and yet almost all of his critics have become gnostics in expounding him, myself not excepted. Wordsworth meant to renovate his readers; the best of them have been comforted, and have even comforted others, but it was not for our comfort that so unique a temperament suffered his giant agonies. We go to the poets to make our souls, Yeats said, thinking of his relation to Shelley and to Keats, but no souls have been made in our own generations by these poets, not even among their most fanatic admirers. Whatever the use of Romantic poetry among us still may be, and doubtless there continues to be great use, it is not, cannot be what these Titans prophesied. Another time, whose presages are nowhere to be found about us, must come if at last this company of visionaries is not to be judged another heroic failure.

CHRONOLOGICAL TABLE

1721	Collins born
c.1745	*Ode on the Poetical Character*
1757	Blake born
1759	Collins died
1769–1778	*Poetical Sketches* (published 1783)
1770	Wordsworth born
1772	Coleridge born
1788	Byron born
1789–1794	*Songs of Innocence and of Experience*
1789	*The Book of Thel*
1790	*The Marriage of Heaven and Hell*
1792	Shelley born
1793	*Visions of the Daughters of Albion*
	Clare born (died 1864)
1794	*The Book of Urizen*
1795	Keats born
	The Eolian Harp
	Darley born
1795–1804	*The Four Zoas*
1796	Hartley Coleridge born
1797	*The Ancient Mariner*
	Christabel
1798	Hood born
	Frost at Midnight
	The Nightingale
	Kubla Khan
	France: An Ode
	Tintern Abbey
	The Old Cumberland Beggar
1798–1800	*The Recluse*
1799	*Nutting*
1799–1805	*The Prelude* (published 1850)
1800	*Michael*
1802	*Resolution and Independence*
	Dejection: An Ode
1802–1806	*Ode: Intimations of Immortality*

1803	Beddoes born
	The Crystal Cabinet
	The Mental Traveller
1804–1808	*Milton*
1804–1819	*Jerusalem*
1805	Wade born (died 1875)
	Peele Castle
	Ode to Duty
1806	*To William Wordsworth*
1812	*Childe Harold's Pilgrimage,* I and II
1814	*Laodamia*
	The Excursion published
1815	*Alastor*
1816	*Hymn to Intellectual Beauty*
	Mont Blanc
	Sleep and Poetry
	Childe Harold, III
	Byron's *Prometheus*
1817	*Limbo*
	Ne Plus Ultra (1826?)
	Endymion
	Manfred
1818	*Childe Harold,* IV
	Beppo
1818–1819	*Prometheus Unbound*
	Hyperion
1819	*The Eve of St. Agnes*
	La Belle Dame Sans Merci
	Lamia
	Bright Star
	Keats's Great Odes
	The Fall of Hyperion
	Ode to the West Wind
	Don Juan, I and II
	Stanzas to the Po
1820	*To a Skylark*
	The Two Spirits: An Allegory
	The Witch of Atlas
1821	*Epipsychidion*
	Keats died
	Adonais
	Cain
	Don Juan, III–V
1822	*The Triumph of Life*
	Shelley died
	The Vision of Judgment

1823	*Don Juan,* VI–XIV
1824	*Don Juan,* XV–XVI
	Byron died
1825–1849	*Death's Jest-Book*
1827	Blake died
1834	Coleridge died
1835	*Extempore Effusion upon the Death of James Hogg*
	Nepenthe
1843–1845	Clare's Asylum Poems
1845	Hood died
1846	Darley died
1849	Beddoes died
	Hartley Coleridge died
1850	Wordsworth died

NOTES

1. Letter to George Cumberland, April 12, 1827.
2. "Adagia," in *Opus Posthumous,* ed. Morse (New York, 1957).
3. *The Necessary Angel* (New York, 1951).
4. See M. H. Abrams, *The Mirror and the Lamp* (New York, 1953), pp. 55–56, 64–68, 288–289, 292–293.
5. "The Eye and the Object in the Poetry of Wordsworth," in *Wordsworth,* ed. Dunklin (Princeton, 1951), pp. 23–42.
6. "Towards Defining an Age of Sensibility," in *Eighteenth Century English Literature,* ed. Clifford (New York, 1959), p. 318.
7. *Anatomy of Criticism* (Princeton, 1957), p. 301.
8. "Collins and the Creative Imagination," in *Studies in English by Members of University College, Toronto,* ed. Wallace (Toronto, 1931), p. 60.
9. *Ibid.,* p. 62.
10. *Fearful Symmetry* (Princeton, 1947), pp. 169–170.
11. *Anatomy of Criticism,* pp. 203–206.
12. See Wallace Stevens' *Credences of Summer,* III.
13. *Fearful Symmetry,* p. 427.
14. The raven is the bird of Odin, the Urizen of Northern mythology.
15. *Fearful Symmetry,* p. 241.
16. *Anatomy of Criticism,* p. 323.
17. *Anatomy of Criticism,* pp. 308 -314.
18. "Notes for a Commentary on Milton," *The Divine Vision,* ed. de Sola Pinto (London, 1957), p. 101.
19. S. Foster Damon, *William Blake* (New York, 1924), p. 358.
20. "Introduction" to *Selected Poetry and Prose of Blake* (New York, 1953), p. xxiv.
21. *Fearful Symmetry,* p. 279.
22. H. M. Margoliouth, *William Blake* (London, 1951), pp. 124–25.
23. David Erdman, *Blake: Prophet against Empire* (Princeton, 1954), pp. 355–356, 369.
24. *Fearful Symmetry,* p. 298.
25. *Ibid.,* p. 332.
26. *Ibid.,* p. 383.
27. From his forthcoming book on Wordsworth. See also the chapter on Wordsworth in his *The Unmediated Vision* (New Haven, 1954).

28. A full discussion is in Abrams, "The Correspondent Breeze: A Romantic Metaphor," available in his *English Romantic Poets* (New York, 1960), pp. 37–54.
29. Pottle, "The Eye and the Object," p. 30.
30. *Anatomy of Criticism*, p. 213.
31. *The Liberal Imagination* (Anchor edition, 1953), p. 147.
32. Humphry House, *Coleridge* (London, 1953), pp. 94–95.
33. For a different emphasis, which has strongly influenced my own, see George Ridenour's *The Style of Don Juan* (New Haven, 1960), pp. 157–158.
34. *Anatomy of Criticism*, p. 216.
35. "On the Character of Rousseau," *Round Table*, no. XXIV.
36. *Fearful Symmetry*, p. 199.
37. *The Style of Don Juan*, p. 1.
38. *Anatomy of Criticism*, p. 234.
39. I am anticipated here by Ridenour, *The Style of Don Juan*, p. 100 n.
40. Ridenour gives a rather different account of "mobility" (pp. 162–166).
41. Ridenour, p. xiii.
42. For a view directly contradictory to my own, see Donald Davie, *Purity of Diction in English Verse* (London, 1953), p. 133; also reprinted in Abrams, *English Romantic Poets*, p. 307.
43. My terms here are derived from Pottle.
44. See my *Shelley's Mythmaking* (New Haven, 1959), p. 139.
45. *Fearful Symmetry*, p. 377.
46. For a full reading of this remarkable lyric see F. A. Pottle, "The Case of Shelley," reprinted in Abrams, *English Romantic Poetry*, pp. 289–305.
47. Geoffrey Grigson, "Introduction," *Selected Poems of John Clare* (London, 1950), pp. 1–20.
48. An acute reading of *Nepenthe*, to which I am indebted at several points, can be found in John Heath-Stubbs, *The Darkling Plain* (London, 1950), which contains the best study of the generation of Beddoes and Darley.

INDEX

Abrams, M. H., 226, 471 n. 4, 472 n. 28
Aeolian harp, 200-02, 225, 288, 301-02, 472 n. 28
Ahania, 32, 85
Albion (in Blake), 24, 32, 54, 72, 74, 307
Amos, 151, 204
Apollo, the Romantic, 12-15, 166, 217, 220, 364, 368, 396-98
Arnold, Matthew, 1, 194, 391
Atlas, 54, 110
Auden, W. H., 150
Augustine, St., 146

Barbauld, Anna Laetitia, 9
Beddoes, Thomas Lovell, 438-44, 456, 458; *Death's Jest-Book,* commentary, 440-44, 458; *Song of the Stygian Naiades,* 444
Beulah, state of (in Blake), commentary, 20-31, 51, 57, 63, 73, 105, 106, 144
Bion, 343
Blake, William: comments on Wordsworth, 125-28, 142, 146, 174; *Ah! Sun-flower,* commentary, 45-46, 68; *Auguries of Innocence,* 36; *The Book of Ahania,* 79, 85; *The Book of Thel,* commentary, 49-53, 314, 369; *The Book of Urizen,* commentary, 71-79, 306; *The Chimney Sweeper,* 41; *The Crystal Cabinet,* commentary, 56-58, 387; *The Divine Image,* commentary, 42-43; *Earth's Answer,* 44; *The Ecchoing Green,* 35; *The Four Zoas,* commentary, 80-97, 283, 317, 433; *The Ghost of Abel,* 254; *Holy Thursday,* 41,

42; *How Sweet I Roam'd,* 17-18; *The Human Abstract,* 42, commentary, 43-44, 74, 180; *Introduction to Songs of Experience,* 44; *Introduction to Songs of Innocence,* 34; *Jerusalem,* 57, 72, commentary, 108-23, 126; *The Lamb,* 35, commentary, 39; *The Little Black Boy,* commentary, 39-41; *London,* commentary, 46-47; *Mad Song,* commentary, 18-19, 445; *The Marriage of Heaven and Hell,* commentary, 64-70, 306, 386; *The Mental Traveller,* commentary, 58-64, 306, 362; *Milton,* commentary, 97-108, 125; *My Spectre around me night & day,* 72-73; *The Shepherd,* 35; *The Sick Rose,* commentary, 44-45; *To Autumn,* 16; *To Morning,* 16-17; *To Spring,* 15; *To Summer,* 15-16; *To the Evening Star,* 17; *To the Muses,* 19; *To Tirzah,* commentary, 47-48, 455; *To Winter,* 16; *The Tyger,* commentary, 35-39, 76, 293; *Vala,* 81; *Visions of the Daughters of Albion,* commentary, 53-56, 335
Boccaccio, Giovanni, 310, 379
Bower of Bliss (in Spenser), 25, 28
Brawne, Fanny, 379
Bridges, Robert, 9
Bunyan, John, 315, 437; *The Pilgrim's Progress,* 20
Burns, Robert, 166
Burton, Robert, *Anatomy of Melancholy,* 379, 387
Byron, George Gordon, Lord: *Beppo,* commentary, 255-57;

Byron, George Gordon, Lord (*cont.*)
Cain, commentary, 253-55; *Childe Harold's Pilgrimage,* commentary, 238-45, 367, 399; *Don Juan,* 3, 193, commentary, 257-72, 326; *I watched thee when the foe was at our side,* 280-81; *Manfred,* commentary, 248-52; *Ode to a Lady,* 276; *On this day I complete my thirty-sixth year,* 279-80; *Prometheus,* commentary, 245-48; *Stanzas to the Po,* commentary, 276-78, 279; *The Vision of Judgment,* commentary, 272-76

Carroll, Lewis, 169
Chapman, George, 50, 392
Chatterton, Thomas, 15, 166, 217, 347, 370
Chaucer, Geoffrey, *The Pardoner's Tale,* 179, 442
Clare, John, 226, 438, 444-56 *passim,* 459; *Badger,* 447; *Birds' Nests,* 456; *I Am,* 451, commentary, 453-54; *An Invite to Eternity,* commentary, 451-53; *Joys of Childhood,* 447; *Pastoral Poesy,* commentary, 448-50; *Poets Love Nature,* 450-51; *The Progress of Rhyme,* 450; *Secret Love,* commentary, 445-46, 451; *The Sleep of Spring,* 451; *To Wordsworth,* 447-48; *A Vision,* 451, commentary, 454-55
Coleridge, Hartley, 203, 204, 216, 434, 438, 445, 459
Coleridge, Samuel Taylor: *The Ancient Mariner,* commentary, 206-12, 213, 234, 386; *Anima Poetae,* 21; *Christabel,* commentary, 212-17, 231, 234, 388; *Dejection: An Ode,* 165, 210, commentary, 222-28, 233, 235, 261, 286, 320, 398, 419, 445, 448, 449; *The Eolian Harp,* 132, commentary, 200-02; *France: An Ode,* commentary, 220-21; *Frost at Midnight,* commentary, 202-05, 210, 234, 434; *Kubla Khan,* commentary, 217-20, 234, 285, 289, 295-96, 364,

387; *Limbo,* 211, commentary, 232-35; *Ne Plus Ultra,* 211, commentary, 235-36; *The Nightingale,* commentary, 205-06, 234; *To Nature,* 232-33; *To William Wordsworth,* 14, commentary, 228-32
Collins, William, 15, 405; *Ode on the Poetical Character,* commentary, 7-15, 85, 105, 217, 364, 402, 404, 438
Cowper, William, 14, 19, 99, 200
Crabbe, George, 196
Crane, Hart, 172, 450; *The Broken Tower,* 9, 301, 460

Damon, S. Foster, 79
Dante, 23, 68, 81, 163, 276, 318, 335, 355, 357, 386-87, 423; *Purgatorio,* 352, 355, 360, 391, 424, 457
Darley, George, 438, 445, 456-59; *The Errors of Ecstasie,* 456; *It Is Not Beauty I Demand,* commentary, 458-59; *Nepenthe,* commentary, 457-58
Davie, Donald, 472 n. 42
De la Mare, Walter, 325
Deism, 94, 173
Demogorgon (in Coleridge), 233; (in Shelley), 250, 309, 310-11, 315-16, 322
Devourer, the, 3, 69, 316-17
Donne, John, 383
Dostoevsky, Feodor, 253

Ecclesiastes, 49, 346
Eden, state of (in Blake), 20, 24, 25, 26, 28, 29, 63, 72, 331, 408
Eliot, T. S., 163, 172
Elton, Oliver, 271
Emanation (in Blake), 32, 61, 73, 335
Empedocles, 306
Enion, 32, 82-83, 86-87
Enitharmon, 32, 60, 77-78, 84-85
Ephesians, 80
Erdman, David, 47, 91
Exodus, 423
Ezekiel, 74, 98, 120, 318-20, 354-55, 364

Ferenczi, Sándor, 175
Frere, John Hookham, 255
Freud, Sigmund, 25, 28, 175
Friedrich, Caspar David, 221
Frost, Robert, 447
Frye, Northrop, 8-9, 12, 14, 19, 21,
    29, 30, 55, 58, 65, 75, 78, 80, 86,
    92, 100, 117, 174-75, 253, 255,
    260, 343

Garden of Adonis (in Keats), 372,
    437
Gardens of Adonis (in Spenser), 21,
    24, 26, 28, 50, 82, 327
Generation, state of (in Blake), 20,
    25, 26, 50, 63, 356
Genesis, 51, 71
Gide, André, *Les Caves du Vatican,*
    209
Godwin, William, 282, 295
Goethe, J. W. von, *Faust,* 248
Golgonooza, 93, 114
Gorki, Maxim, 145
Graves, Robert, 385; *The White
    Goddess,* 58
Gray, Thomas, 8; *Ode to Adversity,*
    187
Grigson, Geoffrey, 444, 445, 446,
    448, 455
Guiccioli, Teresa, 257, 276-77, 279

Hartman, Geoffrey, 142, 144, 145,
    146, 471 n. 27
Hayley, William, 99, 100, 101, 112
Hazlitt, William, 192, 253, 352-53
Heath-Stubbs, John, 458, 472 n. 48
Hemans, Felicia, 196
Heracles, 54
Hobbes, Thomas, 37
Hogg, James, 196
Hood, Thomas, 438, 445, 459
Hopkins, Gerard Manley, *The
    Child Is Father,* 174
House, Humphry, 472 n. 32
Hulme, T. E., 172
Hunt, Leigh, 342, 345, 421

Icarus, 37, 325, 367
Isaiah, 20, 23, 64, 302

Jerusalem (in Blake), 32, 84
Job, Book of, 37, 67, 98, 293, 300-01
Johnson, Samuel: *Life of Cowley,*
    216; *Life of Waller,* 196

Kafka, Franz, 37
Keats, John: *Bright Star,* commen-
    tary, 435-37; *Endymion,* 239, 250,
    289, 342, 344, 367, commentary,
    368-78, 398-99, 429, 456, 457-58;
    The Eve of St. Agnes, 335, com-
    mentary, 378-84; *The Fall of Hy-
    perion,* 234, 352, 377, 391, 392,
    397, 399, 404, 416, commentary,
    421-32, 437, 457; *Hyperion,* 342,
    commentary, 390-99, 424; *La Belle
    Dame Sans Merci,* 361, 377, 383,
    commentary, 384-87, 417; *Lamia,*
    commentary, 387-90; *Ode on a
    Grecian Urn,* 406, commentary,
    416-21; *Ode on Indolence,* com-
    mentary, 420-21; *Ode on Melan-
    choly,* commentary, 413-16; *Ode
    to a Nightingale,* 347, commen-
    tary, 407-12; *Ode to Psyche,* 14,
    132, 365, commentary, 399-407,
    417, 435; *Sleep and Poetry,* com-
    mentary, 363-68, 370, 421, 429,
    445; *To Autumn,* 398, 405, com-
    mentary, 432-35
Kermode, Frank, 172
Kierkegaard, Søren, 392
Klopstock, Friedrich, 101
Knight, G. Wilson, 432

Lamb, Charles, 196-98
Landor, Walter Savage, 153
Lavater, John Casper, 68
Lawrence, D. H., 3, 58, 96
Lear, Edward, 169
Leutha, 54, 101
Lewis, C. S., 58
Linnell, John, 80
Loki, 60
Los, 32, 49, 62, 75, 91, 101, 109
Luvah, 32, 49-50

Margoliouth, H. M., 81, 91
Marlowe, Christopher, *Dr. Faustus,*
    252

INDEX

Martin, John, 221
Melville, Herman, 37, 293
Milton, John, 2, 5, 11, 14, 24, 68,
71, 77, 98, 120, 122, 125-26, 145,
246, 355, 402-03, 409-10, 415, 436;
Lycidas, 197, 343; Paradise Lost,
5, 23, 27, 49, 67, 71, 97, 98, 102,
125, 143, 219, 246, 273, 276, 364,
394, 410, 422
Moore, Thomas, 345
Moschus, 343

Napoleon, 12, 241, 269, 358
Newton, Sir Isaac, 77, 268

Odin, 43, 471 n. 14
Oothoon, 53-56, 106, 108, 132
Orc, commentary, 11-13, 60, 63, 64,
78, 87, 221, 306, 364, 369
Ossian, 15, 54
Ovid, 14, 374, 392

Palamabron, 100, 101, 108
Peacock, Thomas Love, Nightmare
Abbey, 243
Percival, Milton, 26
Percy, Bishop, 15, 207
Plato, 282, 343
Pope, Alexander, 9, 11, 258, 366
Pottle, F. A., 8, 156, 472 n. 46
Pound, Ezra, 172
Prolific, the, 2, 69, 316
Prometheus, 37, 60, 78, 81, 221,
244, 245-48, 252, 260-61, 306-23
passim
Proverbs, 11
Proverbs of Hell (in Blake), 68-69,
70, 366
Pulci, Luigi, Morgante Maggiore,
255
Pye, Henry James, 274

Rahab, 47, 57, 60, 118
Revelation, Book of, 74, 236, 319,
354, 364
Ridenour, George, 258, 260, 472 n.
33
Rilke, Rainer Maria, 235
Rimbaud, Arthur, 450
Rintrah, 65, 100, 101, 105, 248

Robinson, Crabb, 59, 174
Rousseau, Jean Jacques, 144, 156,
238, 239, 240-41, 253, 290, 352-61
passim
Ruskin, John, 60, 171, 175

Satan (in Blake), 32, 100, 101, 250
Satan (Lucifer, in Byron), 253,
273-75
Satan (in Milton), 67-68, 71, 73, 74,
102, 246, 249, 251, 306, 394
Schofield, 99-100, 112
Scott, Sir Walter, 196
Selincourt, Ernest de, 141
Shakespeare, William, 11, 435; As
You Like It, 405; Romeo and
Juliet, 13
Shelley, Percy Bysshe: Adonais, 201,
320, commentary, 342-50, 355;
Alastor, 73, 239, 250, commentary, 285-90, 306, 328, 347, 356,
361, 367, 371, 377, 398, 426, 429,
445, 457, 458; The Cenci, 337,
439; A Defence of Poetry, 302,
321; Epipsychidion, 53, commentary, 335-44, 376; Hymn to Intellectual Beauty, commentary,
290-93, 295, 298, 301, 304, 328,
433, 441; Lines Written in the
Bay of Lerici, commentary, 351-
52; Mont Blanc, commentary,
293-96, 326, 460; Ode to the West
Wind, 113, 220, commentary,
296-302, 305, 349, 353, 367, 433;
Oh! there are spirits of the air,
commentary, 286-87; Peter Bell
the Third, 131; Prometheus Unbound, 249, 283-84, 297, commentary, 306-23, 335, 358, 369, 439;
The Sensitive Plant, 367, 439;
To a Skylark, commentary, 302-
05, 407; To Night, 421; To
Wordsworth, 286; The Triumph
of Life, 144, 240-41, commentary,
352-62, 385, 391, 399, 424, 432,
457; The Two Spirits: An Allegory, commentary, 323-26; When
the lamp is shattered, 350-51,
472 n. 46; The Witch of Atlas,

Shelley, Percy Bysshe (*cont.*)
commentary, 326-35, 339, 369,
390; *The Zucca*, 350
Sidney, Sir Philip, 343, 347
Smart, Christopher, 8, 11, 14, 19,
217
Song of Songs, 13, 15, 20, 383
Southey, Robert, 259, 272-75
Spectre (in Blake), 32, 61, 72, 78
Spectre (in Shelley), 287, 289, 293,
323-26
Spectre of Tharmas, 81-82
Spectre of Urthona, 32, 33, 83, 91
Spenser, Edmund, 5, 10, 11, 13, 15,
24, 27, 50, 110, 111, 325, 384,
415; *Astrophel*, 343; *The Faerie
Queene*, 9, 13, 23, 268, 325, 326,
332, 371; *Hymne of Heavenly
Beautie*, 11; *Mutabilitie* Cantos,
415
Stevens, Wallace, 1, 2, 3, 7, 10, 14,
81, 127, 151, 164, 172, 173, 306,
317, 379, 389, 460; *Angel Sur-
rounded by Paysans*, 127; *Cre-
dences of Summer*, 405-06; *Description without Place*, 133;
Esthétique du Mal, 415; *Mrs. Alfred Uruguay*, 368, 389; *The
Rock*, 140, 173, 415; *Sunday
Morning*, 405, 415, 434
Swedenborg, Emanuel, 64-65

Tennyson, Alfred, Lord, *Tithonus*,
191
Tharmas, 32, 49, 81
Thomas, Edward, 447
Tolstoy, Leo, 145, 182
Trelawny, Edward John, 342
Trilling, Lionel, 175

Ulro, state of (in Blake), 20, 24, 26,
28, 49, 53, 55, 63, 70, 71, 72, 126,
151, 233
Urizen, 32, 44, 49, 60, 62, 65, 182
Urthona, 32, 49, 83

Vala, 32, 60, 84, 361
Vallon, Annette, 131, 157
Virgil, 191, 192, 357; *Aeneid*, 189

Voltaire, 358

Wade, Thomas, 438; *The Coming
of Night*, 460; *The Face*, 460;
The Winter Shore, 460
Waller, Edmund, 9, 11
Warner, William, *Albion's England*,
50
Webster, John, 252
Winters, Yvor, 172
Woodhouse, A. S. P., 9
Wordsworth, Dorothy, 131, 137-39,
158-59, 202
Wordsworth, William: *Animal
Tranquillity and Decay*, 182;
The Borderers, 75; *The Excur-
sion*, commentary, 193-96, 239,
265, 287, 371, 403, 426; *Extem-
pore Effusion upon the Death of
James Hogg*, commentary, 196-
98; *Laodamia*, commentary, 188-
93; *Lucy Gray*, 224, 227-28;
Michael, commentary, 182-84;
Nutting, commentary, 128-31;
Ode: Intimations of Immortality,
61, 135, commentary, 170-77, 187,
224, 225, 226, 227, 228, 231, 261,
285, 288, 290, 292, 301, 359-60,
398, 433, 447-48; *Ode to Duty*,
commentary, 187-88, 229; *The
Old Cumberland Beggar*, commentary, 178-82; *Peele Castle (Elegiac
Stanzas)*, 133, commentary, 184-
87, 229, 262; *Peter Bell*, 224;
The Prelude, 124, commentary,
140-64, 228-32, 292; *The Recluse*,
commentary, 124-28, 402-03; *Resolution and Independence*, 160,
commentary, 164-70, 223; *Tintern
Abbey*, 61, commentary, 131-40,
155, 200, 202, 204, 293, 363, 404,
449

Yeats, William Butler, 18, 77, 111,
172, 173, 235, 310-11, 332-33, 406,
415; *Byzantium*, 218, 321, 332-34,
406; *Sailing to Byzantium*, 9, 218,
405; *The Second Coming*, 63;
Under Ben Bulben, 333-34; *A
Vision*, 58, 174